Research Methods for Postgraduates

Second edition

Edited by

Tony Greenfield

Industrial Research Consultant

A member of the Hodder Headline Group
LONDON
Distributed in the United States of America by
Oxford University Press Inc., New York

First published in Great Britain in 2002 by
Hodder Education, part of Hachette Livre UK
338 Euston Road, London NW1 3BH

www.hoddereducation.co.uk

British Library Cataloguing in Publication Data
A catalogue record for this book is available from the British Library

Library of Congress Cataloging-in-Publication Data
A catalog record for this book is available from the Library of Congress

ISBN 978 0 340 80656 2

4 5 6 7 8 9 10

Production Editor: Anke Ueberberg
Production Controller: Martin Kerans
Cover Design: Terry Griffiths

Typeset in 10 on 13 pt Minion by Cambrian Typesetters, Frimley, Surrey
Printed and bound by Replika Press Pvt. Ltd., India

What do you think about this book? Or any other Hodder Education title?
Please send your comments to www.hoddereducation.com

Research Methods for Postgraduates

Second edition

Contents

List of contributors

Ms Claire Abson
Learning Centre
Sheffield Hallam University
Psalter Lane
Sheffield S11 8UZ

Professor Douglas Altman
ICRF Medical Statistics Group
Centre for Statistics in Medicine
Institute of Health Sciences
Old Road
Headington
Oxford OX3 7LF

Ms Laura Anderson
Bristows
3 Lincoln's Inn Fields
London WC2A 3AA

Dr Karen Ayres
Department of Applied Statistics
University of Reading
PO Box 240
Earley Gate
Reading RG6 6FN

Professor Tom Bourner
Centre for Management Development
University of Brighton
Mithras House
Lewes Road
Brighton BN2 4AT

Mr Ralph Coates
Treetops
3 The Meadows
Cherry Burton
Beverley
East Yorkshire HU17 7RL

Dr Shirley Coleman
Industrial Statistics Research Unit
Stephenson Building
University of Newcastle
Newcastle upon Tyne NE1 7RU

Professor David de Vaus
School of Sociology, Politics and Anthropology
La Trobe University
Bundoora
Victoria
Australia 3083

Mr Felix Grant
14 Severn Avenue
Weston-super-Mare BS23 4DQ

Dr Tony Greenfield
Middle Cottage
Little Hucklow
Derbyshire SK17 8RT

Professor David Hand
Department of Mathematics
Imperial College
Queen's Gate
London SW7 2RH

Mr Mark Hughes
Brighton Business School
University of Brighton
Mithras House
Lewes Road
Brighton BN2 4AT

Professor Garth Johnson
Centre for Rehabilitation and Engineering
    Studies (CREST)
Stephenson Building
University of Newcastle upon Tyne
Newcastle upon Tyne NE1 7RU

Dr Rodney King
6 Keswick Drive
Avon Grove
Hamilton ML3 7HN

Mr Paul Levy
Centre for Research in Innovation
Management
University of Brighton
Falmer
Brighton BN1 9PH

Emeritus Professor Clifford E Lunneborg
Statistics and Psychology
University of Washington
Seattle
USA

Professor Peter Lynn
Institute for Social and Economic Research
University of Essex
Wivenhoe Park
Colchester
Essex CO4 3SQ

Dr Vivien Martin
Open University Business School
Walton Hall
Milton Keynes
MK7 6AA

Dr Andrew Metcalfe
Department of Applied Mathematics
Adelaide University
Adelaide 5005
Australia

Dr Anand David Pandyan
Centre for Rehabilitation and Engineering
Studies (CREST)
Stephenson Building
University of Newcastle upon Tyne
Newcastle upon Tyne NE1 7RU

Professor Roger W Payne
Statistics Department
IACR-Rothamsted
Harpenden
Hertfordshire AL5 2JQ

Mr R Allan Reese
Computer Centre
University of Hull
Hull HU6 7RX

Mr Jim Rowlands
67 Marine Avenue
Whitley Bay
Tyne and Wear NE26 1NB

Mr Jonathan Smith
Population Estimates Unit
Office of National Statistics
Segensworth Road
Fareham
Hampshire PO15 5RR

Dr Hal Sosabowski
School of Pharmacy and Biomolecular
   Sciences
University of Brighton
Cockroft Building
Moulsecombe
Brighton BN2 4GS

Dr Stan Taylor
Director of Quality and Standards
Armstrong Building
University of Newcastle
Newcastle upon Tyne NE1 7RU

Dr Frederike van Wijck
Department of Physiotherapy
Queen Margaret University College
Leith Campus
Duke Street
Edinburgh EH6 8HF

Dr David Williams
Research Services Unit
University of Newcastle
Newcastle upon Tyne NE1 7RU

Preface to the second edition

'This just might be the most useful book any new postgraduate contemplating research could ever buy', wrote John Gribbin in his *New Scientist* review of the first edition of *Research Methods*. Agreement with that view came from postgraduate researchers. Supervisors and teachers welcomed the book as a prop, even *the* main course book, for postgraduate courses in research methods.

Comments and advice flowed in and technology advanced. The time arrived for a second edition. Liz Gooster replaced Nicki Dennis as the publisher's commissioning editor and we worked well together. Fortunately, most of the original contributors were willing to revise their chapters but we needed authors for new chapters and some for a few replacements. The Internet and the World Wide Web are here and they have had a profound influence on the ways of postgraduates. This needed to be reflected in many chapters: for example, those on the library, literature reviews, search for funds, information technology and computers, sources of population statistics. References to further reading via the WWW can be offered for almost every chapter.

Reviewers commented favourably on the first edition; it was considered to be

- a good introduction to many of the skills required by research students;
- offering wide scope and interdisciplinary appeal;
- concise and easy to read and digest; and
- a useful reference on, for example, surveys, sampling results analysis and presentation.

Some chapters, I was told, may be of interest to some students but had little relevance to others. Well, I believe that there is something in every chapter for almost all research students so I asked the authors to refer to many more illustrations of the diverse relevance of their advice. You will find instances of this in, for example, Chapter 28, *Instrumentation for research*, and in Chapter 33, *The value of mathematical models*.

Some comments could not be reconciled. For example, one user said that students from engineering valued this book; another suggested that it was not specific enough for engineers.

Suggestions included:

- more emphasis on the Internet;
- some exciting new developments in using the Internet for teaching and research are coming from chemistry departments around the world; students can send their experimental data across the world and receive it back from computer, spectroscopic or other forms of processing. Similar services for other subjects;
- have a chapter on WAP (Wireless Application Protocol) technology, knowledge-based searches and alerts over the Internet, digital television and other multimedia systems;
- chapter needed on navigating the WWW;
- reflect diversity of software packages;
- more on creativity.

There is certainly much more emphasis on the Internet and on the WWW. The diversity of software packages, particularly for statistical analysis, is discussed. We have four chapters on creativity.

I tried very hard to recruit an author to describe what is happening in chemistry, looking in university departments and in industry, but I failed. 'He didn't ask me,' some reader will say. Well, dear reader, please write to me soon, so that we can start to plan the third edition. Nor could I find an author to tell us about WAP. For these, and other topics, I need suggestions and volunteers.

I should also like your comments about how the book is used. I believe it is a good reference text for any postgraduate student. I also believe it is a good framework for any postgraduate research course. Do you agree?

All the links in this book and an FAQ page can be found at www.arnoldpublishers.com/support/researchmethods

Finally, thanks again to all contributors: those from the first edition for their continuing support and the new recruits for this edition for putting their faith and effort into this publication; and to Liz Gooster for encouraging and helping me in my role as editor.

Tony Greenfield

Preface to the first edition

The government proposed in 1994 in their White Paper *Realising our Potential* that all graduates who wish to study for doctorates should first take a one-year master's course in research methods. Several universities have since introduced such courses and more are planned. This book is a response to that development. It is not intended to be a deeply detailed textbook, rather a set of notes for guidance, to nudge the student's mind into useful avenues, to tell him or her what help is available and to show how he or she can help themselves. This guidance includes many references for further study. As a set of notes it should be useful to all researchers, those studying for doctorates as well as for masters' degrees, for their lecturers too and, indeed, for anybody in any field of research even if a higher qualification is not expected.

The breadth of the subject rules out a single author: none but the most arrogant would pretend to such ability. The publishers and I therefore decided that we should seek contributions from many authors. This posed difficulties of recruitment, of meeting deadlines, of agreeing a common philosophy and adhering to it, and of imposing an editorial style without causing offence to the authors. These difficulties were resolved because there was one clear bond between all the authors: an enthusiasm to help young people to plan, manage, analyse and report their research better than they may otherwise. All of them are busy and successful as researchers and as teachers. I believe that all readers of this book will appreciate how much time and effort, as well as knowledge and experience, the contributors have devoted to its production.

Unusually, this preface is titled *Preface to the first edition*. This is because I have no doubt that there will be subsequent editions. The situation will change with the introduction of more courses on research methods and experience will accumulate. I invite all readers to tell me how it can be improved: what should be added, what should be omitted, and what should be rewritten. But if you like any of it, please write and tell me. I shall forward your comments on to the authors. They deserve your praise.

Tony Greenfield

Thanks (first edition)

I have long recognised a general need for guidance in research methods: my own need as well as that of others. While I was with BISRA (the British Iron and Steel Research Association) that need was expressed by many of the research staff who sought my help with the design and analysis of their experiments and with the writing of their reports. I thank them for encouraging me with their trust. But I also thank two of the directors of BISRA in particular. One was George Wistreich who persuaded me that creativity could be encouraged and indeed taught. Part of Chapter 1 is based on notes that I made at his lectures. The other was Eric Duckworth who insisted that project managers must include detailed experimental design in their research proposals before they could start work on the projects. They needed my help to do this so I was forced to be involved with their work and to learn about their areas of science.

I ran a research methods course for several years in the medical faculty of Queen's University, Belfast, and quickly discovered the need for several contributors. The subject is too wide for a single teacher. The medical statistics and computing staff all contributed as did staff from the library, the university computing service, various departments in the medical faculty and the dean himself, Gary Love. The course students were postgraduate doctors from first-year house officers to senior consultants and professors. I thank them all, lecturers and students, for their continuing encouragement and suggestions for improvements all of which led to the structure of this book.

Nicki Dennis is the commissioning editor at Arnold (as well as being the director of applied science and technology publishing). When the White Paper *Realising our Potential* was published I suggested to Nicki that she should produce a book for guidance of graduates who were starting their research studies. She agreed and asked me to edit the book. I thank her for that decision and for her continuing help and encouragement.

My search for authors revealed a common enthusiasm in a multitalented team. Their individual specialisms have combined into a successful whole and I thank them all: their contributions are great. Most specially, however, I thank Andrew Metcalfe who, as well as writing the whole of Part Six about models, arranged meetings with potential authors and put me in touch with others.

PART 1

Introduction

1 A view of research

Tony Greenfield

INTRODUCTION

Research, depending on your viewpoint, is:

- a quest for knowledge and understanding;
- an interesting, and perhaps, useful experience;
- a course for qualification;
- a career;
- a style of life;
- an essential process for commercial success;
- a way to improve human quality of life;
- an ego boost for you;
- a justification for funds for your department and its continued existence.

To me, research is an art aided by skills of inquiry, experimental design, data collection, measurement and analysis, by interpretation, and by presentation. A further skill, which can be acquired and developed, is creativity or invention.

This book is mainly about the former set of skills, inquiry to presentation. Further useful topics are described, such as: how to find funds; how to protect your intellectual property; and how to find a job when your research is concluded.

First, however, a few words about the origin of this book. It was inspired by the government's proposal in 1994 that all graduates who wish to study for doctorates should first take a one-year master's course in research methods. Whether or not you agree with this, you may agree that some notes for guidance of postgraduate research students would be useful. Some universities have already followed the government's proposal and have created research methods courses. There is already a place for the book. Whether you are studying a master's course in research methods, or doing some research for a master's degree or a doctorate, you can be guided by this book.

However, research is a big subject and it would not be possible to write a single volume about it in any depth. This book is intended to be a general reference on all aspects of research methods and should be used as notes for guidance. Its content is intended to be fairly simple and easily intelligible by most readers. Where necessary, there are references to more substantive texts.

The many viewpoints and components of research methods persuaded me that several contributors would be needed. Fortunately, there are enough qualified people in universities, consultancy and industry, who volunteered eagerly to write one or more chapters each. I asked them to write in a light style that could be read easily with a view to the reader picking up the general themes. I believe that between us we have achieved this but leave it now to you, the reader, to judge.

If there are parts that you do not understand, or that could be expressed more clearly, or if there are important omissions, please write to me or the publishers. Everything can be improved and your opinions will help us.

CONTENTS

The book is divided into ten sections, with several chapters in each. Look through the contents list and see how the topics have been grouped. You may feel that some of the chapters are not for you. For example: do you know how to use the library? Of course you do! But do you really? I suspect that many people who believe that they know how to find the right text at the right time will be happily surprised to discover how much easier the task becomes when qualified guidance is given. Surely you will want to know how to find funds for your research, but 'Ethics? Ethics has nothing to do with my research,' you might say. It has. It has something to do with all research. Read the chapter and learn.

You will run into difficulties. You will find problems of management, of resources, of people. There's a chapter telling you who can help. I suggest you read it before you meet these problems. There are chapters too on planning your work, about keeping documents, about examining your research process and keeping it on course.

There are many types of research and we have classified several of them as: clinical trials, laboratory and industrial experiments, agricultural experiments and surveys. These may seem to be distinct but there is a general philosophy running through all of them, expressed in different ways by the four writers. You may think that because your research fits into one class of research you can ignore the other three chapters in that section. Please make the effort and read those other chapters. You may be stimulated to discover a new slant on your research.

Glance quickly at the section on data analysis and you may think 'I can leave that until much later, when I have some data to analyse'. Scientific method is about observing the world and collecting information so that you can understand the world better. The way in which you do this must surely depend on how you will process the information when you have collected it. The data you collect will depend on how you will analyse that data. Analysis is an essential feature of research and you will make easier progress with your research the more you understand analysis. To some people it is hard and daunting. They would prefer to ignore it. To other people it is a challenge. Whichever is your viewpoint, make it a challenge and face it now. Honestly, the more you understand about how you will analyse and interpret data, the better will be your planning and management of the way you collect it. The design of a good experiment depends on how the data from the experiment will be analysed.

Mathematical modelling and simulation may seem to be remote from the reality that you want to investigate in your research. They are powerful tools in many situations. Social, medical, economic and political systems, as well as physical, chemical and biological, can be described as mathematical models that can then be used in computers to predict the behaviour of those systems under various conditions. This is a useful approach to many types of research. While you read through the examples included in section eight keep asking yourself how each example may relate to your own research project.

Whatever research you do, you must present your results: in a thesis or dissertation, in reports and published papers, and in stand-up talks to live audiences. There are many books about presentation and some are recommended. Three chapters summarise the most useful points.

Other chapters offer good advice about how to buy and use computers and instrumentation, how to sample from populations and interview people, how to protect your intellectual property, and how to progress in your career.

CREATIVITY

Four chapters about creativity have been added to this second edition. As a brief stimulant, however, I have preserved the following paragraphs from the first edition.

Liam Hudson, in *Contrary Imaginations: a psychological study of the English schoolboy* (Penguin, 1972), presents evidence that intelligence and creativity, as features of the human mind, are negatively correlated, but that there are some fortunate people who are both intelligent and creative. This rare combination must be desirable in research where we need both logic and imagination, where we need vision as well as the ability to plan and manage.

But what is creativity?

You are planning your research. You believe that every step on the way must be taken rationally. Indeed, that is the essence of most of this book: to guide you rationally through your work. However, if you look at the most outstanding of creative leaps in the history of science you will see that they were all founded on an irrationality of thought. Well-known examples are: Watt's invention of the separate condenser for the steam engine as he strolled in the country; Poincaré's theory of Fuchsian functions as he boarded a bus; Kekulé's discovery of the benzene ring as he dozed by the fireside. So, be prepared to note any odd thought you might have at an unexpected time in an unexpected place. And don't discard unexpected results.

> *Just because something doesn't do what you planned it to do doesn't mean it's useless.*
> Thomas Alva Edison

Nevertheless, you can bring to bear some methods of intellectual discovery.

- **Analogy**: look for a similarity between your problem and one for which the solution is known. Electrical circuits are envisioned as water flowing through tanks, pipes, pumps and valves; brain function is studied by comparison with computers; the more remote your analogy is from your problem, the more creative will be your solution.
- **By parts**: break the problem into a series of sub-problems that you hope will be more amenable to solution.
- **By random guesses**: Edison used it extensively and brainstorming is a modern version of it.
- **Generalise**: if a specific problem is baffling, write a general version of it; an algebraic model leads to simplified solutions compared with tackling complicated arithmetic head on.
- **Add**: a difficult problem may be resolved by adding an auxiliary sub-problem.
- **Subtract**: drop some of the complicating features of the original problem; this is a trick used in simulation to make it more tractable.
- **Particularise**: look for a special case with a narrower set of conditions, such as tackling a two-dimensional example of a three-dimensional problem.
- **Stretch or contract**: some problems are more tractable if their scale or the range of variables is altered.
- **Invert**: look at the problem from the opposite viewpoint; instead of 'When will this train arrive at Oxford?' ask 'When will Oxford arrive at this train?'.
- **Restructure**: in clinical studies we do not ask if a treatment will cure a disease, but will an inert treatment fail to cure the disease?

- The method of **Pappus**: assume the problem is solved and calculate backwards.
- The method of **Tertullus**: assume a solution is impossible and try to prove why.

Check each of these approaches, asking yourself how you might bring it to bear on your problem. Then, if you need any more stimulation, read the following.

The *Art of Scientific Investigation* by W I B Beveridge, published in 1950 but still, half a century later, stimulating to read;

G Polya's *How to Solve It* offers practical recipes; and

Arthur Koestler's *The Act of Creation* for a discussion of the working of the mind.

2 The research journey: four steps to success

Tom Bourner

INTRODUCTION

Research can seem daunting to those who are new to it. This chapter has two aims:

- to provide an overview of the research journey from start to finish;
- to demystify the business of research.

Most research projects take quite a long time to complete. Research degrees, for example, usually takes at least three years of full-time research. Completing a part-time research degree usually take correspondingly longer. At the start, research can seem like an ill-defined mish-mash of activities littered with hidden pitfalls. When you are in the middle of your research, it is sometimes difficult to see the wood for the trees. In this chapter, I suggest a map for keeping in perspective your research project as a whole. The map is designed to give you an overview of the whole research process as though you were in a helicopter looking down on it so that you can keep it in view from beginning to end.

Research can also seem like a mysterious process: an arcane art practised by the cleverest people, employing obscure jargon and demanding an awesome depth of knowledge. This chapter offers an antidote to this intimidating view of research.

Let us start by considering a problem with which you may be familiar. Suppose that you are a young person wanting to get a flat, how would you go about it? Well, if you're like most people, you would probably collect some literature from estate agents, local newspapers or letting agencies to get an overview of what is available. You would compare the features (such as price, size, location, amenities) of the different flats and make a shortlist of the ones that are most likely to meet your needs. You would probably then personally look over the ones that you had selected for your shortlist. Afterwards, when you have made your decision and you are sitting in your new home, you would probably reflect on the process: the extent to which your flat meets your original aspirations, what your first-hand experience has told you about the housing market, what you have learned from the experience, and so on.

Now, if you take off your flat-hunter's spectacles and put on instead a pair of researcher's spectacles, you will observe some similarities between that process of flat-hunting and the process of research. First, you did a literature review (local newspapers and estate agents' blurbs) to get an overview of the field. Second, you developed a theory of which of the available flats would be to your requirements (your shortlist). Third, you tested the theory by inspecting those on your shortlist. Finally, you reflected on the experience and your results. Stated formally, the process contains four parts:

- Part 1: Reviewing the field
- Part 2: Theory building

- Part 3: Theory testing
- Part 4: Reflecting and integrating

Perhaps this sequence seems familiar. Perhaps you recognise it from other significant decisions you have made in your life: choosing a college, buying a personal computer, choosing a job.

With some decisions, it is not possible to go through all the stages. For example, when you choose a job, the final test of your theory that you have chosen the right job is by doing the job. Unfortunately, this is possible only after you have committed yourself to it. Perhaps that is why so many unsatisfactory job decisions are made.[*]

Once you recognise that you are already familiar with each of the major parts of the research process through your experience of making the larger decisions of your life you will have a valuable resource to draw on. Reflection on those experiences will also give you an indication of the possible pitfalls.

That four-part process can help you to put what you are doing into a broader picture when you start to get bogged down in the detail of research. It can also be useful in designing your research project.

Let us examine the parts of the process in more detail.

PART 1: REVIEWING THE FIELD

Many research projects arise from a study of current thinking in a field. The research project follows from identifying a gap in the literature. Most other research projects arise from awareness of a problem that is worth solving. In either case, a good start is an overview of current thinking in the field.

In case you are impatient with this part of the process and want to start immediately with field work, here are some reasons for spending time and effort on a review of the field:

- to identify gaps in current knowledge;
- to avoid reinventing the wheel (at the very least this will save time and it can stop you from making the same mistakes as others);
- to carry on from where others have already reached (reviewing the field allows you to build on the platform of existing knowledge and ideas);
- to identify other people working in the same and related fields (they provide you with a researcher network, which is a valuable resource indeed);
- to increase your *breadth* of knowledge of the area in which your subject is located;
- to identify the seminal works in your area;
- to provide the intellectual *context* for your own work, (this will enable you to position your project in terms of related work);
- to identify opposing views;
- to put your own work in perspective;
- to provide evidence that you can access the previous significant work in an area;
- to discover transferable information and ideas (information and insights that may be relevant to your own project);
- to discover transferable *research* methods (research methods that could be relevant to your own project.

---

[*] The literature on labour turnover often refers to the period immediately following recruitment as the 'induction crisis', when job expectations are tested by the job realities.

PART 2: THEORY BUILDING

In some ways, theory building is the most personal and creative part of the research process. Some people find it the most exciting and challenging part of the whole business.

In some cases, data collection precedes theory building and, in others, it follows it. Have you ever bought a used car? If so, you may have identified some possibles before narrowing down to a few probables. You collected data and then formed a theory about which of the cars would best meet your needs. In that situation, theory building followed data collection. The process of developing a theory by inspecting individual cases has a special name: *induction*.

Our flat hunting example is another illustration of induction. If each time you are sent the details of a flat in a certain area of town you notice that it is more expensive than you can afford, you may form the theory that all the flats in that area are too expensive for you. Acting on that theory, you may ask the estate agents to stop sending details of flats in that area. That is the process of induction at work again: forming a theory from information about specific instances. Induction is a type of generalisation.

The other side of the coin from induction is *deduction* which involves reaching conclusions about specific instances from general principles. Here is an example of deduction: 'I can't afford to live in Mayfair so don't bother to send me the details of any flats in that part of town'. In this example 'I can't afford to live in Mayfair' is the generalisation and deduction leads me to the conclusion about any specific flat in Mayfair that I can't afford it.

Induction is a thought process that takes you from the specific to the general. Deduction is a thought process that takes you from the general to the specific.

We have seen how a theory can emerge from the data. However, theory can also emerge from armchair theorising; introspection; deduction following a review of the literature; personal experience; a fortuitous remark; a brainstorm; an apt metaphor; or pure inspiration. Creativity has a role to play in all aspects of the research process, but especially in the theory-building part.

I said earlier that data collection can precede theory building and that it can also follow it. In the case of induction, data collection comes first. When data collection follows theory building then it is usually for the purpose of testing the theory. That is the part of the research process that we consider next.

PART 3: THEORY TESTING

> *Experience has shown each one of us it is very easy to deceive ourselves, to believe something which later experience shows us is not so.*
>
> Rogers (1955)

When flat hunting, we wanted to check whether those attractive sounding apartments, reported by the estate agent, would really meet our needs. Likewise, when we are doing research, we will want to check whether the theory (or theories) we have formulated fulfil our hopes and expectations.

The sort of theory testing we do will depend on our ambitions and claims for our theory. If we want to claim that our theory applies *generally** then we may want to use statistical methods (known as *inferential statistics*), which have been developed to enable us to make claims about whole populations from information about a sample from a population.

---

* For example: 'All two-bedroom flats in Mayfair are more expensive than all two-bedroom flats in Leytonstone'.

If, however, your claims are only about the accuracy of your theory in the context of a particular situation[†] then theory testing may involve checking your conclusions (theory) from other perspectives. You may have looked at estate agents' brochures and now you want to look at the flats themselves, talk to the neighbours and so on. In research in the social sciences, the term *triangulation* is used to describe the process of checking if different data sources and different methods allow you to reach the same conclusions.

Theory testing can take many forms. At one extreme, you may simply invite the reader of a research report to test the conclusions against his or her own experiences. The test is: does the reader say 'Aha! I can now make sense of my own experience in a new and convincing way'? However, if the reader is unlikely to have had first-hand experience for testing the researcher's theory, or if the claims being made involve a high level of generality, then the theory testing stage will be more formal and elaborate. At some level, however, theory testing is likely to be part of any research process.

PART 4: REFLECTION AND INTEGRATION

> *Knowledge doesn't exist in a vacuum, and your knowledge only has value in relation to other people's.*
>
> Jankowitz (1991)

Reflection and integration is the last stage of the research journey. There may be many things on which you want to reflect: what you have learned about the process of research; what you could have done differently; what you have learned about yourself. However, there is one matter for reflection that is a crucial part of the research process itself. It will affect how your research is judged and the impact of your research. You must reflect on *how your research findings relate to current thinking* in the field of your research topic.

Your reflection on how your research results relate to current thinking will include your assessment of where your research fits into the field of knowledge. It will contain your assessment of your contribution to the field. In this part of the research process, you are likely to return to your review of current thinking that you made at the outset, and to reassess it in the light of your results. It is as if the current thinking in your field of study is a partially complete jigsaw puzzle and you are detecting where your own new piece of the jigsaw fits in.

Relating the outcomes of your research to current thinking in the field may simply involve showing how it *adds* to what is already known in the field. This would be the case when you have filled a gap in the literature or found a solution to a particular problem in the field. It may involve seeking connections with current thinking. It may involve challenging some parts of the map of the current thinking in the field, so that you will be proposing some reconstruction of that map. It may involve testing the consistency of your research findings with current thinking. It may involve asking 'What if?' questions of your research findings.

Any of these ways of relating your research findings to current thinking in the field may present further questions and new avenues to explore. Successful research usually answers some questions but also raises new ones. It enables researchers to ask questions that would not have been asked before the research. New questions can be an important outcome of research. It is small wonder therefore that the final chapter of most research reports has a section containing suggestions for further research.

[†] For example: 'The flat that suits me best among those whose details I have been sent is Number 10 Railway Cuttings'.

A good practical question to ask yourself is: 'What are the implications of my research results for our understanding in this area?' The implications can take many forms. For example:

- You may have filled a gap in the literature.
- You may have produced a possible solution to an identified problem in the field.
- Your results may challenge accepted ideas in the field (some earlier statements in the literature may seem less plausible in the light of your findings).
- Some earlier statements in the literature may seem *more* plausible in the light of your findings.
- Your work may help to clarify and specify the precise areas in which existing ideas apply and where they do not apply (it may help you to identify domains of application of those ideas).
- Your results may suggest a synthesis of existing ideas.
- You may have provided a new perspective on existing ideas in the field.
- Your work may suggest new methods for researching your topic.
- Your results may suggest new ideas, perhaps some new lines of investigation in the field.
- You may have generated new questions in the field.
- There may be implications for further research.

Most of all, this fourth stage in the research process is about seeking to *integrate* the fruits your own research into current thinking in the field.

SUMMARY AND CONCLUSIONS

It is sometimes difficult to keep in mind the whole research journey when all of your attention is focused on crossing some particularly difficult ground. My purpose in this chapter is to help you to keep the whole research process in perspective when you are engaged in a particular research activity. I have done this by giving an overview map on which the whole journey is plotted in outline. I hope this will help you to *plan* your research journey.

I have related the process of research to the way that you find the information required for the larger decisions in life. You already have much experience to draw upon in planning and doing your research.

I have suggested a four-part research process: (1) reviewing the field; (2) building theory; (3) testing theory; (4) reflecting and integrating.

There is a considerable diversity of approaches to research in different fields, but this four-part framework is sufficiently broad to encompass most research in the sciences, the social sciences and the humanities. Much of the literature on research focuses on different parts of the process. For example, in the social sciences it usually focuses on theory-building, whereas in other sciences it may focus on theory-testing.

Your four parts may not follow this sequence strictly. For example, after you have reviewed the literature you may want to monitor developments in current thinking *while* you are collecting and analysing data. You may engage in some parts of the research process more than once. For example, you may find that data you collect for theory building enables you to test statements found in the literature. Or data collected to test a theory may suggest a new theory so that it becomes an element of theory building.

You may not want to spend the same amount of time and energy on each of the four parts of the process. For example, theory building may be only a token part of your research project if your main contribution lies in testing a theory that you found in the literature. On the other hand, you may direct most of your effort towards theory *building*, so that theory *testing* may be little more than establishing the plausibility of your theory in the light of the data you have collected.

The four parts will be present in almost all research projects, at least conceptually. If one of the four parts seems to be missing from your own research project, you should discuss it with other researchers and, if you are registered for a research degree, with your supervisor. If you intend to omit one of the parts from your own research project, you must be able to state clearly why it has no role.

REFERENCES

Jankowitz, A D (1991) *Business Research for Students*, Chapman and Hall (London).

Rogers, C (1955) Persons or science: a philosophical question. *American Psychologist*, vol. 10. Reprinted in *On becoming a Person* (pp 267–279) (London: Constable).

3 Managing your PhD

Stan Taylor

INTRODUCTION

While the knowledge and skills that you gained as an undergraduate and/or in studying for a Master's degree have given you a basic background in your subject, and perhaps some experience of, and insight into, the process of research, they may not necessarily have equipped you to undertake a PhD. As Salmon (1992, p 51) put it:

> Unlike a certificate, a diploma, a Bachelors or Masters degree, a doctorate does not merely entail the consideration of already existing work within a pre-arranged structure but demands the creation of a personal project. To undertake a PhD is therefore to define oneself as having a contribution to make to the understanding of the area concerned.

Making such a contribution can, in itself, be a daunting and difficult experience, the more so because although you should have the advice, encouragement and support of your supervisor, academic colleagues in the field and fellow-graduate students, ultimately the responsibility is yours, i.e. you stand or fall largely by your own efforts. You have to create the project; you have to undertake the research; you have to write it up; you have to complete on time and submit; you have to defend your thesis at your viva; and if you do all of these things successfully then you personally are awarded the title of 'Doctor'.

However, you have not only to achieve that goal, but, in this day and age, you also have to achieve it within what by historical standards is a relatively short time period. Up until the last decade or so of the twentieth century, the prevailing view was that because they involved making an original contribution to knowledge, PhD theses took as long as they took. But research students in the twenty-first century are now under intense pressures from research sponsors, academic departments and, in many cases, their bank managers to complete within three or, at most, four years of full-time study, or five or six years part-time. Such pressures mean that students must now actively manage both their research and themselves to finish within schedule or as near as possible.

The aim of this chapter is to help you to think about how you are going to manage your PhD. With that in mind, the objectives are to consider

- how to approach your PhD;
- how to start it;
- how to plan it;
- how to organise it;
- how to manage your thesis;
- how to manage your relationship with your supervisor;
- how to manage yourself;

- how to complete your thesis;
- how to prepare for examination.

These objectives form the topics of this chapter and, hopefully, the points made will help you manage your research better and to self-improve your chances of finishing and gaining the degree.

APPROACHING YOUR PHD

If you are thinking about doing a PhD thesis, it makes sense first to enquire about precisely what you are letting yourself in for; that is, what is a PhD thesis?

All universities with PhD programmes have, in their rules and regulations, a definition of a PhD thesis for purposes of examination. While these definitions vary considerably between institutions, they will usually include requirements that the thesis should:

- be on a specified and approved topic;
- constitute a substantial piece of scholarship;
- be the work of the candidate;
- make an original contribution to knowledge;
- in principle, be worthy of publication.

On this basis, then, what you have to do is to specify a topic, have it approved by the relevant university body, produce a substantial piece of scholarship on your own, which adds to knowledge and which is publishable.

This would be fine if there were standard definitions of 'substantial', 'scholarship', 'own work', 'original contribution' or 'publishable'. While there are some common elements in the interpretation of what these terms mean (see e.g. Phillips and Pugh 2000, pp 58–73; Cryer 2000, pp 57–82), there are of course substantive variations both between and within academic subjects. As Partington *et al* (1993, pp 67–68) have suggested, at one extreme, the PhD can be seen as a multi-volume exhaustive account of a subject produced entirely by independent study, opening up new vistas in the discipline, and ready to go into proof as a major book; at the other, it may be seen as the application of extensive research training to produce a narrow account of a detailed aspect of a phenomenon tackled as part of a research team and leading to an article or two in specialised journals. Between these extremes of the individually produced blockbuster and the narrow demonstration of ability to apply research training lies a range of other conceptions of theses embodying a diversity of characteristics.

If, then, the nature of the beast remains elusive, what can you do? By far the best strategy is to go to the library and look at a few successful theses recently written in a cognate area to that which you are considering, and ask yourself:

- Were they on big topics or relatively narrow ones?
- Did they involve a massive amount of detailed research or was this limited and narrowly focused?
- Were they the product of a single scholar or was their considerable attribution of contributions by colleagues?
- Did they aim to open up broad new fields of knowledge or push the barriers out slightly in a tightly-defined area?
- What made them publishable?

By these means, you should hopefully have a reasonably clear idea of what, at the end of three or four years, you should expect to be able to achieve, and so you can embark on your own PhD.

STARTING YOUR PHD

Many PhD students in the sciences and engineering are recruited to undertake a specific piece of research, which has been planned by their supervisor(s), i.e. they can step into a ready-made research project. But others, particularly in the arts, humanities and social sciences, are unsure about precisely what they want to do in their research and so the first few weeks or months are spent in deciding upon a topic. This usually involves looking at other work on, or relating to, the broad area, seeing where there are significant gaps/areas of disagreement/problems/conflicting interpretations, reflecting, refining, and coming up eventually with a detailed research proposal.

This can be a frustrating, difficult and demoralising experience, as your initial ideas and expectations often turn out to be too ambitious and you find yourself thrashing around in an intellectual vacuum and moving from the macro-level of your subject through the meta- and so to the micro-level in the search for a topic. You should, however, receive strong support at this stage from your actual or potential supervisor, who should act as a sounding board for your ideas and give you the benefit of his or her experience and that of appropriate colleagues. With such assistance you should eventually come up with a topic which, following Moses (1992, pp 9–13) and Rudestam and Newton (1992, pp 10–11), is:

- *viable* – can be tackled with the available or specified obtainable resources, including a good supervisor with relevant experience and expertise in the area, the library, computing facilities and laboratories;
- *do-able* – can be done by someone with your knowledge and skills or with specified additions to these, and within a reasonable period of time;
- *sustainable* – will hold your interest and maintain your commitment over a period of several years;
- *original* – has the potential to make an original contribution to knowledge;
- *acceptable* – conforms to the requirements and standards that examiners may apply.

Both you and your supervisor must be reasonably satisfied on all of these counts before you proceed further with the thesis.

PLANNING YOUR PHD

When you were an undergraduate or a postgraduate taking a taught course, you worked to a plan, that of your degree programme, which organised and directed your work over the duration of your studies. Postgraduate research is no different in so far as it needs to be conducted to a plan as well; one of the central causes of dropping out is failure to plan, resulting in loss of direction and time. But what is different is that it is now your responsibility, in conjunction with your supervisor, to draw up a plan and to direct your studies accordingly.

While PhDs vary hugely in their structures and format and in how they are tackled, most involve the nine components of:

1. review and evaluation of general and specific literary and other sources in the area of the topic;
2. identify the gap/problem/issue/conflict or other trigger for the research and formulate appropriate investigations/potential solutions questions/theories/alternative interpretations;
3. decide upon an appropriate paradigm/conceptual framework/methodology within which to do the research; specify concepts, theories, hypotheses, statistical procedures and significance levels before you embark on survey or experimental work;
4. tackle the substantive research, involving one or a combination of:
    *   reading original documents
    *   subject interviewing
    *   elite interviewing
    *   mass interviewing
    *   scientific fieldwork
    *   scientific experimentation
    *   problem-solving
    *   computer modelling
5. sift, check, and analyse material;
6. interpret findings/results and assess their implications for the initial focus of the inquiry;
7. reformulate the field of knowledge in the light of findings;
8. summarise what your research has achieved, how it has been achieved, what conclusions have been reached and, if appropriate, directions for future research;
9. write the drafts of your thesis.

These are the core components of most theses. There may be more, depending on the topic, which will define your tasks over the next few years.

While it is difficult to assign precise time values to each of these components and some, of course, may overlap, you should, in conjunction with your supervisor, try to plan a schedule for completing the stages of the research within a reasonable time limit.

So you may, for example, plan in outline to spend the first six months refining the topic, reviewing and evaluating the literature, and dealing with methodological questions, 18 months undertaking the substantive research, three months analysing, interpreting and reformulating, and three months gluing the whole together, writing your summary and conclusions, and finally polishing the thesis for submission. Then, with these broad boundaries in place, you may be able to break the components up into sub-components and try to set targets for their completion.

It is vital that, when you specify time for each of the components of the thesis, you should make a clear allocation for writing up that part of your work. This is critical for five reasons:

1. It gets you straight into the habit of writing rather than leaving this until the end when it can be difficult to acquire.
2. It encourages you to reflect upon what you have done before you go on and may highlight problems/avenues of exploration.
3. It provides a continuing record of your achievements so far.
4. It enables your supervisor to see exactly what you have done and to advise how to proceed.
5. If you write throughout you build up a portfolio of your work, which you can then fashion into the shape of the final thesis rather than face beginning from scratch to assemble your research (and often finding that the sum of unconnected parts fails to add up to a thesis).

Your plan, then, should embody time for writing up each component. An example of such a plan, including writing time, is presented by Phillips and Pugh (1994, p 85), and this can be adapted for your own use.

ORGANISING YOUR PHD

With an outline plan in place, you now have to decide how you are going to try and meet it in a organised way. This involves organising your time, working conditions, and materials.

Time

As a postgraduate student you are responsible for managing your own time and, without any sort of preparation for this, it is – as one student reported to Welsh (1979, pp 33) – all 'too easy for the postgraduate to spend his [her] time pottering about' and fall behind.

Many universities now recognise that it is necessary to offer graduate students assistance with time management and include a session in the appropriate induction programme, while others allow postgraduates access to courses run for the academic staff. Additionally, Cryer (2000, pp 117–24) offers excellent and detailed advice on time management.

If you feel that things are beginning to slip, you might consider:

- dividing your days into blocks of (say) two hours and keeping a diary of what you have done in that period;
- reviewing this and calculating the time you spent on your thesis and the time you lost through distractions of one kind or another;
- reorganising your day to ensure adequate working time and to minimise unwanted distractions.

Regular reviews of this kind can enable you to establish and maintain a stable pattern of work and help you to adjust psychologically to postgraduate study.

Working conditions

The demands of doctoral study are, or can be, very intense, and you need an appropriate working environment where you can read, reflect, think, evaluate and write. In line with this, the national body which represents postgraduates, the National Postgraduate Committee (NPC 1995), has produced guidelines, including the provision of:

- office space, preferably within the department where students are based with designated maximum numbers;
- necessary equipment with a minimum of a desk, chair, lamp, bookcase and lockable filing cabinet;
- where appropriate, a carrel in the library or bench space in the laboratory;
- access to computing facilities, preferably ones dedicated to postgraduate use;
- private common space for postgraduates to study when necessary on their own;
- access to the departmental staff common room and to the postgraduate common room for social purposes.

You should, preferably before signing up for a PhD, ensure that, as far as possible, these facilities are available to you. If there are deficiencies, you should bring these to the attention of your department as factors likely to delay your research and completion.

Materials

In the course of your PhD, you can expect to accumulate a vast amount of materials relating to your research, and it is important that you organise these properly. There is nothing worse than writing up and finding that you cannot trace the precise source of that key point or that your reference is inadequate and have to interrupt the flow while you trek to the library to sort it out. You should:

- find out which referencing system you will be expected to use in your thesis and note the exact requirements for footnotes or end notes and for your bibliography;
- assume anything that you read may eventually be cited and take full details of the reference. A master list of these should be stored in a card index or, even better, a database, which can then later be manipulated and sorted to form your bibliography;
- establish a filing system and file your materials under appropriate headings (this may be manual or computerised, but in the latter case copies must be backed-up regularly);
- index your filing system so that it is easy to find any document.

Organisation of your material in this way should mean the minimum of delay while you are doing your research, particularly writing up, and hence the least interruption to your creative flow.

MANAGING YOUR THESIS

The creation of a plan for your PhD and organisation of your work is one thing, but it is hard to stick to it. While books and articles suggest that research consists of a seamless unrolling of the advancement of knowledge, in practice it may be two steps forward and one back, not to mention several sideways. Common problems with theses include the following.

- *Drifting from the topic*: as the research progresses, highways and byways of new exploration open up which just have to be investigated because they could be vital. So every avenue is investigated until you become lost in the maze of possibilities and unable to find your way back to where you should be at that stage.
- *Difficulties with the methodology*: particularly for arts, humanities and social science students, there may be a need to establish a conceptual framework for the research and to establish the appropriate methods to be used. This can require you to grapple with a whole range of philosophical, theoretical, empirical and experimental problems, and it can require a major effort to try and identify, tackle and resolve these, particularly when you are really itching to undertake the substantive research.
- *Frustration with the substantive research*: you can expect a range of problems to occur as you undertake the substantive research – evidence that you can not obtain as easily as you hoped, experiments that do not work, apparently promising lines of enquiry that turn out to be dead ends, simulations that do not run properly. The list is endless.
- *Inconsistencies in findings*: with the substantive research accomplished, you experience difficulties in analysing and interpreting it – the evidence is contradictory; the experiments yield unexpected results; the cast-iron assumptions are apparently falsified; the simulation results defy predictions; variables behave badly; and so on.

Any or all of these experiences – and you are almost bound to meet them – can throw your planning out of gear, but there are several things that you can do to prevent problems getting out of hand. These include the following.

A regular review of your progress

Your supervisor is responsible from an institutional standpoint for reviewing your progress, but this can entail anything from weekly through to annual reviews. If your meetings with your supervisor are infrequent and/or irregular, you should set aside time on a regular basis and ask yourself:

* What did I plan to achieve by this stage of my research?
* What have I actually achieved?

In this way you can identify shortfalls, hopefully at an early enough stage to correct them.

Acknowledge the existence of a problem

As an undergraduate or Masters' student, you may have sailed through with effortless brilliance and it can be an immense shock to encounter problems of the kinds outlined above, and acknowledging them can be seen as weakness or failure. But such problems are experienced throughout virtually the entire research community, and admission should not be conceived of as a weakness, but as a strength. So, if you are falling behind, acknowledge that there is a problem, reflect upon the reasons why, and try to identify a solution.

Seek help

If you cannot quite define the problem or cannot find a solution, do not simply pace your room waiting for inspiration and sink into the slough of despondency, seek help. You can find this from:

* *The literature*: there are several books dealing generally with problems of researching a PhD (for example, Phillips and Pugh 2000; Cryer 2000) or with PhDs in particular subject areas (for example, Allan and Skinner 1991; Beynon, 1993; Blaxter *et al* 1996; Burnham (ed) 1997; Frost and Stablein 1992; Murrell 1990) or with specific problems such as writer's block (Hall 1993) which may offer help and assistance.
* *Fellow-graduate students*: they may well be experiencing similar problems or, if further on in their studies, have met them and sorted them out, so they may well be able to assist and/or provide support and encouragement. Some departments now try to promote such mutual self-help by organising graduate-only workshops on a regular basis or by *mentoring*, whereby a student near completion lends a sympathetic ear to those students at earlier stages.
* *A member of your department*: junior members of your department will probably have fairly recently completed a PhD themselves, and will be able to point you in the direction of how to solve difficulties. Sometimes colleagues may take an interest in your research and become, in effect, informal mentors, and there is some evidence (Lyons *et al* 1990, pp 277–285) that such support improves both the self-confidence of graduate students and their performance.
* *Your supervisor*: your ultimate source of assistance should be your supervisor who is charged with guiding you through your research on behalf of the university and who is, or should be, an expert in the broad field of your thesis and the processes and problems of research.

YOUR RELATIONSHIP WITH YOUR SUPERVISOR

You should enjoy a supportive and productive relationship with your supervisor, one that starts as 'a master [or mistress] pupil relationship and ideally end(s) up as almost equal colleagues' (SERC 1983, quoted in Young *et al* 1987, p 28). These days, most supervisors receive at least some training in their responsibilities and often have to serve an apprenticeship period 'shadowing' an experienced supervisor before undertaking duties on their own (Elton *et al* 1994, pp 24–37). Consequently, the chances are that you will have a good experience, provided of course that you play your part and

- turn up regularly for supervisory sessions;
- take a constructive approach to criticisms and comments made (it can be painful to have pet theories criticised by your supervisor but this is not nearly as bad as having them shot down in flames by your eventual examiners);
- treat supervisions in a business-like way as an opportunity to review your achievements so far and to set realistic objectives for progress (as an aide memoire it can be very useful immediately after the meeting to jot down summary notes of what was said, what you agreed you would do, and when you agreed to do it by).

What happens, however, when your supervisor, your ultimate source of assistance, feels unable to help because of your subject matter, or is unable to find adequate time, or is disinclined to assist?

- *Inability to help*: it may be that, while your supervisor has a general expertise within the field, he or she is unable to assist with the specifics of your research, i.e. your work has moved beyond what he or she feels totally confident to supervise. In this case, he or she should at least have an extensive knowledge of the research network in the field and be able to point you towards sources of assistance outside your institution and, possibly, outside the country. Whereas, a few years ago, it was difficult to conduct a domestic or international dialogue about your research problems, this has of course been greatly facilitated by the Internet, which can be a very useful resource for graduate students.
- *Unable to find time*: all academics are under severe pressures to perform in research, teaching and administration, and time is at a premium, especially in institutions where postgraduate supervision is considered to be part of research activity and no allowance is made for this in allocating other duties. However, that said, it is no excuse for the occasional horror stories about postgraduates having most of their meetings with supervisors in railway stations or airports or receiving comments on their draft chapters months after they have been handed in for comments. If an academic agrees to supervise you then he or she takes on a commitment and should be prepared to fulfil it.

    If you are having problems, consult your university's guidelines for supervisors and, if available, postgraduate charter, and point these out to him or her. (If your institution has neither of these, the National Postgraduate Committee (1995) has produced *Guidelines on Codes of Practice* and you should consult these.) If you still experience problems, then have a word with the head of the graduate school or department and/or a new supervisor may be the only way forward.
- *Unwilling to help*: supervisors may be unwilling to help because, in their judgement, it oversteps the boundaries between supervising your research and doing it for you. This may reflect

a traditional view of a PhD as a venture made worthwhile because it is performed alone and is heroic, with the weak falling off the mountain, or alternatively, it is a very real concern that, to continue the analogy, you are asking him or her to put in the supports and then carry you to the summit. If you are stuck and your supervisor proves unwilling to help or evasive, you should try and discuss the matter and resolve it. If that fails and you feel your feet giving way and are not thrown a rope, again consider taking the matter further.

Disagreement between co-supervisors: over the past decade or so, there has been an explosion in multi-disciplinary research, in which students are often co-supervised by staff drawn from diverse disciplines, and in collaborative research with industry, where students have both an academic and an industrial supervisor. Where co-supervisors have similar perceptions of the research project, there should be no difficulty. But, where supervisors have, because of their different backgrounds or interests, dissimilar perceptions of the project, this can leave students as 'piggy in the middle' to the detriment of their research.

Students being jointly supervised need to be alert to signs of explicit or implicit disagreement between their supervisors and, as far as possible, ensure that they are discussed and resolved as early as possible in the research project. If differences persist, then it may be worth taking this up with the Head of Department or other responsible senior figure.

MANAGING YOURSELF

In addition to managing your thesis and your relationship with your supervisor over the course of your studies, you also have to manage yourself. That is, you must cope with the personal problems of postgraduate life. These can include initial adjustment, isolation and loneliness as you get into your research, and mid-thesis crisis.

Initial adjustment

At school and, to a lesser extent, as an undergraduate or a postgraduate on a taught degree, your programme of studies was mapped out for you and you had to meet deadlines set by your department for the delivery of work. As a postgraduate, you are, as noted in the quote at the start of the chapter, responsible for mapping out your own programme of study and for implementing it. This can be a liberating experience. Possibly for the first time in your life you are your own boss. But it can also be a frightening experience and it is not unusual for postgraduates in their first few months to feel as if they have been cast adrift on a stormy sea without a clear course to steer by. While, a few years ago, this period was regarded as one you had to survive to continue the degree, many institutions now offer help in the form of comprehensive induction programmes that are designed to help PhD students acquire appropriate skills, while training programmes for supervisors are now placing greater emphasis upon the need to support supervisees during this critical period. So, if you do feel lost and adrift, you are by no means alone and you should seek and expect support to help you to adjust to postgraduate life.

Isolation and loneliness

At school and as an undergraduate you studied in company. It can come as a shock to find yourself spending much of your time working on your own without human contact, and you can become isolated and depressed in consequence. Again, a few years ago working alone was considered by many to be a necessary evil, but now some universities recognise the need to offer support to postgraduates. Academically, this may take the form of formal graduate supervisions involving not just the customary one, but possibly two or three graduates, the use of graduate mentors, graduate-led workshops and seminars or, increasingly, through separate graduate schools. Socially, graduates may be brought into contact with each other by such schools or by university or departmental postgraduate societies that organise a range of events, or through participation in student societies.

If these things are not done by your institution or they are not enough and you still feel isolated and on your own, the answer may be a graduate self-support group. This usually consists of a few students, not necessarily from the same subject area, meeting once a week or once a fortnight to discuss their progress, or lack of it, and helping each other in other ways. You should establish some appropriate ground rules, for example with regard to confidentiality and the making of constructive rather than destructive remarks, and try and help each other.

Mid-thesis crisis

One phenomenon that has been widely observed (see Phillips and Pugh, 2000, pp 79–80; Cryer 2000, pp 218–19) is the tendency towards a crisis in mid-thesis. You are now well into your research, churning it out day after day, and you become bored with the whole thing and ripe for distractions that will take your mind off the drudgery of your research and entertain you. While there is no simple solution to this problem – if you want to complete you have to continue the research – it can be beneficial to take a short break and then come back to it with a fresher mind. However, if you contemplate this, do stick to a defined break – there are many ex-PhD students who took a breather from their studies and then procrastinated and procrastinated about returning until it was far too late.

COMPLETING YOUR PHD

With the mid-thesis crisis overcome and the substantial research and the analysis complete, you still face what can be the momentous task of assembling all that you have done over a period of three or four years, perhaps more, into a thesis. This task will be much easier if you have written draft chapters as you went along, but these rarely fit together perfectly and work is still required to produce a coherent and cohesive account.

You have followed an intellectual journey across unknown territory. Think of yourself as the explorer producing a guidebook to where you have been and what you have seen and discovered in the process. As the author of the guidebook, you need to explain:

- your starting point and why you decided to embark on the journey (the literature and the deficiencies revealed by evaluation which led you to undertake the research);
- how you decided to undertake the journey (the methodology);
- the route you followed and the discoveries you made on the way (the substantive research chapters);
- how, in the light of the above, you redrew the route (analysis and interpretation);
- where you arrived at the end of your journey, how it differed from your starting point, and where you go from here (conclusions, knowledge added, and directions of future research in the subject).

You should start by, literally, drawing an outline map of these points. Ensure that the various stages link together and are reasonably consistent with each other so that, in general, the route is clear and can be followed easily. Then, within each part of the route – each chapter – you need to decide what must be said to take your reader through that stage and lead him or her onto the next one, bearing in mind that the deviations up highways and byways that were so fascinating to you might be irrelevant to others. Concentrate on the essentials and leave extraneous materials to footnotes, end notes or appendices.

If you do this you should have a master-map of the route as a whole and detailed guides to each of the sections of it: a template for your thesis. You should now try this out on your supervisor and ask for his or her comments before proceeding. Otherwise, when you have completed the draft you may find major flaws in the structure that necessitate a major re-write.

How much am I going to write?

You not only need to decide what you are going to write about, but also how much you will write in total and for each part of the thesis.

With regard to the total, many institutions have word limits on PhD theses, and it is important that you find out what these are and what they include, e.g. whether they relate just to the text or whether they include the bibliography and any appendices as well.

Perhaps more importantly at this stage, you need to allocate at least rough targets for each part of the thesis. Here, the key thing to think about is what you need to do to convince your examiners that your research is worthy of the award of the degree. Examiners are, as Cryer (2000, p 227) has pointed out, familiar with the general literature and the available methodologies, and their real interest is in the original scholarship of the thesis. So, for example, you should certainly not aim for half of your thesis to be taken up by the literature review, a further quarter by the methodology, and only a quarter for the original scholarship. In fact, some institutions produce guidelines (for an example see Blaxter, Hughes and Tight 1996, p 217). You should find out if your institution has any similar guidelines, or, if not, work out an appropriate distribution and agree it with your supervisor.

What style am I going to write it in?

A PhD is, of course, a work of scholarship, and the thesis will have to be written in the style known as 'academic writing'. While there is no objective definition of academic writing, it can be said to be characterised by explicitness of intention, clarity and coherence of argument and analysis, a respect for the conventions of writing in the subject or discipline, the substantiation of points by evidence, and by explicit linkages between what you are writing, what has gone before, and what is to come.

In deciding upon a style, it can be very useful to ask your supervisor(s) to identify a particular thesis or paper which is a 'model' of academic writing in your discipline and to discuss it with them before starting your own writing.

How will I go about the writing process?

One of the features of the PhD experience is that it almost always takes far longer to write up the thesis than was allowed for in the planning. The reason for this is that you now have the benefit of hindsight for the research project as a whole, and this should yield new insights and connections that you then build into the final draft. However, while this is an essential part of writing a PhD thesis, it almost always means that you end up writing against the clock, and to do this you need a high degree of self-management.

By definition, self-management is an individual thing, i.e. it depends on your preferred writing routines. Some people work best with set times each day for writing and need no interruptions; some work best intermittently and need to have background music, etc.; some work best with targets, e.g. 1000 words a day, no matter how long it takes. It is important that you identify your preferred writing routine, whatever it is, and, as far as possible, stick to it. In doing so, it may be helpful to remember what Delamont *et al* (1997, p 121) have identified as the golden rules of writing. These are:

- The more you write, the easier it gets.
- If you write every day, it becomes a habit.
- Tiny bits of writing add up to a lot of writing.
- The longer you don't write, the more difficult it is to get back in the habit.

Drafting and Submission

Once you have a first draft you should show it to your supervisor(s) and ask whether, in principle, it is likely to make the grade. If not, your supervisor(s) should indicate the additional work required; if it looks likely to pass, you can begin the process of polishing the rough diamond into a final draft.

When, usually after several iterations, you have produced the final draft, it goes back to your supervisor for a re-read and, with luck, the green light to go ahead and submit the thesis. In some institutions, it is a requirement that your supervisor approves your thesis for submission, while in others it is the decision of the candidate. In the latter case, if your supervisor still has reservations, you would be well advised to pay heed and do any additional work or writing to satisfy them before formally submitting.

When all is done and dusted and you do decide to submit, you should check your institution's regulations. Usually, you are required to give notice of submission, and you may have to conform to a range of stylistic conventions. Only when you are satisfied on this score can you print off the usually multiple copies to be bound and submitted to your institution.

PREPARATION FOR EXAMINATION

When you have formally submitted and the university is satisfied that your thesis meets its regulations, the wheels are then set in motion for the process of examination, beginning with the appointment of examiners. In this respect, practice varies between universities, but there will normally be two, one from your department (but not usually your supervisor) and one external.

While there is not, and indeed should not be, any formal procedure for consulting candidates about the external, your head of department and/or supervisor will normally be asked for nominations and they may raise the matter with you and present some possible names. If you have reservations, such as that Dr So and So in your department has consistently been sceptical of the value of your research or that Professor A N Other outside might take unkindly to the fact that your thesis has refuted his or her life's work, you can and should raise these. There is, of course, no guarantee that your preferences will be taken into account and it may be that you end up with Dr

So and Professor Other. If you do fear foul play, then in many universities it is possible to have your supervisor present at your viva (taking no part in the proceedings but able to observe) and in the unlikely event of perceived victimisation, there are usually appeal procedures that involve a fresh reading by a third examiner.

When examiners have been appointed, there is usually a hiatus of anything from a few weeks to several months while they read, digest, and form opinions about your work, following which they arrange the statutory oral examination, the viva voce.

While vivas play a part in most institutions at undergraduate level, this is usually limited, and for many postgraduates the viva on their thesis is a novel experience and it can be a daunting prospect. So it makes sense to, first, think about the possible purposes of your viva and, second, to prepare yourself for the experience.

You have already given your examiners written evidence of your abilities in the form of your thesis, and the purpose of the viva is to gain additional evidence relating to your suitability to be awarded the degree of PhD. Such evidence will normally be of two kinds, one relates specifically to issues arising from your thesis, the other, more generally, to your professional competence as a scholar.

As each PhD thesis is unique, there are no generic templates detailing what you are likely to be specifically asked about your work, but you can gain some insights into possible questions if you:

- check the publications of your examiners, which may yield clues as to their likely interests;
- look at published guidelines for external examiners in your own or in adjacent subject areas. In the case of some disciplines there are highly detailed guidelines, e.g. in psychology (British Psychological Society/UCosDA, 1995), and there are also suggested guidelines in Partington *et al* (1993, pp 74–75) for assessing theses based on experiments and on documentary studies;
- asking competent colleagues/friends to read your work and identify possible issues that could be taken up.

With regard to more general questions, as well as scrutinising your thesis, examiners will need (Partington *et al* 1993, p 77) to be satisfied that

- the thesis is substantially your own work;
- you have developed skills in research at this level;
- you have an understanding not just of your thesis but of the general field to which it relates; and
- you have fully thought through the implications of your work.

You need, then, to be prepared for questions concerning these areas as well; in particular, to show that you are fully familiar with what you have written, have a thorough mastery of the methodology to demonstrate your research skills, are aware of the wider literature pertaining to your field, and are clear about what your research means for your subject.

Thus prepared, a mock viva can help as a final step before the big day. Many departments now arrange these for their students by arranging for members of staff, preferably those who have been externals themselves, to read the thesis and ask you appropriate questions before giving you feedback on your performance. This can be invaluable in anticipating lines of inquiry and in improving your presentation skills. With these sharpened up, you should be ready for the real thing.

Before the viva, your examiners should have been in contact with each other to identify the strengths and weakness of your thesis and to reach a preliminary verdict and, upon this basis, to decide upon the objectives of the viva. They may

- pass the thesis as it stands or with minor amendments and use the viva to discuss the latter;
- pass the thesis as it stands or with minor amendments subject to satisfaction in the viva on your subject knowledge and professional competence;
- regard the thesis as genuinely marginal and use the viva to probe problem areas of your thesis and determine whether you otherwise meet the standard for the award of the degree; or
- regard the thesis as unacceptable as it stands and use the viva to guide you towards the reasons.

Where there is no doubt that the thesis meets or exceeds the standards, humane examiners will put you out of your misery and tell you at the start of the viva that they intend to recommend that you be awarded the degree, perhaps subject to minor changes. However, even if your thesis is fine, other examiners may follow the letter of the law and give you no clue at the start as to the purpose of the viva and interrogate you at length on it to establish your subject and professional credentials. So, prolonged questioning is by no means necessarily an indication of failure, and you should not be disheartened by it.

Usually, if you have not been informed at the start, at the end of the viva you will be asked to leave while your examiners confer, and then brought back in and given an informal indication of the result prior to the formal recommendation to the university. This may be

- the immediate award of the degree;
- the award of the degree subject to minor revisions to be completed within a specified period;
- the referral of the thesis for major revisions followed by re-submission and re-examination; or
- the award of a lower research degree;
- that no award be made.

If the outcomes are either of the last two, you may wish to consider an appeal, and you should consult your university's procedures. If your thesis is referred, your examiners should give you a detailed list of the work required before re-submitting the thesis. If the degree is to be awarded subject to minor revisions, again you should receive a detailed list of the changes that have to be made and then the revised thesis is re-submitted to the internal examiner. Subject to his or her certification that the changes have been made within the time limit specified, the degree is then awarded.

CONCLUSIONS

The road to a PhD is a long and hard one with many pitfalls on the way. However, as I hope this chapter has shown, you can improve your chances of gaining the degree by actively seeking to manage the processes of starting, planning, reviewing, undertaking, completing, and preparing for examination. While such management will not turn an inadequate thesis into a successful doctorate, the absence of such management can, and in the past often has, meant that a promising topic has come to nothing, i.e. the thesis has been abandoned. So, as you work for your PhD, remember that while you are being examined explicitly on your ability to make an original contribution to knowledge, you are also being examined implicitly upon your ability to manage your studies and yourself, and you need both abilities to be awarded a doctorate.

REFERENCES

Allan, G and Skinner, C (1991) *Handbook for Research Students in the Social Sciences* (London: Falmer).
Beynon, R (1993) *Postgraduate Study in the Biological Sciences* (London: Portland).

Blaxter, L, Hughes, C and Tight, M (1996) *How to Research* (Buckingham: Open University Press).

Burnham, P (1997) 'Surviving the Viva' in P Burnham (ed) *Surviving the Research Process In Politics* (London: Pinter).

British Psychological Society and UCoSDA (1995) *Guidelines for Assessment of the PhD in Psychology and Related Disciplines* (Sheffield: CVCP).

Cryer, P (2000) *The Research Student's Guide to Success*, 2nd edn (Buckingham: Society for Research Into Higher Education/Open University Press).

Delamont, S, Atkinson, P and Parry, O (1997) *Supervising the PhD: A Guide to Success* (Buckingham: Society for Research Into Higher Education/Open University Press).

Elton, L and Task Force Three (1994) 'Staff development in relation to research' in O Zuber-Skerritt and Y Ryan *Quality in Postgraduate Education* (London: Kogan Page, pp 24–37).

Frost, P and Stablein, R (1992) *Doing Exemplary Research* (Newbury Park, CA: Sage).

Green, H (1998) *The Postgraduate Viva: A Closer Look* (video) (Leeds: Leeds Metropolitan University).

Lyons, W, Scroggins, P and Bonham Rule, P (1990) *The Mentor in Graduate Education*. Studies in Higher Education, 1   5(3), pp 277–85

Moses, I (1992) *Supervising Postgraduates* (Campbelltown: Higher Education Research and Development Society of Australia).

Murray, R (1997) *The Viva* (video) (Glasgow: Centre for Academic Practice, University of Strathclyde, Glasgow).

Murrell, G (1990) *Research in Medicine: A Guide to Writing a Thesis in the Medical Sciences* (Cambridge: Cambridge University Press).

National Postgraduate Committee (1995) *Guidelines on Accommodation and Facilities for Postgraduate Research*; and (1995) *Guidelines on Codes of Practice for Postgraduate Research* (Troon: NPG).

Partington, J, Brown, G and Gordon, G (1993) *Handbook for External Examiners in Higher Education* (Sheffield: CVCP).

Phillips, E and Pugh, D (2000) *How to Get a PhD*, 3rd edn (Buckingham: Open University Press).

Rudestam, K and Newton, R (1992) *Surviving Your Dissertation* (London: Sage).

Salmon, P (1992) *Achieving a PhD – Ten Students' Experience*. (London: Trentham).

Welsh, J (1979) *The First Year of Postgraduate Research Study* (Guildford: Society for Research Into Higher Education).

Young, K, Fogarty, S and McRae, S (1987) *The Management of Doctoral Studies in the Social Sciences* (London: Policy Studies Institute).

4 Documenting your work

Vivien Martin

Whatever type of research you do, you will need to keep records of what you do, how, when, where and why. You may not think that this is important; you may even think that you will easily remember everything and can write it up later. You won't, and you can't!

WHY DOCUMENT?

Your perception of what you do and why you are doing it will change in subtle ways as your research progresses. As you become clearer about some aspects, you forget earlier doubts. As your findings accumulate, you form firmer ideas. If some findings do not confirm hesitant proposals, you are likely to reform them or forget them and may concentrate on those that seem to offer interesting results. Much of the richness of your original thinking and planning is lost, and hesitant directions that do not look immediately rewarding may be prematurely closed. Without good records you will forget earlier ideas.

Research is often discussed more for its results than for its processes. In planning your research you will have studied research methods and taken time to make a plan of your proposed work. You may think in terms of the broad question you plan to address and the ways in which you will explore the question. You will consider the research methods and try to choose appropriate ones for your intended study. You will probably plan the process carefully to ensure that your data collection is suitably rigorous. You will intend to write your 'Methods' chapter explaining how you have planned. However, you may not have thought about how you will demonstrate that you worked in a methodical way.

Many people declare their intentions in the 'Methods' section and then jump straight to describing results. You would expect to have to substantiate your results, to offer supporting evidence for everything you claim to have found. So why not expect to do the same for your methods, for the process you have used to collect and analyse your data? Experienced researchers know that the plan is only the starting point and that many annoying and illuminating hitches will occur between plan and report. Much of the learning for you and your reader will be in the detail of the process planned and the discovery of what really happened; why changes were made, what could have been anticipated and what could not, what caused time to slip and which expectations were unrealistic.

One advantage of having records of your process is in being able to supply and use the detail of the whole story whenever you may need it. If all goes reasonably well, you can use the detail to substantiate your discussion of the planned and the actual methods used. If anything goes wrong you can use the detail to explore and explain. Some researchers despair if their original idea or hypothesis seems to be either unprovable or even disproven. But with good records of the process there is still much to say about why this might have happened and perhaps evidence to recommend a different approach another time.

One more good reason for methodical record keeping is that at least you are writing something and you won't have to face the intimidating blank sheet when you start to write up the full report. You will have a lot to start with and it will contribute to many sections including

- the introduction of why you are doing what you are doing;
- the background for the study;
- the context;
- the choice of methods; and
- the report of findings.

It may also contribute to your discussion of strengths and weaknesses in the study. How can you ignore such potential value from what is simply a little self-discipline?

In many areas of work it is essential to use recording methods (including journals, laboratory notes and software files) as everyday documenting procedures. These records have to be kept in a way that fulfils the purpose of recording, and the resulting records have to be available to those with authority to use them, consult them and inspect them. There may be issues of confidentiality and, if the records contain information about individuals who could be identified, the records may be subject to the legal conditions regarding data protection. These conditions are no different for a researcher and you should ensure that your proposals for record keeping are legal, conform to any regulations within the organization in which you are researching and are approved by the relevant ethics committee if there is one for your area of research.

HOW TO DOCUMENT?

The methods that you choose for keeping records of your research will reflect the type of research and the conditions in which you are working as a researcher. Your record-keeping system can be a great help if you plan it carefully and acknowledge the possibility of your own weaknesses from the start. The system you plan can be designed to compensate, in part, for your personal weaknesses. If you recognise that you do not always make careful notes or keep all the details that might be needed later, design a system for yourself that will always jog your memory whilst you are able to remember the detail. For example, if your work will include interviewing people, use a record form that requires you to fill in the essential information. If you conduct a number of telephone interviews, you could record these on a form that will prompt you to keep a full record. You can design a form as the basis of your recording system by thinking of the essential information that you would need if you had to return to ask more, perhaps as much as a year later. As a starting point I suggest that you need to record:

- the date of interview,
- the name (of person being interviewed),
- the name of interviewer if you are not conducting all the interviews yourself,
- how the interview was conducted (in person or by phone),
- contact details of the interviewee (address, phone number, e-mail),
- the title of interviewee if the nature of the work or affiliations are an issue, possibly the address and contact details of any relevant organisation,
- the purpose of the interview,
- the content of the interview (this may be a verbatim recording, if necessary), and

- any agreed action (this may include giving the interviewee an opportunity to review the record kept of the interview).

In addition you may want to include other headings relevant to your research.

When you begin a research project it often seems that it is so fresh in your mind that you think you will always remember the people and organisations involved. However, it is amazing how quickly such details slip your mind and how quickly your interests and concerns can move to a different focus.

If your records are to be of use to you, there are some characteristics that are essential to try to achieve. Records must be accurate or they will be misleading. They must be relevant to the research that you are conducting. The record must be written clearly, an illegible record is useless. The record must be as complete as possible; this often means that it should include, as a minimum, details of the source of the data, the full or summarised content and the date the record was made. This information in a record will help you to decide how reliable it is for potential use in your research.

Consider using different methods of recording for different stages or different aspects of the study so that the method used fits as naturally as possible with the way in which you are working. There are several methods that you might consider using.

Diary

Keep a diary or journal of the research from first idea to completion of write-up. The diary might be handwritten in a hardback book or in several small notebooks that you date and number as you fill them. You might prefer to use file paper and ring files so that you can rearrange the pages as themes emerge (but if you do this, number or date the pages so that you can remember where they originated). You may prefer to keep the diary in a computer program, but this would restrict you to making entries only when you have access to the computer.

You may also consider using the diary as a major part of your research and to analyse its contents occasionally. There are software programs with search facilities that can help you to do this. Other ways of pulling out themes and recurring issues once there is enough material in your diary include

- using highlighter pens,
- applying different coloured Post-its to significant pages,
- colour coding entries with stick-on dots,
- using coloured pens, or
- photocopying and cutting and pasting to make up reconstructed pages.

A useful source of further information about this approach is in Judith Bell's (1993) book, *Doing Your Research Project*.

In some research, you might ask your respondents to keep diaries. You might do this to elicit recurring issues, maybe to identify critical incidents in their work or lives, perhaps to identify their problem areas and responses to problems. People are often prepared to collaborate to assist in research and will often agree to keep a diary for a researcher. However, if you have a particular focus in your research it will be necessary to give clear directions about the focal area, the types of issues that you would like them to address and the length of time that you would like them to keep the diary. If your research is not so closely focused and you want them to join you in conducting a broad inquiry into the issues that they encounter over a period of time, make that clear to them. This approach to research brings some other issues into consideration. If you ask people to keep personal records with the expectation that they will reveal the contents to you, you are asking for access to very personal matters. Before you set off into research of this nature, consider the implications of forming such a relationship with your prospective respondents. In *Collecting and Interpreting Qualitative Materials*, Denzin and Lincoln (1998) offer very helpful thoughts about the responsibilities of a researcher who engages in an enquiry into the experiences of others.

Recording observations

In a study involving observation, you will need a way to record the issues relating to your research rather than everything that is going on. Are you an outsider observing a setting or are you a participant observer? What are the implications of each position?

Your note making will need a mixture of writing, diagramming, mapping and drawing. The setting will need to be recorded in terms of anything that may impact on your data collection. This might include a map of the setting (showing physical features such as doors, windows, furniture, if it is a room). If the research concerns movements of people or animals, this will need to be shown, probably using diagrams to show paths taken and timing, perhaps coded to indicate who moved or how the movement was made. You may find it helpful to devise grids to tick as things occur or checklists of things to look for and mark off. Observations that include listening to speech or sounds will need to be recorded in some way, perhaps with tape recordings or perhaps with diagrams showing the frequency of speech and types of interaction. Video recording might be sensible in some studies, but similar issues arise as for photography.

Bell (1993) introduces methods suitable for recording interaction between people. In any study of this sort you will need pilot studies to derive a good method for recording observations and to be sure that you record what you intend. You will also need to check that you do not change the setting too much by the use of your recording process. For example, if you choose a method of recording that is not unobtrusive you might accidentally change how your subjects behave by attracting them to look at the interesting diagrams you are drawing!

Could you benefit from structured observation, such as activity sampling with a strict framework for when and how observations will be made and recorded? More information about how to do this can be found in *Management Research* by Mark Easterby-Smith *et al* (1991).

To some extent, the method you choose for recording observations will relate to your approach as a researcher and it would be wise to be aware of the approaches used traditionally by your discipline or related disciplines. Anthropology field notes record observations, as do the interaction diagrams used by social scientists and the activity samples of organisational behaviour practitioners. Your choice of method should relate to the traditions and expectations of your disciplinary area.

Laboratory notes

Laboratory notes apply more to experimental research. If you set up an experiment to prove your hunch, you will need to keep very accurate and methodical records to defend your findings. You should be careful to establish a method of note keeping from the beginning of your studies so that your records are consistent. You must even record mistakes and omissions, such as missed entries or lost information. The planning is very important, so consult the literature from your discipline, for example Plutchik (1974) on experimental research in psychology. It can be very helpful to look at recent work in your area of study to see how other people have kept records, particularly if there are examples of similar research. Remember that the records you keep might have to be inspected by others if your claims are to be verified, so ensure that notes are clearly written and could be understood by someone else.

Recording voices

If your research involves interviews or focus groups, how will you record what people say? People usually speak more quickly than a researcher can write, so although it is often possible to make notes, catching verbatim quotes is more difficult. You may think your notes are sufficient, but they will be your précis of what you have heard, a brief analysis of what was said, not what was *actually* said. One way to record what was actually said is to explain to the interviewee that you need to write down every word and that pauses will be needed. This is often acceptable if the interview raises questions that require thoughtful answers. It is sometimes more acceptable than tape recording.

Audio tape recording is the obvious way to record sound but it does have some hazards. The first consideration is the effect of having an obvious tape recorder between you and your interviewee or group. It can inhibit conversation and it can present difficulties of confidentiality if respondents might be recognised and would rather be anonymous. If you are tempted to record but not to tell respondents, consider the ethical issues and the constraints your covert approach might bring in terms of the use of your data. You might also consider what the consequences might be for you or the subjects of your recording if you were found out. *Focus Groups: Theory and Practice* by Stewart and Shamdasani (1990), outlines the issues you will need to consider if you are planning to hold a focus group to obtain data.

If you think that tape recording would not present particular problems for your interviewees, it is best to explain why you want a recording, how you will use it and then to record openly. Plan to have an appropriate time available on the tape so that you do not have to disrupt the interview to change it. Choose the tape recorder with care and ensure that it can record effectively in the setting, particularly in group work. Learn how to use it confidently before you are in the interview. Be cautious about using mini tapes and the very small recorders because you might eventually want to copy the tape or to edit bits from it, at which time you will need more versatile equipment and standard audio tape size. Consider the advantages and disadvantages of using voice-activated equipment, as the pauses between voices might be significant and important. You are likely to find a pause facility on the machine useful when you play back to make notes. Some researchers recommend using a variable speed playback to help at the analysis stage.

If you are not a good note maker, consider using a personal dictaphone to record your research process, the thoughts and additional ideas that occur and what actually happens as you go along. This is essentially the diary approach, but keeping an oral diary instead of a written one. You will need to write something eventually if you are making a research report, but you could then refer to your recordings and quote passages as appropriate or you could have a typed transcript made as you complete tapes.

Whenever you use tapes, do be sure to label them as you use them with date and contents. If you use a large number of tapes, consider how you will file them so that it is easy to find any particular one when you want it later. If the tapes are crucial to your research, consider making back-up copies.

If your research will require you to document long oral reports, other concerns arise relating to the personal nature of biographical accounts. You may need to keep a very detailed record containing personal information about the individual's life and experience. *Recording Oral History* by Yow (1994) is a helpful text and offers examples of forms that you might use.

Card index

For some record-keeping, the card index is ideal. It may seem old-fashioned or associated too much with office files, but there is a very practical advantage in its portability and the portability of packs of file cards. Researchers can carry a few cards around with them and use them wherever they are to make an instant record. The cards can be filed in a system once you are back in your study area. An example of this is to use cards to record the sources in a literature search, perhaps to note key quotes. The cards can be arranged in a helpful sequence at the point when you write the literature review, then rearranged when you compile your bibliography.

Computer database

The main advantage of a card index over a computer one used to be portability, but laptop computers have now changed this. If you have access to a laptop, check the software now available to help researchers at many stages of research. There are some very useful software packages that will link stages of the literature review in a similar way to a manual system with card files. Some of the popular bibliographic packages include: Pro-Cite, Reference Manager, EndNote Plus, Papyrus and Bib/Search. You should record the full reference for every book or journal article that you might want to list in your final bibliography; the publication date and details and the page numbers that are particularly relevant.

Your searches will probably include web pages. For bibliographic purposes, you should keep similar records; the full URL, the correct title of the resource and the author's name if possible, also note the date(s) that you used the site. It is useful to keep records of your online searches so that you can save time if you need to re-visit sites. Make sure that you keep a copy of the copyright statement on a page that you might want to refer to and note any citation instructions. You will also need to note the last date on which you visited a site mentioned in your references. If you enter into any e-mail correspondence, remember to save the documents, as these too can be useful references.

If your research involves collection of a considerable amount of data from which you will make a content analysis, consider putting the whole data collection into a package which will subsequently help with the analysis through the use of key words and phrases. You may be able to do this directly with a laptop if you can key in your data as you collect them. With a desktop model it may be less convenient and you should consider the advantages and disadvantages carefully if it will mean transcribing written notes that might be used effectively without being computerised.

Again, a computer can be used very effectively for diary keeping and for keeping a personal log of progress through the research process.

Mapping and making diagrams

Some sorts of research will involve complex ideas that can be described and recorded visually as maps. This can be useful if there is not yet an obvious sequence or priority, such that making lists may be less appropriate. Maps and diagrams may also allow ideas to be linked in ways that would be difficult with sequential writing.

Mind-mapping is one approach that works very well for some people. It can be used to develop detailed thoughts around a central theme. You write the theme in a central bubble and then draw branches out from it as related thoughts arise. The main thoughts are the lines out from the bubble and branches from these represent aspects of the main idea. More information about this method can be found in *Use Your Head* (Buzan 1989) and other books by Tony Buzan. The method is useful at the early stages of generating ideas and connecting them. Some people like to use this method to explore their first thoughts about an idea, as you might if you were carrying out a brainstorming session with a group of people. It is also very useful in planning chapters of writing and mapping out how to report various aspects of research studies. Another use of the mind-map is to make a quick record of a day or an event when it is more important to catch the elements and associated thoughts and feelings than to make a linear time-related record.

More conventional mapping may be useful in research records to record where something is located or to record differences over time when the research relates to physical changes in an environment or the use people or animals make of an environment. More comment on this method was made earlier in the section on recording observations.

Another recording system for group work is cognitive mapping, which is familiar in strategy development workshops in business and management research. The idea is based on mapping perceptions of the setting and has connections with the Repertory Grid technique. Groups can work with coloured cards and walls of flip chart paper to map out issues and relationships and the group map can be the basis of subsequent planning. More information about how to use this can be found in *Management Research* (Easterby-Smith *et al* 1991).

Remember that diagrams can save the use of a lot of words and explanations. Consider use of flow diagrams, Venn diagrams, multiple cause diagrams, fishbone diagrams and force-field diagrams.

Drawing

Drawing is less formal than mapping. You might make a drawing of something as a record, a traditional approach of many archaeologists, palaeontologists and other researchers whose work involves recording objects.

One way to use drawing is as a projective technique. For example, I might ask you to make a drawing of your research as you see it at the moment. You might draw yourself struggling to climb a mountain or disappearing down a black hole, or perhaps more cheerfully relaxing on a beach in the sun. The drawing could be the basis of a discussion about why you chose the images and what this means for you in terms of the progress of your research. The drawing would record the initial stimulus for the discussion and could be part of your record keeping of the process of your research. This has been described in words and, clearly, words could be used for this process instead of drawing. For example, you might use metaphor to liken your feelings as a researcher to something else, such as 'As a researcher, I feel like a fish out of water'. Once you, or a colleague, have said this, it is possible to explore the feelings that have prompted the remark and to look for ways in which this person can be supported to feel more at home as a researcher.

With individuals or groups you might construct a *Rich Picture*. The idea of this is to capture a situation in as much of its complexity as possible, showing all its component groups and individuals, sites and connections, communications, conflicts, inputs and outputs, and messy areas. Draw it with pictures, symbols and connecting lines, in any way that makes sense to the individual or the group. If you draw it in discussion with a group, you will capture the discussion and the ideas of the group. For an individual it captures the thought process and the personal perception. These can be used only as a record, but are more usually the first stage in making an analysis of problem areas and muddled systems. In its most formal form, this is part of a process called *Soft Systems Analysis* as described in the book by Peter Checkland (1981), *Systems Thinking, Systems Practice.*

Photographs in record keeping

If your research concerns something that can be communicated effectively in visual records then it may be appropriate to use photographs. Consider all the usual research issues in deciding how and when to use them, because the subjective choice of viewpoint, span of view and selectivity are all choices made by the recording photographer. If you take photographs yourself to support your research, make sure you record:

- when you took it (date and time),
- where from,
- what you were looking at, and
- the reason why you took it.

The last point is important because of the delay in processing and the possibility that you will look at the prints and wonder what one or two were supposed to be about. When you look at the subject you photograph you know exactly what you are focusing on, but the camera will record everything evenly unless you are sufficiently skilled to ensure that you focus on your subject and reduce the importance of everything else. If you are not a skilled photographer, you will need your notes to make good use of the prints. If you use the prints in writing up your research, you will need to reference them and to link them to your text. An example of use of photographs in research is their use in marketing research. A researcher was evaluating potential shop sites in different high streets, looking at which areas had the most people shopping at particular times of the day. Photographs taken regularly from the same spots were used with maps of streets with shops marked on them and the numbers of people present at each time were noted. The photographs added visual information that was richer than the other methods could produce alone.

Memoranda and correspondence

As soon as you start to research, you will produce and receive all sorts of related notes, phone calls, e-mails, letters, comments. Consider right from the beginning how you might keep these in an accessible form in case they are useful later. It is easy to lose the more trivial things, including scraps of paper with notes and phone numbers, handwritten memos and letters that you write yourself requesting information. A personal example of why keeping these somewhere is important can be found when I wrote off for college prospectuses, for some of my own research, put them all in a box and pondered about how to analyse them but did not use them for several years. The original idea changed and developed and I went to use these prospectuses in a comparison with current ones. I found that they were not consistently dated and that some prospectuses were for one academic year and some for another, so I needed my original letter to fix the point at which the prospectuses had been requested. It was sheer luck that I found a copy of that letter. Now I file all correspondence relating to research even if it does not seem immediately relevant.

It is easy to disregard e-mail messages as part of the correspondence that contributes to your research records. If you anticipate using e-mail for anything related to your research, think about how you will file this correspondence. It is easy to form the habit of copying all relevant e-mail messages, those you send and those you receive, into your permanent records. You can then file them according to their respective topics, as you would file paper records.

Memoranda of all sorts can influence and shape research and might subsequently be seen as crucial to the formation of your research idea. Try to record how you became interested in doing a particular piece of research. If it relates in any way to photographs you discovered in the attic or an article in a newspaper or a set of receipts or bus tickets, keep all the evidence. For this type of material, I suggest just putting things in a cardboard box labelled research rather than trying to develop a filing system. When you want to retrieve something you will soon find out if you need a more sophisticated system.

Storage and retrieval

Records are no use at all unless you can retrieve them when you need them, preferably quickly and accurately. If all else fails, throwing everything relevant into a cardboard box will at least preserve the material, but the task of retrieval may be so daunting that you never actually get round to searching for the item you want. Some thought given to the storage of records and retrieval of data will pay off later! Consider storing in date order, in topics, in themes, in labelled envelopes, in transparent envelopes in ring files, in labelled boxes, in card files, in computer files: much depends on your material and your own preferred methods. There is little in the research process that is more annoying than having to retrace your steps to find the exact reference for a quotation or the exact source of a piece of information.

REFERENCES

Bell, J. (1993) *Doing Your Research Project* (Milton Keynes: Open University Press).
Buzan, T (1989) *Use Your Head* (London: BBC Books).
Checkland, P (1981) *Systems Thinking, Systems Practice* (London: Wiley).
Denzin, N K and Lincoln, Y S. (eds.) (1998) *Collecting and Interpreting Qualitative Materials* (London: Sage).
Easterby-Smith, M. *et al* (1991) *Management Research, an Introduction* (London: Sage).
Plutchik, R (1974) *Foundations of Experimental Research* (London: Harper and Row).
Stewart, D W and Shamdasani, P N (1990) *Focus Groups: Theory and Practice* (London: Sage Publications).
Yow, V R (1994) *Recording Oral History* (London: Sage).

5 Word processing tips

R Allan Reese

TIPS

Writing is hard for most of us. Eventually you must write your thesis (see Chapter 37 for guidance). It will be very hard if you leave that task until you have finished your research. Far better to write small sections as you progress, at the same time as you are making notes. Write a little at a time and write often. Keep a research log, in a bound book, so that you can jot down what you have read, discoveries, ideas, events, meetings, any observations, thoughts and advice, in strict sequence. When you come to write up your findings, this will help you to trace how and when you made progress.

Transfer your notes regularly from your research log into computer documents. This will be good preparation for editing your notes into your finished thesis. Also, the act of copy typing your notes will focus your mind on them and stimulate further thoughts.

Do not assume that writing a thesis is like a very (very) long essay or scientific paper. The regulations vary considerably between universities and conventions vary between disciplines, so check carefully what is expected of you. However, it would be a great disappointment if you completed three or more years of research without having something new and interesting to add. Research students are expected to develop their communications skills, so let us take that literally and hope that your thesis will be readable, and read, by more than just the examiners who are paid to do so. A word processor gives you many tools that you can exploit to make writing less burdensome and more productive, and to add value to the product. The following tips aim to persuade you to see a word processor, such as Word, as more than a typewriter that churns out repeated drafts.

Multiple files open

Have several files open whenever you are writing. Apart from the text you are working on, use another window for notes. Or two extra windows: one for notes you are working from, and another for new ideas. A word processor saves the list of 'recently used files' after each session, and can be programmed to open set files when restarted. Software that emulates the sticky notelets used in offices is also very cheap and effective.

Words and meaning

Whenever you come across a technical or jargon word, or any word that might be misunderstood or whose meaning is contentious, mark it *how??* as something to add to your glossary. Incidentally, a *technical* word is not the same as a *jargon* word. The former is a word that is needed in a specific technical situation. The latter is used pretentiously or falsely to give an impression of special

knowledge. Technical words should be explained. Jargon should be avoided. Using an odd character sequence (such as the ?? above) as a flag allows you to carry on writing. You can later use the
Find command to find all the words you want to explain.

Glossary

Build your own glossary and thesaurus of your topic to ensure that

- you recognise what are specialised or jargon words,
- you understand the special vocabulary of your field and that you *share* that understanding with
  your supervisor and peers; and
- you can explain your special terms or usage to a wider audience.

Something that is obvious or commonplace to you and your daily contacts may be a complete
barrier to readers elsewhere, or a few years on. Published research not uncommonly gives the
impression (true or false) that words or phrases have been used formulaically; they establish group
identity and membership, but have no precise significance. Communication has broken down.

Find and replace

Find and replace can save you time and improve your writing. For example, you might type cryptic abbreviations for complex but frequently used words or phrases that can then be expanded
later. You will then more readily notice if you are overusing stock phrases, and ensure that technical terms are used consistently. Check, in particular, that acronyms are used consistently, are
spelled out at least once when first used and are included in the glossary.

Spell checkers

Spell checkers confirm only that a word is in the stored list. They do not confirm that you have
chosen the right word. Use your glossary to create your own custom-spelling list, and add to the
exceptions file words that you use specifically. The spell-checker will then waste less time on your
specialist vocabulary, and will highlight commonplace words for you to check as correct in *your*
context. The skill of writing comes, first, from the choice of words, so have a dictionary on hand
(either as a book or online) as you work.

Style formats

Use **styles** (a technical term in word processing, meaning the application of a set of formatting
features to a piece of text) rather than explicit formatting. Use styles for headings, for standard
paragraphs, and for quoted paragraphs, which should be indented and single-spaced. Incidentally,
Word's default normal paragraph (unspaced and unindented) does not match any accepted standard. Learn to create new styles. Not only will your work be more consistent, but you will think in
terms of the meaning to the reader: This is the *Title of a Book*, whereas this is *emphasised*.

Style checkers

While I should like to recommend the tools that check 'grammar and style' as enthusiastically as
spell-checkers, the truth is that they can be misleading and time wasting. The checking tools built

into mainstream word processors do not, for some reason, match the performance and sophistication of standalone programs from ten years earlier. Many users turn the feature off, while all who use it in the majority of cases disagree with the 'improvement' suggested by the software. The benefit is to focus your attention on features of the text. Personally, I use the style checker only to note when sentences have dragged on for too long and sometimes split the ideas into separate sentences.

Outline

Use **outlining** to establish a logical skeleton to your thesis and to help you navigate round it. *Planners* are writers who plan the outline first and then expand it. *Discoverers* are writers who write free text before imposing a structure. Other strategies for writing have been described, and you may well vary your approach at different times. With outlining, you can view your thesis as various levels of headings, or as the full text. Outlining can create and insert a *Table of Contents* from your headings, adding the page numbers automatically.

Keep copies . . .

When you work on a valuable file, such as your thesis, make frequent copies. Do not rely on the automatic backup that keeps only one previous version on the same disk as your working version. Make extra copies, with the file or directory name indicating a sequence number or date so that you can retrace the development of your text.

. . . on floppy disks, zip disks, CD-R or anything portable

Backup disks are cheap. Although files on a university file server may be very secure, it does no harm to make copies onto floppy disks that you can store elsewhere. If you do most of your writing on a home machine, make copies and store them at your workplace. Or post them home to Mum.

Graphics

A single graphic may form a larger file than all of the text in your thesis. When including computer graphics, do not physically insert them into the working file. Either use OLE (Object Linking and Embedding) linkage and display a 'place-holder' while you are writing, or just insert a note to yourself as a reminder to insert the graphic in the final stages of laying out the text. A thesis does not need elaborate desk-top publishing (DTP) page layout, and your graphics or pictures can easily appear on pages by themselves.

Line spacing

True double-spacing with a proportional font, such as the ubiquitous Times Roman, looks *dreadful* and is difficult to read. This is because the inter-word spacing is so much smaller than the inter-line spacing. Most readers will accept one-and-a-half line spacing on your word processor as 'double-spacing'. It looks better and saves you time and paper when printing.

Fonts

A font is a style or design of type. Two classes of font are those with serifs and those without serifs (called sans-serif), serifs being the tiny decorations at the extremities of the main strokes of characters. Fonts with serifs include Times, Goudy and Baskerville. Sans serif fonts include Gill, Arial and Univers. Serif fonts are generally used for large bodies of text because tests show they speed up comprehension and are preferred by adult readers. Sans serif types are more suited for display, such as text headings or as labels in figures. The contrast helps to distinguish the main text from an insertion.

Font sizes

Heights of type characters are measured in points. There are approximately 72 points to the inch (a little more than 28 to the centimetre). The minimum font size for a thesis is 6 pt (honest – it was in British Standard BS8241) and the default in Word is 10 pt, but on A4 paper, with standard margins, this gives rather too many words for comfort across each line. Make your main text 11 pt for improved readability and less eyestrain.

The best overall advice for student writers comes from the regulations of Southampton University: 'It is not only courteous but also in your own interests to ensure that examiners can read the thesis easily.'

RECOMMENDED READING

Matthews, J R, Bowen, J M and Matthews, R W (2001) *Successful Scientific Writing: a Step-by-step Guide for Biomedical Scientists*, 2nd edn (Cambridge University Press).

Zinsser, W K (1998) *On Writing Well: the Classic Guide to Writing Non-fiction* (6th revised and updated edn (Harper Reference).

6 Ethics of research

Tony Greenfield

Kant's wonder
Two things fill my mind with ever-increasing wonder and awe the more often and the more intensely the reflection dwells on them:
> *the starry heavens above me*
> *and*
> *the moral law within me.*

Critique of Pure Reason
Immanuel Kant (1724–1804)

INTRODUCTION

This chapter is about the ethics of well designed and executed research; it is about honesty in analysis and reporting of results.

It is *not* about moral questions relating to projects such as experiments using aborted foetuses, or the release of genetically altered viruses for the control of crop pests, or the development of weapons of war.

The ethics of medical research have rightly demanded attention, which has led to legislation, international agreements and declarations, regulatory authorities and local committees empowered to approve and monitor research projects. This emphasis, which arises from human concern, has extended to research about animals and the environment. There has been much publicity and debate in all media about the ethics of research in these areas.

If you are researching in some area of medicine, either human or animal, or into some aspect of the environment, you will almost certainly have thought about the ethical aspects of your intentions. However, if your research is in some other area such as sociology, education, physics, chemistry, materials, electronics, computing, mechanics or industrial manufacturing, you may think that there are no ethical questions for you to consider.

You would be wrong to think that. Fraud is an obvious ethical matter but, surprisingly, so are experimental design, planning, management, execution and publication.

If you know yourself to be thoroughly honest, you must be confident that you will never be deliberately unethical. Unfortunately, no matter how good a person you are and how well intentioned, there is the possibility, indeed it is very likely, that you will be inadvertently unethical, insomuch as you infringe the accepted code of research behaviour. Anybody who embarks on research is at risk of such inadvertent unethical behaviour. Avoidance demands good advice at all stages. Where will you find that advice? Start here and follow the leads.

BACKGROUND

We start with some definitions and, in the rest of the chapter, look at some good principles and bad behaviour.

Ethics, in its widest sense, as the principles of good human behaviour, is one of the issues for which philosophers have striven to provide guidance. Plato, in about 400 BC, proposed that there were *forms* of all things, including a *form of the good*. We could never experience true forms, but could at least approach them through knowledge.

For Plato, bad behaviour was the result of ignorance. Despite the enormous influence of his ideas, especially on religious belief, few people today would accept them in their original guise. For example, philosophers of the postmodern school hold the view that there are no absolute standards, and that morality can only be culturally determined.

There have been many philosophers, and theories, in the intervening years. Kant emphasised the *will* and the importance of intention. His categorical *imperative* is stated by Russell (1946) as: 'Act as if the maxim of your action were to become through your will a general natural law'. The utilitarians, Jeremy Bentham and others, concentrated on consequences, and the 'greatest-happiness to the greatest-number' principle. Their ideas had a great, and generally highly beneficial, influence on British government during the middle of the 19th century, and probably still exert their influence today. Nietzsche's intense individualism was in stark contrast to this. He argued that such paradigms would stifle creativity.

The works of the major philosophers are not usually easy reading and, given the other demands on your time, you may think a more appealing understanding of ethics was given by Charles Kingsley in his children's adventure *The Water Babies*:

> *She is the loveliest fairy in the world and her name is Mrs Doasyouwouldbedoneby*

If philosophers cannot agree on the basic principles of ethics, and commentators cannot always agree about the correct interpretation of their work, it is hardly surprising that there is even more diversity of opinion about the practical application of those principles. Some philosophers, such as Nietzsche, had their ideas grotesquely misrepresented, and then reinterpreted in a more generous light. Hollingdale's translation of Nietzsche's *Thus Spake Zarathustra* sold well in the late 1960s. Despite all the controversy, there is enough common ground to establish codes of conduct which are generally accepted.

CODES OF CONDUCT

Most professional organisations have their own codes of conduct that are largely about the ethical standards that are expected of members. One of the best known of these codes of conduct is embodied in the *Declaration of Helsinki*. This was first adopted by the World Medical Association (WMA) at Helsinki in 1964. There have been several amendments since then. The latest was at the WMA meeting in Edinburgh in 2000.

Even if your research may be far removed from 'biomedical research involving human objects', which is what the Helsinki declaration is about, you should read it. Many of the points can be interpreted more widely. One, from an early edition of the declaration, that clearly applies to all research, without exception, and that includes yours, is:

> *It is unethical to conduct research which is badly planned or poorly executed*

This has been restated in the latest edition as:

> *The design and performance of each experimental procedure involving human subjects should be clearly formulated in an experimental protocol*

My view is that this principle should apply to all research, whether or not involving human subjects.

Here is a further selection of points:

- ... research ... must conform to generally accepted scientific principles ... based on adequately performed ... experimentation and on a thorough knowledge of the scientific literature.
- Every ... research project ... should be preceded by careful assessment of predictable risks in comparison with foreseeable benefits ...
- In publication of the results of ... research ... preserve the accuracy of the results. Report of experimentation not in accordance with the principles ... should not be accepted for publication.
- The research protocol should always contain a statement of the ethical considerations involved.
- Special caution must be exercised in the conduct of research which may affect the environment.

Since all research involves the collection, analysis, interpretation and presentation of data, some points from the codes of conduct of statisticians are worthy of mention.

The Royal Statistical Society declares:

- Professional membership of the Society is an assurance of ability and integrity.
- ... within their chosen fields ... have an appropriate knowledge and understanding of relevant legislation, regulations and standards and ... comply with such requirements.
- ... have regard to basic human rights and ... avoid any actions that adversely affect such rights.
- ... identities of subjects should be kept confidential unless consent for disclosure is explicitly obtained.
- ... not disclose or authorise to be disclosed, or use for personal gain or to benefit a third party, confidential information ... except with prior written consent.
- ... seek to avoid being put in a position where they might become privy to or party to activities or information concerning activities which would conflict with their responsibilities.
- Whilst free to engage in controversy, no fellow shall cast doubt on the professional competence of another without good cause.
- ... shall not lay claim to any level of competence which they do not possess.
- ... any professional opinion ... shall be objective and reliable.

Some points from the code of conduct of the Institute of Statisticians (now merged with the Royal Statistical Society) were:

- The primary concern ... the public interest and the preservation of professional standards.
- Fellows should not allow any misleading summary of data to be issued in their name.
- A statistical analysis may need to be amplified by a description of the way the data were selected and the way any apparently erroneous data were corrected or rejected. Explicit statements may also be needed about the assumptions made when selecting a method of analysis. Views or opinions based on general knowledge or belief should be clearly distinguished from views or opinions derived from the statistical analysis being reported.

- Standards of integrity required of a professional statistician should not normally conflict with the interests of a client or employer. If such a conflict does occur, the public interest and professional standards shall be paramount.

None of these points needs elaboration. You can judge which apply to your research. However, thinking in terms of medical research, the ethical implications of statistically substandard research may be summarised as:

- **misuse of patients:** put at risk or inconvenience for no benefit; subsequently given inferior treatment;
- **misuse of resources:** diverted from more worthwhile use;
- **misleading published results:** future research misdirected.

It is worth remembering that:

> *precise conclusions cannot be drawn from inadequate data.*
>
> *Biometrika Tables for Statisticians*
> Pearson and Hartley (1966)

POLITICS

Facts are sometimes distorted for political advantage. The ways in which this is done may also be applied in scientific research, so some discussion of them is appropriate with a warning to be on your guard.

There is no official code of conduct about 'official statistics', those tables and graphs that are published by government departments and reach the public through newspapers, radio and television. However, there is wide concern in Britain, and in most countries in the world, about the way that governments handle the figures. In Britain, for example, we are told that unemployment figures are expected to fall again, that the economy is recovering, that the poor are better off and that more is being spent on the National Health Service. Can we believe such statements?

Some tricks of official statistics:

- burying unfavourable statistics in a mass of detail;
- changing definitions (what constitutes a major hospital project; items included and method of calculation of the retail prices index; who is unemployed);
- discrediting authors of unfavourable reports.

CUTTING CORNERS

Some of these guidelines are illustrated in the following anecdote from my own experience.

Pharmaceutical companies are naturally eager to conclude clinical trials quickly and favourably. This eagerness constitutes a commercial pressure on clinical research departments or agencies, and all others involved. This is fair enough provided no corners are cut and the highest ethical standards are maintained. Generally this is so, but sometimes statistical analysis reveals that it is far from the case. What should I, the statistician, do then?

I believe that I must state my opinion firmly, without fear of loss of business or even of a libel action. I should do this just as if the trial had been conducted properly and the results had been entirely favourable, with the expectation that the company would respect and honour my work and opinion.

The following example is of a trial that was designed and conducted by a pharmaceutical company. The data, already coded and entered into a computer file, came my way for analysis because the company was in difficulties, some of which will be revealed.

The trial was an open, randomised, phase three, multicentre study (see Chapter 19). The protocol specified that 150 eligible patients would be recruited by 12 investigators. In fact 32 patients were recruited by five investigators, one of whom recruited only one patient. Of those 32, only 21 patients were clinically evaluable and only seven were microbiologically evaluable.

The general conclusion was that nothing useful emerged from this study except for a strong message to the pharmaceutical company that they must pay closer attention to the design, planning, management and execution of trials than had been exhibited in this case.

Scientific integrity demanded comments on these aspects of this study. Recall that the *Declaration of Helsinki* (1975), states (section 4.2):

> It is unethical to conduct research which is badly planned or poorly executed.

It is generally accepted, by medical research ethics committees, that if the number of patients is too small to obtain a useful and significant result, then patients will have been submitted fruitlessly to inconvenience, discomfort, doubt of outcome, and to risk. Such a trial would be unethical.

The writers of the protocol assumed that if there were a 75 per cent evaluability rate, approximately 112 of the 150 patients would be eligible for efficacy analysis. In fact 21 of the recruited patients were clinically evaluable (65 per cent).

The assumptions of a cure rate of 85 per cent for the better of the two treatments and a 23 per cent difference between the two, with a significance level of 0.05 and a power of 0.8, indicated that 112 patients would be sufficient to detect that difference. In fact, the total cure rate was 43 per cent and there was far from enough information to test for any differences of outcomes between the two treatment groups. No differences were indicated.

It was improper to embark on this trial without confidently expecting 150 eligible patients to be present. There was nothing in the protocol to show that the necessary number would present in a specified time. In fact, a time was not specified. Having embarked on the study it was not ethical to stop it, without clear evidence that one treatment was inferior, before the specified number of patients had been recruited.

The data collection form provided for the collection of 1488 items of information on each patient. Much of this information, particularly relating to return visits, was returned as blanks.

Catch-all data forms may have a semblance of thoroughness to the uninitiated, but they demonstrate a lack of forethought and an absence of scientific planning. Apart from demographic data collected to demonstrate the success of random allocation of patients to treatments and the general homogeneity of the sample, all other data collected in a clinical trial should be related in some way to clearly stateable hypotheses.

The only hypotheses implicit in the protocol, although not explicitly stated, were:

1. There is no difference in the clinical improvement rates between the two treatments.
2. There is no difference in the microbiological responses between the two treatments.
3. There is no difference in the incidences of adverse events between the two treatments.

These are straightforward hypotheses that may have been tested if 150 patients had been recruited. If any of the many variables of haematology, blood chemistry, medical history, age, sex, race, height and weight, surgical procedures and other medications could have influenced the outcomes, then the relevant hypotheses should have been stated. It could be left to the statistician to decide how to use these extra variables and what multivariate techniques to apply. However, the expected relationships should be stated in advance so that they could be taken into account in sample size determination.

A medical research ethics committee may have been misled by the protocol into believing that the study was well designed and would be well executed. The section on statistical methods contained an 'outline of statistical analysis plan' which appeared to be thorough. However, a responsible and careful committee would also look at the data collection form and question its potential, not only for collecting the necessary data, but also for facilitating data processing and statistical analysis. They may question first the desirability of collecting so much information and how it was proposed to use it all in testing hypotheses. The plan suggested tabulations and complete listings but without any indication of how these would be interpreted. While clinical judgement may be needed to assess the effect of a treatment, it is not an appropriate tool to use when data recorded from clinical trials are interpreted. Clinical judgement is not necessarily reproducible between investigators, whereas formal statistical analysis is reproducible.

The most striking feature of the data collection form was that there was no indication as to how the data were to be coded and entered into computer files. The consequence of this failing was that the data had been entered into the computer files in formats that are very difficult to manage.

Pharmaceutical companies should understand that it is usual to have a pilot study to test data collection forms for their suitability for

* use by investigators;
* coding for data entry; and
* statistical analysis.

The investigators had not generally completed the forms properly. This may be because the forms were badly designed. Haematology and clinical chemistry data called for individual assessment of 'significant abnormality', which was not defined. If it was intended to be 'outside normal ranges', this could be left to calculation provided the laboratory normal ranges were given, although it is well known that these are contentious. The normal ranges were provided for the various centres but the data collection forms had not been designed to include this information. Because the data collection forms were poorly designed, they could not be expected to encourage cooperation by the investigators, who responded by leaving many questions unanswered, or improperly answered. If the regulatory authorities were aware of the nature of this study, it is likely that they would admonish the company for conducting trials unethically.

The results of this trial were not satisfactory. This is because the trial was poorly designed and inefficiently and incompletely executed, and because the data forms were badly designed and unsuitable for data coding, computer entry, and statistical analysis. The unavoidable conclusion was that the conduct of this trial was not ethical. As the statistician responsible for analysing the data and reporting the results, that is what I told the pharmaceutical company.

FRAUD

While much unethical science is inadvertent, caused mainly by poor management, there is a long history of scientific fraud reaching back several centuries. Charles Babbage, who was Lucasian professor of mathematics at Cambridge University (a chair held by many great scientists including

Isaac Newton and Stephen Hawking), published a book in 1830 entitled *The Decline of Science in England*. Read that again. The date was *eighteen* thirty.

One chapter in his book was about scientific fraud, and he described four methods of fraud: Hoaxing, Forging, Trimming, and Cooking. To these I would add Obfuscation. For the first four, I cannot do better than quote him directly.

Hoaxing

> In the year 1788, M Gioeni, a knight of Malta, published an account of a new family of Testacea of which he described, with great minuteness, one species. It consisted of two rounded triangular valves, united by the body of the animal to a smaller valve in front. He gave figures of the animal, and of its parts; described its structure, its mode of advancing along the sand, the figure of the tract it left, and estimated the velocity of its course at about two-thirds of an inch per minute. . . . no such animal exists.

There have been many more hoaxes since Babbage's day, including the saga of the Piltdown man.

Forging

> Forging differs from hoaxing, inasmuch as in the latter the deceit is intended to last for a time, and then be discovered, to the ridicule of those who have credited it; whereas the forger is one who, wishing to acquire a reputation for science, records observations which he has never made. . . . The observations of the second comet of 1784, which was only seen by the Chevalier D'Angos, were long suspected to be a forgery and were at length proved to be so by the calculations and reasoning of Encke. The pretended observations did not accord amongst each other in giving any possible orbit.

Statistical methods now exist to discover forged data. Examples may be found in industrial research and in clinical trials. If you are tempted to forge your data, be warned. A good examiner will detect your forgery and you will be humiliated.

There can be great pressure on students to complete research projects within the time specified by the university rules or before their grants expire. Under such pressure students may be tempted to forge data that they never observed. Or, if a student has made some measurements but they do not properly meet expectation, he or she may be tempted to cook the results. Cooking is described below by Babbage.

Trimming

> Trimming consists in clipping off little bits here and there from those observations which differ most in excess from the mean, and in sticking them on to those which are too small . . . the average given by the observations of the trimmer is the same, whether they are trimmed or untrimmed. His object is to gain a reputation for extreme accuracy in making observations . . . He has more sense or less adventure than the cook.

Cooking

> This is an art of various forms, the object of which is to give to ordinary observations the appearance and character of those of the highest degree of accuracy.

One of its numerous processes is to make multitudes of observations, and out of these to select those only which agree, or very nearly agree. If a hundred observations are made, the cook must be very unlucky if he cannot pick out fifteen or twenty which will do for serving up.

Another approved receipt, when the observations to be used will not come within the limit of accuracy, is to calculate them by two different formulae. The difference in the constants, employed in those formulae has sometimes a most happy effect in promoting unanimity amongst discordant measures. If still greater accuracy is required, three or more formulae can be used.

It sometimes happens that the constant quantities in formulae given by the highest authorities, although they differ amongst themselves, yet they will not suit the materials. This is precisely the point in which the skill of the artist is shown; and an accomplished cook will carry himself triumphantly through it, provided happily some mean value of such constants will fit his observations. He will discuss the relative merits of formulae ... and with admirable candour assigning their proper share of applause to Bessel, to Gauss, and to Laplace, he will take that mean value of the constant used by three such philosophers which will make his own observations accord to a miracle.

Obfuscation

Obfuscation means 'to make something obscure'. It is a deliberate act that is intended to convey the impression of erudition, of being learned, of great scholarship. Hence it is fraudulent. There is a style of academic writing, increasingly common in recent years, that is long-winded with long paragraphs, long sentences, long words, passive statements and tortuous structures (see Chapter 37). It is intended to deceive and it does so easily because the reader, even an examiner, is tempted to skim such verbosity and subsequently fears to confess he has not understood every word.

It is a trick that is apparent today in many academic papers and theses but it was not uncommon a hundred years ago.

> *The researches of many commentators have already thrown much darkness on this subject, and it is probable that, if they continue, we shall soon know nothing at all about it.*
>
> Mark Twain

Perhaps some people cannot help writing obscurely, but if a postgraduate research student does so we should be suspicious.

> *People who write obscurely are either unskilled in writing or up to mischief.*
>
> Peter Medawar

Unnecessarily esoteric mathematics should be avoided. For example, it is not necessary to preface straightforward calculus, as applied to an engineering problem, with references to Hilbert spaces and sigma fields. Simple numerical examples can be a great help to your readers.

ADVICE

How can you, an inexperienced student, know how to avoid any of the problems, to be sure that your research is ethical? Only by seeking advice. The librarian is there to help you (Chapter 13); your supervisor is there to help you (Chapter 9); there are statisticians.

WHY STATISTICIANS?

A statistician is objective. Although he or she may know little about your special subject, a statistician can advise you about how to do things fairly, how to achieve balance, how to measure and record information (which is what research is about), how to analyse data (Chapters 29 and 30), how to design your experiments (Chapters 19 to 24), how to avoid making too many measurements, how to be sure you are making enough, how to avoid bias, how to achieve high precision, how to present your results clearly and succinctly.

In measurement and analysis, 'Hard science is easy. Soft science is hard.' Anything qualitative is so difficult to measure, analyse and interpret that special care must be taken to avoid subjective judgement and misinterpretation, either inadvertent or deliberate.

> *When you can measure what you are speaking about and express it in numbers, you know something about it: when you cannot measure it, cannot express it in numbers, your knowledge is of a meagre and unsatisfactory kind. It may be the beginning of knowledge, but you have scarcely in your thought advanced to the stage of science.*

> Lord Kelvin

The researcher's prayer
Grant, oh God, thy benedictions
On my theory's predictions
Lest the facts, when verified,
Show thy servant to have lied.

May they make me BSc,
A PhD and then
A DSc and FRS,
A Times Obit. Amen.

Oh, Lord, I pray, forgive me please,
My unsuccessful syntheses,
Thou know'st, of course – in thy position –
I'm up against such competition.

Let not the hardened editor,
With referee to quote,
Cut all my explanation out
And print it as a note.

> *Proceedings of the Chemical Society*, January 1963, pp 8–10
> (Quoted in *A Random Walk in Science*,
> an anthology published by the Institute of Physics in 1973)

REFERENCES

Babbage, C (1830) *The Decline of Science in England* (London: Fellowes).

Nietzsche, F W (1969) *Thus Spake Zarathustra: a book for everyone and no one*, translated with an introduction by Hollingdale, R J (Harmondsworth: Penguin Books).

Pearson, E S and Hartley, H O (1966) *Biometrika Tables for Statisticians*, Vol. 1, 3rd edn (Cambridge University Press).

Russell, B (1946) *History of Western Philosophy* (London: George Allen & Unwin).

PART 2 | Support

7 Research proposals

David Williams

INTRODUCTION

A good research proposal is one that gets the research funded. With intense competition for funds, having a good research idea is not enough; it has to be well presented and clearly aimed at meeting the objectives of the funding source if it is to stand out from all the other applications. Each proposal should therefore be customised for a particular sponsor, but some general principles to bear in mind when drafting any proposal are given below.

PLAN THE PROPOSAL

Proposals that are put together at the last minute are seldom successful. Care needs to be taken to identify the most suitable sponsor and to check that what you propose falls within the remit of the sponsor and preferably in a priority area. Most sponsors will produce handbooks or annual reports that lay out the objectives of the sponsor and the research areas or projects currently being funded. It is worth reading these carefully to get to know the sponsor's policy. If you are not sure whether you have an appropriate project, make a few preliminary enquiries by telephone to the sponsor.

Find out about the application procedures.

- What are the deadlines?
- Must the application be in a particular format?
- Are there application forms?

Most sponsors will issue guidelines for applications to the schemes they offer. The research councils send application forms and information booklets to each university. Your departmental or central administrative office should have bulk supplies. You may have to contact other sponsors directly for information.

WRITING THE PROPOSAL

Follow carefully any rules and formats specified by the sponsor. They may appear bureaucratic or silly, but the sponsor probably has a good reason for them and it is their money. If you do not follow the rules, your application may be rejected at the first stage, before the research programme has even been assessed.

You will address two audiences in the proposal:

- the *specialist academic referees* who will assess the detailed research case you have presented; and
- *non-specialists* who are on the board or panel to assess the wider context of the work proposed.

It is important to address this second audience also.

Wherever possible, try to avoid using technical language that non-specialists would not under-stand, particularly in sections of the proposal that deal with the objectives and wider benefits of the work proposed. In all proposals, you should try to answer the following questions.

What are you trying to do?

Sponsors have finite budgets and cannot make open-ended commitments. They like projects that have a recognisable conclusion, even if the area of research may be continued by follow-up propos-als. You need to define the scope of your application by giving the *aim* of the proposal and some specific *objectives*. These will be the criteria by which you, and the sponsor, will be able to judge the success of the research you do.

Why do this research?

Why is this research important? State why you believe it meets the objectives of the sponsor and why they should fund it. Give the *background* to the proposal, outlining the intellectual problem that has to be solved. Show you are really up to date in the field by stating what previous work has been done in the area by you or others, particularly work funded by that sponsor, and particularly by any researchers who may be referees or on the panel assessing the proposal.

What will be the benefits if the research is successful? Industrial sponsors have always been required to evaluate the financial benefits of research, but there is an increasing trend for publicly funded research to justify its contribution to wealth creation and the quality of life.

Why you?

You may have made a strong case for the research to be carried out, but you need to show the spon-sor that you are a suitable or, since most major sponsors receive many applications in similar areas, *the* most suitable researcher to do it. Demonstrate your expertise by citing relevant publications or works, and projects that you and any collaborators have completed successfully.

What will you do?

Describe the *research programme*. This is usually the main section of the application and you should state clearly what the various tasks within the work programme are and who will carry them out (collaborators, assistants, technicians). Define the *methodology* that will be adopted: types of surveys, techniques or concepts to be used. Identify appropriate *milestones* at significant points during the research. These may be the production of some deliverables such as reports and prototypes, or events such as seminars or meetings of the collaborators. The sponsors may wish to evaluate the progress of the research through the timely achievement of such milestones.

What resources will you need?

The resources you will require should be based on the programme of work you have defined. It is in no-one's interest to submit a proposal with resources inadequate to carry out the project success-fully, and top-up grants can be hard to come by. The particular resources that may be charged to the project vary considerably from sponsor to sponsor, so it is imperative to read carefully the financial terms and conditions of the particular sponsor scheme to ascertain what costs may be included in the proposal and what costs must be found from the applicant's institution or other external sponsors. Your finance office or equivalent should be able to give you advice. For all resources requested, there must be a justification in the application. They fall into the following general headings.

Staff

Not all sponsors will pay for the time of academic staff (such as lecturers) on the project, but most sponsors will pay all the costs of employing research support staff on the project (such as research associates, technicians). Explain how you will use such staff. For example, if you are asking for a senior researcher rather than a research assistant, state why a person of this grade is necessary for the project. Such staff are generally paid on nationally agreed terms and conditions, which include annual pay rises and increments. You should check whether the sponsor will automatically supplement the grant for pay rises, or whether such rises need to be built in to the costs of the proposal. This can be a significant sum for projects lasting several years.

Travel and subsistence

You should include realistic costs for travel and subsistence for the purposes of the project. Not all sponsors will pay for you to attend conferences overseas.

Consumables

Consumables include general running costs and materials used in the project. Such items generally need not be itemised but you should justify the funds requested in the proposal.

Equipment

You should specify large items of equipment that you require, giving details of the particular item, supplier and cost or quotation. Justify the purchase of the equipment rather than rental, and indicate the time the equipment will be used on the project. Note that some sponsors will not necessarily pay the full cost of equipment purchased.

Other items

Think carefully about any other resources you may need and other costs that may be charged to the sponsor, such as recruitment and advertising costs.

Indirect costs (overheads)

You should include costs for services provided by the institution but which cannot be attributed specifically to the project. These include personnel costs, finance costs, staff facilities, training, library and other central facilities, and departmental services. These are real costs that will be incurred if you proceed with the project, and will have to be met by your department or institution if you do not receive funding from the sponsor. Much of the indirect costs result from the employment of additional staff. They are usually expressed as a percentage of total staff costs, and are generally close to 100 per cent of such costs. That is, the indirect costs of a project are usually about the same as the total staff cost on the project.

It is therefore important that you recover as much of the indirect costs as possible from the sponsor. Some sponsors, such as the research councils, have a fixed level (currently 46 per cent) for such costs. Most universities have their own policies on charging for indirect costs, your finance office will be able to advise you on the appropriate costs at your institution.

WHAT IS THE PRICE?

When you have determined the *cost* of the resources you will need to carry out the research, you must decide on a *price* to charge the sponsor. The research councils and some other sources of publicly funded research have detailed financial conditions for grants which largely determine the price you should charge. For other projects, particularly from industrial or commercial sponsors, there is more flexibility.

There are many factors that may influence the price, but perhaps the most important is the long-term benefit that you or your institution may expect to receive, either financially or in other ways. If the research is long-term or basic, and may be expected to generate academic publications or future research projects, then there may be an agreement to share the costs with a sponsor by, for example, not charging the full indirect costs. If the research is commissioned by a sponsor that places restrictions on publication, or requires transfer of intellectual property to the sponsor, then you should not be expected to subsidise such research and may wish to set a price covering the full costs of the project and also opportunity costs for loss of intellectual property rights.

When you quote a price to a sponsor you should always make it clear that it is exclusive of VAT. Your finance office will tell you if the project is liable for VAT.

CAN YOU MANAGE THE PROJECT?

Sponsors will want to ensure that their money is well spent and will look in the proposal for a plan for *project management*. This should include details of

- who is in charge of the overall project;
- who is in charge of the various tasks or sections of the programme;
- how all the activities will be coordinated;
- time scales; and
- milestones.

A diagram of the project plan will help and can save space where the length of application permitted is limited. For example, you could use a simple bar-chart (Gantt chart) which shows the list of tasks and the time required to complete them; or, for more complex projects, you could include a network (PERT) diagram.

BEFORE YOU SUBMIT

- Check again that the proposal meets all the necessary criteria of the sponsor in case you overlook them when you revise the proposal with collaborators.
- Get someone else in your department or someone familiar with the research area to read and comment on the proposal.
- Check how many copies need to be submitted to the sponsor and the deadline for receipt.
- Allow plenty of time for final typing or printing and photocopying of the proposal.
- Many application forms require a signature of an administrative authority. Find out in advance who this is at your institution and allow plenty of time. Administrators are busy people too.

IF YOU ARE UNSUCCESSFUL

Try to get feedback from the sponsor as to why your proposal was not funded. If it was because of some aspect of presentation, or because of a minor technical reservation that you feel able to address, or simply that the sponsor did not have sufficient funds at that time, then it may be worthwhile revising the proposal in the light of feedback and re-submitting it. If it was rejected because it did not address the sponsor's objectives or priorities then you might be better re-writing the proposal and submitting it to a different sponsor.

IF YOU ARE SUCCESSFUL

It is not uncommon to be awarded less than you asked for. It is also not uncommon for the sponsor still to want the full research programme. You must decide whether or not you can do the research with the resources offered, or if you need to curtail the research programme and outputs. If you think there is a problem, discuss it with the sponsor. It is in no-one's interest for a research project to have reduced its chances of success because it has inadequate resources.

From many sponsors you will receive a contract to be signed. This will contain various financial and administrative conditions as well as terms for doing the work. Conditions will include

- the start and end dates of the contract, when the money will be paid;
- if it is a fixed amount of money or if you will be reimbursed only for what you spend;
- who owns the intellectual property rights;
- what happens if you or the sponsor terminates the project early.

These are important conditions that can affect the way you do the work, and you should read them carefully. Do not sign any contract before seeking advice from your finance office. If necessary, negotiate with the sponsor to achieve mutually acceptable terms.

THE FUTURE

Do not wait until the project is finishing before you submit further applications. Plan in advance, particularly for those sponsors who are already funding you. Keep in touch with them. Send them reports from your current research. If your current research is producing results, consult your sponsors about how you may both get good publicity from the work. Keep them interested by offering to put in position papers for possible future research areas or topics. And start planning your next application.

REFERENCE

A source of publications for your guidance is:
Universities UK, Woburn House, 20 Tavistock Square, London WC1H 9HQ, UK. Tel: +44(0)20 7419 4111.
www.UniversitiesUK.ac.uk

8 Finding funds

Tony Greenfield

The provision of funds can be a major hurdle when you plan postgraduate research. The Higher Education Careers Services Unit (CSU) offers advice and has published a booklet, *Prospects: Postgraduate Funding Guide*, of which this chapter is a distillation with CSU's permission. The guide is designed to be a starting point in your search for postgraduate funding and presents most of the options available to you. The guide is also reproduced on www.prospects.ac.uk. The website provides information about research opportunities and includes information on funding provision where appropriate.

Most public funding is provided by the research councils, the Arts and Humanities Research Board (AHRB), Students Awards Agency for Scotland, Department for Education and Employment, Department of Higher and Further Education, Training and Employment (Northern Ireland). Competition for Research Council and AHRB awards is intense, with only a small number of successful candidates. Between them, the Research Council and AHRB provide around 8000 postgraduate studentships. Unlike undergraduates, postgraduates are not eligible for loans from the Student Loans Company. Some postgraduates take out a career development loan (CDL), although these are only available for certain vocational courses.

MAJOR COSTS

You will have two types of expense: fees and cost of living. Although tuition costs for UK students are subsidised through grants paid to institutions through the Higher Education Funding councils, most postgraduates have to pay a contribution towards them.

Some postgraduates receive a Research Council award that covers both tuition fees and living expenses. Others support themselves through a combination of public and private finance. Some receive funding from charities, foundations or trusts. Many are entirely self-funded. Competition is fierce but, if you meet the eligibility criteria, you should apply for awards.

Some bodies, especially smaller charities and trusts, provide funds for specific subject areas. Some provide grants for study in foreign countries, for humane scientific research or for particular areas of medical study. Some employers will contribute to course fees and other costs or will allow paid time for study or research. You should ask for support if your research is relevant to your employers' business.

BENEFITS

If you are a part-time postgraduate, you may be eligible for housing benefit, council tax benefits and other benefits. There are extra allowances for disabled students. For further information, contact SKILL on www.skill.org.uk. Check with your local Benefits Agency about the most up-to-date rulings. The website is www.dss.gov.uk/ba.

BE INFORMED

The more you know about how funding works, the more chance you will have of finding some. Make sure that you investigate every possible funding source and make sure that you are fully aware of dates, deadlines and eligibility criteria. Ask, first, your university careers service. Talk to current postgraduate students and discover how they fund themselves. Ask your department head or your supervisor if there is any institutional support.

The AGCAS careers information booklet, *Postgraduate Study and Research*, is available free at your careers service. Most careers services' websites include postgraduate funding sections. The University of Newcastle (www.careers.ncl.ac.uk/students/pages/rfesfund.html) has a particularly good funding section with links to funding sources. The University of Wolverhampton's institution map includes a research-funded sites page (www.scit.wlv.ac.uk/ukinfo.uk.map.res.html).

Some careers services can give you access to a searchable database, Funderfinder. A web-based system, Moneysearch, is also available at some institutions. The most comprehensive source of information on funding opportunities is the *Grants Register*, published annually by Macmillan. The Charities Aid Foundation publishes the *Directory of Grant Making Trusts* annually.

PUBLIC FUNDING

The most important sources of funding for postgraduates in the UK are the research councils and the Arts and Humanities Research Board. These are government-funded agencies for the support of research. There are six research councils:

- Biotechnology and Biological Research Council (BBSRC)
- Engineering and Physical Sciences Research Council (EPSRC)
- Economic and Social Research Council (ESRC)
- Medical Research Council (MRC)
- National Environment Research Council (NERC)
- Particle Physics and Astronomy Research Council (PPARC)

There is also the Arts and Humanities Research Board (AHRB). Contact details and major areas of interest of the research councils can be found at the end of this chapter, on page 61.

All the research councils award studentships to individual postgraduates. Only a small percentage of applications are successful. Funding is easier to obtain in the sciences and in engineering than in the arts and social sciences.

The research councils provide a variety of awards. The most common are

- Standard research studentships for PhD or MPhil students on programmes of up to three years full-time and five years part-time;
- Research masters training awards (MRes) usually for one year;
- Collaborative Awards in Science and Engineering (CASE). These are similar to standard research studentships but involve collaboration with a partner in industry, a public body or government research unit. Funding for these awards comes from both the Research Councils and the collaborating body.

Some of the councils offer industrial CASE awards, where the collaborating body defines its own research project within the council's remit. There are also joint interdisciplinary awards such as the ESRC/NERC joint studentships that are similar to standard research studentships.

Research council awards may cover some or all of the tuition fees, a payment straight to the institution, a maintenance grant (often called a *stipend*) and a contribution towards travel, fieldwork, academic materials and other expenses. Additional sums may be available for disabled students and those with dependants. CASE awards are usually worth more than standard research studentships.

To be eligible for a research council award, you must be ordinarily resident in the UK throughout the three years preceding your applications. This does not include living in the UK while you are a student. You should also have a first-class or upper second-class honours degree from a UK higher education institution, although there are exceptions to this. The research councils are responsible for postgraduate awards to students who live in Northern Ireland but who also wish to study in Great Britain. The Department of Higher and Further Education, Training and Employment (DHFETE) is responsible for students from Great Britain who wish to study in Northern Ireland and for students from Northern Ireland who want to stay there.

Unless you are applying for an ESRC research competition studentship, you should not apply directly to the research councils. Each council reviews academic departments and programmes and publishes an approved list. Research studentships are allocated by programme area. You should apply directly to the department in which you want to study. The department then forwards selected applications to the research council for consideration. Departments usually do this in June each year. The Students Awards Agency for Scotland (SAAS) offers studentships for research programmes.

INSTITUTIONAL FUNDING AND EMPLOYMENT

Your university or other institution can provide detailed information on institutional funding and employment. There are two main areas of such funding: teaching studentships and research scholarships. Graduate teaching assistantships (GTAs) and graduate research assistantships (GRAs) are the most common forms of institutional support. Under these schemes, postgraduates receive direct payment (usually the equivalent of a research council grant) or the waiver of their fees, or sometimes both, in return for teaching or research duties. Some institutions offer assistantships only to those students who have failed to get a research council award.

More research students than taught course students become GTAs because they spend longer within a department. Since it is important that GTAs received proper training and support, as well as payment, for their work, it is usual for them to advance through several stages. Most departments restrict the type of teaching that can be done in the first year to basic marking, tutorial or demonstration duties. By the final year of a research degree, GTAs may be employed as temporary lecturers with all associated duties. Most universities and funding bodies allow full-time postgraduates to teach up to six hours a week.

GTA guidelines are less specific for part-time research students. In some institutions, there are restrictions on the hours that they can teach.

Employment conditions for GTAs vary between institutions. Some offer either full-fee or bursary studentships. Bursary students have to pay their own tuition fees.

If you are thinking of becoming a GTA then you should look at the National Postgraduate Committee website on www.npc.org.uk for useful advice and guidelines.

OTHER SOURCES OF FUNDS

Alternative funding bodies range in size from the Wellcome Trust, the world's largest medical research charity, to the British Federation of Women Graduates, which offers a few cost of living bursaries for female postgraduates in the second year of their research degrees.

INTERNATIONAL STUDENTS

Students who wish to do postgraduate research in the UK should explore all options in their home countries. Start with your education ministry. The British Council has offices in many countries and will offer advice. If there is no British Council office, try the British Embassy, Consulate or High Commission. Even if you obtain a scholarship, you still need to be sure that it is enough to meet all of your costs. The British Council warns you to be especially careful if you have only a partial scholarship or if you intend to bring your family. Your local British Council office should have up-to-date information on the costs of living in the UK. Other useful addresses can be found at the end of this chapter, on page 64.

Copies of the *Postgraduate Funding Guide* can be ordered from www.prospects.ac.uk

ADDRESSES AND PROGRAMME AREAS OF RESEARCH COUNCILS IN THE UK

Biotechnology and Biological Sciences Research Council (BBSRC)

Polaris House
North Star Avenue
Swindon SN2 1UH
Tel.: 01793 413348
www.bbsrc.ac.uk

Biomedical sciences; biochemistry and cell biology; genes and developmental biology; animal sciences; plant and microbial sciences; engineering and biological systems, agri-food.

Engineering and Physical Sciences Research Council (EPSRC)

Polaris House
North Star Avenue
Swindon SN2 1ET
Tel.: 01793 444000
www.epsrc.ac.uk

Chemistry; engineering for infrastructure and the environment; engineering for manufacturing; general engineering; IT and computer sciences; materials; mathematics; physics.

Economic and Social Research Council (ESRC)

Polaris House
North Star Avenue
Swindon SN2 1UJ
Tel.: 01793 413043
www.epsrc.ac.uk

Area studies; economics; economic and social history; education; human geography; linguistics; management and business studies; multi-disciplinary; planning; politics and international relations; psychology; social anthropoly; social policy; socio-legal studies; sociology; statistics; research methods and computing allied to the social sciences; science, technology and innovation.

ESRC subjects overlap with those of the Arts and Humanities Research Board in some areas.

Medical Research Council (MRC)

20 Park Crescent
London W1N 4AL
Tel.: 020 7636 5422
www.mrc.ac.uk

Natural Environment Research Council, (NERC)

Polaris House
North Star Avenue
Swindon SN2 1EU
Tel.: 01793 411667
www.nerc.ac.uk

Earth observations; Earth sciences; freshwater sciences; marine and atmospheric sciences; terrestrial sciences.

Particle Physics and Astronomy Research Council (PPARC)

Polaris House
North Star Avenue
Swindon SN2 1SZ
Tel.: 01793 442118
www.pparc.ac.uk

Particle physics; astronomy and astrophyscis; solar system science

Arts and Humanities Research Board (AHRB)

10 Carlton House Terrace
London SW1Y 5AH
Tel.: 020 7969 5205/5212
www.ahrb.ac.uk

English and American studies; media/communication studies; other languages, literatures and cultures; linguistics; visual and performing arts; history of art/architecture; history; philosophy; history and philosophy of science; theology; divinity and religious studies; archaeology; classics; law.

Some of the AHRB's programme areas overlap with the ESRC's

ADDRESSES AND PROGRAMME AREAS OF SOME ALTERNATIVE SOURCES OF FUNDS

British Federation of Women Graduates

4 Mandeville Courtyard
142 Battersea Park Road
London SW11 4NB
Tel.: 020 7498 8037
http://homepages.wyenet.co.uk/bfwg

Scholarships for postgraduate research for women. Applicants must be in at least their second year of research at time of application.

BFWG Charitable Foundation

28 Great James Street
London WC1N 3ES
Tel.: 020 7404 6447
bfwg.charity@btinternet.co.m

Grants for living expenses for women graduates while registered for research at an approved institution in Great Britain.

Carnegie Trust for the Universities of Scotland

Cameron House
Abbey Park Place
Dunfermline
Fife KY12 7PZ
Tel.: 01383 622148
www.geo.ed.ac.uk/carnegie/carnegie.html

Full-time research for three years within the UK.

Institution of Electrical Engineers

Savoy Place
London WC2R 0BL
Tel.: 020 7240 1871
www.iee.org.uk/Awards

Electrical, electronic, manufacturing or information engineering.

Institution of Mechanical Engineers

Northgate Avenue
Bury St Edmunds
Suffolk IP32 6BN
Tel.: 01284 763277
www.imeche.org.uk/prizes

Science or practice of mechanical engineering.

Institution of Mining and Metallurgy

77 Hallam Street
London W1N 6BR
Tel.: 020 7580 3802
www.imm.org.uk

The Royal Society of Edinburgh

22–26 George Street
Edinburgh EH2 2PQ
Tel.: 0131 240 5000
www.ma.hw.ac.uk/RSE/

Travel scholarships for engineering graduates from Scottish universities; research studentships on the ageing process.

The Royal Society

6 Carlton House Terrace
London SW1Y 5AG
Tel.: 020 7451 2547
www.royalsoc.ac.uk

Rutherford scholarships for candidates under 26. Natural sciences; experimental physics.

OTHER USEFUL ADDRESS

Foreign and Commonwealth Office
London SW1A 2AH
Tel.: 020 7270 1500

Department for International Development
The Association of Commonwealth
Universities
John Foster House
36 Gordon Square
London WC1H 0PF
Tel.: 020 7387 8572

Overseas Research Students Awards Scheme
29 Tavistock Square
London WC1H 9HQ
Tel.: 020 7419 5499

The Fulbright Commission
62 Doughty Street
London WC1N 2LS
Tel.: 020 7404 6880
www.fulbright.co.uk

International Federation of University Women
8 Rue de l'Ancien-Port
Geneva, CH-1201
Switzerland
Tel.: ++41.22 731 23 80
www.ifuw.org

British Council
Bridgewater House
58 Whitworth Street
Manchester M1 6BB
Tel.: 0161 957 7755
www.britcoun.org

9 Who can help?

Shirley Coleman

INTRODUCTION

You have started your postgraduate studies – well done. Who can help you with ideas, support and encouragement? This chapter looks at supervisors and what to do if they are no use. It looks at what help is available from other academic staff, librarians and technicians. It also looks at a wide range of other sources of help including public services, government departments, trade unions and industrial companies. Even if you feel you have enough help, contact with these various sources can be very interesting and useful later on in your career. These experiences may add that little extra sparkle that will make your research excellent rather than just very good.

SUPERVISORS

The potentially most useful resource is your personal supervisor. His or her task is to help you through your studies, to get the best from them and finish successfully, and be ready to take up suitable, gainful employment. Some supervisors, however, are not too keen to dedicate sufficient time to you and this can be very frustrating.

If you look on the bright side, and assume your supervisor is conscientious, and interested in your studies, then what can you expect?

You can have regular meetings at which you summarise your work to date or since the last meeting. This means that you keep a good record of your activity throughout your period of study. Your supervisor can add his or her own thoughts and ideas to yours and can offer suggestions that might spark further ideas in one or other of you. As well as you keeping an eye on published work and the advances in your field, your supervisor can be doing the same. This is useful as you can keep tabs on much more work and be more likely to stumble upon relevant information.

Besides providing technical support and inspiration, a good supervisor will deal with all the administration to do with your study. This could include the important question of choosing appropriate (and hopefully sympathetic) external examiners and applying for time extensions. The exact title of your thesis, if you are writing one, or of any publication, is very important; remember, it will follow you around on your CV and job applications for ever more, so a good supervisor will help you choose the best wording, which will allow you to adapt your past to suit your future.

A good supervisor can help you to meet academics and others who may be interested in you and your work. He or she may become a life mentor for you, helping you to find employment after you finish studying. If you have to defend your study in a viva voce, a beneficent, supportive supervisor is a great asset as well as a comfort, especially if you are borderline.

Poor supervisors may be unwilling to see you or may not concentrate fully when you try to discuss your work with them.

If your supervisor is poor, what can you do about it? You can try to improve your availability and flexibility about when meetings are held; you can try to improve the quality of the presentation of your work. Your enthusiasm may ignite the interest of your supervisor, if you are lucky. If not, at least you will feel that you have done your best to improve the situation. In the final analysis, if none of these efforts have any effect, you just have to try to carry on regardless and look further afield for people to be involved with. It is worthwhile considering why your supervisor is under-performing. Sometimes supervisors are too busy; it is not always a good plan to go to study with someone whose fame is meteorically rising. They will not have much time for you. Perhaps you or your project bores your supervisor. Another possibility, however, is that your supervisor thinks you are highly competent, are doing a good job and do not need their help. Although this may be a flattering concept, it is also a nuisance as everyone can benefit from the input and interest of an eminent mentor, but again, unless you go to great lengths to prove your incompetence, there is not much you can do except get on as best you can on your own. Try to avoid becoming too self-centred. In a few years' time, you yourself will have forgotten most of the vital details you are struggling with now.

In the rare (hopefully) cases where a supervisor is actually incompetent or maleficent, what can you do? You can try to change to another supervisor without becoming too involved in accusations and unpleasantness. Be careful how you choose another supervisor; someone who is keen, conscientious and compatible may be the best even if he or she is not the most renowned. Ask previous tutees how helpful they found their tutor. Try to check whether they are likely to move jobs or retire – racing them up the stairs or challenging them to tennis is not a reliable test! If it is not possible to change your supervisor or it is too late, the best you can do is keep a good record of your work. Do not rely on the supervisor at all but use the other resources (suggested in this chapter) in case you need to defend yourself later. Be positive and think of your traumatic period of study as good training for coping with later life. After all, if you are careful, no one can stop you from doing your work, writing it up and passing successfully. This is more use than making a big fuss and trying to upset a structure with an inertia that might have appealed to you initially as a stable environment in which to study. If you do need to take matters further, you can always discuss your problems with the head of department, or dean of the faculty. If these people are unhelpful or you wish to go further, seek advice from the students' union and student affairs officers before you do anything rash. Academics have long memories.

Even if you have a good supervisor, other sources of help can provide you with practical examples of where your study is relevant. This makes your work more interesting and allows more unusual questions to be asked when you are interviewed for further study or jobs later.

ATTRACTING IDEAS

Try advertising yourself! If possible, it is a good plan to give a talk or seminar about your work early on in your study. That way you get help in terms of ideas and suggestions from your audience and you can check what other work is being done in your field and by whom (this reinforces your own literature search).

ACADEMIC SOURCES OF HELP

Academic members of staff are usually happy to spend a few minutes discussing ideas arising from their own studies which interest you. It is often better just to drop in rather than be too formal. You can always ask their secretaries when it is a good time to catch them.

The authors of relevant papers in journals that you have come across during your study are also likely to be enthusiastic about discussing their work with you. Use the 'address for correspondence' on the papers to contact them. This sort of pro-activity not only provides you with state-of-the-art ideas but also gets you known and may be useful when you are looking for a job. You can combine a visit to more distant authors with the summer holidays, but remember to take some presentable clothes with you, and a notepad!

Conferences often have attractively reduced rates for students and are usually well worth the money and effort of attending. You can cross-examine authors of relevant presentations and make some useful contacts for sharing ideas, help and inspiration. Occasionally there are conferences especially for postgraduate students. The subject matter will be wide ranging but such events provide a good opportunity to make a presentation and to share your experiences with other post-graduates.

Universities and colleges usually run a series of seminars and lectures during term-time; again, the subject areas covered will be wide but these events are often well worth attending.

OTHER SOURCES OF HELP

Libraries

Help may be available from a surprising number of diverse sources as well as the more obvious places. University, college and public libraries are a standard starting point. Besides the books and journals available, try talking to the specialist libraries who have a vast pool of information at their fingertips. Government publications are surprisingly rich in all sorts of facts and figures; the monthly publication, *Social Trends*, for example, will tell you how many died from falling off ladders in the preceeding month.

Have a look at the reports from government and other research institutes; they may give you some good ideas and contacts.

Government departments

The Department of Trade and Industry (DTI) has local offices that you can visit. You can find out which companies are involved in the latest initiatives and who you should contact to ask about them.

The Department of Trade and Industry jointly sponsor, with various companies, the Teaching Company Scheme, in which graduates are employed by a University as a Research Associate for two years but actually work full time in a company on a specific project. These projects may be relevant to your study and the list of current programmes could be very useful.

Other government departments may offer help and ideas, for example the Central Statistical Office. There is also the European Commission and the various ministries, for example the Department for Environment, Food and Rural Affairs (DEFRA).

Local services

Town halls and civic centres have excellent information facilities and are able to supply data on many aspects of the local economic and social scene. Try looking up your city, county and local councils in the telephone book.

The local Chamber of Commerce is a good source of literature and contact names and addresses. It may be able to put you in touch with appropriate trades societies or trades unions. These are also involved in research and may be willing to help you. The Chamber of Commerce will also have literature from the Institute of Directors, Confederation of British Industry and other institutions.

Miscellaneous

The financial pages in newspapers give useful information about companies. Keep a scrapbook of any articles that are relevant to your area of study.

Keep a check on the activities of local colleges and schools; they sometimes have project competitions in very interesting subject areas.

Groups of students may work with a local company and you could make use of the same contact.

Hospitals have personnel dedicated to disseminating information. They also have staff libraries you may be allowed to browse through if your study is in an area associated with health.

Technical support

Laboratory staff know a lot more about the way things work than you can learn from a book, so make sure you are on good terms with them and listen carefully. Materials and equipment supply companies are very happy to furnish literature and demonstrations to postgraduate students. You may expect them not to be interested in you as you have no intention of buying anything but, on the contrary, they see you as future customers and people with influence. They will be very keen to promote their products.

Companies

University or other careers services are probably the best places to learn about companies of interest to you. Usually, the information is readily available for you to look at without having to make an appointment or talk to anyone. There is nothing more satisfying when you go to visit someone than knowing more about their company's business than they do! You can try to organise your own visit with a specific person in the company or you can contact their public relations department and try to join a factory tour. In either case, remember to dress the part and take a notebook.

Making a visit

Arrange the visit when you are sure you are ready – do not risk having to cancel. Read up as much as possible about the place and the people who work there. Be clear in your mind what it is that you want to know or want to look at. Write out a checklist to be sure you don't forget anything. Double check your travel arrangements and take a map. Allow plenty of time to get there and plenty of time afterwards in case you are invited to stay for lunch, tea, evening meetings, etc. Wear appropriate clothes. Afterwards, write a quick thank-you note saying briefly what benefits you gained from the visit. That way they will be happy to have you back and will remember you if you apply for a job there!

Internet

All of the above can be researched from the comfort, or otherwise, of your computer via the Internet. One of the advantages of surfing the net is the global perspective it gives. One of the disadvantages is that you may feel that the field is expanding out of control. You should find, however, that eventually you start recognising the same things turning up again and again, and that is the beginning of getting to grips with the subject.

Be careful not to spend too many hours looking at the computer screen and playing with the mouse – time flies when you're having fun! Make sure you jot down the addresses of any pages that interest you, just in case you can't find them again, and print off interesting, relevant information so that you can read it at your leisure, for example in the bath, on the beach or in a bus.

There is still some information that is not public enough to be put on the web but which is not secret enough to be kept from you, so the Internet is complementary rather than alternative to the other sources of help.

Family and friends

Do not forget this valuable collection of committed supporters. Explain your ideas to them and try to cope with their common-sense comments – they often say things that can make you think very deeply about what you are trying to do. In most write-ups, you need a layman's introduction, abstract or summary; try reading your attempt to a friend and see whether they can understand it. An outside view will help you to bring out the important points more clearly.

SUMMARY

In summary, there are many sources of help if you have the energy to go out and seek them. The benefits will be widespread in terms of making your study more interesting and relevant and in the advantages such action provides in your future career.

PART 3 | Tools of research

10 Information technology and computers

R Allan Reese

INTRODUCTION

All popular technologies go through phases. They start by being exciting but limited to enthusiasts; when they become available to the public at great expense, they can be trendy and desirable; if, however, a mass market develops, it removes the cachet of ownership and leads to driving down of costs. From the consumer's viewpoint, the movement is from wild claims to blind acceptance. You may become reliant on the technology, but indifferent to it until it fails. Consider how your daily routine would change were there no electric light.

The time of writing appears to be a point of transition. At the end of the 1990s, the Internet was available only to a minority and was promoted, by the press and the UK government, as essential for every future consumer and worker. Stocks in any new Internet or high-tech company were grabbed at any price, with the main fear that an underclass unable to keep up with the 'information society' might develop. At the end of 2000, it is reported that a majority of the UK population have access to the Internet at work or home, but are using it for specific and limited purposes. Most of the remainder do not expect to buy a computer for home entertainment, although without doubt they are using the Internet for activities such as banking and shopping. Internet companies have failed, just as non-Internet companies do, and consumers have found that goods ordered online still need to be physically delivered. Computer prices continue to drop, or computers at the 'market price' provide more features.

For academic work, however, the computer and the Internet are firmly established as a basic and vital prerequisite.

Your university or department will undoubtedly offer advice and facilities when your research involves complex calculations or large amounts of data. This chapter therefore addresses the needs of students who nevertheless must rely on information technology to get to grips with the ever-increasing volume of literature and to produce the substantial piece of writing that is a dissertation. The same considerations will, however, be relevant to the former group of students. It is often assumed that using a word processor is intuitive or too trivial to be taught to advanced students, but, as with any tool, a computer can be used more, or less, effectively.

We can assume you have access to personal computers. These are most likely to be PCs, implying compatibility with the Microsoft software and usually running some version of Windows. Or they may be Macintosh computers, which run a different operating system MacOS. They are unlikely to be anything else unless you are in a specialist computer science department, where you might meet systems such as Unix, Linux or X. We also consider, below, some other alternatives that bridge the gap between computers and 'personal information managers' (PIMs); these are pocket-sized machines that your department will almost certainly not supply, but which might greatly enhance your effectiveness in handling information. Whatever the machine, you control it and receive feedback through an interface that provides input (keyboard, mouse, etc) and output (screen, speakers, etc). The interfaces listed so far (Windows, OS, Linux, etc) are operating systems, programs that control the internal workings of the computer.

You, as a researcher, are more concerned with applications, the programs that carry out specific tasks. Marketing pressures ensure that the popular applications are available under any operating system, with a similar set of controls as seen by the user. At times, however, anyone who uses more than one type of computer will be confused by the differences, like a driver who gets into a different car and switches on the lights, mistaking them for the wipers.

Apart from the preferences in makes of computer and applications, you may find your access to university computers is inadequate. Machines may not be available when you want them, although 24-hour access rooms are sometimes provided. They may not be where you want them, unless you are prepared to spend every hour in the office or laboratory. Most seriously, you will be competing for the use of public-access computers with every other student. As both student numbers and the expectations of individual students grow, universities cannot provide facilities to meet the need, and will increasingly demand that students provide for themselves.

Fortunately, the features required in a computer for most research are quite basic, and a second-hand computer or one considered obsolete for the current consumer market may be more than adequate. Of course, if you want a computer for playing DVD movies or the latest interactive multimedia games, then you need to buy an appropriate model. However, a computer that will be a research tool can be more ruthlessly specified; researchers with families may consider it essential to have a games or entertainment system, but separate from their research computer!

Let us consider the components of a computer system, in particular for a personal computer for your home or university accommodation.

COMPUTER HARDWARE

The first item mentioned is usually the processor; indeed, it is often used to name the system, as in, 'a Pentium III system'. Several manufacturers now produce alternative chips at a range of prices, and as long as the overall machine is compatible with the software you wish to run, you will probably be unaware of any distinctions in performance. While specialist magazines provide detailed 'benchmark' tests, these compare the performance of systems using specific tasks designed to exercise the chips. Such tests typically show a variation of less than two to one within a range of machines competing in the market, and you will not notice such differences in practical use. Choosing appropriate software and learning to use it effectively will save you far more time.

The next feature mentioned will be the amount of internal memory, or RAM (Random Access Memory). This is the working space used by the processor, quite distinct from the permanent storage for files. The best advice is, unfortunately, to go for a system with as much RAM as you can afford. Unfortunately, because the skills of writing programs that run in limited amounts of memory have been neglected and lost; commercial assumptions over the past 20 years have been that every new program, and each revised version, can demand a system with ever more memory, and users will upgrade or replace their computers. The 1995 edition of this book described systems with 8 MB (megabytes) of RAM and suggested 16 MB as desirable. Current systems come with between 64 MB and 256 MB as standard.

Storage for software or information files is provided in the first instance on internal 'hard disks'. Again, the details of the technology do not matter, and the description 'hard' is purely historic.

What does matter is the capacity, and, again, the sheer data-holding capacity has shown dramatic growth. Large disks are needed mainly because of the growth in animated graphics for games and the convergence with video technology. A single complex image may contain several megabytes of data (one megabyte is about one million characters), although elegant data-compression techniques mean this can be reduced. Video at 25 frames per second means that even large hard disks can be filled rapidly. PC systems are now typically offered with 20 or 30 gigabyte disks (one gigabyte is about 1000 megabytes), enough to store the name, address and personal details of every person in the UK without the need for abbreviations. In contrast, your PhD dissertation will contain, say, 100 000 words or about 600 000 characters of text at the end of your years of effort. Whatever you have on the hard disk, you will want to make back-ups so that the information is not lost if your computer is damaged, lost or – as it surely will be – replaced.

Most PCs still come with a standard 3.5-inch floppy disk drive. Such disks have a capacity of about 1.5 MB, and are therefore totally impractical for backing up large hard disks. Nevertheless, as just noted, your dissertation files will fit onto a floppy disk, perhaps with images omitted. Floppy disks are very cheap and robust, so it makes sense to make several copies of valuable files and store them at different locations.

Less common, and less standard, are various types of higher-capacity magnetic disks. The Zip drive provides for disks with either 100 MB or 250 MB capacity, and the Jaz drive for up to 1 GB. Apart from the higher capacity, these are much like floppy disks, and the drive itself can be built into the computer or plugged in as a portable accessory. The speed of data transfer with such drives is typically far slower than that of the built-in hard disk, but they can provide a substantial back-up capacity. Despite the name, the Zip drive does not impose the software data compression provided by WinZip, PKZip or similar programs. Nevertheless you can 'zip' files using such software and thus store far more information on a Zip or Jaz disk than its nominal capacity suggests.

The CD (compact disc) has, for several years, been the *de facto* standard way to distribute software, as it is fast, cheap to produce and very robust. The fact that a CD cannot be overwritten by accident is, for this purpose, an advantage over magnetic disks. CD players are now very cheap and are almost an essential component. Apart from the convenience for installing software, standard CD drives will play music CDs, either through headphones plugged into the drive or through the computer's sound card and speakers. Music while you work may be, according to your taste, a small extravagance or the feature that preserves your sanity.

The limitation that CDs used to be read-only has, in the past year or so, been overcome. Many home systems now come with a CD writer or re-writer. These have not yet evolved to a single standard; in particular, there is a distinction between CDs that can be written and erased, and those that can be written only once. Whichever you have, a single CD can hold about 500 MB (0.5 GB) of files, so is comparable with the Zip and Jaz drives but more portable to other computers. A CD writer can be added to most PCs, but requires some understanding so that data are transferred at the appropriate rate for burning the disk. The speed of writing CDs is generally much slower than that for reading in the same drive. MiniDisks (MD) use a different technology; having been promoted over several years as the digital alternative to audiocassettes, they appear to be gaining acceptance for reproducing music from MP3 files, but as yet MDs have not gained favour for general data storage.

CDs are gradually giving way to DVDs (strictly speaking, this stands for Digital Versatile Disk, but because of the use for movies is often interpreted as Digital Video Disk), again driven by the needs of the entertainment industry. Whether you want to play DVD movies on your computer is a matter of personal choice, but clearly the next product range will include the DVD drive as standard and may provide for writing your own DVDs as the replacement for home videotape.

When you buy a complete system, it will come with input and output devices: keyboard, mouse and display. VDU displays remain the default provision for desktop systems while portable (laptop) computers require lightweight LCD or plasma screens. Either display will work with any computer, as the data connections are identical, so the distinction remains mainly on the grounds of cost. Unfortunately, there seems little development in terms of making displays larger and more ergonomic; while we have seen PCs with multiple linked screens so that more windows could be visible at once, these were expensive custom-built computers. The vision of a true 'desk top', to work on several documents at once, remains a vision. (See Chapter 5 for hints on working with text.)

Other current devices, often bundled with the PC as a sales package, include digital cameras (still or video), scanners for turning documents into computer files, sound input, and printers. All apart from the last would be novelties within academic research, but potentially highly useful. You might, for example, take pictures during your fieldwork and store them as an *aide memoire* or part of the research diary, even if they may not figure in the dissertation. Digital sound is more a specialist area, and while there are excellent voice recognition systems for dictation in special circumstances (most especially for disabled users), these do not yet match the keyboard for speed and accuracy in normal use. Digital editing of moving video is an area that may develop in the home computing market and may therefore become widespread. At the time of writing, it is in the upper reaches of processing and storage capacities. A printer remains essential despite all predictions of the paperless office; proof-reading on screen and on paper are different in feel and a proof-read on paper can be more reliable if you do not have practice of on-screen proof-reading.

NETWORKS

All the items listed so far would comprise a standalone computer system that you could use without reference to any other system. Buy such a computer and you literally plug it together (usually with no difficulty because each plug only fits one socket) and switch on the power. Joining a network, or the Internet, requires one more connection, and allows you to communicate from your computer to many others, fetching information or exchanging messages. You need to link your computer in the first instance to an Internet Service Provider (ISP).

Most large organisations, including probably all universities, run private computer networks on their premises. The physical wiring for such a network is maintained by the local computer service, and they will advise you how to connect to it. This usually involves adding a special 'network card' inside your computer. My own university, for example, provides such cards and every student study-bedroom has a local network socket. Once you are connected, your computer will give access to the same facilities as on the public-access computers for all students.

If you do not have a local network socket, you can still connect to other computers through a standard telephone line. Your computer is connected to the telephone socket through a modem, a device that enables the computer to dial telephone numbers and connect to other computers (to be precise, to the modem on that phone number). The modem can also interact with fax machines, so you can fax a document via the computer, without having to print it out and sending it using a traditional fax machine. In contrast to the local network, for which you will probably not be charged, using the standard phone line will involve some commercial agent. A special telephone line capable of delivering data at a higher rate (ISDN and, more recently, ADSL) is an option, but not essential, and you may not see better performance for the higher cost if the speed is limited by some other part of the Internet. At the time of writing, charges vary widely and you need to investigate and consider your own pattern of use. Students living away from their university area will, however, almost certainly find it expensive to dial straight through to the university's own modem lines; look for a local ISP to whom you connect by phone, then connect to your university through the Internet. Despite the problems and the relatively slow speed of modem-based connections, Internet use by telephone or cable-company connections looks likely to remain a growth area, and competition is driving down the costs. Using your phone line for computer access has the drawback that callers often find your number engaged; the phone companies are quick to point out that they will install a second line, of course at a very special price.

You can therefore set yourself up with a personal computer at a price to suit any pocket, from a couple of hundred pounds for a second-hand computer able to handle your dissertation writing, to a couple of thousand pounds for a current model with the latest home entertainment features. The principle for buyers remains as ever: decide what you will use the computer for, buy one that slightly exceeds your specification to allow some growth, but do not throw away money on features you do not understand and almost certainly will not use. Once set up, running costs should be small, in terms of electricity, cost of consumables (disks, paper) and telephone charges. But do not forget to include costs of software licences in your calculations. We consider in a later section some of the software applications that you either need to run or may find add to your effectiveness.

You may be confused, when using a network, by not knowing where your files are actually stored. There are disk drives that are physically in the machine on your desk, but you also have the use of disk space on the computer at your ISP. E-mail sent to you arrives initially at your ISP's machine. When you log on and read your mail, the message appears on your screen and has probably been physically copied onto your PC and deleted from the ISP. The distinction is important as e-mails that you want to keep must be treated like other files, and you must make your own back-up copies for security. Conversely, when you wish to make some of your own files accessible to other people (in the shape of your website), you might compose the pages on your PC but then copy them onto the ISP machine, where your provider takes on the responsibility for allowing others to read your pages (but not change them). You can run a website that is physically on your own machine, but then *you* would have to allow anyone else to access to your PC, an invitation to hackers and vandals.

Another consideration, which is not restricted to networked computers but becomes more pressing in such systems, is to protect your computer against viruses. Viruses and related programs (worms, trojan horses, etc) attract much media interest, but most are more an irritation than a hazard; they usually cause little damage, especially if removed quickly. On the other hand, new viruses are created all the time and old viruses continue to circulate – as, incidentally, do hoax messages describing 'particularly dangerous' computer viruses. Be assured, we have all been caught out, and hopefully learned from the experience. Prevention is better than cure, so do buy one of the major anti-virus programs as part of your basic system. Install it (or have it installed) and have it running constantly. Of course, the program's list of viruses has to be kept up to date, but this can be done over the Internet, provided you trust the anti-virus company to run a secure website.

WHERE DO YOU NEED YOUR COMPUTER?

The ideal is that technology should save you work, but taking notes in longhand and transcribing them onto the computer may take more time than relying on a paper-based system. You may therefore assume that a portable (laptop) computer would be more desirable. Laptops that meet all the requirements above are certainly available. The advantage is that the machine can be taken almost anywhere: to the library, laboratory, even (within reason) into the field. Portability is an advantage when travelling or moving home. The disadvantages are that laptops are more expensive and, generally, less durable than office machines, if only because they are always on the move. A portable machine is also, by definition, easier to steal, which adds to the urgency to keep back-ups of all valuable files.

You can have the best of both an office and a portable system, by choosing a portable device that provides only the features you need away from your base. While an insurance salesman or an engineer may require access to all their data and specialised calculations when meeting customers, you need to consider what operations you will use when in the library, laboratory or out collecting data. Quite possibly, a small device that allows you to store notes will be sufficient, provided those notes can be transferred easily onto your PC. Palmtop computers, personal information managers (PIMs) and notebook computers all provide such features for a couple of hundred pounds. They have the advantage of instant access when switched on – no waiting for a long boot-up – and good battery life. The built-in software usually comprises a diary system and address book, as well as a simple word processor and spreadsheet for basic tables. Data are transferred to your PC via disks or by linking the two machines through a wire or without (WAP, or Wireless Applications Protocol, being a buzzword). The files themselves can then be used with the standard applications.

Some students find personal technology exciting and effective. A hand-sized device that allows you to hand write notes using stylised letters on the screen with a plastic stylus may make you more efficient, or it may strike you as an irritating gimmick. Devices with a small touch-sensitive screen may allow you to sketch and store diagrams. Whatever you choose to buy, the fact that it is your own money should make you critical as to its true worth, but the ability to evaluate, take up and exploit appropriate tools will be a central element in your research training.

APPLICATIONS

The uses of computers and range of programs is limited only by your imagination. Colleagues or the literature will bring to your attention specialist programs for so-called vertical markets or research areas. Principles worth restating are that you should avoid wasting time by recreating software that already exists, and that you should understand the limitations of computers as machines if, ultimately, you do have to write software. The last point is summed up in the epigram: *computers do what you tell them to do, not what you want.* The ubiquitous provision of spreadsheets has particularly contributed to an assumption that any answer that comes off the computer has to be correct. That is not to condemn the software, only to remind you that anyone who programs a computer has to ensure that appropriate checks are built in; these include checking that the input data are complete and appropriate and that any calculations are appropriate for a finite-precision machine, using the methods of numerical analysis. Check and check again!

HANDLING INFORMATION

Most of the tasks for which you need your own computer do not require you to be a programmer. Calculations, as such, are a very minor part of information technology (IT); far more important are communication, searching, storage, sorting and retrieval, all of which can be carried out using widely-available tools. The most popular are so widely used that they are often assumed to be 'standard', but, in the words of another epigram, 'the great thing about standards is that you can have so many'. True standards, established by international bodies, are very few and very restrictive. Commercial programs, in contrast, may change arbitrarily and give rise to problems in the exchange of information or maintaining continuity. One fundamental problem for academic users is that of character sets: academic writing almost certainly requires reference to names of people from many countries, and even simple tasks such as quoting equivalent sums in several currencies can be thwarted. Searching for a name or keyword that includes an accented or non-English character may fail to find many references. IT has added immensely to our effectiveness as researchers, but use it with care.

The names 'Internet' and 'World Wide Web' are often used interchangeably. The distinction is that the Internet refers to the physical collection of all hardware attached to open networks through communications links, while the Web is the collection of information that is available through those links. Before the Web was created as a way to make information public and widely available, accessing information from another computer required that you could log on, so each person needed an account and password on every computer they might use. The Web was welcomed at first as the largest collection of information open to everyone. As it has grown, several problems have become apparent. Information may be put up as an experiment or an initial enthusiasm; it then remains incomplete and out of date, often with no indication of its age or provenance, maybe even an embarrassment to the organisation that did not plan or resource for continued support. The quality of information on the Web varies greatly, as there is no quality control or editorial support. The sheer volume of material can be overwhelming, especially when a search term brings up an unexpected and irrelevant theme. Internet search engines can give a misleading impression of completeness. In practice, searching the Web is like fishing in the sea; you pull in the gear and see what it has caught, but you have no idea how much was missed. On a positive note, however, if you catch what you want, you are delighted.

An Internet browser, the program that fetches and displays Web pages, will probably come with your computer: Microsoft's (hereafter MS) Internet Explorer and Netscape Navigator are the best known owing to the 1999 lawsuit in the US Supreme Court. Such programs allow you to type a Universal Resource Locator (URL) or Internet address and contact the appropriate computer. How quickly the information can be displayed will be affected by how large and complex it is, how far away it is, how fast your computer can talk to your ISP, and how busy the rest of the Internet is at that instant. Progress in fetching the files is usually reported on the screen, and it is helpful to get in the habit of watching this. An unfortunate snag is that the report describes progress regarding one file at a time, and a page may be built up from several or many files, each containing a block of text or an image. Hence the counter can get up to 100 per cent, only to start again while not displaying any part of the page. More informatively, it also reports the instantaneous rate at which information is being received, which may vary from zero to a few thousand bytes per second; comparing this with the data transfer rate for your modem will usually convince you that the speed is determined by factors outside your control. Buying a new computer or modem, or paying a higher rental for a faster phone line will not achieve any immediate improvement. Commercial Web pages containing animated adverts are particularly long-winded to fetch. This is particularly irritating when you are paying for the connection or ISP use by the second, less so if you can do something else and not run up a time-related bill.

Finding useful Web pages is, literally, a hit and miss affair. There may be an existing home page for your special interest, or someone may have created a page of links. Web search engines can be useful in turning up links that no other method would locate. As a real example, having seen the Spanish film 'Beltenebros', I was still ignorant as to the meaning of its title, but typing that word into a search engine brought up a collection of references to the film, the book on which it was based, the use of the name in Don Quixote, and the original basis in Dark Age myths. The more unusual the search term, the more likely you will find a manageable number of relevant pages. As a counter example, attempts to find Kenneth Clarke's book 'Civilization' through the net failed, because the spellings should be 'Clark' and 'Civilisation'. Good search engines can be found at www.infind.com, www.askjeeves.co.uk (but do not be misled by the suggestion that it understands English sentences), and www.google.com.

Whenever you find something useful on the Web, you may want to find it again. The possibilities (under the File menu of your browser) are to print the page being viewed, to download it and save it in a file, or to remember the URL as a 'bookmark'. The first two methods preserve the page at the instant you viewed it; the last remembers only how to revisit the remote file, which may change or disappear. Consequently, it is advisable when citing material on the Web (which you may need to do in your dissertation) to quote the URL and the date you viewed it. Printing and downloading both fail at times, for reasons implicit in the way the page was stored. If you try the standard operation and it fails repeatedly, it is probably not your fault, so contact the author of the Web page or your local support service.

Most Web pages are stored as text commands in HyperText Mark-up Language (HTML) or slight variations. HTML provides information for your browser to interpret and display, and usually you will see what the author of the page intended. Sometimes the Web-page author has made inappropriate choices or assumed your browser will behave differently, so some pages may appear to you as unreadable (for example, because text and background are the wrong colour) or as gibberish (if the character set has been swapped). Pages may also contain links to other types of file, which may require a further piece of software to interpret, usually termed a plug-in. Your browser will usually warn you that it is about to download a file, and the browser may then fetch and install the plug-in program without further instructions from you. Downloading any such file leaves your PC open to the possibility of importing a virus, hence the warning, and you have to decide whether to trust the Web page you are viewing. One common way to spread viruses is through pin-up screen-saver pictures. Anti-virus software, kept up to date, will almost certainly detect such a virus and protect your computer.

LITERATURE SEARCHES

Cold-searching on the World Wide Web is as unpredictable as prospecting, and you may find fool's gold or a real nugget. There are, however, particular sites that no researcher can ignore, where you can search through comprehensive reference lists of books and journal papers. Students in the UK should consult www.theses.com for a list of doctoral and masters theses accepted at UK universities since 1971, with bibliographic details and keywords for all and abstracts for the most recent work. The Web of Science (wos.mimas.ac.uk) is a more general service covering a very wide range of journals and other databases. The output from reference lists usually includes an abstract and the works cited within each publication. Searches can be made by keyword or by looking for work that cites a given reference. Thus, you can work back from the latest papers or forward from a classic reference to see where your work might fit.

Quality databases like these, backed by commercial support companies, are not free to all users, and usually require a log-in to identify yourself. Apart from those just mentioned, many major libraries (such as the British Library and the Library of Congress) make their online catalogue (OPAC) available to scholars. Fortunately, you should not need to register separately for each such database. You register instead under a national UK academic system called Athena, so if this has not been offered to you, you should ask at your library.

Access to citation databases and OPACs has revolutionised the research process. Although you have saved the time and expense previously used in travelling to specific libraries and searching along physical shelves, you now risk being overwhelmed by the volume of literature apparently available. Any keyword may bring up thousands of hits, and even when you have refined your search to exclude blatantly unrelated uses, you may still have too many references to make further filtering a simple matter. Using an OPAC also makes clear a feature of bibliographic records: the content of each is complex and arbitrary, with anything from one author to hundreds (for example, Dunham, I and 217 co-authors 'The DNA sequence of human chromosome 22', *Nature* **402**, 1999, pp 489–495), not to mention editors, series editors, and also translators. Different conventions apply to journal papers, books and other types. Furthermore, in addition to the basic reference, you may want to store extracts to quote or your own comments and ideas. All these considerations lead to one conclusion: that a good bibliographic database will be central to your research.

Do not be tempted to write your own software or use a general-purpose database program (for example, MS Access) for this task. Apart from the amount of detailed knowledge about the literary conventions that you would need, specialised bibliographic programs have the advantage of interfacing with the major word processors. The effort you expend at the start of your research in setting up the database, and keeping it up to date with all sources you consult, will be rewarded when you need to cite these sources in your dissertation. Software then brings together your database and your word-processed text, inserting an appropriate reference marker in your text and marking the database entry for inclusion in the list of references. Several excellent bibliographic programs are available (EndNote, Papyrus, Reference Manager, being just three examples), and your choice should be guided by local advice and compatibility with fellow workers, as much as by technical distinctions. Although not automatic or trivial, it is usually possible to move lists of references between alternative systems, or to download sets of references from the major online databases so that you can start your research database with a list of sources to investigate.

The power of such a system becomes apparent when your reference list has built up to some hundreds or thousands of references. Personal bibliographic programs provide standard fields for items such as author, title, year, etc. They then offer a variety of free-text fields for your 'added value'. Your own keywords, copied quotations (and remember to include the page number for subsequent checking!), and added comments, critique or research questions, all provide ways to search and to link previously unrelated work. That may be where your own original idea becomes patent.

WRITING

The word processor is the assumed tool of any academic writer. A few very successful writers stick with a manual typewriter, on the basis that the rhythm and physicality help them to maintain their output. A few privileged senior staff stick with the process of dictation and revising – on paper – drafts produced by a typist. Writers who do not have unlimited use of a secretary, find almost universally that, having tried a word processor, they would not go back to any other way of writing (Zinsser 1998). The ability to make words visible, to rethink and delete or move them, and produce successive drafts without having to type anything apart from the changes, should make us all better and more productive writers.

Your choice of software will again be influenced by the support available and the need to be compatible with colleagues. Remember, though, that word processors have been largely developed for use in offices, a market that is much larger and more affluent than that of authors, of whom academic authors form only a part. Office documents are usually short compared with a book, and contain standard text that is copied between many documents. The popular word processors therefore contain many features that are irrelevant to you, fail to provide features that could be invaluable, or make them clumsy to use in the academic setting. Many users report, for example, that documents in MS Word have been inexplicably lost or corrupted. Attempts to explain such losses have implicated the MASTER DOCUMENT feature that allows several files to be treated as one large whole, and the use of large numbers of footnotes. Both of these features are likely to occur in academic writing, and the only helpful advice is, again, to ensure that you make frequent back-up copies and keep them away from the working draft.

The major, and immediately obvious, feature of writing with an office word processor is that the display is WYSIWYG: What You See Is What You Get. Although widely assumed to be the natural way to work, this has, at times, been questioned, and you need to be particularly careful to check that what you see on the screen will be what appears in print. The need for academic writers to use multiple languages (if only for names in the list of references) and the inclusion of mathematics, chemical formulae or other special symbols (for example, currencies) are all potential pitfalls. Moving files between versions of the same program, between different types of computer, or even between similar computers running 'the same' software, have all at times caused problems. These may be caused by actual incompatibilities, such as the software and printer assuming different fonts. They may be caused by features of the software, 'feature' being the term used for something that does not work as you expected but was intentional in the software, as opposed to a 'bug'. Office word processors are strong on 'auto-format' and 'auto-correct' features, which may change the appearance or meaning of what you type.

One alternative is to use a structural mark-up system in which, instead of highlighting a piece of text and applying a visible style, you need to state the intended function in the text, for example 'title' or 'emphasis'. A separate process then interprets the function as an appropriate style. For example, a word that should be stressed in a sentence would be shown as *italic* on a printed page, but might be coloured or made to flash on a screen, and would be emphasised in a voice-output. The attraction of such a system is that the file is no longer locked into a single program, but can be viewed and edited on any text editing program. The assumption of HTML as a standard for creating Web pages demonstrates the power of such systems, and even popular articles on how to create Web pages generally advise users to learn something of HTML rather than rely entirely on a WYSIWYG editor. The system recommended by this author is L^AT_EX (Lamport, 1994), which was initially conceived with academic writing in mind.

Whatever software you use to format your dissertation, the process of writing involves choosing words and placing them in order. The standard advice on this is to start early and practice often; writing a dissertation is not like writing a series of essays or one very long scientific paper. Features of the word processor that may assist you in the task of writing are listed in chapter 5.

E-MAIL

Electronic mail is the glue that binds any modern academic community. The usefulness of understanding how and where your own e-mail is stored as you read it has been mentioned. Similarly, it is helpful to understand how other people's e-mail readers ('Mail User Agent' or MUA) differ from yours, so that you do not send them messages that are useless or cause anxiety.

First, you need to distinguish between e-mails to individuals, where you can establish a dialogue and agree on mutual standards, and e-mails to groups of individuals. E-mail lists are a vital source of information and assistance but may have hundreds or thousands of members that include distinguished members of your research community. The main system that maintains e-mail lists in the UK is www.jiscmail.ac.uk, and you can browse that site to find lists relevant to your research, view the lists of members' names, and read the archives of messages.

E-mail was originally a text-based service, and for simple use you just type a message and send it. Sending to a list is no more difficult than sending to an individual: you send to the list address and a computer program copies your message to each list member as an ordinary e-mail. The immediacy of e-mail is the root of many problems, especially when someone responds to a message and replies to the list rather than to the individual. (This is the basis of a hoary but funny e-mail parable: how many list members does it take to change a light bulb? You can find out on the Web if you want.) It is also commonplace to have the effect of an e-mail ruined by a misspelt, wrong or omitted word, so one rule worth imposing on yourself is to read it at least twice to check the spelling before sending any e-mail. And do not send any message you would be offended to receive yourself.

The second problem when using email is that some MUAs make it easy to add non-text items as attachments, which can be computer files of any type. Mail agents that are linked to word processors are particular culprits; to send a message composed in the word processor, which therefore might contain formatted text, they will turn every message into an attachment that is an HTML file. Users whose MUA works in plain text will therefore see the message as a jumble of text and commands. Or the MUA may send the message as a file appropriate for that word processor, so any recipient who does not have compatible software will not be able to open the file. The MUA may even send every message in multiple formats, making every message more than twice as large as it should be. This is amplified when the message is sent to a list and respondents quote it in full when making a reply. In general, avoid using attachments except when you are sure that the recipient can open the file and will want to receive the information. In particular, never send attachments to an open list, but send a message describing the file and why you wish to send it. Then send it to individuals who request it.

Used properly, e-mail is a major tool in your research. The style of exchanges within e-mail lists has itself been a topic of research, and the anonymity (you have a name, but nothing else) and speed of exchanges leads to lively and candid discussion. Some students have commented on the apprehension they felt before sending their first query or request to a list, knowing that this would go immediately to hundreds of potential colleagues or competitors. Many more have commented after their first exchanges to thank the list members who immediately responded with constructive and thoughtful ideas. There really is no need now for any research student to feel isolated.

DATA COLLECTION

Computers were originally developed for computation, and may still be associated with quantitative, numeric data and the traditional sciences. As described above, a large proportion, probably the overwhelming majority, of modern use is concerned not with numbers as such, but with storing and retrieving textual information. Internally, all values are coded as voltages or magnetic charges, but that does not usually concern you. What matters is that what you type in can be retrieved or manipulated in predictable ways.

The collection and capture of data is very often the most time consuming and expensive portion of your research. Within a PhD project it is also one of the most difficult to make efficient and effective. Advisors on data analysis are, sadly, all too frequently moved to say, 'If only you had come for advice before collecting all these data. . . .' Here are some brief comments to suggest good practice.

Minimise copying: if only to save on time and costs. Older researchers may still remember the times when data were collected on field sheets and transcribed onto 'computer coding sheets' for 'data entry clerks' to type. Much effort was then expended on proof-reading and checking. You will have to decide what is practical and acceptable, but effective use of technology at the point where data are collected may be highly efficient. It may also increase the confidence of other people (including interviewees), who see you as professional and effective.

Concentrate on accuracy: this includes validity, ensuring that everyone involved understands the same concepts and definitions. Avoid cryptic or complex codings, as these make it easier for data errors to slip through. For example, it is better to code yes and no initially as 'y' and 'n', female and male as 'f' and 'm', rather than use 1 and 0.

Double-check where possible: so that your data collection does not assume that everything is always completely right first time. This may involve some duplication or redundancy, which have negative connotations, or may be presented as 'triangulation' – checking that results are consistent and correct, clearly a virtue.

Balance completeness with validity: a good maxim here is that it is better to have an approximate answer to the right question than a precise answer to the wrong question.

Minimise human involvement: the point made above about using natural codings applies equally when entering data on the computer. Do not attempt to recode data on the fly as you enter it. If some later analysis requires numeric values, changing the codes is a straightforward task for the computer. Investigate whether there are facilities for data capture directly from forms (Optimal Mark Reading, OMR, or Optical Character Recognition OCR) or by eliminating forms, for example, by taking a laptop computer into an archive room. On the other hand, if data have to be copied from field sheets, treat this as an opportunity to scan the data. You will be amazed at the way you, as the primary researcher, will spot interesting or anomalous values during simple copying. A hired hand will not have the knowledge or motivation to do this.

Allow for exceptions: data collection rarely goes smoothly. In open-minded research it will often be the answers you did not anticipate that are most informative. Most questionnaires allow for this by having a category 'Other' and allowing respondents to write in extra answers or explanations. Such extra information has to be incorporated into the analysis, so needs to be stored with other, more tabular, data.

A website and source of free, but high quality, software for data capture is run by the World Health Organisation (WHO). Their examples and documentation refer to disease outbreaks, but the software can be applied to any topic. See www.cdc.gov, in particular Epi-Info.

DATA STORAGE

There is a widespread misconception that because you have some 'data' then it must be held in a 'database'. This is untrue and unhelpful, as a database is, by definition, a system of several related files or tables. Most databases, as constituted on personal computers, add a layer of complexity and inefficiency to the process of analysing research data. To establish whether or not a database system is truly required, I propose the following criteria, *all* of which must be met:

1. large volume of data, which is suggested to mean a gigabyte or more
2. complex file structure
3. long-term use, with data subject to continuing accumulation or incremental update
4. absolute accuracy and consistency needed on a micro-scale
5. frequent accesses to small subsets, or demands for instant answers to ad hoc queries, and
6. data shared by more than one person.

In contrast, academic work at PhD level generally involves small datasets (typically less than 1 Mb), collected and used over a limited timescale. Some measurement or recording errors will inevitably creep in and will be tolerated because they do not affect the gross results. The data structure may alter during the project, but is unlikely to be subjected to a formal analysis by a computer scientist. Projects involve one or very few people, all of equal status (relative to the data!). At the end of a project the data may be archived, but this must be in a generalised form to allow it to be picked up by future workers with probably different software (Reese 1990).

Spreadsheets are very convenient for entering and storing data. One strength is, however, also a weakness. As was stated in the previous section, you need to be able to type in exceptional values and comments as the data are captured. The spreadsheet allows this admirably, but you must be careful, when transferring data from the spreadsheet to another analysis package, to check how irregular cells have been converted. Have dates been misunderstood as text or annotated numbers been treated as missing?

DATA ANALYSIS

Chapter 11 describes specialised software for statistical analysis of quantitative data. Recent years have seen a growth in the use of computers to analyse and interpret qualitative or textual data, such as interview transcripts, written text or descriptions of objects (www.gsr.com.au is a source of information and software). There has also developed a realisation that the two modes of investigation are often complementary – data may emerge by noting or counting occurrences of features in qualitative data, or quantitative data may be 'fuzzy' rather then precise.

CONCLUSIONS

Whatever your personal feelings about them, it is inevitable that you will use computers throughout your research: from the initial stages of planning and searching the literature, through data collection and analysis, during the interpretation of your results and for interacting with other researchers all round the world, and to support the hard work of bringing all the results together in written form.

REFERENCES

Lamport, L (1994) *LaTeX: A Document Preparation System*, 2nd edn (Addison-Wesley, Reading, MA).
Reece, RA (1990) *University Computing*, 12, pp 52–60.
Zinsser, W (1998) *On Writing Well*, 6th edn (HarperCollins).

11 Choosing and using software for statistics

Felix Grant

I assume that you already recognise the need for statistical analysis at some level, and that you already know, or will soon decide, what techniques are appropriate to your needs and purposes. Consequently, I shall not advise you on what statistical methods you need. Advice on this can be found in other chapters. I shall, instead, advise on how to choose the software aids most appropriate to you in applying those methods once they have been selected. Questions to consider are:

- What can you afford?
- What sort of person are you?

WHAT CAN YOU AFFORD?

Can you afford to buy (or persuade someone else to buy) new software, or must you rely on what is already available? At the time of writing, the cost of statistics software ranges from under £100 (about 100 Euros or US dollars) to over £1000 (about 1800 Euros or US dollars). It will be wise to investigate your position in this regard at an early stage. There is no point in identifying an ideal solution if it is not accessible to you. If your institution, employer or sponsor has a standard program in place, they may be reluctant to buy something else. In that case, you have to decide whether the price of purchase is justified by the advantages offered. Even if you persuade someone else to make a purchase, or if you are factoring in the cost of software for a funding body bid, you will still need to provide a cost-benefit case to justify the outlay in terms of time savings and/or improved productivity.

If you cannot match your ideal package with realities of supply, all is not lost. You may be able to borrow facilities. If even a restricted range of options is available to you, the advice here will equip you to choose between them. If all else fails, knowing what you want will at least help you to make best use of the software provided.

With the questions of cost decided, the ultimate check must obviously be whether or not a software package embodies or enables the techniques you have chosen or, perhaps, parallel equivalents. This is a matter of detailed examination of the manufacturer's literature, application of your own subject area knowledge and follow-up enquiries, which we will consider in more detail towards the end of this chapter. Before you can make sound decisions about the capacity of a package, though, you must first make a realistic assessment of your own relation both to statistics and to software in general.

WHAT SORT OF PERSON ARE YOU?

All software is trying to provide a perfect balance between power, ease of use and affordability. But where that perfect balance lies varies from person to person. What sort of person you are is an important factor in choosing the best tools for your purposes. Don't let anyone tell you that only the mathematics or statistics wizard can do valuable research. There are as many approaches to research as there are researchers or study areas, and using software to complement your strengths in other areas is as valid as using it to amplify your reach in one where you are already secure. Also, depending on the work you are doing, very different blends of rigour and intuition may be your best ally. With that in mind, ask yourself some honest questions – and answer them candidly.

Do you delight in statistical methods, or do you fear them? Are you happy with detailed mathematical work at university level, or does it fill you with dread? Do you willingly delve into the workings of the software tools that you already use, or do you just want them to work smoothly and not bother you with detail? Do you enjoy programming or is it a closed book to you?

The answers to these questions will take you a long way towards your final choice. If you can cheerfully call yourself confident in all four respects, you may prefer products that emphasise power and flexibility. If, on the other hand, you feel confident in none of them, your priority will be maximum support and ease of use. In most cases, of course, you will be somewhere between the two extremes and looking for some intermediate balance of power with usability.

How much statistical work do you really need to do? And are you a visual thinker or a symbolic puzzle solver?

The most efficiently powerful tools for a strong mathematician with confidence in both the underlying statistical methods and programming practice are those that overtly present themselves as a high level language and offer a Command Line Interface (CLI) at which you type your requirements. If you are a visual thinker from the arts or humanities, however, with little or no background in any of these areas, a far better solution is a program built around a Graphical User Interface (GUI), which mimics or uses the methods and software that you already know – and you even may be better off with one of the more extensive technical graphics packages.

Very few products, these days, are entirely within either camp. Most offer at least a basic form of both methods – but there is a great variation in the emphasis that is placed on one or the other. I will cover the two ends of the spectrum first, then move on to look at the packages that occupy the middle ground. Finally, I will look at some special cases that do not fit into these neat compartments.

I will use specific products as examples; I have selected them because I know them well, and can recommend them all, but you should look beyond the specifics to general principles that will help you match available tools to your particular tasks and needs. Remember, too, that this is a fast-changing area: by the time this book is published, changes and developments will have occurred in many products. I shall assume that you are using the increasingly dominant 'Wintel' platform. This is a personal computer with an Intel or compatible processor chip, running Microsoft Windows. If that is not true in your case, the general considerations in this chapter will still be valid but not all of the specific products will be available to you. Many products are available on one or more alternative platforms; some are not.

EMPHASISING THE GRAPHICAL

Starting from the GUI end of the range, we will first look at the technical graphics option. You should seriously consider whether such software might do all you need. This sector of the market is well suited to exploratory statistics, and visualisation is a large part of that approach.

The current generation of scientific graphics packages includes various basic statistical functions. Some (such as *StatGraphics Plus*, from Manuguistics Corp) regard this as part of their core function, while for others (*Axum* from MathSoft and *SigmaPlot* from SPSS, for example) analysis is a value-added addition to a primarily visualisation function. For many purposes, graphic visualisations will tell you what you want to know. All the graphics packages are slightly different so it is worth examining them all for particular techniques that might meet your needs. Diamond, from SPSS, to take a particularly striking example, offers a fractal foam tool that allows, at the time of writing, the most intuitive exploration of relatedness between numerous aspects of your information.

If your analysis needs are more than can be met by such software, consider the other side of the same coin: will a statistical analysis package provide the graphics you need? You may need both types of software, but usually not. It makes little sense, for example, to acquire both *Axum* and MathSoft's analysis package *S-Plus* (see below), when both include the same graphics capability. Think carefully about your actual needs; consult with your supervisor and others with experience in this area.

Moving on from these *visualisation crossover* solutions, we come to a body of statistics tools that emphasise one or other of the *Window, Icon, Menu, Pointer* (WIMP) approach to analysis rather than a programming or a command line.

You may be familiar with a spreadsheet program, most likely with Microsoft's Excel spreadsheet, part of the Microsoft Office suite of programs that have swept the board as far as standard products are concerned. You may want to continue using this spreadsheet. You may even *have to* continue using it, if you need to exchange data and results with other people. Spreadsheets are valuable tools, and can be used to great effect for basic statistical work if you know how to get the best from them; but you should be aware of their limitations. In particular, some statistical spreadsheet functions become unreliable if you push them too far; and you will, in many cases, work harder for the same results than you would in a proper statistical package. Nevertheless, most analysis and visualisation products allow you to leave your data within your spreadsheet for general management purposes, import it for analysis, and perhaps even export the analyses back to Excel.

You must organise your spreadsheet in the way the receiving product will expect to find it, with variables in columns and cases in rows (or, in database terms, each column is a field and each row is a record) and some spreadsheets are better supported than others. Excel generally gets the best support for current file versions. Data from Lotus 123 often have to be saved in older file formats such as WK1. Users of Corel's otherwise excellent *Quattro Pro* have the hardest ride; although a few packages will read this format directly, most require the mild inconvenience of an intermediate file saved in some other supported format. Nevertheless, whatever your spreadsheet you can share its contents with your analysis software. For users of Excel, probably the easiest package to use (at the time of writing) is release 5 of *Unistat*, from the company of the same name.

Unistat is actually a separate, stand-alone product with its own built-in *datasheet* (datasheet is what most statistical packages call their specialist internal spreadsheet array). It is also, however, specifically designed to be hidden within other products and it comes out of the box ready to integrate seamlessly with Excel. Once *Unistat* is installed, you have three options: run Excel alone, run *Unistat* alone, or run Excel with *Unistat* as an add-in extension; the third option does not use a separate datasheet at all, and you need do no conscious importing or exporting. Highlight the Excel columns you want to analyse or visualise, select a function from the three new items that *Unistat* has placed on your Excel menu, and *Unistat* will kick in automatically to operate on the highlighted data. When you have what you want, click one of four output buttons on a new toolbar at the top to export it to your choice of destination: back to Excel, out to a Word report, into an HTML formatted web page or onto the Windows clipboard for use in some other suitable program. Statistical work from spreadsheet data does not get much easier than this.

Another package that makes the most of the GUI approach, but in a completely different way, is *Statview*. This is one of a range of products tailored to different needs from the giant SAS Institute. *Statview* originated on the Apple Macintosh platform (where it is still available) and brings a view of things that is somewhat different from the Wintel norm, but the differences are all positive.

To *Statview*, everything is an *object*. Each of your variables (such as age, intensity, salinity, colour) is an object. A graph of a relationship between those variables is an object. An analysis of the way in which a variable is distributed is an object. At first sight, this is strange (especially if you are used to spreadsheets) but it has tremendous advantages once you look more closely. The objects have a physical presence on your screen, and they can be picked up and dropped on each other. If you want to investigate the relation between two variables, for example; just open a scattergraph object with a mouse-click, then drag the two variables into it. *Statview* is particularly popular in the medical and health sciences, but it also has a good record of success for users with no prior experience of statistical work at all. The object-based approach is a good analogy for everyday, hands-on experience of working with things or ideas. *Statview* also allows you to save an analysis you have done as a new object, so you can use the same method again, just by dragging and dropping new data into it.

If you are not afraid to deal directly with statistical ideas, prefer a free-standing package with a conventional worksheet approach to your data, but want to stay in the WIMP category, a strong contender is *Stat-100* from Biosoft, offering remarkable value for money at a price well below its specification. Probably the lowest priced package around at the moment, it demands very few system resources, will run on older versions of Windows and on older machines or small crowded notebooks, yet will do most of what more expensive competitors can do. It is also a very effective partner to some of Biosoft's other, more specialised tools (see the Special cases section below). There is a more sophisticated sibling, *Stat-200*, still low-priced at double the cost, but that belongs in the middle ground.

TAKING DIRECT COMMAND OF YOUR SOFTWARE

At the other extreme from these graphical environments, we find the overtly programming approaches.

Perhaps the purest and best known of these is *Genstat*, a statistical programming language developed from the more general Fortran by the statistics section at IACR specifically for statistical analysis. Marketed by NAG, it concentrates on analysis, giving graphical and text output in very stripped-down form, with presentational aesthetics taking a back seat to clarity. If you are confident in Fortran and want to build your own highly efficient routines focused on your own needs, this is a good place to start the investigation of software for your chosen route. *Genstat* does have a Windows interface for interactive exploration of data, but its users usually see this as a tool for preliminary investigation before getting down to serious batch processing.

At this end of the scale, my warnings about the use of statistical functions in spreadsheets apply with even greater force, but the spreadsheet program itself can still be used to great effect as a container and low-level organiser of your data. As before, most programs will import data from widely used spreadsheets, particularly Excel. If your preferences, constraints or working software environment predispose you to remaining within Excel for the analysis itself, despite the problems,

NAG again have a solution in the form of their *Statistical Add-ins for Excel*, a package of Fortran routines that integrate as an Excel add-in to provide command line function call access.

Many products in this category could, perhaps, be placed in the Middle ground, since their WIMP interfaces are so highly developed. Mathsoft's *S-Plus*, for example, is built around Lucent's powerful S programming language, and it is through direct access to that aspect that a user will use the facilities available to maximum effect. Despite this, however, *S-Plus* installs on your computer to present you with a graphical exploration interface as powerful as any; the language is hidden behind the WIMP front end until wanted. Despite appearances, *S-Plus* would be an expensive and overpowered purchase for most users who want a graphical program, but it is an excellent choice if you want exploratory and visualisation capacity on top of a programming environment.

If you are mathematically as well as statistically confident, you may want to investigate the use of generic mathematical tools with programming or command line facilities as an alternative to dedicated statistical ones (see the Special Cases section).

GOING FOR THE BEST OF BOTH WORLDS

The range of products available for this most popular category is vast. *Stat-200*, Biosoft's big brother to *Stat-100* in the graphical group, is a good introduction. Both GUI and programmed approaches coexist on more or less equal terms in the same package. It is, primarily, an interactive exploratory package that makes full use of the sophisticated WIMP facilities in 32-bit versions of Windows; it has, nevertheless, a procedure language that enables a considerable degree of batch automation.

The middle ground also includes, for example, Statsoft's *Statistica*, an immensely powerful modular package that integrates with other Statsoft products to provide anything from basic descriptives through to full blown control of a factory. *Statistica* is a WIMP-driven package, conceived from its very earliest days as a graphic tool. It has, however, a programming language that enables any degree of batch automation, allows control of other programs or subservience within them and can be used to build specialised turnkey systems.

Another interesting and widely used member of this group is *Minitab*, which has, in many ways, taken the opposite development route to *Statistica*. *Minitab* originated as a command line program, has evolved towards the WIMP model and now straddles the two approaches. In the version current at the time of writing, the screen is divided horizontally with the WIMP menu and tool bars at the top, a session window below, and a datasheet at the bottom. Operations selected from the menu are echoed in the session window as commands; these can be copied, pasted, edited, and executed or stored as batch processes from a command line. Command sequences can also be written from scratch in the session window and executed directly without recourse to the menus at all.

SPECIAL CASES

I have concentrated primarily on general-purpose statistics software, but there are specialised tools out there for many and more focused purposes, either in their own right or alongside the more general products.

Design of Experiments (DoE)

One of the big growth areas in recent years has been the computerised design of experiments. Industry is the economic engine here, and agriculture was the crucible where the techniques evolved, but DoE is applicable to every study where any control at all can be exercised over the collection of data: from literature to physics and everything in between. DoE is essentially a particular application of standard methods, but purpose-designed software support simplifies its application considerably.

Increasingly, DoE tools at some level or other are built into general products (particularly the high end ones) and these may well suffice for your needs. If you are going to make intensive use of these methods, however, it is worth considering the dedicated packages that are available. *DesignEase* and *DesignExpert* from Stat-Ease Corp and the *DoE-Fusion* products by S-Matrix are both excellent. Both companies offer two levels of power to suit your needs, and both achieve their ends in different ways to suit different user psychologies.

Closely related to DoE is sample design software, such as the excellent *nQuery Advisor* from Statistical Solutions.

Mathematics in the round

Useful as statistical analysis software is, it does not answer every need. In certain circumstances, and if you are sufficiently relaxed with mathematics, both analysis and modelling can be more efficiently and rapidly productive using general mathematical methods. Products such as *Mathematica*, *Mathcad*, *Maple* and *Matlab* (all in different ways) can provide invaluable support or even replacement for their dedicated statistical cousins. On the one hand, you may want to work exploratively with formulae in natural notation, using the speed of a computer to build up rapidly an intuitive model for data features that resist conventional methods. Or you may find that building your own numerical approaches from fundamental mathematical building blocks enables you to shake off preconceptions and attack intractable problems in new ways.

Other special purpose tools

If your study is particularly concerned with a particular aspect of your data, there may well be an established way to deal with it that offers greater efficiency than a general analytical product. Search the web, and/or the available literature, for references to your particular concerns in relation to software.

For example, if you are concerned with highly peaked data (which occurs in fields as diverse as aeronautics and art history), a suitably framed search may turn up two very different but equally valuable avenues to explore. One relies on the focused use of a generic package, *S-Plus*, which uses modified kernel routines. The other uses a specialist program designed for the purpose: *Peakalyse*, from scientific software supplier Biosoft.

Peakalyse is one example of the many specialist software tools that are available not only from Biosoft but from plenty of other companies. There may be one company that already produces exactly what you want. In Biosoft's range you will find products (apart from *Peakalyse*) for purposes such as assay analysis, curve-fitting, data extraction from published plots, and mixture characteristics, amongst others.

SUITABILITY FOR YOUR PURPOSE

General considerations

What I have been able to give here is no more that a broad sketch of the range of software products from which you must select the best tools for your needs. With that sketch in mind, decide the *type* of software product you would ideally like to use and the types that you would prefer to avoid if possible. Then, from the detailed knowledge of your own study before you, start by making a list of the essential statistical techniques to be employed, and a subsidiary list of the desirable ones.

At this point, as you survey the market and make a detailed examination of feature lists on websites and manufacturers' literature, you will either find that several products serve your purpose or that none matches your needs perfectly and you must seek to make a second choice fit the bill. The first, happy, state of affairs is most likely if your needs match your skills closely; the second is more probable if there is a mismatch in either direction. Either way, you should delve more deeply in order to choose between the candidates.

Ask to try out the software, to get a feel for it in your own hands and context. Increasingly, companies are making time-limited demonstration copies available for web download. Ask for the names of satisfied customers and then approach those customers with a request for brief hands-on experience. Talk to colleagues and others in your area, or who are like you as a person. Join mailing lists (see the Help and support section below).

If you are unable to match needs with techniques on offer, are there ways to achieve your ends through other techniques that *are* available? If you have the confidence, can your required techniques be synthesised from others, achieved by modifying others, or built from scratch by programming them yourself with the facilities provided? Can you pair up a main package with a specialised one (or more) to get the combination you need?

It is worth approaching the publishers of those products that come closest to what you are seeking. They have a tremendous store of accumulated in-house experience, and will often come up with a solution that had not occurred to you. In some cases, they will even make modifications to provide what you want. After all, if you want it then so, perhaps, do other potential customers.

Help and support

Minitab and *Statistica*, although about as different as they can be, both originated in the academic system. This is still very visible in their approaches to users: when you buy these products you are also buying into a system of user support which knows how people like you learn to use their statistical tools. They are not the only ones. *Systat*, for example, is another. It has one of the best manual/tutorial sets around for the non-statistician.

This is one of the many issues you should consider and which has nothing to do with statistics: how much help and support are you going to need, and who will provide it? If you are secure in your abilities within the context of your subject, you are free to choose from the whole gamut of software that the market can offer. If you are going to rely on sources of help amongst those around you, you will need to consider the need to stay within their range of experience and/or adaptability. If you are inexperienced, unsupported and nervous, you should look carefully at the support resources available to you.

Support resources do not have to come from the manufacturer or publisher of the product (although they often do so). There are Internet news and discussion groups, and mailing lists for some widely used products (*Genstat*, for example, has a thriving user list). Some products have also spawned a large number of textbooks (*Minitab*, again, is notable in this area). Look for books that mention your particular area of study in connection with particular products. There may be valuable support from those who have gone before. Search the web, that most prolific source of the latest information, and contact them.

AND FINALLY . . .

Never forget that statistics software is only a tool, no more useful than what you do with it. Allow statistics to strip away the undergrowth and reveal the true form of your data, and allow software to take the drudgery out of the process, but never, ever, allow either of them to usurp your own understanding, experience, intuition and independent powers of thought. Like all power tools, they are dangerous if they are not fully in your control, but liberating as long as you remain in charge.

12 The Internet

Karen L Ayres

INTRODUCTION

Over the last few years the Internet (see page 79 for the distinction betweeen the Internet and the World Wide Web) has greatly expanded and, consequently, contains a vast amount of information that is potentially useful for postgraduate research in all subject areas. This information is usually provided either by individuals, in the form of personal home pages (see Chapter 40), or by university departments, companies or other organisations.

There are several ways in which research students can use the Internet. As well as a reference tool for gathering background information about a subject, or learning about specific formulae or new approaches, there are various freely available software packages that you can download and install on your own computer. In addition, many journals now publish their articles online, and individual researchers often include preprints of their articles on their web pages for others to access.

The fact that the Internet contains so much information means that sometimes it can be difficult to locate sites of interest. Consequently, using the Internet for research can be daunting. However, with practice and patience you can learn how to use it efficiently.

I shall give only a brief introduction to using the Internet for academic research. For more details, see, for example, Basch and Bates (2000).

ACCESSING THE INTERNET

Recent advances in communications technology mean that a computer is no longer needed to access the Internet. Internet-televisions are now available. These connect to the telephone line in the same way as do personal computers with modems. In addition, WAP (Wireless Application Protocol) mobile phones are increasing in popularity, although these currently only allow connection to specially formatted pages, not the entire Internet. However, at present, most people use a computer of some sort to connect to the Internet, and so we focus on computer-based browsing in this chapter.

To view pages on the Internet you need to install web browsing software on your computer. This software reads the computer code underlying the page (written in HTML, see Chapter 40), and displays the information on your computer screen. The two main browsers (both freely available) are

- Netscape Navigator
  http://www.netscape.com/download/
- Microsoft Internet Explorer
  http://www.microsoft.com/windows/ie/default.htm

For a guide to using Netscape Navigator see, for example, Turlington (1998), and for Internet Explorer see Freeze and Freeze (1999).

If you want access from home, rather than via your college's computer network, you will need an account with an Internet Service Provider (ISP). Several companies (including supermarkets and other high street stores) now offer free Internet connection: you only pay the price of the telephone call for the time you are connected. If you are buying a new personal computer (Chapter 10), ask the sales assistant for details about Internet connection (new computers usually include, as standard, some software allowing you to connect easily to the Internet).

SEARCHING FOR INFORMATION

There are a number of Internet search engines that provide a quick and easy way to search databases of web pages for the keywords you specify. Unless you know in advance the web address of the page you want, you will usually have to use one or more of these search facilities to locate the information you require. Popular search engines include

- AltaVista   http://www.altavista.com/
- Excite   http://www.excite.co.uk/
- Google   http://www.google.com/
- WebCrawler   http://www.webcrawler.com/
- Yahoo!   http://www.yahoo.com/

In most cases, a list of several hundred pages is returned as a result of your search, some of which will no longer be accessible. These sites are usually listed in order of matching content, so those containing more of your specified keywords appear at the top of the list. To obtain a shorter list, specify more keywords, or insist that they *all* appear somewhere in the page for it to be listed (to do this you usually need to include a plus sign, +, between each keyword when initiating the search, or enclose the keywords in quotation marks " " if they constitute a set phrase). If you are searching for general information rather than a specific site, use more than one search engine, as you may obtain different results with each.

RESEARCH RESOURCES

As well as using the general internet search engines listed above, you can find suitable sites to visit while attending conferences and seminars, where other researchers will include their website addresses in their presentations. In addition, fellow researchers in your department (especially your supervisor) will be able to suggest good sites to look at, and your department may even maintain a web page of useful links. If not, you can consider compiling your own page of useful websites for your subject area (see Chapter 40 for details of how to create your own web page). Some sites that may be useful to researchers are given below. There are many more and you should search the Internet to find others that are more specific to your area of research.

Lists of useful sites

The following sites provide links to web pages covering specific areas of interest: a more general database of Internet resources covering several subjects is maintained by BUBL, and is located at http://bubl.ac.uk/link/

- The Bioinformatics Resource
  http://www.hgmp.mrc.ac.uk/CCP11/
- Statistical Science Web
  http://www.maths.uq.oz.au/~gks/webguide/
- OMNI: Organising Medical Networked Information
  http://omni.ac.uk/
- ChemDex (International Directory of Chemistry)
  http://www.chemdex.org/
- Social Science Information Gateway
  http://www.sosig.ac.uk/
- Art and Humanities Research Board links
  http://www.ahrb.ac.uk/links/

Free software

The Internet is a useful place to find good quality free software for your computer. For example, the following word processing packages can be downloaded free:

- L^AT_EX and T_EX (mathematical typesetting programs)
  http://www.tug.org/ctan.html
- Sun StarOffice (word processor, spreadsheet, and other office-related facilities)
  http://www.sun.com/staroffice/

Free tools for viewing documents (such as electronic journal articles and preprints) that have been created in a specific format include.

- Microsoft Word and Excel file viewers
  http://www.microsoft.com/downloads/
- Ghostscript and Ghostview – viewing PostScript files
  http://www.cs.wisc.edu/~ghost/
- Adobe Acrobat Reader – viewing PDF (Portable Document Format) files
  http://www.adobe.com/products/acrobat/readstep.html

More specialised software packages are also available, for example the following statistics packages:

- BUGS – for 'Bayesian inference Using Gibbs Sampling'
  http://www.mrc-bsu.cam.ac.uk/bugs/
- R – general statistics package (similar to the S language)
  http://www.gnu.org/software/r/R.html
- DJGPP – a free C/C++ computer programming language compiler
  http://www.delorie.com/djgpp/

For details about other software available, see the following sites:

- GNU Project and the Free Software Foundation
  http://www.gnu.org/
- CNET Shareware.com – searchable database of shareware programs
  http://shareware.cnet.com/

or look for information via Internet search engines.

Online journals

Several journals now publish their articles on the Internet, as well as in paper format. To access the electronic versions of the articles, you must have a subscription to the journal. In some cases, you may access the site from a recognised institution that subscribes.

The advantage of online journals is that articles often appear on the Internet before the paper version reaches the library (particularly in the case of overseas journals). You therefore have immediate access to the latest articles as soon as they are published. Furthermore, most online journals provide searchable databases of their tables of contents, allowing you to identify which articles you need (some also provide automatic e-mail alerts, notifying you about the contents of new issues). Each journal also usually includes advice for potential authors on its web page.

Some journals do not include electronic versions of articles on their own website, but instead make them available from specialist database sites. For example, several journals can be accessed from the ingentaJournals facility (http://www.bids.ac.uk/journals/browse/ap/es), which is maintained by the Bath Information Data Service (BIDS).

In most cases, articles from only the last few years are available on the Internet so it cannot replace the library as the primary tool for a literature review (see Chapter 13 for further details on using libraries). The main exception is for those journals that have been completely archived in for example, JSTOR, an online Journal Storage facility at http://www.jstor.ac.uk/ (http://www.jstor.org/ for the US version). Again, subscription is required at either the individual or institutional level to download files, but articles are available in different formats, and generally from the first issue to within about five years of the current date.

As well as downloading full-text versions of articles, the Internet is useful for providing lists of relevant articles that you can subsequently obtain elsewhere. Chapter 13 includes an introduction to the use of citation indexes and other databases for obtaining listings of suitable literature. Many such searchable indexes are now on the Internet, such as BIDS (http://www.bids.ac.uk/) and MIMAS, the Manchester Information And Associated Services facility (http://www.mimas.ac.uk/).

Other useful resources

There are several other useful resources on the Internet. For example:

- Many universities offer online tutorials on certain subjects, including notes that you can download.
- The major funding councils maintain their own sites, providing details about the funding opportunities that they offer (see Chapter 8).
- Details can be obtained about professional societies dedicated to your subject, and membership application forms downloaded.
- Online bookstores (for example Amazon, at http://www.amazon.co.uk/) allow for simple purchasing of research-related texts.
- Introductions to statistics (for example StatSoft's Electronic Statistics Textbook at http://www.statsoft.com/textbook/stathome.html) provide guidance about techniques for analysing data.

JOB OPPORTUNITIES

While studying for a postgraduate qualification, you need to be aware of current job opportunities in your area of research, so that you can apply in good time for a suitable post before the end of your studies. The Internet provides an easily accessible source of current job vacancies both at home and abroad, in addition to other methods of job seeking (see Chapter 42).

When searching for jobs on the Internet, you should first look at the website maintained by your university careers service. This is likely to contain a list of jobs currently available at your university, as well as links to other careers sites. Web and e-mail discussion groups may carry job adverts as well, so you can periodically check archives of such groups if available.

There are many websites that list current job opportunities: your careers service can provide you with a list, but I have found the following useful:

- Jobs.ac.uk   http://www.jobs.ac.uk/
  Searchable database of currently available jobs in UK universities – also provides weekly e-mails of new postings.
- Guardian Unlimited Jobs   http://jobs.guardian.co.uk/
  Searchable database of currently available jobs primarily in the UK, but also some worldwide, plus useful careers information and links to other sites.
- NewScientistJobs   http://www.newscientistjobs.com
  Searchable database of science-related jobs appearing in *New Scientist* magazine: currently this site requires registration before allowing access to the database (registration is free). E-mail alerts of new jobs can be requested.
- Monster.co.uk   http://www.monster.co.uk/
  Searchable database of jobs available worldwide, plus useful careers advice. Allows you to create your own online account so that details on specific jobs can be e-mailed to you.

Some Internet careers sites allow you to create and save a personal profile, so that details about jobs of particular interest can be forwarded on to you. Others allow more general lists to be e-mailed to you on a regular basis. Check several sites periodically for details of the latest career opportunities.

WORDS OF WARNING

Although the Internet contains much information useful for research, there are some problems. Since the content of a website is not peer-reviewed in the same way as a journal (with the exception of online journals) there cannot be the same level of confidence in the correctness of any information found on the Web. You should therefore take extra care to verify for yourself, as far as possible, any results and theories that you obtain from the Internet. A further problem is that information is often out-of-date. Always check the 'last updated' details on a webpage to ensure that the information you obtain is likely to be relevant. For example, a page giving details about DNA profiling techniques that has not been updated since 1995 is unlikely to be useful for learning about current practices (which typically now use different methods to obtain profiles).

The Internet is also subject to the same rules regarding intellectual property rights as other forms of information provision (see Chapter 41). If you cite results, formulae, or other opinions expressed on a webpage, you should give full details of the source, including its web address and author if appropriate.

Finally, the best way to discover how useful the internet can be to your research is to start searching it regularly. And remember to bookmark any sites that are particularly interesting to your research project, so that you can easily revisit them when you need to.

REFERENCES

Basch, R and Bates, ME (2000). *Researching Online For Dummies.*(I.D.G. Books).

Freeze, WS and Freeze, JT (1999). *SAMS Teach Yourself Internet Explorer 5 in 24 Hours* (Indianapolis, USA: SAMS).

Turlington, S (1998). *SAMS Teach Yourself Netscape Communicator 5 in 24 Hours* (Indianapolis, USA: SAMS).

13 Library and information services

Claire Abson

INTRODUCTION

You have probably used a university library as an undergraduate. However, as a postgraduate, whether on a taught course or pursuing your own research, you will need to be a more independent library user. After you have found and interrogated appropriate sources for your subject area, you will also need to evaluate their usefulness and accuracy.

There are ever-increasing volumes of information available to researchers, both official academic refereed sources and unofficial sources, more and more of them accessible electronically. It would be impossible to do justice to all the sources available for different subject areas in an introductory chapter. Indeed, with the pace of technological change and new sources becoming available all the time, such an introduction would be out of date by the time it is published. Instead, in this chapter, I shall point you towards ways in which to locate, evaluate and make effective use of the information that is available to you, and also how to get the most out of your library or learning centre, whatever your subject area and institution of study.

KNOW YOUR LIBRARIAN

Most university libraries have dedicated staff responsible for particular subject areas, and it is a good idea to find out who your librarian is. The level of support you can expect will vary but, at the very least, there should be someone with the job of ordering library materials for your subject area. That person should also be knowledgeable about information databases and other appropriate sources, and will probably have some responsibility for training students to seek information effectively. They may have special arrangements for training staff and researchers, or they may be willing to see you on a one-to-one basis and deal with your particular needs. If they are unable to do this, they should certainly be able to provide you with the information you need to get started, either in paper format or, increasingly, electronically, possibly via a set of web pages.

DEVELOP THE SKILLS YOU NEED

Before you begin to search for information, you will need to think about precisely what you are looking for. It is much better to be as specific as you can when you first start searching for information, as it will save time in the end. Think about words and phrases you would use to describe your topic. Probably most of the sources you will use to direct you towards relevant information will be electronic and they will all be searchable in slightly different ways. Some will be searchable by putting in free text, where you will need to be familiar with what are known as 'search operators', the connecting words you use to string your search terms together. Other sources will have boxes in which you can type your search terms that will connect them together for you. More detail on electronic databases and other sources will be described later, but whatever sources you use, a well planned search strategy is invaluable.

A search for information about women in the workplace, for example, will require you to think about the words you use. 'WOMEN and WORKPLACE' would be obvious, but there is a lot that you would exclude with that. Most databases will allow you to use a 'wildcard' where you can replace a letter with a symbol, commonly a question mark, and the database will pick up that word with any letter in that position. For example it might be sensible to replace WOMEN with WOM?N so that you would pick up the word 'woman' as well. In addition, the term 'workplace' is only one way of describing a place of work or a place in the workforce. Work, office, factory, labour market: these are all ways you might describe this. You may not want to include work in the home. A better constructed search, therefore, might look something like:

WOM?N and (WORK or WORKPLACE or OFFICE or FACTORY) not HOME

You can probably think of other valid descriptions yourself for this example. This is not an exhaustive list, but it illustrates the importance of thinking about the search before you start. As you begin interrogating different sources, you will need to experiment. In addition, as your search generates relevant results, you will find that the sources you are using can also help you. Many library catalogues and databases attach subject descriptors to the references to books and other materials. These may give you clues as to other search terms you can use.

You will probably begin by searching for books on your chosen topic, and the mechanics of this will be described later. However, as you will no doubt be aware from your undergraduate studies, information comes in many different formats. Which of these formats is key to you depends very much on your subject area and, in addition to planning your search, you need to think about other factors, for example:

- **Currency**: how up to date does the information need to be? If you are a scientist, the sources you access must be current. If your research is in the humanities or social sciences, this may not be so important.
- **Nationality**: is the country of origin of the book or journal or database important? If you are engaged in educational research, you may be interested in material relating only to the education system in the UK.
- **Language**: if you don't speak any language other than English and do not have access to a translater, there is little point spending time trawling through references to material where the original is in French or Spanish.
- **Academic refereeing**: legitimacy and quality will be touched on later but, depending on your area of research, the validity of a newspaper article as against an article in a journal validated by experts in the field of study may be crucial.

In other words, you will need to think about what you want to exclude from your search as well as what you want to include. Most of the library catalogues and databases you use will allow you to make selections relating to some or all of the above, possibly before you even input your search. If you are unsure about how to begin constructing your search strategy, or you encounter problems, your librarian will be able to help you.

TRACKING DOWN BOOKS

The software and interface will vary but, essentially, most academic library catalogues, or OPACs (Online Public Access Catalogues) are the same. They will generally allow you to search the library's holdings by author name, book title, keyword or subject heading, and there may be other more complex or refined searches you can perform. You may find that your institution includes other materials in the catalogue, such as media materials or student dissertations. If you have used an online catalogue of any kind as an undergraduate you will pick up a new system quite easily.

You will progress beyond the limits of books fairly quickly as you make inroads into your research project, certainly books held by your own university library. However, you will probably need to identify and consult books relevant to your topic that your university library does not hold. It is becoming easier and easier to do this. Most university libraries now make their online catalogues available via the web and, if your library has its own web pages, it will have made links to gateways to allow you to access these. If not, your subject librarian will advise you on how best to do this. Some university and research libraries working in similar areas (geographically or in terms of their status or the nature of their collections) have put their holdings together to form union catalogues. These will allow you to search several library collections at once by inputting a single search. A good example of this is COPAC, which brings together the holdings of 19 of the largest university research libraries in the UK and Ireland. The catalogues of the British Library are also accessible via the web. There may be other institutions with a strong research profile in your subject area (your research supervisor should be able to advise you on this) so you may find it useful to search their catalogues individually if they do not belong to a consortium.

Obtaining books from other libraries for consultation can be more problematic. Visits to other libraries to consult material is usually possible, unless, for example, you are in Aberdeen and the book is in Plymouth. An Inter-Library Loan is another option and this will be explored in more detail later.

JOURNAL ARTICLES AND ELECTRONIC SOURCES

Once you have formulated your search strategy and considered your priorities, you will need to identify the sources that can direct you towards the most relevant information. This is where the advice of your librarian is invaluable. If you require current information, for example, the librarian may be able to direct you towards any academic refereed journals published online and to which your institution subscribes. It is increasingly common for journals to be published in this way as, in addition to cutting costs, the information is available much more quickly. If your area of study is in the sciences or in business and management, you will find full-text electronic journals are now commonplace. This is less common in the humanities and other social sciences but the picture is changing. Alternatively, your librarian will be able to advise you which information databases are the most appropriate for your topic and help you to track down relevant journal articles. If you are returning to study after a break, you may have used paper-based abstracts and indexes in the past. The information databases you are now likely to encounter began as electronic versions of these paper-based abstracts and indexes, but there are still a few key sources remaining in paper format. Also key sources have become more sophisticated and, in some cases, do far more than simply reference journal articles.

Information databases are commercial sources that your library buys in on CD-ROM or buys access to via the web. You can use your carefully composed search strategy to search online for references to journal articles or, in some cases, the full text of journal articles. Databases that contain only references to journal articles will usually give you an abstract, or summary of the article content, to guide you as to whether or not the full article is going to be relevant to you. The subject focus, the national bias and the language coverage will vary from one database to another, even where the databases cover the same broad subject area. The time you have spent thinking about exactly what sort of material you require, and what you do not want, will help you decide which databases to concentrate on, and will help your librarian to advise you most effectively.

If you are accessing a database that gives you only references to journal articles, the references it contains are likely to bear no relation to the journal holdings of your university library. You will probably be able to find some of the journals referred to in your search results, but you will have to obtain some materials from elsewhere. In the previous section I outlined the possibilities for accessing other university library catalogues. These should give you details of journal holdings of other institutions as well as details of book collections.

Databases are a reliable source of information. You are being referred to a piece of work published in a journal of recognised academic quality. However, that is not to say that resources freely available on the Internet and, as such, not subject to the same rigorous academic processes are not valid. You just need to evaluate the sources you use more carefully.

In this chapter I have already introduced you to ways in which you might evaluate the usefulness of a particular database for your research needs. However, if you are making use of Internet resources, you need to assess the quality as well as the appropriateness of the information. There is no point reinventing the wheel, though. Your first port of call should be gateways and other sites where the evaluative work has been done on your behalf, generally by practitioners or librarians in the field. Your library may have its own set of web pages linking you to relevant resources in particular subject areas. Even if it doesn't, your librarian should be able to direct you towards relevant subject gateways where that work has been done.

When you do need to trawl the web for resources, there are additional criteria you should apply to evaluate the usefulness of a website:

- Is the information accurate (factually and in terms of spelling and grammar)?
- What, if any, research or evidence is it based on?
- Where has it come from? Who wrote it? Might the authors be biased?
- Does it make reference to any published sources of information?

(Paraphrased from Cooke 1999, p.63)

The Internet is unquestionably a valuable source of information, but be sure you have a full understanding of the origin and nature of the source you are using.

ACCESSING OTHER LIBRARIES

Your own university library will almost certainly *not* hold all of the relevant books and journals you require, so it will be necessary to obtain them from elsewhere. In this chapter, I have described the benefits of searching the catalogues of other libraries. Where there are other local institutions with a strong research profile in your subject area, it may be easy for you to visit their libraries and consult material yourself. It would be prudent, however, to consult a librarian first. The situation regarding access to other libraries is improving but some institutions may allow you through their doors only with a letter of introduction!

The alternative to visiting another university library would be to obtain material on Inter-Library Loan, but different institutions' policies vary enormously in this area. You may find that your university library will allow you to request as many items as you require on Inter-Library Loan. Others may limit you to a small number as an individual, or your school or department may have an allocation to distribute as it sees fit. Familiarise yourself with the local situation, and plan very carefully what you request and what materials you try to obtain yourself. You should also plan carefully in terms of time. Journal articles can usually be obtained fairly quickly, but books can take some weeks. The British Library may have a copy already on loan to someone else. Many university libraries refuse to lend books outside their own institutions.

STUDYING AT A DISTANCE

It is becoming increasingly common for students to work at a distance from their institutions of study. As a result, university libraries have done a lot of cooperative work in recent years to put measures in place that recognise this.

As information databases are increasingly becoming available via the web, there may be scope for you to work not only from outside the library but also from outside the university. If you have Internet access at home, ask your librarian what is accessible from outside, and what system of passwords you might need to access the relevant resources. Remote access to electronic resources is becoming increasingly common. It is also increasingly possible to visit other university libraries for reference purposes and, in some cases, particularly if you are studying part-time, to borrow materials. This can depend on whether or not your university library is party to any local or national reciprocal arrangements, and your librarian will be best placed to advise you on this.

Your university library may also provide some specialist support for students studying at a distance, such as by postal loans of materials.

KEEP A RECORD OF WHAT YOU HAVE DONE

One of the most important things to remember when conducting research is to keep an accurate record of anything you use. Keeping notes on index cards, ideally in the correct format, will make your life considerably easier when you come to write up your research. If, during your undergraduate degree, you have not been required to produces references and bibliographies in a standardised format, you should familiarise yourself with one of the systems. The Harvard referencing system is the most commonly used (see Chapter 37). The library may even produce guides to referencing and bibliographies that you can take away. Alternatively, there are Internet sources that will take you through referencing all types of materials, from books and journals through to citing a video or a webpage you have used.

Do not forget to keep a record of searches you have done on the library catalogue, on information databases or on the internet. With so many information sources at your disposal it is easy to forget exactly what you have searched and which combinations of words and phrases you have used. Keep a note and you will avoid repeating work. Some online databases will allow you to save a search strategy you have used so that you can return to it later. If you are keen to keep up to date with the very current research on a topic, for example, you might want to revisit a frequently updated source, perhaps monthly. Be aware of how long the system will retain your search strategy; it won't be forever! However, where this kind of service is available, it will save you a lot of time and ensure you are completely up to date.

CONCLUSION

I have given you enough guidance for you to begin searching for material to support your research. The means of accessing quality information are changing constantly, and what constitutes the latest technology today will probably be out of date in two years' time. Electronic journals have not yet overtaken paper journals in most subject areas. However, as electronic textbooks are now a reality, it may only be a matter of time before access to academic texts is almost wholly electronic. If your computing skills are in need of updating then you must update them. Your supervisor, or your librarian, will point you in the right direction for help, even if they are unable to help you themselves.

Nevertheless, although the means of accessing information may be changing constantly, certain truisms remain. Your research still needs to be

- well planned – do your thinking before you start;
- timely – give yourself plenty of time to obtain the materials you need;
- thorough – check out all of the information sources at your disposal;
- accurately recorded – write, or save, everything you do.

If you do all of the above you will be able to make best use of the wide (and widening) variety of information sources at your disposal.

REFERENCE

Cooke, A (1999) *A Guide to Finding Quality Information on the Internet: Selection and Evaluation Strategies* (Library Association Publishing).

14 Searching in unfamiliar fields

Michael Hal Sosabowski and Tom Bourner

A STRATEGY FOR SEARCH

While many students of this book will be pursuing research that follows soon after their undergraduate academic studies, others may have found their ways into research through their professional occupations, such as history, engineering, law, medicine, social services, chemistry and human resources. We call the latter *practitioner researchers*. The two routes have contrasting approaches to literature searches. One seeks to describe a detailed background to the research area, showing the history of what has gone before in order to establish a wide context, and to support arguments for a new theory. It is *intensive*. The second seeks to discover current knowledge that will help to answer a well-defined question. It is *extensive*. This latter is reflected in present-day methods and teaching of *evidence-based medicine* (Sackett, *et al* 1996) and *evidence-based management*. Evidence-based practice requires the practitioner to obtain evidence of the up-to-date knowledge in the field.

The two approaches are contrasted in Table 14.1.

Professional practitioners often face problems for which their academic background and professional studies provide them with little or no familiarity. The search to establish 'what is already known about this problem' is not likely to involve drilling deeper within a known subject discipline. The search must be far and wide for where the problem, or some variation of it, has been encountered in other fields. A structured approach is needed.

We describe here a recursive process for literature search by people researching in fields where they have little or no familiarity with the literature. The elements of the strategy are:

Table 14.1 Approaches to literature searching contrasted

	Literature search in higher education	Literature search in professional practice
Intensive or extensive search	Intensive search (drilling down)	Extensive search
Relationship to academic disciplines	Intra-disciplinary	Inter-disciplinary and search outside of current disciplines
Starting point of search	The state of current knowledge in the field	A problem or an opportunity
Key question for search to answer	What are the gaps in the current literature on this topic?	Who has ever encountered this problem, or some variant of it, and what possible solutions have been suggested or tried?

1. focus on core journals and key authors as well as seminal articles
2. identify potentially significant works, journals and people by applying the principle of duplication of references
3. ensure convergence on the set of articles that are most relevant to the issue under investigation by applying the principle of diminishing returns to search.

SEARCHING IN UNFAMILIAR TERRITORY

We focus here on just one form of literature to present our strategy: *journal articles*. In our experience, this is the most useful source of up-to-date thinking on a subject. Reasons for this include:

- Journal articles usually contain brief reviews of the relevant literature in addition to an account of the method, research findings and how the findings add to what was previously known.
- Academic journals are refereed and this provides some quality control.
- The journals are usually published several times each year so they are likely to be relatively up-to-date.
- Journals are the vehicles through which researchers have traditionally shared their findings with other researchers so they are published in forms designed to enable researchers to find them through a literature search. Thus, for example, they often contain keywords and abstracts designed to enable other researchers to find them in a literature search.

Although we focus on journal articles, the strategy applies to other forms of literature.

We present the search strategy as a set of stages as we feel that will be most helpful to the practitioner researcher.

Stage 1. Search profile

Summarise the starting point for the literature search in the form of a *search profile*. A search profile defines the scope of the search. It provides a preliminary answer to the following questions:

- What is the topic of this research?
- What is the research trying to find out? What is the research question?
- What is the aim(s) of the research investigation?

We illustrate the method at the end of this chapter with a specimen search profile. Producing a search profile will concentrate your mind and force you to clarify what is within the scope of your investigation and what lies outside of it. As the literature search proceeds, the scope of the research is likely to change and it is important to acknowledge that and not regard the search profile as a straitjacket. Its purpose is to provide sufficient clarification of the research topic and definition of the scope of the research to enable the process of the literature search to start.

Stage 2. Keywords

What words best describe the subject matter of the research? Keywords can be words, combinations of words or short phrases. The keywords will be the way into the literature of the research topic. How many key words should you start with? The more you use the more likely you are to find your way into relevant literatures. The basic procedure here involves two steps:

1. generate as many plausible keywords as possible, and then
2. rank them in terms of their relevance.

See the later section on keywords for guidance on ways to generate keywords.

Stage 3.   Starter references

Use the highest ranked keywords to search for relevant journal articles.

Collections of periodical/journal indexes come in a variety of forms: printed, CD-ROM or via the web. You can use an electronic database (CD-ROM or web) to search through years of journal indexes easily, rather than having to scan volume after volume manually. The database of journal indexes that you select will depend on the area of your research. This presupposes that you can already identify the subject discipline in which the issue is located. Keywords, on the other hand, enable you to search across subject disciplines. It is easy to start with a web-based book supplier such as Amazon.

Use the information in your search profile to focus your search. Most databases provide a *keyword search* facility. You may also have the opportunity to specify parameters, such as year(s) and whether you want to do a national or an international search. Focus your search at this stage to obtain a list of journal articles that will be of direct, rather than vague, relevance to the issue you wish to research.

Once you have produced a list of journals, identify and obtain the ten articles that look most promising, judging by their titles and abstracts.

Stage 4.   Seminal works, core journals and key people

Identify works that have been particularly influential in the field, the *seminal works*, the journals that are most likely to publish articles on the topic, the *core journals*, and the people who are also working on the issue, the *key people*. Core journals may not all lie within the same field of study as categorised by traditional academic disciplines. For example, a search on 'managing professional change through action research' is likely to yield core journals covering a range of academic disciplines.

Use the references cited in the ten articles to identify

- articles and books that are mentioned more than once; these are the potential seminal articles;
- journals that are mentioned more than once; these are potential core journals for the topic of interest;
- authors who are mentioned more than once; these are likely to include the key people researching and writing about the topic of interest.

This stage can be completed with various degrees of meticulousness. At one end of the scale you can inspect the references for duplication of published work, journals or authors respectively. At the other end of the scale, you can type all of the references listed in all of the articles into a document and then use cut-and-paste to produce an alphabetical list of titles of the works cited, names of the authors and titles of the journals. Duplications become conspicuous in this process. This may seem a time-consuming approach, but a significant proportion of the references will need to be keyed in at some stage, if only to provide a list of references for the final report of the research.

A short cut would be a preliminary scan across all the references and highlight only those that look at all plausible and thereafter work only with the highlighted articles.

An intermediate position on the 'meticulousness' scale would be to key into a table just the names of the authors, the titles of the works cited, and the names of the journals or publishers. Most commonly used word-processing packages allow rows to be moved around easily and this facilitates the rearrangement of rows to display the duplications.

Stage 5. Seminal articles

Assemble the articles and other works, such as books and reports, you identified while finding the duplications.

Stage 6. Core journals

Each of the core journals should publish an index of contents at regular intervals. Look at the indexes of contents of the core journals for the last few years to identify the most recent articles addressing the topic of the research, or closely related issues.

Stage 7. Key people

Use a *citation index* to look for other published work by the authors you have identified as potential key people in the field. A citation index is a regularly updated index that lists works cited in later works. It includes a list of the sources from which the citations were gathered. Researchers use it to locate sources related by subject to a previously published work. For example, a search in a citation index for Dr Smith's work will reveal all the articles that have cited or referred to Dr Smith. This will enable you to identify what else the authors have written that is relevant to the topic in question. You may also wish to send some authors a note, perhaps by e-mail, to explain your interest in the topic. You could, for example, enclose a list of your top ten references to date and ask them to add any notable omissions from your list, including anything else that they have written on the topic. You may get back copies of work that is so new it has not yet been published.

Stage 8. Further iterations

Stages 5, 6 and 7 will have generated additional references. Select, from them, a handful that look most promising and repeat the process from Stage 4 onwards to identify additional potential seminal works, core journals and key people. This process can then be repeated until no new works, journals or people are found. The principle of diminishing returns to search should ensure that the process will not continue indefinitely. The eight-stage process is summarised in Fig. 14.1.

KEYWORDS

Generate as many plausible keywords as possible and then rank the most plausible ones in terms of their relevance to the research topic. The following list of ways to generate plausible keywords

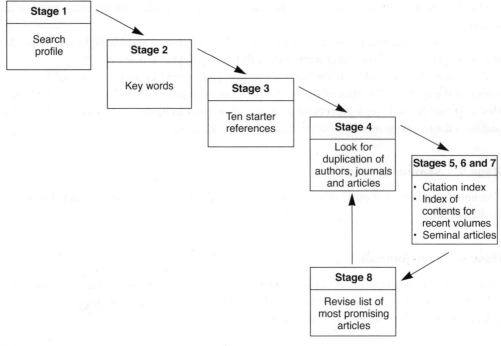

Figure 14.1 The literature search process

is a selection of the ideas resulting from a brainstorm of MBA students on a creative problem-solving course on this theme.

1. Use a dictionary
2. Use a dictionary of synonyms and antonyms
3. Use known academic journals/trade journals
4. Use the contents/index pages of a relevant book
5. Do an Internet/Intranet search
6. Use the contents pages and bibliography of other dissertations
7. Look at keywords in other people's published articles in journals to get an idea of what makes a good set of keywords
8. Talk to practitioners
9. Check for regulatory body
10. Use one keyword and Amazon.com
11. Annual reports of organisations in the field
12. Mindmaps/brainstorming
13. Rich pictures
14. Journal articles/references in articles
15. Newspapers and other media
16. Focus groups/action learning set
17. Library catalogues
18. Newsgroups
19. Trade conferences
20. Conference proceedings

CONCLUSIONS

When you need to search the literature in an unfamiliar field, or across unfamiliar fields, you need a structured approach to avoid the frustrations of a haphazard hunt. We believe you will succeed in your search if you follow our eight-stage process. You will find further guidance in Bourner *et al* (1999) and in Egger *et al* (2001). In conclusion, we offer the following example.

SPECIMEN SEARCH PROFILE

Topic

Development of professional doctorates in England during the 1990s

Research question

What is the rationale for the development of professional doctorates?

Aim of the investigation

Discover the thinking behind the development of professional doctorates in England in the 1990s.

Parameters

Time: 1990 to present; the more recent the better.
Place: Unrestricted; anywhere in the world
Languages: English only in the first instance

Keywords

1. Doctorate
2. Doctor of
3. Professional doctorate
4. Practitioner research
5. Taught doctorate
6. Continuing professional development
7. Work-based learning

REFERENCES

Bourner, T, Bowden, R and Laing, S (1999) A national profile of research degree awards: innovation, clarity and coherence. *Higher Education Quarterly*, 53(3), pp 264–280.

Egger, M, Davey Smith, G and Altman, D G (eds) (2001) *Systematic Reviews in Health Care. Meta-analysis in Context* (London: BMJ Books).

Sackett, D L, Rosenberg, W M, Muir Gray, J A, Haynes, R B and Richardson, W S (1996) Evidence-based medicine: what it is and what it isn't. *British Medical Journal*, 312(7023), pp 71–72.

PART 4 | Creativity

15 Darwin and creativity

Rodney King

CHARLES DARWIN

In 1859, Charles Darwin published his famous treatise on evolution, *The Origin of Species*. In that year, Darwin engraved into our language the phrase: 'Survival of the fittest', a phrase he borrowed from Herbert Spencer.

Few eminently creative individuals provide such a rich background to the evolution of their creative work as Charles Darwin on his Theory of Evolution by Natural Selection. His methodology, the impact of his theory on orthodox religious beliefs, and his theory's significance for the understanding of our heritage make it a prime choice for reviewing the creative process. But how did Darwin arrive at his Theory of Evolution by Natural Selection?

In his book, *The Act of Creation*, Arthur Koestler (1971) coined the word 'bisociation' to signify the linking of two unrelated planes of thought or knowledge. This is illustrated in Fig. 15.1.

There are many examples of *bisociation* in the history of science and technology: Kepler linked ocean tides with the movement of the moon; Gutenberg linked a wine press with the problem of printing many copies of a document. But what happens before and after the creation of an idea? Activities such as 'preparation' and 'verification' are not evident in Koestler's model. They are developed in Fig. 15.2: *the creative web for macro-projects*. I will discuss this creative web more at the end of this chapter. It is a more realistic model upon which to base the development of Darwin's Theory of Evolution by Natural Selection. This is shown in Table 15.1.

There were three phases in Darwin's development of his theory: 1809–1831; 1831–1838; 1858–1859. He was born in 1809 and died in 1882. In the first phase (1809–1831), Darwin's level of potential creativity was at the lowest. Although he was an avid beetle collector and remained so throughout his life, he may have had relatively little knowledge about a theory of evolution. Nevertheless, he might have been exposed early to ideas on evolution because his grandfather, Erasmus Darwin, had developed a theory of evolution based on the inheritance of acquired characteristics.

At Edinburgh and Cambridge universities, he met leading scientists in zoology, botany and geology. Through his hobbies as a beetle collector and bird-watcher as well as his participation in entomological and geological tours, he was acquiring knowledge and skills of observation, abstraction, classification and recording. These events occurred in Darwin's peripheral creative space, since his training at university first focused on medicine and later on divinity. The events in his peripheral life space made him particularly worthy of consideration for the post of naturalist on the vessel, HMS Beagle.

In the second phase of Darwin's creative web, he embarked on a five-year (1831–1836) voyage as a naturalist on the HMS Beagle. In retrospect, and by default, this phase may be considered as the time in which Darwin defined and established his core domain and strong interest in a theory

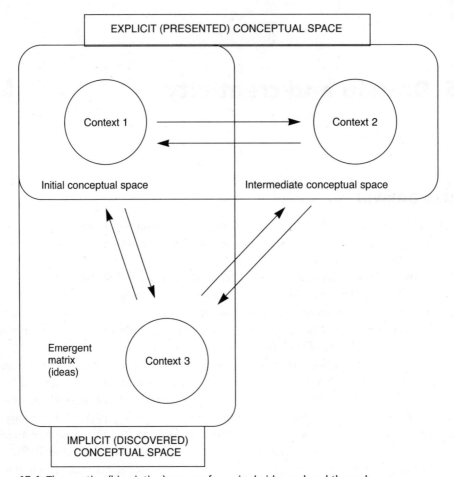

EXPLICIT (PRESENTED) CONCEPTUAL SPACE

Context 1

Context 2

Initial conceptual space

Intermediate conceptual space

Emergent matrix (ideas)

Context 3

IMPLICIT (DISCOVERED) CONCEPTUAL SPACE

Figure 15.1 The creative (bisociation) process for a single idea or breakthrough

of evolution. After the journey, his level of potential creativity was more than average. He had acquired deep and practical knowledge of his core domain. And he was able to pose the significant question: how and by what mechanism does the evolution of species occur? By defining his project-problem after collecting data and information, Darwin contradicts the classic CPS (creative problem solving) model, which recommends that a problem be first defined.

Darwin started his first notebook on the transmutation of species in 1837 and soon after formulated his Monad Theory of Evolution (Weisberg 1993). In the light of subsequent available fossil evidence, however, Darwin abandoned his Monad Theory of Evolution. Darwin was looking for a theory that would fit the mass of data and information he had acquired during his five-year voyage. Darwin's theory-building could be assumed to follow the trial-and-error or recursive pattern illustrated in the creative web; see Fig. 15.2.

In 1838, Darwin's peripheral interest or 'external' life space seriously impacted his ideas in his core domain. As the story goes, he read for amusement Thomas Malthus's *Essay on Population*. Thereafter, he got the insight for the Theory of Evolution by Natural Selection. Darwin's insight could be explained using the model for bisociation in Fig. 15.1.

My theory is that, on reading Malthus's paper (Context 2), the key idea of 'survival of the fittest' emerged in Darwin's matrix of emergent ideas (Context 3). Darwin then made an unexpected but

Table 15.1 Darwin's real-time creative web

Creative 'life space'	Activities in Core/Peripheral/Remote Domains							
		Lifetime beetle collector; Erasmus Darwin's Theory of Evolution	Edinburgh University: Divinity/Cambridge University: Medicine; Entomological & geological tours			(a) Reading of Malthus's essay	(a) Letter from Wallace	Lifelong beetle collector
Implementation space	(7b) Acceptance/Implementation						(f) Mild reception at the Linnaean Society	(e) Overwhelming reception and acceptance of The Origin of Species
	(7a) Presentation						(e) Reading of Darwin & Wallace's paper to the Linnaean Society	(d) Publication of The Origin of Species
Solutions space	(6) Evaluation & Verification of Outputs (Syntheses)				(c) Rejection of Monad Theory of Evolution		(d) Proof-reading of Darwin & Wallace's paper	(c) Proof-reading of The Origin of Species
	(5) Execution & Testing of Solution-paths (Syntheses)						(c) Editing/revision of The Origin of Species	(b) Editing/revision of whole of The Origin of Species
Methods space	(4) (Unexpected) Synthesis of One or More Solution-path(s) 'Illumination'				(b) Formulation of Monad Theory of Evolution	(b) Restatement of theory as three principles	(b) Start of writing of The Origin of Species/ Darwin & Wallace's paper	(a) Continuation and completion of writing for The Origin of Species
	(3) Reengineering, Exploration, and Generation of 'Objects'/ 'Incubation'					(c) Idea of evolution through natural selection		
Problem-definition space	(2) Preparation, Immersion and Acquisition of Database of Knowledge (Data and Information) & Skills			(a) Naturalist on HMS Beagle; observing and documenting animal and plant life	(a) First Notebook on transmutation of species	(a) Reading of Malthus's essay	(a) Letter from Wallace	
	(1) (Creative) Problem-finding/recognition/ procurement/definition			(b) How and by what mechanism does evolution occur?				
Conceptual spaces	Module(s) Time	1809– Pre-uni.	1825-1827/ 1827-1831	1831-1836	1837	1838	1858	1859

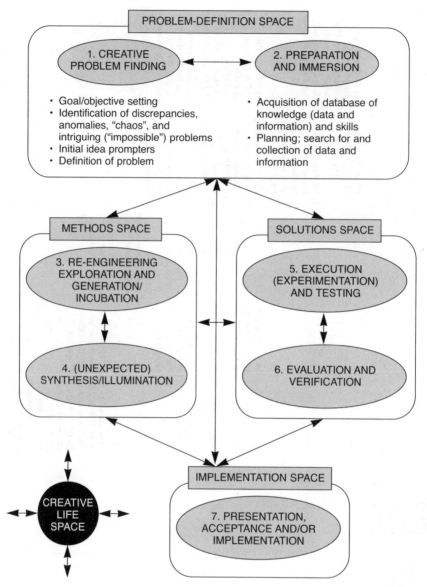

Figure 15.2 The creative web for macro-projects

coherent link with his long-standing question on the mechanism for the evolution of species (Context 1). It is at this moment that the explicit conceptual space (Contexts 1 and 2) bisociates with the implicit conceptual space (Contexts 1 and 3). The result is 'illumination', which in popular parlance is called the 'aha!' experience. No wonder, Darwin remarked, that the idea 'at once struck' him; for at that instant, the three contexts form a triangle and are unified in a single space.

After reading Malthus's essay, Darwin restated his theory as three principles (Weisberg 1993). However, for various reasons, probably including the avoidance of conflict with orthodox religious views and interests, Darwin did not publish his revised theory. Meanwhile, he published papers on his observations of coral reefs, insects, and geological formations in South America.

The third and final phase (1858–1859) in Table 15.1 covers the publication of Darwin's seminal work, *The Origin of Species*. Once more, it was an external event in Darwin's life space that acted as a catalyst for publishing the book. In 1858, Darwin received a letter from Alfred Russell Wallace in which Wallace summarised a Theory of Evolution by Natural Selection and asked for Darwin's comments as well as help in getting the theory published; Wallace's was an independent discovery on which Darwin remarked, 'I never saw a more striking coincidence.' Wallace had also read Malthus's essay and, after an 'incubation' of 12 years, linked the idea of 'survival of the fittest' with the question of the origin of species.

Darwin and Wallace jointly wrote and published a paper on the Theory of Evolution by Natural Selection that was read to the Linnaean Society in London. There was no discussion or interest on the paper. A year later, Darwin published *The Origin of Species* and provided compelling evidence for the validity of his theory. Only then did professional and public interest in the theory surge, and the survival of the fittest has since remained in public consciousness.

By the time Darwin published *The Origin of Species,* all variables had high ratings in the equation for the level of potential creativity: he had amassed deep knowledge and sharp skills in core as well as peripheral domains; he had honed his creative thinking strategies and tools using trial-and-error explorations (feedback); his creative life space was also extensive. He also had strong motivation. And, as he writes in his autobiography, he was 'ambitious to take a fair place among scientific men.' In short, the chance of Darwin having a breakthrough, in particular unifying the various strands of evolution theory and providing comprehensive evidence to back a unified theory, was high. And deliver he did. No wonder that in the struggle for survival among the competing theories of evolution, Darwin's Theory of Evolution by Natural Selection did emerge as the fittest. Patrick Matthew had published a similar theory in 1831 and earlier evolutionists included Anaximander, Erasmus Darwin, and Comte de Buffon.

THE CREATIVE WEB FOR MACRO-PROJECTS

The creative process at the macro-level (Fig. 15.2) features four main conceptual spaces:

- problem-definition space;
- methods space;
- solutions space;
- implementation space.

The creative life space is considered as a set of external factors. The model contains a maximum of seven modules and covers basic creativity and innovation. Each module can be regarded as a task or sub-project. In practice, the modules in a particular space would flow into one another so that they could not be regarded as separate or distinct; for example, modules 3 and 4. All the modules in the basic creativity area (problem definition and methods spaces: modules 1 to 4), solution, and implementation spaces are interconnected into the creative web and their relationships are recursive. The creative web illustrates problem solving in space rather than in time.

Although we live in the constancy and flow of time, we solve problems spatially; the space may be physical and/or conceptual (abstract). In the creative web, as in jigsaw puzzles, there is no fixed path or set of modules to the solution of problems. What is important is that the problem solver at least visits the problem-definition space, the methods space, and the solution space.

In some creative problems, the problem solver may even start with the solutions space, for example by answering the questions: 'What am I going to create? What end product do I want?' This approach is applicable to, for example, the design of questionnaires when the output or desired results are first specified and then the corresponding questions are formulated. The creative web in Fig. 15.2 therefore presents a general framework and can be used for a wide variety of creative projects. In research, the creative web can be used as a framework for structuring and programming the whole or selected modules of a research proposal. The creative micro-process (see Fig. 15.1) can be used together with creativity strategies and tools, within any module. Breakthrough insights could occur before, during and after specific tasks.

CONCLUSIONS

Creativity, ideas management, and creative problem solving are central to innovative research. Creativity cannot be described adequately by a single definition or process. It mainly involves novelty, utility, and the process of problem solving. Although both goal-directed and organic approaches are involved in problem solving, I suggest that the goal-directed approach or creative problem solving (CPS) more directly relates to postgraduate research. The suggested framework for creative problem solving is the creative web.

In the literature, many tools and techniques are offered to enhance creativity, ideas management, and problem solving. These tools and techniques can be synthesised in a conceptual framework that allows the use of all tools and techniques. In Chapter 17, I offer *Versatile thinking* as a framework, within which tools and techniques of creativity, ideas management, and problem solving can be integrated. The tools of versatile thinking include the versatile matrix and map.

REFERENCES

Koestler, A (1971) *The Act of Creation* (London: Pan Books).
Weisberg, RW (1993) *Creativity* (New York: W. H. Freeman.)

16 When to use creativity

Rodney King

CREATIVE THINKING

Creative (non-linear explorative) thinking is complementary to logical (linear critical) thinking. Each is one-half of total thinking and is a set of tools for mining, exploring and re-engineering knowledge as well as skills. Where logical thinking seems largely inadequate, creative thinking can be used; where creative thinking seems largely inadequate or inappropriate, logical thinking should be used.

I summarise my view of thinking, expression and problem solving in the acronym, BEAR: Bring Every Available Resource. The BEAR strategy is illustrated in Fig. 16.1. In the BEAR strategy, creative and logical thinking exist on a continuum. You should be prepared to use any thinking strategy or tool to achieve your objective. When both creative and logical thinking are highly developed, internalised, and integrated in a philosophy of versatile thinking, the quality, quantity, breadth, depth, unexpectedness (surprise/novelty), and coherence (utility/value) of outputs in many domains would tremendously increase. Creative or versatile thinking is not a substitute for domain-specific knowledge and skills.

However, in what situations does creative thinking offer advantages over logical thinking? Creative thinking is more effective and efficient than logical thinking in three types of case.

Case Type I.   Situations of creative (verbal, visual and kinaesthetic) perception, expression and construction

Examples include when novel perceptions and ideas as well as unexpected (surprising) but coherent outputs are required, as in radical innovation, discovery, invention, design and scenario-presentation.

Case Type II.   Situations of apparently impossible tasks and problems

Examples include situations, tasks and problems that are perceived as impossible, intractable, unsolvable, extremely difficult, complex and non-routine. Such situations inherently contain problems that could be described as 'ill-defined' or 'well-defined but having solution-paths that are unknown or impossible to attain.'

Case Type III.   Situations of (anticipated) unproductive logical thinking

Creative thinking may be more effective and efficient than logical thinking in producing outputs that are unique, novel and imaginative. Logical thinking often leads to converging and similar solution-paths, while creative thinking results in diverging, unexpected and unique solution-paths.

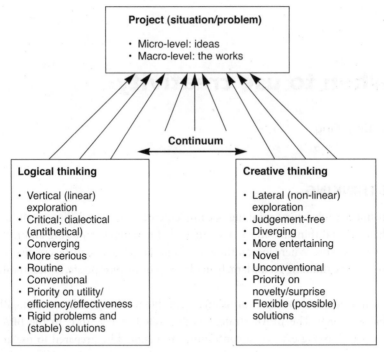

Figure 16.1 The B.E.A.R. strategy in cognitive situations

The three types of cases relate to each other, especially in macro-projects. In advanced academic research, Case Type II seems most relevant as it is problem-oriented. Any task or pending situation can be reframed as a problem, for example, by introducing creative question-leads such as:

- In how many, and different, *ways* could I (achieve a particular task)?
- In how many, and different, *places* could I (achieve a particular task)?
- What if (wishes/fantasies/dreams/nightmares/taboos/contradictions)?

The word 'different' in the first two question-leads could be replaced by one or a combination of the following:

- *right-brain adjectives:* unexpected, novel, surprising, unlikely, delightful, shocking, sensational, bizarre, strange, unusual, unconventional, unthinkable, unfamiliar, entertaining, dramatic, taboo, forbidden, controversial, intriguing, beautiful, awesome;
- *left-brain adjectives:* effective, efficient, excellent, much improved.

Ordinary or close-ended situations can be made more explorable by adding a creative end-phrase such as '. . . in future.' To generate even more ideas, the personal pronoun 'I' in creative question-leads could be replaced by the name of a person(s) whose creativity, knowledge, and skills you most admire. Reframing through such conceptual questioning would greatly increase the chances of producing creative solutions.

Tasks during postgraduate research include the following.

General

- Review literature
- Obtain data and information; explore and generate ideas

- Structure and present ideas, especially as diagrams
- Overcome writer's block
- Meet deadlines; achieve targets
- Find and solve apparently impossible problems of interest to yourself and 'clients'
- Organise, store, and manage materials as well as ideas
- Discuss ideas
- Solve personal problems, include the avoidance of distractions
- Write the thesis, dissertation, or chapters

Problem-definition space

- Choose a research topic or task
- Explore a topic
- Discover anomalies and important issues
- Make hypotheses and suggestions

Methods space

- Identify trends, patterns, and relationships; explore situations
- Analyse situations, data, information, problems and causes
- Design surveys and questionnaires
- Design experiments
- Theorise, include the development and testing of models

Solutions space

- Gain insights, perceive connections, and envision solutions
- Explain and summarise ideas
- Synthesise and construct, include the making of scenarios
- Evaluate alternatives and select preferred alternative(s)

Implementation space

- Communicate or express ideas, findings, and results
- Present reports, including the final dissertation or thesis

These tasks can be reframed as problems. Here, a problem is defined as an obstacle, resistance, and/or missing link that inhibits the path(s) to a desired space or state. For other criteria for defining a problem, see Mayer (1992). Problems may be open-ended or close-ended (Rickards 1988). Open-ended situations are usually systems with weak or no integration between elements, while close-ended situations are generally integrated systems or systems with strong internal linkages. Table 16.1 shows relationships between types of problems, methods, and solutions in a problem space. For more details on the characteristics of problem spaces, see Mayer (1992). Levels of solutions depend on levels of problems, and vice versa. Vertical problem solving is usually more useful for close-ended problems. The table can be used to classify problems as well as to determine problem solving strategies that are required and types of solutions that are expected.

Table 16.1 Types of problems, methods, and solutions in a problem space

Level	Problem-definition space/ Type of problem	Methods space/ Recommended means	Solutions space/ Expected outcomes	Nature of outcomes
	General/ open-ended problems: • ill-defined • broad • weak linkages • fluid (flexible) boundaries • 'inventive' • 'impossible' • 'soft' data and information	• Conceptual (lateral) exploration • Generic creativity strategies and tools • One-line (sentence) strategies	• Conceptual solution-paths or solutions, e.g. general strategies • Multiple (possible) approaches	• Broad; at policy level • Points to 'direction' of detailed solution(s) • Further exploration would be required, especially using conceptual and domain-specific methods • Generally, least-time consuming
1.2	*Specific* open-ended problems: • domain-specific • more detailed • 'soft' to 'hard' data and information • explicit contradiction(s)	• Conceptual (lateral) and detailed (vertical) exploration • Generic as well as detailed creativity techniques and instruments • Domain-specific knowledge and skills • Strategies having two or more sentences	• Detailed solution-paths, e.g. specific strategies (Non-)unique solutions	• More specific; at strategic level • Point to 'area' of detailed solution(s) • Further exploration using domain-specific methods and templates may be required • Time-consuming
2	Close-ended problems: • well-defined; detailed • specific • strong linkages • rigid boundaries • 'routine'; conventional • domain-specific • 'hard' data and information • specific obstacles or contradictions	• Conceptual and detailed domain-specific exploration • Domain-specific or operational knowledge and skills • Vertical methods and templates • Detailed procedures or answers	• Narrow solution-paths and detailed (operational) solutions e.g. action plans or detailed instruments • Unique answer(s) or solution(s) • Product or artefact	• Specific; at 'shop' level • Point to 'spot' of solution(s) • Implementable results • Generally, most time-consuming to realise

The previously described tasks of dissertation or thesis work fall under general open-ended problems. Consequently, conceptual explorations would first be recommended and general strategies would be expected as solutions to the question of generating new ideas and approaches for each task. To obtain detailed strategies subsequently, open-ended research tasks could be initially transformed to close-ended problems; for instance, by repeatedly asking, 'How?'

REFERENCES

Mayer, RE (1992) *Thinking, Problem Solving, Cognition* (New York: WH Freeman).

Rickards, T (1988) *Creativity at Work* (Hampshire: Gower).

17 Synthesis and evaluation of creativity

Rodney King

I have synthesised an approach to creativity, ideas management, and problem solving that I call *versatile thinking*. Versatile thinking rests on four interconnected pillars:

- Template theory for versatile creativity
- Pattern and Object (PAO) thinking
- Versatile matrix of strategies for thinking
- Versatile map for problem solving.

The versatile matrix and map are elements of PAO thinking, but I consider them important enough to be treated as separate pillars of versatile thinking. A simplified version of versatile thinking is presented in this chapter; only the versatile matrix and map are presented.

SIMPLIFIED VERSATILE MATRIX

Creativity tools are usually applied to open-ended or ill-defined problems; they focus on lateral rather than vertical exploration. Vertical, as well as lateral tools should be used to explore knowledge spaces fully and to obtain highly creative solutions. Vertical tools and templates are domain-specific and more suited to close-ended problems: that is, problems that have convergent solution-paths or known solutions. Lateral or creativity tools can be used to explore problems that have unknown solutions as well as known but inaccessible solutions. I therefore regard creativity tools as a subset strategies for versatile thinking. On the whole, creativity tools are more efficient in the context of open-ended problems, especially those problems that are ill-defined, perceived as impossible, or require alternative solutions.

Creativity tools and techniques can be classified according to strategies for thinking. Table 17.1 is a simplified versatile matrix that contains creativity tools and techniques related to versatile thinking. The strategies are adaptations and extensions of the 'thirteen tools of the world's most creative people' (Root-Bernstein and Root-Bernstein 1999). The matrix is a comprehensive classification system for creativity tools and techniques in the literature. The strategies are classes of objectives for creativity tools and techniques.

The strategies in Table 17.1 are not mutually exclusive: some creativity tools and techniques appear in several classes. For instance, mind mapping, analogy, and 'paoisms' belong to several strategies. An important aspect of the versatile matrix is that the strategies, tools and techniques relate to the modules in the creative web (Chapter 15, Fig. 15.2) in terms of problem-definition, methods, and solution-spaces.

The rating of the strategies in Table 17.1 is subjective and based on my personal experience. The

Table 17.1 Versatile matrix™ of strategies for thinking

Item	Description of strategy (Verbal/Visual/ Olfactory/Kinaesthetic/Gustatory)	Tools for generating ideas and/or re-engineering objects	Problem-defn space	Methods space	Solutions space
1	Observing, being curious, and reflecting	Deep questioning; Checklist; Meditation; CreaLogic; paoisms; Observing anomalies and patterns	3	2	2
2	Envisioning and planning	Visualisation; Day-dreaming; Story-telling; Scenario-making; Goal setting; (Fantasy) Forecasting	3	2	3
3	Recording, managing and presenting	Mind map; Concept map; Tables; Matrices; Graphs; Charts; Diagramming; Storyboarding; Record management; Mnemonics; Object-map; Object-templates	3	3	3
4	Exploring	Brainstorming; Mindstorming; PMI; questions; Checklists; Analogies; Diagramming; 'Roaming'; Lotus blossom; Categorising; Typologies	3	2	2
5	Abstracting, structuring and classifying	Questions: How? How?; Why? Why?; Templates; Summarising; Analogies; CreaLogic; Paoism	3	1	2
6	Escaping, speculating and relaxing	Lateral thinking: Po; Random 'objects'; Challenging/reversing assumptions and boundaries: What if?; Travel; Sleeping; Taking breaks	2	2	1
7	Deconstructing, analysing and evaluating	Attribute (component) listing; Graphs; Matrices; Morphological analysis; Root-cause analysis; Fishbone diagram; Critical (dialectical) analysis; Force-field analysis; How? How? SWOT analysis; Systems thinking; Weighted index; Voting	2	3	3
8	Patterning and modelling	Copying; Imitating; Parallel worlds; NLP; Pattern language; Prototyping; Discovering and creating templates; Analogising; Composing	2	2	2
9	Using analogy, creaLogic and paoisms	Analogies; Synectics; CreaLogic; Paoisms; Analogic; Metalogic; Similes; Metaphors	2	2	3
10	Using multi-level, multi-phase and multi-dimensional 'objects'	Multiple perspectives (roles): Six thinking hats; Six coloured eyes; Spatial thinking; CreaLogic; Paoisms; Multi-temporal thinking	3	3	3
11	Empathising and body thinking	Personal analogies; Meditation; Paoisms; Acting; Introspecting	2	1	2
12	Acting, playing, simulating and energising	Role playing; Tinkering; Humour; Experimenting; Visual Modelling; Poetry; Improvising; Dancing	2	3	2
13	Transforming	Manipulation or re-engineering verbs, e.g. SCAMPER; Reframing	2	3	3
14	Connecting, unifying, combining, and synthesising	Forced connections (fitting); Bisociating; Metaphorming; Circle of opportunity; Modelling; Sculpting	2	3	3
15	Possessing and displaying 'creative' attitudes and behaviour	Affirmations; Practising 'creative living'; Idea quotas; Creative journaling; Aphorisms; Lateral thinking puzzles; Creative hobbies	2	1	2
16	Enhancing creative life space	Joining creative people and Internet creativity groups; Creative adventure; Hobbies; General interests	2	2	2
17	Combining the above strategies	Creative problem solving (CPS) models; TRIZ; Versatile thinking; Creative Whack Pack; Thinkpak; Theory of constraints; Problem-situated learning and transformative game	3	3	3
18	Using miscellaneous strategies	Domain-specific expertise; External consulting	2	3	3

Key: 1 = barely useful; 2 = quite useful; 3 = highly useful
References for strategies and tools: Root-Bernstein and Root-Bernstein (1999); Michalko (1991, 1998); Higgins (1994); Siler (1997); von Oech (1992); De Bono (1994); PAO Thinking

ratings are to be used as a guide. If your experience is different, the ratings could be modified. Using the matrix and ratings, however, you can select exploratory strategies and creativity tools that are most relevant to your targeted objective, problem, or task. Tools and techniques in a research domain could be catalogued using the versatile matrix, for example TRIZ, which Genrich Altshuler (1996) describes in his book *And Suddenly the Inventor Appeared*. TRIZ is the Russian acronym for the 'Theory of Inventive Problem Solving'. It is a hot topic in product development but it could be restructured as a generic creativity tool using the versatile matrix. Finally, the versatile matrix can be used to develop novel conceptual strategies for solving open-ended problems in postgraduate research.

My approach to creativity and problem solving is encompassed in the BEAR (Bring Every Available Resource) strategy, described in Chapter 16. Many and diversified creative strategies should be used to obtain multiple perspectives as well as information-rich problem-definition, methods and solutions spaces. In general, the richer the information in the problem space, the greater the chances of finding problems and solutions that are not only highly novel and valuable but also rare.

As shown in Table 17.1, the most versatile strategies and tools belong to 'Recording, managing and presenting', 'Using multi-level, multi-phase and multi-dimensional "objects" ', and 'Combining the above strategies'. I suggest that you learn the former two categories of strategies and their corresponding tools before the others. All strategies are useful in a problem space; some strategies to a higher degree, others to a lesser degree.

VERSATILE MAP

The versatile map is a template for solving all types of problems, such as

- routine and creative ('impossible') problems;
- mathematical and non-mathematical problems.

The versatile map can be used to collect data and information as well as to manage them. As an object-map, the versatile map (see Fig. 17.1) combines ideas from mind mapping (Buzan and Buzan 2000) and concept mapping (White and Gunstone 1993).

In the literature on creativity and problem solving, there is much confusion in the use of the terms 'mind map' and 'concept map'. Sometimes, the terms are used interchangeably. In this chapter, mind map refers to the Tony Buzan's classic mind map, which is a hierarchical diagram with a central theme and one word per link (line between two nodes). In contrast, a concept map refers to a network (two or more central themes) or a hierarchical diagram where words, phrases and/or sentences are written on links as well as in closed shapes such as circles, 'bubbles' or 'ovals'. Alternative names for generic concept maps include cognitive maps, cluster diagrams, tree diagrams, oval diagrams, and system maps. Examples of special-purpose concept maps are objective trees, relevance trees, flow charts, decision trees and critical path diagrams. Traditionally, mind maps include pictures and drawings on lines but there is no reason why pictures and drawings cannot be included in concept maps. In conclusion, a mind map can be regarded as a special case of a concept map.

One advantage of the versatile map is that it facilitates holistic problem-solving since the problem-definition, methods and solutions spaces are simultaneously seen and explored. Another advantage is that the versatile map can be used to manage ideas and tasks in each module of the creative web:

1. Creative problem-finding;
2. Preparation and immersion;
3. Reengineering, exploration, and generation/incubation;

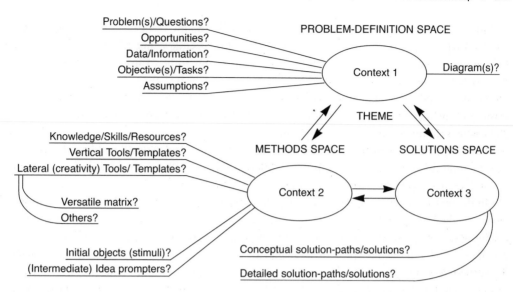

Figure 17.1 Versatile map for problem solving

4. (Unexpected) synthesis/illumination;
5. Execution (experimentation) and testing;
6. Evaluation and verification;
7. Presentation, acceptance, and/or implementation; creative life space.

A versatile map is a multi-centric mind map, in which information is recorded as in both a classic mind map and a concept map. A mind map predominantly has one word written per link, whereas a concept map has phrases, sentences, paragraphs and other objects recorded on links or inside closed shapes. Other rules associated with classic mind mapping, such as 'basic ordering ideas', colour coding and the maintenance of horizontal lines for writing are used in versatile maps. My prepared versatile maps are mainly verbal. Visual/verbal versatile maps are more information-rich but verbal versatile maps are quicker to develop, especially by hand.

Unlike concept maps, the nature of relationships or 'generative rules' is hardly described on the lines of versatile maps. Thus, versatile maps are spatially efficient; they consume space economically. The common but invisible description of relationships at nodes in a versatile map or mind map includes: 'is related to'; 'belongs to'; 'consists of'; 'is a category (division) of'. It is important to remember these descriptions when reading versatile maps.

In the versatile map shown in Fig. 17.1, only three central objects are shown; each central object can be regarded as the central theme on a mind map. The three objects correspond to the problem-definition (context 1), methods (context 2) and solutions (context 3) spaces. The detailed modules of the creative web are omitted for clarity; these modules can be added when desired. For micro-creative projects involving conceptual problem solving or the generation of one-line (phrase or sentence) strategies, the three central objects would suffice. However, for macro-creative projects, such as in advanced research or detailed problem solving, all modules of the creative web should be considered and added to the three central themes of problem-definition, methods and solutions-spaces. Details can be obtained from generated one-line strategies or solution-paths, for example, by repeated abstractions, such as asking, 'How? How?'

All creativity strategies, tools and techniques, especially from the versatile matrix, can be used within the framework of the versatile map. The same is true for vertical (domain-specific) tools and templates. There is no limit on the size of paper for versatile maps; I prefer to draw or print the template on an A3 size paper in horizontal format. Sometimes, I use A2 size paper; on rare occasions, I use A1 size paper.

When I use the versatile map, I add words, sentences, paragraphs, drawings and/or tables to the existing branches of the template. I call this 'mindstorming'. It is a cross between mind mapping and brainstorming. Mindstorming simply means suspending judgement while I write down ideas using the rules of one word per link and paragraphs, or large-sized 'objects', within a closed shape. In the literature, brainstorming connotes a different process. When mindstorming is used on a versatile map, the process is known as 'object-mapping.'

On the versatile map, mindstorming is used to populate and enrich with ideas, the problem-definition, methods and solutions-spaces. In mindstorming, there is no right or wrong answer. If an answer does not appear worthwhile, it can be categorised under the branch of '(intermediate) idea prompters'. Such intermediate prompters might later generate strategies or solutions that can then be included in the solutions-space. When mindstorming, I usually play the role of a 'paoist', whose maxim is: 'every object in the universe is connected.' The ideas on a versatile map can therefore be generated intuitively, randomly and systematically with the view that everything will eventually be connected.

Based on ideas in the Template Theory and PAO Thinking, I have developed a checklist of generic questions that can be used with the versatile map. This is the *versatile checklist*. In the questions, the word 'object' may refer to a situation, task, activity, problem, opportunity, objective or project. For postgraduate research, typical activities can be found in Chapter 16.

For best use of the versatile map, I recommend that you convert given issues to 'impossible' situations, tasks and problems. The versatile checklist could facilitate the generation of 'impossible' situations, tasks and problems. An alternative approach for generating an 'impossible' or 'inventive' problem can be found in the ideal solution method in the *Theory of Inventive Problem Solving*, which has the Russian acronym 'TRIZ'. More situations can be generated by considering contexts 1, 2 and 3 as 'present', 'past' and 'future' spaces respectively or as 'input', 'processing' and 'output'.

Table 17.2 Versatile checklist

---

1 (a) Do you think a template exists for ['object']?

    (b) Which types of templates are similar to ['object'] in core, peripheral/parallel and remote domains?

2 How many and different ways of ['object'] exist in core, peripheral/parallel and remote domains?

3 To which classes of structural templates does ['object'] belong: stone-heap, chain, tree and/or web-templates?

4 (a) What are the rules for generating ['object']?

    (b) Which concepts, theories, hypotheses, laws, formulae, diagrams, charts and/or models could be related to ['object']?

5 What basic rules for ['object'] could be violated or broken?

6 Which rules cannot be violated or broken?

7 In how many and different ways could ['object'] be:

    (a) observed, recognized, discovered, obtained and explored?

    (b) deconstructed and analysed?

    (c) adapted and modified?

    (d) combined, synthesised, 'sculpted' or constructed?

    (e) envisioned and transformed?

    (f) presented and/or implemented?

8 What are (creaLogical) alphabets, vocabularies, and patterns of ['object'] in core, peripheral/parallel, and remote domains?

9 Which further strategies, tools and techniques from the versatile matrix could be used?

It is in the realm of the 'impossible' that we best exercise our creative muscles and discover inventive solutions that can be transferred to the context of ordinary problems. In solving 'impossible' problems, a problem solver breaks mind sets and paradigms as well as develops habits and strategies for widely exploring knowledge spaces. 'Impossible' situations encourage 'impossible' problem finding and solving as well as use of the BEAR strategy. If you develop the habit of bringing every available resource – the fantasy and the rational, the fun and the serious, the improbable and the probable – to any situation, extraordinary thinking processes would become normal. The chance of coming up with a highly creative work would consequently be higher.

HOW TO EVALUATE CREATIVE IDEAS AND WORKS

So the problem space has been investigated, multifarious lateral and vertical tools have been applied, and myriad solution-paths and solutions have been generated. What happens next? From the modules in the creative web, the most appropriate solutions should be selected. But how?

Approaches to evaluating and selecting solutions can be categorised as qualitative and quantitative. Qualitative approaches usually deal with soft information and are mainly used for shortlisting and/or group evaluation. Common qualitative methods include:

- intuition (aesthetic sensibility or visual inspection using binary categories such as impressive/not impressive, beautiful/not beautiful, acceptable/not acceptable);
- classification or sorting of alternative solutions using spider diagrams (Majaro 1991), grids, tables, affinity diagrams, sticking dots, clustering (Rickards 1988).
- voting or (experts') consensus on preferences;
- checklists (using binary categories of yes/no, satisfied/not satisfied);
- negative brainstorming (Couger 1996, Majaro 1991).
- critical analysis (advantages/disadvantages, SWOT: strengths/weaknesses/opportunities/threats; force field: forces for/forces against).

The rating scales for qualitative analysis are mainly nominal and ordinal. In qualitative analysis, the objectives of evaluation are subsumed in the selection of rating scales, especially in critical analysis. Methods of critical analysis are used for both preliminary and final selection of preferred solutions.

In contrast to qualitative approaches, most quantitative methods are based on explicit objectives and criteria that are rated on ordinal and interval scales. In general, quantitative methods are more time-consuming than qualitative methods and therefore more applicable to shortlisted alternatives. The most commonly used category of quantitative approaches are multi-criteria methods.

Of the multi-criteria methods, the weighted index method using a matrix or table (Couger 1996, Majaro 1991, Proctor 1995) is the most popular. The index is a score or number on an interval scale, which permits the ranking and selection of alternative solutions. In this chapter, the criteria for creativity are novelty (N), utility (U) and rarity (R); if innovation or application of ideas is an issue, then a corresponding criterion and weight should be introduced. Each criterion can be rated on a scale from 1 to 10 ; 1 indicating 'lowest' and 10 the 'highest'. If each criterion is to be weighted, then the weights for novelty, utility and rarity would respectively be as follows: w/n, w/u and w/r.

Consequently, the weighted creativity index or exhibited creativity for a solution would be given by:

Exhibited creativity (EC) = w/n (N) + w/u (U) + w/r (R)

To facilitate arithmetic calculations, the sum of the weights could be 100 per cent, so that the value of each weight would theoretically range from 0 to 100 per cent. Within any project, the values of a set of weights should remain constant. Using this formula, the exhibited creativity for alternative solutions can be calculated and ranked. The alternative with the highest score would be the most creative solution.

CONCLUSION

Properly applied, versatile thinking would increase your level of potential creativity by laterally increasing your knowledge space. Versatile thinking, however, is not a substitute for domain-specific expertise or vertical knowledge. To maximise your creativity, you should combine versatile thinking with a deep knowledge of your domain as well as a high quality of interaction in your creative life space.

This chapter is far from being the last word on creativity, ideas management and creative problem solving, or even versatile thinking. For instance, only a simplified version of versatile thinking is presented in this chapter. Sections of versatile thinking such as object-templates, creaLogic, paoisms, and pattern learning are omitted due to the limitation of space. Nevertheless, it is hoped that the presented instruments of the versatile map and matrix would facilitate your skills of creativity, ideas management and problem solving.

Like many skills, the mastery of creativity, ideas management and creative problem solving comes with regular practice. During your research, you should therefore try to use the versatile map when collecting and exploring ideas as well as when confronting complex tasks. It might also be useful to take a detailed look at some of the tools that are briefly described in the versatile matrix and apply them to specific problems in your research. The tools are referenced in the literature as well as websites listed in the next chapter.

There is no agreement on the value and effectiveness of creativity tools. There is no guarantee that using listed creativity tools or the versatile map would produce 'original' ideas for your research. Using such tools, however, you could unearth areas that you would have otherwise overlooked. The greatest value of versatile thinking may lie not in producing original areas but in facilitating ideas management and conceptual problem solving in your research. If versatile thinking is measured mainly against these latter criteria, then its value in research would be more discernible. Finally, as in the case of Charles Darwin, the road to many great discoveries begins with ideas management and the posing of apparently impossible questions. I hope versatile thinking is useful to you in both activities.

APPENDIX

Practical example of versatile thinking

Versatile thinking can be applied to the following situations:

1. Situations of creative perception, expression and construction
2. Situations of apparently impossible tasks and problems
3. Situations of (anticipated) unproductive logical thinking

In this example, versatile thinking is applied to a situation of case type 2. A student is about to start doctoral research work in the field of regional development planning. The student is interested in research in the area of eco-development and is currently exploring the topic of 'writing a thesis'. The student hopes to discover novel ways to approach the research study.

Concepts and tools of versatile thinking could be applied to the scenario in several ways. The main task in the given scenario could be expressed as 'write a thesis'. So, in the centre of the triangle in the versatile map and just below word 'THEME?', I record the phrase 'writing a thesis'; see Fig. 17.1. The original versatile map was prepared using A3 size paper.

Next, I convert the given task to an 'impossible' problem by using the question-lead: 'In how many and different ways could I (achieve a particular task)?' For this scenario, my 'impossible' question is: 'In how many and different ways could I *write a thesis that will win a Nobel prize?*' Using the versatile map, I write this question on a line that extends from the branch of 'PROBLEM(S)/ QUESTION(S)?' In writing this question, I observe, as in the case of a classic mind map, the rule of one word per line. This rule facilitates the addition of alternative words below the link, which is a line between two nodes. For instance, below the link containing 'I' on the branch of 'PROBLEM(S)/ QUESTION(S)', substitute names such as Linus Pauling, Albert Szent-Gyorgyi and Richard Feynman are added. These persons would provide multiple perspectives on the 'impossible' question. Similarly, the word 'dissertation' could be added below any link containing 'thesis.'

Using a process of mindstorming (brainstorming), I extend and add information to all branches of the versatile map. All ideas are written down, even those that appear impractical, far-fetched or absurd. During mindstorming, judgement and 'idea killers' such as 'That's not practical!', 'That's ridiculous!' and 'It won't work!' are suspended. Provision is made for absurd ideas in the branches of 'INITIAL 'OBJECTS' (STIMULI)?' and '(INTERMEDIATE) IDEA PROMPTERS?' This approach reflects the BEAR strategy, which encompasses the maxim: 'Bring Every Available Resource'. In my experience, to be creative means to think from the impossible through the improbable to the probable.

There is no particular order in which the branches are selected and information is added. However, all phrases and sentences are written so that they are coherent when read towards contexts 1, 2 and 3. Some expressions, such as those on the extended branches of 'PROBLEM(S)/QUESTION(S)', were therefore written in reverse order: starting from the end of a branch and proceeding inward. Fresh branches (basic ordering ideas) such as 'OBSTACLE(S)/ CONSTRAINT(S)?' could be added to the 'closed shape' for contexts 1, 2 or 3.

The versatile matrix was used to select creativity techniques that were applied to the versatile map. Of particular use was the versatile checklist (Table 17.2) where 'object' is replaced by 'write a thesis'. The nine questions in the versatile checklist were used to generate additional ideas that were then written on the branches of the versatile map. The checklist questions reflect creativity techniques such as 'analogies', 'deep questioning' and 'challenging/reversing assumptions and boundaries'.

A richly populated versatile map is shown in Fig. 17.2. When sentences appeared too long or inadequate space existed, sentences were written in closed shapes. Some symbols have been drawn adjacent to the branch of 'DIAGRAMS'; these symbols reflect my analogy of the 'impossible' problem, which is a blindfolded person shooting at a moving target. Solving this analogical problem could provide possible solutions for the original problem.

When used, especially with 'impossible' or open-ended problems, the versatile map provides useful insights and alternative conceptual solutions. It is left to the problem-owner to select the most appealing solution, which could be a particular conceptual solution or a combination. With the given scenario, versatile thinking produces some novel and interesting ideas, of which the research student might not have originally thought.

A versatile map is open-ended and therefore, never complete. For more detailed results, conceptual solutions could be converted to detailed solutions by repeatedly asking, 'How? How?'

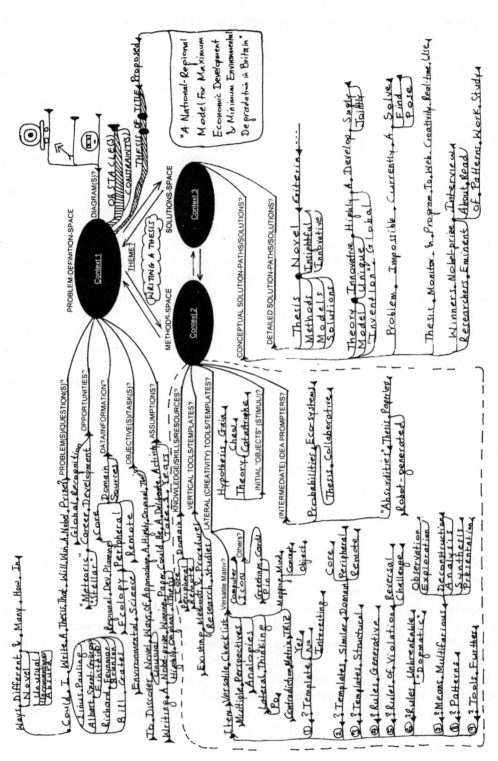

Figure 17.2 Versatile map for a proposed research study

Table 17.3 Real-time creativity web for a proposed research study

Creative 'life space'	Activities in Core/Peripheral/Remote Domains	Interact with colleagues and other people in core, peripheral, and remote domains; try to relate ideas and discussions. Join Internet mailing lists that are related to proposed research study; explore 'creative' hobbies.					
Implementation space	(7b) Acceptance/ Implementation				Obtain, from supervisor, comments and approval of contents of articles (chapters)	Discuss, with supervisor, content and style of draft thesis.	Defend thesis.
	(7a) Presentation				Present/revise articles (chapters) on key topics and themes of research.	Present draft of thesis.	Print and submit final version of thesis.
Solutions space	(6) Evaluation & Verification of Outputs (Syntheses)			Evaluate alternative topics and approaches.	Innovatively analyse and interpret results. Establish limits or range of validity of model(s), experiment(s), or survey(s).	Summarise main conclusions and findings. Revise/edit all chapters and prepare draft of thesis. Collate chapters.	Discuss revised draft of thesis and obtain supervisor's approval.
	(5) Execution & Testing of Solution-paths (Syntheses)		Consider alternative topics and approaches.		Develop and test hypotheses/model(s). (Design and conduct experiments/surveys.) Write and edit articles (chapters) that are relevant to topics of research study.	Write chapters for thesis.	Revise draft of thesis.
Methods space	(4) (Unexpected) Synthesis of One or More Solution-path(s)/ 'Illumination'				Develop testable hypotheses. Formulate more concrete explanations and ideas.		
	(3) Reengineering, Exploration, and Generation of 'Objects'/ 'Incubation'			Explore novel hypotheses and suggestions. Generate novel ideas.			
Problem-definition space	(2) Preparation, Immersion, and Acquisition of Database of Knowledge (Data and Information) & Skills		Innovatively review relevant literature in core, peripheral, and remote domains. Innovatively collect data and information.				
	(1) (Creative) Problem-finding/ recognition/ procurement/definition	Innovatively find and explore topics, themes, hypotheses, methods, and situations: Innovatively identify 'gaps' of knowledge as well as 'anomalies'.					
Conceptual space(s)	Module(s) Month No.	6	12	18	24	30	36

A by-product of the exploration and in line with the 'impossible' problem of the versatile map is a title for the proposed thesis: 'A national–regional model for maximum economic development and minimum environmental degradation in Britain'. Once again, this is an exploratory title and could be investigated further using the same or another versatile map. A real-time creative web for the proposed thesis is shown in Table 17.3. The table depicts a program (activity) chart that could be used to plan and monitor work for the proposed thesis. An advantage of the real-time creative web is its focus on creativity, in particular, creative problem finding and solving. It is important to note that Table 17.3 reflects one of many approaches for programming a doctoral research study. Whichever approach is used, the student should discuss the proposed plan with the supervisor of the research project.

REFERENCES

Altshuler, G (1996) *And Suddenly the Inventor Appeared* (Massachusetts: Technical Innovation Center).
Buzan, T and Buzan, B (2000) *The Mind Map Book* (London: BBC Books).
Couger, JD (1996) *Creativity & Innovation* (Massachusetts: Boyd & Fraser).
De Bono, E (1994) *De Bono's Thinking Course* (London: BBC Books).
Higgins, JM (1994) *101 Creative Problem Solving Techniques* (Florida: The New Management Publishing Company).
King, R (1999) PAO Thinking. http://www.ozemail.com.au/~caveman/Creative/PAO/
Majaro, S (1991) *The Creative Marketer* (Oxford: Butterworth-Heinemann).
Michalko, M (1991) *Thinkertoys* (California: Ten Speed Press).
Michalko, M (1998) *Cracking Creativity* (California: Ten Speed Press).
Proctor, T (1995) *The Essence of Management Creativity* (Hertfordshire: Prentice Hall).
Rickards, T (1988) *Creativity at Work* (Hampshire: Gower).
Root-Bernstein, R and Root-Bernstein, M (1999) *Sparks of Genius* (Boston and New York: Houghton Mifflin).
Siler, T (1997) *Think Like a Genius* (London: Bantam Press).
Von Oech, R (1992) *A Whack on the Side of the Head/Creative Whack Pack* (California: Creative Think).
White, R and Gunstone, R (1993) *Probing Understanding* (London: The Falmer Press).
Zlotin, B, Zusman, A, Kaplan, L, Visnepolschi, S, Proseanic, V and Malkin, S (1999) *TRIZ Beyond Technology*. www.triz-journal.com/articles.htm.

18 Software and websites for creativity

Rodney King

SOFTWARE

Creativity, ideas management and problem solving comprise such a wide field that almost any software could be regarded as suitable for this field. In this chapter, the focus is on software packages and websites that specifically deal with the manipulation of ideas in order to generate novel ideas and products. Most of the software operates in MS-Windows.

Generic software for creativity and ideas management includes

- word processing software;
- outlining and graphic organisers;
- presentation (drawing) software;
- database software;
- memory management software.

Generic software for problem solving would include project management software. These generic software packages are rigid with regard to idea generation and manipulation in creative situations. Although not meant to stimulate the creative process, the software could be used to facilitate creativity and ideas management.

Table 18.1 shows 25 software packages that have been developed with a view to creativity, ideas management, and problem solving. This is an overview and not a critical appraisal of available software. More information on the software packages could be obtained from the associated websites. The comments in the table are valid at the time of writing; information rapidly changes on the Internet and websites evolve.

The purposes of the software packages vary from dedicated applications for mind mapping, concept mapping and cognitive mapping to multifarious applications and ideas management. Of the dedicated applications, mind mapping and brainstorming tools are the most popular. A few applications involve questions and random words for the generation of creative solutions.

Of the listed software, two packages use a system of templates and checklists to facilitate creative problem solving. Most packages do not explicitly present a Creative Problem Solving (CPS) model. Only ten packages describe procedures for solving creative problems.

Most of the listed software is commercial. Eleven websites offer trial versions of their software, while in four websites no offer is made. Two websites, however, offer 'lite' versions of their commercial software. Some individuals and organisations freely offer their software as shareware or free suite.

Another 25 websites on creativity, ideas management and problem solving are listed in Table 18.2. I have used the descriptions of 'minimal' for less than five offered items, 'moderate' for between five and ten offered items, 'many' for more than ten offered items; this ordinal scale is

Table 18.1 Some software for creativity, ideas management, and problem solving

Description of software	Creativity and ideas mngt.	Creative problem solving	Free software?
Axon Idea Processor http://web.singnet.com.sg/~axon2000	Many and diverse tools & techniques	Templates and checklists	Axon Lite
BatMemes www.winsite.com/ingfo/pcwin3/misc/batmemes.zip	Random words	No CPS model	Shareware
The Brain www.thebrain.com	Ideas management	No CPS model	Free trial version
Brainstormer www.jpb.com/creative/brainstormer.html	Brainstorming tool	CPS procedure	30-day free trial
Brainstorming www.brainstorming.co.uk	Brainstorming and other tools	CPS procedure	30-day free trial
Creativity Unleashed www.cul.co.uk/software/index.htm	Diverse tools	CPS procedure	Free suite
Decision Explorer www.banxia.co.uk/demain.html	Cognitive mapping	No CPS model	Free trial download
The Electric Mind http://softseek.zd.net/Business_and_Productivity/	Brainstorming tool	No CPS model	Free trial version
ForeSight www.circle-of-excellence.com/fs/ex_fsght.htm	Many and diverse tools	Templates; checklists	Free suite
IdeaFisher www.ideafisher.com	Brainstorming tool	CPS procedure	Not available
Idon www.idonresources.com	Ideas management	CPS procedure	Free demo
Imagination Engineering www.cul.co.uk/software/imeng.htm	Diverse tools	CPS procedure	Free (limited) version
Info Select www.miclog.com/isover.htm	Ideas management	No CPS model	Not available
Innovation Toolbox www.infinn.com/toolbox.html	Diverse tools	CPS procedure	30-day free trial
Inspiration www.inspiration.com	Concept mapping	No CPS model	30-day free trial
MindManager www.mindman.co.uk	Mind mapping	No CPS model	21-day free trial
MindMapper www.winsite.com/info/pc/win3/misc/mindmap.zip	Mind mapping	No CPS model	Shareware
Serious Creativity www.sixhats.com	Lateral thinking	CPS procedure	Free demo
Simplex www.basadursimplex.com/software.htm	Ideas management	CPS procedure	Not available
SmartDraw www.smartdraw.com	Drawing/ Graphics	No CPS model	30-day free trial
SolutionsMap www.solutionsmap.com	Questions	CPS procedure	Not available
SuperMemo www.supermemo.com/english/down.htm	Memory Ideas mngt.	No CPS model	Freeware: SuperMemo 7
ThoughtPath www.thoughtpath.com	Synectics and other tools	CPS procedure	Not available
VisiMap www.coco.uk	Mind mapping	No CPS model	VisiMap Lite
Visual Mind www.visual-mind.com	Mind mapping	No CPS model	30-day free trial

Table 18.2 Some other web sites on creativity, ideas management, and problem solving

Description of web site	Creativity and ideas management tools & techniques	Creative problem solving	Articles?
Center for Studies in Creativity www.snybuf.edu/creative/hist.html	Minimal	Minimal	Many
Create-It www.create-it.com	Minimal	Minimal	Minimal
Creativity Management http://pcbs042.open.ac.uk/b882/B882hmpg.htm	Many	Many	Many
Creative Think www.creativethink.com	Minimal	Minimal	Minimal
The Creative Thinking Association of America www.thinkoutofthebox.com	Minimal	Minimal	Minimal
Creativity & Innovation www.buzancentre.com/creative.html	Minimal	Minimal	Minimal
Creativity Unleashed www.cul.co.uk	Many	Many	Many
The Creativity Web www.ozemail.com.au/~caveman/Creative	Many	Many	Many
Directed Creativity www.directedcreativity.com	Many	Many	Many
Edward de Bono www.edwdebono.com	Minimal	Minimal	Minimal
Enchanted Mind www.enchantedmind.com	Many	Minimal	Many
Infinite Innovations Ltd www.infinn.com/index.html	Many	Many	Many
Inspiration Resources www.cmcsite.com/tools.htm	Many	Many	Many
The Innovation Network www.thinksmart.com/articlespersonal.html	Many	Many	Many
Michael Michalko www.creativethinking.net	Minimal	Minimal	Minimal
Minciu Sodas Laboratory www.ms.lt	Minimal	Minimal	Many
Mind Tools www.demon.co.uk/mindtools/page2.html	Moderate	Minimal	Many
MultiCentrix www.multicentric.com/index.htm	Minimal	Minimal	Moderate
National Center for Creativity Incorporated www.creativesparks.org	Minimal	Minimal	Minimal
Quantum Books www.quantumbooks.com/Creativity.html	Moderate	Moderate	Moderate
Technique Library Home Page http://www5.open.ac.uk/b822/	Many	Many	Many
TRIZ www.triz-journal.com	Minimal	Moderate	Many
Visual Communication-Creativity www.wisc.edu/agjourn/trumbo/creat1.html	Minimal	Minimal	Minimal

subjective. Note that quantity and quality are not the same. The quantity of information on a website might be minimal but that does not mean that the quality of information is minimal.

The websites in Table 18.2 are characterised by two extremes:

1. websites that offer many tools, techniques and articles on creativity, ideas management and problem solving;
2. websites that offer minimal tools, techniques and articles.

In general, commercial websites offer minimal items. Many items are offered by some commercial websites as well as individuals. The offer on other websites is between the two extremes.

PART 5 | Research types

19 Randomised trials

Douglas Altman

INTRODUCTION

A randomised trial is a planned experiment that is designed to compare two or more forms of treatment or behaviour. Randomised trials were originally developed in agriculture (Chapter 21) as a means of getting valid comparisons between different ways of treating soil or plants, where it was known that there was inherent variability in the land being used (such as drainage or exposure to wind). The same principles extend to numerous other disciplines where a comparison of procedures or treatments is needed, in particular when humans are being studied (such as in education or medicine).

The key idea of a controlled trial is that we wish to compare groups that differ only with respect to their treatment. The study must be prospective because biases are easily incurred when comparing groups treated at different times and possibly under different conditions. It must be comparative (controlled) because we cannot assume what will happen to the patients in the absence of any therapy.

Clinical trials merit special attention because of their medical importance, some particular problems in design, analysis and interpretation, and certain ethical problems. The methodology that is used was introduced into medical research over 50 years ago. The most famous early example was a trial of streptomycin in the treatment of pulmonary tuberculosis (MRC 1948). This chapter concentrates on randomised trials of health care interventions, better known as *clinical trials*. They share all the general features of such studies in all fields, but have several additional problems, such as allocation bias, blinding and ethics, which do not apply in other areas. This chapter illustrates the way in which the design and analysis of research studies have to be tailored to individual circumstances.

Although clinical trials can be set up to compare more than two treatments, I will concentrate on the two-group case. Often, one treatment is an experimental treatment, perhaps a new drug, and the other is a control treatment, which may be a standard treatment, an ineffective *placebo*, or even no treatment at all, depending on circumstances. Some trials compare different active treatments, or even different doses of the same treatment.

This chapter provides a brief overview of a complex topic. There are several books devoted to clinical trials, of which those by Pocock (1983) and Matthews (2000) are particularly recommended. The papers by Peto *et al* (1976) and Pocock (1985) give a useful discussion of some of the trickier problems; see also Chapter 15 in Altman (1991).

TRIAL DESIGN

Random allocation

A vital issue in design is to ensure that, as far as possible, the groups of patients receiving the different treatments are similar with regard to features that may affect how well they do. The usual way to avoid bias is to use *random allocation* to determine which treatment each patient gets. With randomisation, which is a chance process, variation among subjects that might affect their response to treatment will, on average, be the same in the different treatment groups. In other words, randomisation ensures that there is no bias in the way the treatments are allocated. There is no guarantee, however, that randomisation will lead to the groups being similar in a particular trial. Any differences that arise by chance can be at least inconvenient, and may lead to doubts being cast on the interpretation of the trial results.

While the results can be adjusted to take account of differences between the groups at the start of the trial, the problem should be controlled at the design stage. This can be done with *stratified randomisation*. In essence, this involves randomisation of separate subgroups of individuals, such as patients with mild or severe disease. If you know in advance that there are a few key variables that are strongly related to outcome they can be incorporated into a stratified randomisation scheme. There may be other important variables that we cannot measure or have not identified, and we rely on the randomisation to balance them out. It is essential that stratified randomisation uses *blocking*, otherwise there is no benefit over simple randomisation. Allocations to each treatment are balanced within each consecutive series, or block, of patients within each stratum. For example, blocks of size of six will include three patients on each of two treatments ordered randomly within the block. A different form of blocking is described in Chapter 21.

While randomisation is necessary it is not a sufficient safeguard against bias (conscious or subconscious) when patients are recruited. The treatment allocation system should thus be set up so that the person entering patients does not know in advance which treatment the next person will get. A common way of doing this is to use a series of sealed opaque envelopes, each containing a treatment specification. For stratified randomisation, two or more sets of envelopes are needed. For drug trials the allocation is often done by the pharmacy, who produce numbered bottles that do not indicate the treatment contained.

Blinding

The key to a successful clinical trial is to avoid any biases in the comparison of the groups. Randomisation deals with possible bias at the treatment allocation, but bias can also creep in while the study is being run. Both patients and doctors may be affected in the way they respond and observe, by knowledge of which treatment was given, especially if the outcome is subjective, such as reduction in pain. For this reason, neither the patient nor the person who evaluates the patient should know which treatment was given. Such a trial is called *double blind*. If only the patient is unaware, the trial is called *single blind*. In a double blind trial, the treatments should be indistinguishable.

When there is no standard beneficial treatment, it is reasonable not to give the control group any active treatment. However, it is often better to give the control group patients an inert or placebo treatment than nothing. First, the act of taking a treatment may itself have some benefit to the patient, so that part of any benefit observed in the treatment group could be due to the knowledge/belief that they had taken a treatment. Second, for a study to be double blind, the two treatments should be indistinguishable. Placebo tablets should therefore be identical in appearance and taste to the active treatment, but should be pharmacologically inactive. More generally, when the control treatment is an alternative active treatment rather than a placebo the different treatments should still be indistinguishable if possible. In some circumstances, such as in most surgical trials, it is impossible to disguise the treatment. In such cases it helps to have the patients' outcome assessed by someone who is blind to which group they are in.

Many clinical trials show some apparent benefit of treatment in the placebo group, and there are often side-effects too. Without a placebo, we cannot know how specific any benefit (or harm) is to the active treatment.

Sample size

For parallel group studies, the calculation of sample size is based on either a *t*-test or a comparison of proportions. Sample size calculations are based on the idea of having a high probability (called 'power', and usually set at 80 to 90 per cent) of getting a statistically significant difference if the true difference between the treatments is of a given size. Unfortunately, specifying this *effect size* is not easy.

In common diseases, such as heart disease, small benefits are worthwhile. Detecting small effects requires large trials. For example, a trial designed to have a high probability of detecting a reduction of mortality from 30 per cent to 25 per cent would need at least 1250 patients per group.

Ethical issues

One of the main ethical issues is the provision of adequate information about the trial and the treatments to potential participants. In general, the patient should be invited to be in the trial, and should be told what the alternative treatments are (although they will not know which they will get). The patient can decline, in which case they will receive the standard treatment. If the patient agrees to participate they may have to sign a form stating that he/she understood the trial. *Informed consent* is controversial because many patients may not really understand the information they are given. There are some cases where it is not possible to get informed consent, for example, when the patients are very young, very old or unconscious.

No doctor should participate in a clinical trial if he/she believes that one of the treatments being investigated is superior, and the doctor should not enter any patient for whom he/she thinks that a particular treatment is indicated. In other words, the ideal medical state to be in is one of ignorance: the trial is done because we do not know which treatment is better. This is sometimes called the *uncertainty principle*.

The methodological quality of a trial is also an ethical issue. A trial that uses inadequate methods, such as failing to randomise, and thus fails to prevent bias may be seen as unethical. Likewise, having an adequate sample size is often considered to be an ethical matter.

Outcome measures

In most clinical trials, information about the effect of treatment is gathered about many variables, sometimes on more than one occasion. There is the temptation to analyse each of these outcomes and see which differences between treatment groups are significant. This approach leads to misleading results, because multiple testing will invalidate the results of significance tests. In particular, just presenting the most significant results as if these were the only analyses performed is fraudulent.

A preferable approach is to decide in advance of the analysis which outcome measure is of major interest and focus attention on this variable when the data are analysed. Other data can and should be analysed too, but these variables should be considered to be of secondary importance. Any interesting findings among the secondary variables should be interpreted rather cautiously, more as ideas for further research than as definitive results. Side effects of treatment should usually be treated in this way.

Alternative designs

The simplest and most frequently used design for a clinical trial is the *parallel group design*, in which two groups of patients receive different treatments concurrently. The most common alternative is the *crossover design*, in which one group of all the patients are given both treatments of interest in sequence. Here, randomisation is used to determine the order in which the treatments are given. The crossover design has some attractive features, in particular that the treatment comparison is *within-subject* rather than *between-subject*. Because within-subject variation is usually much smaller than between-subject variation, the sample size needed is smaller. There are some important disadvantages, however. In particular, patients may drop out after the first treatment, and so not receive the second treatment. Withdrawal may be related to side-effects. In addition, crossover studies should not be used for conditions that can be cured or which may be fatal.

Lastly, there may be a carry-over of treatment effect from one period to the next, so that the results obtained during the second period are affected. In other words, the observed difference between the treatments will depend upon the order in which they were received. Crossover trials are covered well by Senn (1993).

A variation of the parallel group trial is the *group sequential trial*, in which the data are analysed as the data accumulate, typically at three, four or five time points. This design is suitable for trials that recruit and follow up patients over several years. It allows the trial to be stopped early if a clear treatment difference is seen, if side effects are unacceptable, or if it is obvious that no difference will be found. Adjustment is made to significance tests to allow for multiple analyses of the data.

In some situations, groups of individuals are randomised, usually for logistic reasons. Such studies are common in health education, for example. In such trials, the group is the unit of randomisation rather than the individual. Special considerations are necessary in the design and analysis of such trials, as described by Donner and Klar (2000).

One further type of design is called the *factorial design*, in which two treatments, say A and B, are compared with each other and with a control. Patients are randomised into four groups, who receive either the control treatment, A only, B only, or both A and B. This design allows the investigation of the interaction (or synergy) between A and B. It is rarely used in clinical trials, but it is becoming more common. Such designs (and more complex ones) are standard practice in agricultural field trials and in industrial research (see Chapters 20 and 21).

Protocols

As with all research, an important aspect of planning a clinical trial is to produce a protocol, which is a formal document outlining the proposed procedures for carrying out the trial. Pocock (1983) suggests the following main features of a study protocol:

1. Background
2. Specific objectives
3. Patient selection criteria
4. Treatment schedules
5. Methods of patient evaluation (outcome measures)

6. Trial design
7. Registration and randomisation of patients
8. Patient consent
9. Required size of study
10. Monitoring of trial progress
11. Forms and data handling
12. Protocol deviations
13. Plans for statistical analysis
14. Administrative responsibilities

A detailed protocol must accompany an application for a grant for a trial, and the local *ethics committee* will also require most of the above information. As well as aiding in the performance of a trial, a protocol makes the reporting of the results much easier as the introduction and methods section of the paper should be substantially the same as sections (1) to (9) above.

Many difficulties can be avoided by having a pilot study, which is valuable for assessing the quality of the data collection forms, and for checking the logistics of the trial, such as the expected time to examine each patient (which affects the number that can be seen in a session).

ANALYSIS

The general methods for the statistical analysis of data, described in Chapters 29 and 30, apply to clinical trials and you should read those chapters. Several specific problems arise in the analysis of clinical trials, some of which are considered here. A fuller discussion of bias in analysis is given by May *et al* (1981) in addition to the textbooks referenced.

Comparison of entry characteristics

Randomisation does not guarantee that the characteristics of the different groups are similar. The first analysis should be a summary of the baseline characteristics of the patient in the two groups. It is important to show that the groups were similar with respect to variables that may affect the patient's response. For example, we would usually wish to be happy that the age distribution was similar in the different groups, as many outcomes are age-related.

A common way to compare groups is with hypothesis tests, but a moment's thought should suffice to see that this is unhelpful (Altman and Doré 1990). If the randomisation is performed fairly we know that any differences between the two treatment groups must be due to chance. A hypothesis test thus makes no sense except as a test of whether the trial was indeed randomised. In any case, the question at issue is whether the groups differ in a way that might affect their response to treatment. This question is clearly one of clinical importance rather than statistical significance. If we suspect that the observed differences (imbalance) between the groups may have affected the outcome we can take account of the imbalance in the analysis, as described below.

Incomplete data

Data may be incomplete for several reasons. For example, occasional laboratory measurements will be missing because of problems with the samples taken. It is important to use all the data available and to specify if any observations are missing. In addition, some information may simply not have been recorded. It may seem reasonable to assume that a particular symptom was not present if it was not recorded, but such inferences are, in general, unsafe and should be made only after careful consideration of the circumstances.

The most important problem with missing information in trials relates to patients who do not complete the study. Some patients may be withdrawn by their doctor, perhaps because of side-effects. Others may move to another area or just fail to return for assessment. Efforts should be made to obtain at least some information regarding the status of these patients at the end of the trial, but some data are still likely to be missing. If there are many more withdrawals in one treatment group, the results of the trial will be compromised, as it is likely that the withdrawals are treatment-related.

A further difficulty is when some patients have not followed the protocol, either deliberately or accidentally. Included here are patients who actually receive the wrong treatment (in other words, not the one allocated) and patients who do not take their treatment, known as *non-compliers*. Also, sometimes it may be discovered after the trial has begun that a patient was not, after all, eligible for the trial.

The only safe way to deal with all of these situations is to keep all randomised patients in the trial. The analysis is thus based on the groups as randomised, and is known as an *intention-to-treat analysis*. Any other policy towards protocol violations will depart from the randomisation, which is the basis for the trial. Also, excluding some patients involves subjective decisions and thus creates an opportunity for bias. In practice, those patients who are lost to follow up and thus have no recorded outcomes will need to be excluded, but all other patients should be included. The absence of outcomes for all patients causes major difficulties in both analysis and interpretation (Lachin 2000).

Adjusting for other variables

Most clinical trials are based on the simple idea of comparing two groups with respect to one main variable of interest, for which the statistical analysis is simple. We may, however, wish to take one or more other variables into consideration in the analysis. One reason might be that the two groups were not similar with respect to baseline variables. We can thus perform the analysis with and without adjustment. If the results are similar, we can infer that the imbalance was not important, and can quote the simple comparison but, if the results are different, we should use the adjusted analysis. Imbalance will only affect the results if the variable is related to the outcome measure: it will not matter if one group is much shorter than the other if height is unrelated to response to treatment. The use of restricted randomisation designed to give similar groups (such as stratified randomisation) is desirable as it simplifies the analysis of the data.

Subgroup analyses

Even with a single outcome variable there is often interest in identifying which patients do well on a treatment and which do badly. We can answer some questions like this by analysing the data separately for subsets of the data. We may, for example, redo the analysis including only male patients, and then only female patients. Subgroup analyses like these pose serious problems of interpretation similar to those resulting from multiple outcome measures. It is reasonable to perform a small number of subgroup analyses if these were specified in the protocol. However, if the data are analysed in numerous ways in the hope of discovering some 'significant' comparison, or because some aspect of the data suggests a difference, then they must be recognised and identified as exploratory.

INTERPRETATION OF RESULTS

Single trials

In most cases, the statistical analysis of a clinical trial will be simple, at least with respect to the main outcome measure, perhaps involving just a *t*-test or a *chi-squared* test. Interpretation seems straightforward, therefore, but for one difficulty.

Inference from a sample to a population relies on the assumption that the trial participants represent all such patients. However, in most trials, participants are selected to conform to certain inclusion criteria, so extrapolation of results to other types of patient may not be warranted. For example, most trials of anti-hypertensive agents, such as beta-blocking drugs, are on middle-aged men. Is it therefore reasonable to assume that the results apply to women too, or to very young or very old men? In the absence of any information to the contrary, it is common to infer wider applicability of results, but the possibility that different groups would respond differently should be borne in mind. This issue is discussed by Ellenberg (1994).

All published trials

In many fields, there have been several similar clinical trials, and it is natural to want to assess all the evidence at once. The first thing that becomes apparent when looking at the results of a series of clinical trials of the same treatment comparison is that the results vary, sometimes markedly. We would expect to see some variation in treatment effect because of random variation, and should not be worried by it. The confidence interval for the treatment benefit observed in a single trial gives an idea of the range of treatment benefit likely to be observed in a series of trials of the same size.

A relatively recent development has been the move towards the identification, methodological appraisal, and (optionally) a pooled statistical analysis of all published trials to obtain an overall assessment of treatment effectiveness. Such a study is known as a *systematic review*, and the analysis combining results from several studies as a *meta-analysis* (this latter term is sometimes used for the whole exercise) (Egger *et al* 2001). Systematic reviews can show a highly significant overall treatment benefit when most of the individual trials did not get a significant result. Again, this is to be expected, as many clinical trials are too small to detect anything other than an unrealistically huge treatment benefit. However, this new type of study has generated many new challenges for statisticians.

ASSESSING THE QUALITY OF CLINICAL TRIALS

As hinted above, not all trials are done well. In addition, many studies have found that inadequate reporting of trials is widespread. The CONSORT statement, first published in 1996, has provided a widely accepted basis for the reporting of trials, and many medical journals expect authors to follow these recommendations (Moher *et al* 2001). Fuller reporting of trials should greatly assist in the assessment of the quality of the methodology used in a trial, and thus help the reader judge the reliability of the results.

While there are many aspects of the quality of a trial, the most important are those relating to steps taken to avoid bias, such as randomisation and blinding. Empirical evidence is accumulating that failure to use such methods does indeed lead to bias (Altman *et al* 2001).

REFERENCES

Altman, DG (1991) *Practical Statistics for Medical Research* (London: Chapman and Hall).

Altman, DG and Doré, CJ (1990) Randomisation and baseline comparisons in clinical trials. *Lancet,* **335,** pp 149–153.

Altman, DG, Schulz, KF, Moher, D, Egger, M, Davidoff, F, Elbourne, D, Gøtzsche, PC and Lang, T for the CONSORT Group (2001) The revised CONSORT statement for reporting randomized trials: explanation and elaboration. *Annals of Internal Medicine,* in press.

Donner, A and Klar, NS (2000) *Design and Analysis of Cluster Randomisation Trials* (London: Arnold).

Egger, M, Davey Smith, G and Altman, DG (eds) (2001) *Systematic Reviews in Health Care. Meta-analysis in Context* (London: BMJ Books).

Ellenberg, JH (1994) Selection bias in observational and experimental studies. *Statistics in Medicine* **13** pp 557–567.

Lachin, JM (2000) Statistical considerations in the intent-to-treat principle. *Controlled Clinical Trials* **21** pp 167–189.

Matthews, JNS (2000) *An Introduction to Randomised Trials* (London: Arnold).

May, GS, DeMets, DL, Friedman, L, Furberg, C and Passamani, E (1981) The randomised clinical trial: bias in analysis. *Circulation* **64** pp 669–673.

Moher, D, Schulz, KF and Altman, DG for the CONSORT Group (2001) The CONSORT statement: revised recommendations for improving the quality of reports of parallel group randomized trials. *Lancet,* in press.

MRC (1948) Streptomycin treatment of pulmonary tuberculosis. *British Medical Journal* **2** pp 769–782.

Peto, R, Pike, MC and Armitage, P *et al* (1976) Design and analysis of randomised trials requiring prolonged observation of each patient. I. Introduction and design. *British Journal of Cancer* **34** pp 585–612.

Pocock, S (1983) *Clinical trials: a Practical Approach* (Chichester: Wiley).

Pocock, S (1985) Current issues in the design and interpretation of clinical trials. *British Medical Journal* **290** pp 39–42.

Senn, S (1993) *Cross-over Trials in Clinical Research* (Chichester: Wiley).

20 Laboratory and industrial experiments

Tony Greenfield

INTRODUCTION

Experimental design and analysis is an essential part of scientific method.

Every experiment should be well designed, planned and managed to ensure that the results can be analysed, interpreted and presented. If you do not do this you will not understand properly what you are doing and you will face the hazard of failing to reach your research goals, of wasting great effort, time, money and other resources in fruitless pursuits.

Other chapters in this book (Chapters 29 to 32) are about the analysis of experimental data. This chapter is about the design of experiments.

An *experimental design* is:

> *the specification of the conditions at which experimental data will be observed.*

Experimental design is a major part of applied statistics and there is an immense amount of literature about it. In this chapter, I present only those aspects of experimental design that have most to contribute to the physical sciences, specifically to laboratory and industrial experiments. Such experiments are aimed primarily at improving products and processes.

Descriptions are necessarily brief and selective. Please read this chapter as an introduction and a reference. There are many good books on the subject and a few of the best are listed at the end of this chapter.

There are many types of experimental design. In this chapter, I describe a range of designs, selected for their usefulness to the physical sciences, including manufacturing and industries, and leading from the simplest to the more complex. These are:

Descriptive

A sample of several test pieces, all from a standard material, is tested to determine the elementary statistics of a characteristic of that material. You may, for example, wish to report the mean and the standard deviation of the tensile strength of a standard material.

Comparative

Comparison against a standard

You may wish to compare the characteristic of a new material against a specified industry standard. You would test a sample of several pieces and ask if there was sufficient evidence to conclude that the measured characteristic of this material was different from the standard specification.

Comparison of two materials with independent samples

You may have two materials, perhaps of different compositions, or made by slightly different processes, or, even if they are claimed to be of the same composition and made by exactly the same process, they are made at different places. You wish to determine if they have the same or different properties so you test a sample of several pieces from each material. These samples are independent of each other.

Comparison of two materials by paired samples

You may have two materials and you wish to determine if they have the same or different properties. However, you wish to ensure, in the presence of uncontrollable outside influences, to make a fair comparison. For example, you may wish to expose samples of structural steel to the weather and measure their corrosion. One approach would be to expose test pieces in pairs, each pair comprising one item piece of each material. The data to be analysed would be the difference in corrosion measured between each pair by weighing them separately.

Response

Factorial experiments

When new materials or manufacturing processes are being developed there are usually several variables, or factors, that can influence a material property. Experiments to investigate the effects of several variables should be designed in which all of those variables are set at several levels.

> **Warning:** There is a widespread belief, still taught in schools and to undergraduates, that the best approach is to experiment with one variable at a time and to fix all the others. That approach is inefficient, uneconomic, and will not provide information about interactions between variables.

Two-level factorial experiments, in which each factor is set at two levels, high and low, are widely used during development studies.

Response surface exploration with composite designs

In the final stage of a development study, when you are seeking the conditions (such as the values of composition and process variables) that will yield the best value of a material property (such as the highest value of tensile strength), additional points must be added to factorial experiments so that the curvature of the response can be estimated. These designs are known as *augmented* or *composite designs*.

Inter-laboratory trials and hierarchical designs

Another class of experiment used in industry is the inter-laboratory trial for the purpose of estimating the repeatability of test results within each of a set of laboratories, and the reproducibility of test results between laboratories. These are described more fully in several text books and in a British Standard (BS 5497).

Similar issues arise when comparing variability within and between batches of product.

PRINCIPLES OF EXPERIMENTAL DESIGN

Statistical analysis of experimental results is necessary because of variation: *all test results vary*. This variation must therefore be considered when experiments are designed.

Descriptive experiments

In a descriptive experiment, a characteristic of a standard material will be reported from the analysis of measurements on several test results. For example, the mean tensile strength of a sample of several test pieces will be calculated. This is unlikely to be the true value of the underlying population mean. If you calculated the mean tensile strength of another sample of several test pieces it would be different. The calculated sample mean is therefore only an estimate, a *point* estimate, of the underlying population mean. In reporting it you should report an interval in which you can confidently expect the population mean to lie: a *confidence interval* for the population mean.

This confidence interval depends on three things:

1. the variation of test results, expressed as the variance or standard deviation of the measured material property;
2. the number of pieces tested in the sample;
3. the degree of confidence of the interval, loosely interpreted as the probability that the population mean is truly in that interval, usually as a percentage (for example: a 95 per cent confidence interval).

The variation will have to be determined from the experiment. The number of test pieces must be specified before the experiment is done. The degree of confidence is the choice of the experimenter and should be specified before the experiment is done. Ideally, the experimenter should specify how large a confidence interval, and with what confidence, they would like. For example, they may specify: sample mean value ± 1.0 N/mm^2 with a confidence of 95 per cent. The experiment would then proceed in four stages.

Stage 1 A preliminary experiment to estimate the underlying population variance and/or a review of similar experiments reported in the literature

Stage 2 A calculation of the sample size N needed to estimate the specified confidence interval using the variance estimated in Stage 1

Stage 3 Test measurements on a sample of N pieces

Stage 4 Calculation of the estimated mean, standard deviation and confidence interval

These four stages are described fully in the referenced textbooks.

Comparative experiments

Statistical analysis of test results should never be regarded simply as a set of calculations leading to a clear-cut conclusion, such as 'the effect is significant' or 'there is no significant effect'. The conclusion depends on the circumstances of the experiment and on the intentions of the experimenter, which should be declared before the tests are done. For example, the circumstances of an experiment may ordain how likely an effect is to be declared as statistically significant *if it exists*; the intentions of the experimenter will include a statement of what they consider to be a *technically* significant effect.

Four major steps must be taken before starting an experiment.

Step 1 State the alternative inferences that can be made from the experiment

Step 2 Specify the acceptable risks for making the wrong inference

Step 3 Specify the difference that must be demonstrated statistically so as to be of technical significance

Step 4 Compute the necessary sample size

These four steps are described more fully below and are described in detail in the referenced text-books.

Step 1   State the alternative inferences that can be made from the experiment. These should be stated as alternative prior hypotheses

When two materials are to be compared according to some property, the most usual comparison is between the mean values of that property. Even though the sample mean values $\bar{x}_1$ and $\bar{x}_2$ will differ, is there sufficient evidence to infer that the mean values of the underlying populations (μ_1 and μ_2) differ? If there is not sufficient evidence you cannot refute the claim that the means of the underlying populations are the same. An assumption that they are the same is known as the null hypothesis (H_0). An assumption that they are different is known as the alternative hypothesis (H_a).

These hypotheses may be stated symbolically as:

$$H_0: \ \mu_1 = \mu_2$$
$$H_a: \ \mu_1 <> \mu_2$$

In this case, the experimenter is concerned about *any* difference between the population means. This will lead to a two-sided test.

If the experimenter is interested in a new material only if it has a greater mean strength than the standard material, a one-sided test will be used and the alternative hypotheses will be:

$$H_0: \ \mu_1 = \mu_2$$
$$H_a: \ \mu_1 > \mu_2$$

The distinction must be made *before* the experiment is done. The calculation of the sample size depends on the distinction.

Step 2   Specify the acceptable risks for making the wrong inference. The wrong inferences are called the type one error and the type two error with probabilities α and β respectively

The possible inferences from a two-sided test may be understood from Table 20.1. A *type one error* occurs when the experimenter accepts the alternative hypothesis (H_a) although the null hypothesis (H_0) is true. The probability of this occurring is α. Usually α is specified as 0.05 (a five per cent chance).

Table 20.1 Possible inferences from a two-sided test

		Inference	
		$\mu_1 = \mu_2$	$\mu_1 <> \mu_2$
Truth	$\mu_1 = \mu_2$	correct probability $= (1 - \alpha)$	type one error probability $= \alpha$
	$\mu_1 <> \mu_2$ or $\mu_1 - \mu_2 = \delta$ where δ is not zero	type two error probability $= \beta$	correct probability $= (1 - \beta)$ which depends on δ

Table 20.2 Burst strengths (kPa) of filter membranes

Batch one	Batch two
267	284
262	279
261	274
261	271
259	268
258	265
258	263
258	262
257	260
256	259
251	246
250	241

A *type two error* occurs when the experimenter accepts the null hypothesis (H_0) although the alternative hypothesis is true. The probability of this occurring is β, which depends on the difference between the population means ($\mu_1 - \mu_2$). Usually, β is specified as 0.05 or 0.10 for a specified difference of technical importance. The probability of detecting this difference is $(1 - \beta)$. Thus, if β is chosen to be 0.05 and the experiment is designed accordingly there is a strong chance (a probability of 0.95) that the specified difference will be detected if it truly exists. More generally, a plot of the probability $(1 - \beta)$ of correctly detecting a true difference (Δ) against Δ is known as *the power curve of the test*.

Unfortunately, it is common for experiments to be done without consideration of β or the power and consequently important true effects may remain undetected. For example, consider the burst strengths (kPa) of two batches of filter membranes as shown in Table 20.2.

Suppose that a purpose of the experiment was to detect any difference exceeding 10 kPa. A power calculation ($\alpha = 0.05$) shows that with only 12 results for each batch there is a probability of 0.75 of detecting a difference if it exists. Sample sizes of 23 would be needed to give a probability of 0.95 of detecting that difference.

Step 3 Specify the smallest difference (δ) of technical significance, which should have a specified probability $(1 - \beta)$ of being detected

The purpose of many experiments is to discover an improvement in a material property of that which is being tested. In other experiments, the purpose may be to show that, under different circumstances, there is no substantial difference in the material property.

In either case, the experimenter should be able to state the smallest difference that they would regard as likely to have a practical or technical significance. For example, how much stronger, in terms of tensile strength, should one material be over another to make its selection preferable for a particular application? One per cent, or 2 per cent or 0.5 per cent? It may depend on the application.

The specification of this smallest difference (δ) is essential to the design of a comparative experiment.

Step 4 Compute the necessary sample size

There are several formulae for calculating sample size. The correct choice of formula depends on the type of comparative experiment (comparison against a standard, comparison of two materials with independent samples, comparison of two materials by paired samples) and on whether the proposed comparison test is one-tailed or two-tailed. The information needed in any of the calculations is the choice of α, β, δ and an estimate of the variance (σ^2) of the underlying population.

The choices of α, β, δ depend entirely on the opinions and purposes of the experimenter, as already explained. An estimate of the population variance (σ^2) may often be obtained from earlier experiments or from the literature. Otherwise a preliminary experiment of at least five test pieces must be done to obtain that estimate.

Response experiments

Introduction to response experiments

Much research and development in the materials sciences is intended to establish relationships between materials properties and other factors that the technologist can control in the production of those materials. The properties are called *response variables* (also called *dependent variables*). The other factors that influence the response variables are called *control variables* (also called *independent variables*). The control variables are usually composition variables and process variables. All of these variables must be measurable.

- The variable we are most interested in studying is often called the *response* variable because it changes in response to changes in other variables. In addition, it is usually a characteristic of a product by which we judge the usefulness of the product.
- For example, we may be doing an experiment about the production of an artificial silken thread. The process involves the stirring of a mixture and the tensile strength depends, at least partly, on the stirring speed. In this case, tensile strength is an important property of artificial silk. It seems to respond to stirring speed so it is a response variable. We show it along the vertical, or Y axis.
- The variable that we think is influencing, or controlling, the response variable is, in this case, stirring speed. We call it a *control* variable and show it along the horizontal, or X, axis.

All of the variables that may influence the response are collectively called *explanatory* or *predictor variables*. Sometimes there are other variables that may influence the response variables but which cannot be controlled, although they can be identified and measured. Common examples are the temperature and humidity of a factory workshop atmosphere. These variables are called *concomitant variables* (also called *covariates*).

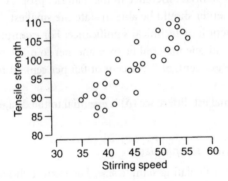

Figure 20.1 Graph showing tensile strength (response variable) against stirring speed (control variable)

The experimental design is the specification of the values of the control variables at which the response variables will be measured. The experiment should be designed according to the expected relationship between the response variable and the control variables. The expected relationship is a hypothesis. The hypothesis should be formulated as an algebraic model that can be represented in terms of the measurable variables.

The experimental design would be very simple and few observations would be needed to fit the model if the expected relationship could predict the results exactly. However, there are several reasons why this cannot be achieved:

- The exact relationship cannot be known; the model is only an approximation to reality.
- All measurements may be subject to time dependent errors that we cannot identify but which show their presence by trends in the observed values of response variables.
- All measurements are subject to random errors; these represent other unidentified variables that, taken together, show no pattern or trend.

The experiment must therefore be designed so as to reduce the influence of these unknowns.

The statistical objectives of designed response experiments are to specify

- the number of observations;
- the values of the control variables at every observation;
- the order of the observations

with a view to

- ensuring that all effects in the model can be estimated from the observed data;
- testing the reality of those effects by comparison with random variation;
- ensuring that all effects can be estimated with the greatest possible precision (reducing the influence of random variation);
- ensuring that all effects can be estimated with the least possible bias, or greatest accuracy (reducing the effects of time dependent errors);
- suggesting improvements to the model;
- keeping within a budget of effort and cost.

Factorial experiments

Two-level factorial experiments. The two-level factorial design is fundamental to experimental design for the physical sciences.

When there is good reason to believe that, over the range of values of a control variable, the dependent variable is related to the control variable by a linear function of the form:

$$y = a + bx \tag{20.1}$$

where y is the response variable, x is the control variable, and a and b are coefficients to be estimated, then a and b can be estimated with the greatest precision if all observations are divided equally between the two ends of the range of x. A common fault among experimenters is to divide the range into $N - 1$ equal parts (where N is the number of planned observations) and to make one observation at each end and at each of the division points. A few intermediate points may be desirable as a check on the believed linearity if curvature is suspected.

In equation (20.1), the effect on y of a change in x of one unit is represented by the coefficient b, which is the slope of the line. Another way of representing the relationship between x and y is achieved by using a different notation. In this notation, the independent variables (the xs) are called factors and are represented by capital letters: $A, B, C, \ldots$

The range of a factor is specified by the two ends of the range: the high and the low values of the factor. These are represented by lower case letters with suffixes. For example, in the single factor experiment, the high and low values of factor A would be a_1 and a_0 respectively. This lower case notation is also used to represent the observed values of the dependent variable at the corresponding observation points.

The effect of factor A on the dependent variable (y) over the complete range of factor A is equal to:

$$(\text{mean value of } y \text{ at point } a_1) - (\text{mean value of } y \text{ at point } a_0)$$

which can be expressed as:

$$\text{effect of } A = \bar{y}(a_1) - \bar{y}(a_0)$$

or, more briefly,

$$A = a_1 - a_0 \tag{20.2}$$

Note a further abbreviation in that the capital letter A is used to denote the effect of factor A.

Similarly, the mean value of y is simply

$$M = (a_1 + a_0)/2 \tag{20.3}$$

Now consider two factors, A and B, which can be represented as two variables in a plane with the dependent variable y along a third dimension perpendicular to the plane. The design is shown in Fig. 20.2

The high and low values of B are b_1 and b_0. If observations of y are made only at points defined by the extreme ranges of the two factors, there are four points that can be denoted by the combinations of letters as: a_0b_0, a_1b_0, a_0b_1 and a_1b_1. The notation can be abbreviated further to represent these four points as: (1), a, b, ab. The symbol (1) denotes the observation point at which all the

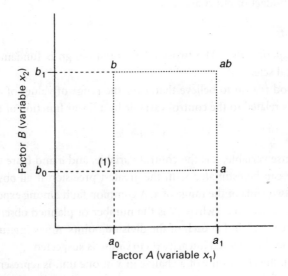

Figure 20.2 Graph showing two-factor design

factors are at their low levels. The point a is where factor A is at its high level but factor B is at its low level. The point ab is where both factors are at their high levels. The rule is that the high and low levels of factors are represented by the presence or absence, respectively, of lower case letters.

Analysis is almost as easy as in the single factor case. Using the combinations of lower case letters to represent the values of y observed at the corresponding points, the average effect of factor A is:

$$A = \frac{a+ab}{2} - \frac{(1)+b}{2} \qquad (20.4)$$

That is: the effect of A is the difference between (the mean value of y observed at all the points where A was at its high level) and (the mean value of y observed at all the points where A was at its low level).

Similarly:

$$B = \frac{b+ab}{2} - \frac{(1)+a}{2} \qquad (20.5)$$

The interaction of factors A and B may be defined as the difference between (the effect of A at the high level of B) and (the effect of A at the low level of B). It is denoted by AB. Thus:

$$AB = (ab - b) - (a - (1)) \qquad (20.6)$$

This is exactly the same as: the difference between (the effect of B at the high level of A) and (the effect of B at the low level of A).

The estimation of these effects is equivalent to fitting the algebraic model:

$$y = \beta_0 + \beta_1 x_1 + \beta_2 x_2 + \beta_{12} x_1 x_2 \qquad (20.7)$$

where y is the response variable, x_1 and x_2 are two control variables and $\beta_0, \beta_1, \beta_2$ and β_{12} are algebraic coefficients.

Least squares regression analysis (Chapter 30) is widely used for analysis of these and other experiments to be described. Computer software is available for this analysis, which includes the estimation and testing of coefficients in equations such as equation (20.7).

Two-level fractional factorial experiments

These principles of design and analysis of two-level factorial experiments can be extended to experiments involving any number of factors. See Fig. 20.3 for an illustration of a three-factor situation. However, the number of observations in such an experiment increases exponentially with the number of factors. If there are n factors, the number of observations is 2^n. Thus:

Number of factors	Number of observations
1	2
2	4
3	8
4	16
5	32
6	64
7	128
8	256
9	512
10	1024

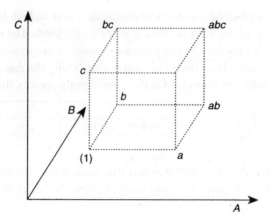

Figure 20.3 The three-factor situation

It is not unusual to have experiments with seven or more factors (control variables). Thrift demands an experiment with only a fraction of the experiments in a full design. If a suitable fraction can be found, the resulting experiment is called a two-level fractional factorial.

The theory and method of constructing these fractional experiments is described in textbooks. In addition, software is available for the automatic design and analysis of these experiments (see the Bibliography and the end of this chapter).

Composite designs

Whereas two-level factorial experiments, and their fractions, are suitable for fitting models that are linear in the main effects and including interactions, they are not suitable for estimating the curvature of response, if it exists. For example, if there is a single control variable, equation (20.1) may be suitable either if the relationship is genuinely linear for all values of x, or if the region of the experiment is on either the rising or decreasing slope of a quadratic response.

However, if the experiment is to be done in a range of x that is close to the peak (or trough) of the quadratic response, then curvature will have a major effect and must be estimated. This is particularly important if a purpose of the experiment is to estimate the value of x for which y is a maximum (or minimum).

Equation (20.1) must then be augmented as:

$$y = a + bx + cx^2 \tag{20.8}$$

Similarly, equation (7) must be augmented as:

$$y = \beta_0 + \beta_1 x_1 + \beta_2 x_2 + \beta_{12} x_1 x_2 + \beta_{11} x_1^2 + \beta_{22} x_2^2 \tag{20.9}$$

Designs for these augmented relationships are called *augmented* or *composite designs*. The theory and methodology of constructing them is described in several textbooks. Software is available for constructing and analysing them. Analysis is usually by least squares regression.

An example

Figure 20.4 shows how a catheter is fixed to a valve body. It enters through the A-channel and expands into the C-channel where it is held by a bush which is pressed into the end of the catheter.

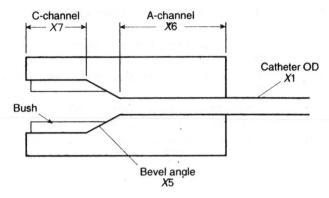

Figure 20.4 Catheter fixed to a valve body

The purpose of the experiment was to discover the dimensions such that the catheter would be gripped with maximum security. The assembly is put into a tensile tester and the force is gradually increased until the catheter is pulled out. The response variable ($Y1$) is the disassembly force measure in newtons.

There are some constraints in the dimensions. The C-channel ID must be greater than the bush OD. The C-channel ID must be greater than the A-channel ID. These constraints are avoided by using differences in variables $X3$ and $X4$.

The control variables (measurements in mm, except for $X5$) are:

		Low	High	Increment
$X1$	catheter OD	1.7	1.8	0.05
$X2$	bush OD	1.6	2.0	0.1
$X3$	C-channel ID – bush OD	0.20	0.45	0.05
$X4$	C-channel ID – A channel ID	0.00	0.10	0.05
$X5$	bevel angle	30°	90°	5°
$X6$	A-channel length	3.0	5.5	0.5
$X7$	C-channel length	0.5	4.0	0.5

The experiment was designed, using DEX, to fit a model that included all quadratic effects and the first-order interactions: $X1.X2$, $X1.X3$, $X1.X4$, $X1.X6$, $X1.X7$, $X3.X5$, $X4.X5$. The choice of interactions was based on experience, mechanical judgement and analysis of earlier trials.

The designed experiment has 47 observations, of which the first 32 comprise a quarter of a 2^7 factorial. The following 15 observations are axial and are centre points that are added to estimate curvature as quadratic terms in the model. Thus, this is a composite experiment constructed by augmenting a fractional two-level experiment. It achieved its purpose of discovering the conditions that would yield a maximum disassembly force for the catheter valve. You can see a further explanation of the designed experiment on p.420 of Metcalfe (1994).

BIBLIOGRAPHY

Atkinson, AC and Donev, AN (1992) *Optimum Experimental Designs* (Oxford: Oxford University Press).
Box, GEP and Draper, NR (1987) *Empirical Model-Building and Response Surfaces* (New York: Wiley).
Box, GEP, Hunter, WG and Hunter, JS (1978) *Statistics for Experimenters. An Introduction to Design* (New York: Wiley).

Diamond, WJ (1981) *Practical Experimental Designs for Engineers and Scientists* (New York: Van Nostrand Reinhold).

Greenfield, T *DEX: a Program for the Design and Analysis of Experiments* (Little Hucklow, Derbyshire: Greenfield).

Grove, DM and Davis, TP (1992) *Engineering Quality and Experimental Design* (Harlow: Longman Scientific and Technical).

Metcalfe, AV (1994) *Statistics in Engineering* (London: Chapman and Hall).

Montgomery, DC (2001) *Design and Analysis of Experiments* (New York: Wiley).

Wu, CFJ and Hamada, M (2000) *Experiments* (New York: Wiley).

21 Agricultural experiments

Roger Payne

INTRODUCTION

Experiments are a fundamental part of agricultural research. Indeed, much of the theory of design and analysis of experiments was originally developed by statisticians at agricultural institutes. The methods are useful, however, in many other application areas. Consequently, this chapter should be of interest to all researchers, whether or not their chosen area of study is agriculture.

The aim of the chapter is to cover the main principles of the design and analysis of experiments. Further information can then be obtained either from the books listed at the end of the chapter, or from your local statistician.

First, we consider the basic experimental *units*. In a field experiment, these may be different *plots* of land within a field. In animal experiments, they may be individual *animals* or perhaps pens each containing several animals. There is a great deal of practical expertise involved in setting out, managing, sampling and harvesting field plots. The accuracy of these aspects can be vital to the success of an investigation, and potential field experimenters are encouraged to read Dyke (1988, Chapters 2–6) for further advice.

BLOCKING

The units frequently have either an intrinsic or an imposed underlying structure. Usually this consists of a grouping of the units into sets known as *blocks*. For example, the animals in an experiment may be of several different breeds (this would be an intrinsic grouping). Alternatively, in a field experiment, you might decide to partition up the field into several different blocks of plots. The aim when allocating plots to blocks is to make the plots in each block as similar as possible: to try to ensure that pairs of plots in the same block are more similar than pairs in different blocks. Often this can be achieved by taking contiguous areas of the field as blocks, chosen so that the blocks change along a suspected trend in fertility. However, blocks need not be contiguous. For example, in an experiment on fruit trees you might wish to put trees of similar heights in the same block, irrespective of where they occur on the field. Blocks need not all have the same shape. In a glasshouse you might find that the main variability is between the pots at the side and those in the middle. So you could have two L-shaped blocks around the edge, and other rectangular blocks down the middle. The key point is that you should think about the inherent variability of your experimental units, and then block them accordingly. Further advice can be found, for example, in Dyke (1988, Chapter 2) or Mead (1988, Chapter 2). An important final point is that you should remember the blocking when you are planning the husbandry of the trial. For example if you cannot harvest all the units of the experiment in one day, you should aim to harvest one complete set of blocks on the first day, another set on the second, and so on. Then any differences arising from the different days of harvest will be removed in the statistical analysis along with the differences between blocks, and will not bias your estimates of treatments.

More complicated blocking arrangements can also occur, and are described later in the chapter. The alternative strategy of fitting spatial covariance models to the fertility trends is also discussed below.

TREATMENT STRUCTURE

The purpose of the experiment will be to investigate how various treatments affect the experimental units. In the simplest situation there is a single set of treatments – perhaps different varieties of a crop, or different amounts of a fertiliser, or different dietary régimes for animals. Figure 21.1 shows the field plan of a simple example in which fungicidal seed treatments to control the disease take-all were examined in a *randomised complete block design*.

In this design, the units (in this case field plots) are grouped into blocks as described in the section on blocking. Each treatment occurs on one plot in every block, and the allocation of treatments to plots is randomised independently within each block; so here, a random permutation of the numbers 1 to 3 was selected for each block and used to determine which treatment was applied to each of its plots. Designed experiments are usually analysed by analysis of variance. Figure 21.2 shows output from GenStat for Windows (Payne 2000a,b, Harding *et al* 2000). This system was developed by statisticians at an agricultural research institute, and so it has especially comprehensive facilities for the design and analysis of experiments.

First there is an *analysis of variance* table that allows the effects of the treatments to be assessed against the inherent variability of the units. The variability between the blocks is contained in the *Block stratum*, and the variability of the plots within the blocks is in the *Block.Plot stratum*. Within the *Block.Plot* stratum, the *Seed_treatments* line contains the variability that can be explained by the assumption that the seed treatments do have differing effects, and the residual line contains the variability between units that cannot be explained by either block or treatment differences. The *mean square* (m.s.) for blocks is over nine times that for the residual, indicating that the choice of blocks has been successful in increasing the precision of the experiment. Similarly, the variance ratio (v.r.) of 12.05 for *Seed_treatments* suggests that the treatments are different. The analysis will also provide tables showing the estimated mean of the units with each treatment, usually (as here) accompanied by a standard error to use in assessing differences between the means.

It is important to realise that the analysis is actually fitting a *linear model* in which the yield y_{ij} on the plot of block i to receive treatment j is represented as follows:

$$y_{ij} = \mu + \beta_i + t_j + \varepsilon_{ij}$$

150	150	100	0
0	100	150	150
100	0	0	100

Figure 21.1 An example of a randomised complete block design

```
***** Analysis of variance *****

Variate: Yield

Source of variation      d.f.         s.s.           m.s.         v.r.       F pr.

Block stratum             3         2.39990        0.79997        9.12

Block.Plot stratum
Seed_treatments           2         2.11449        1.05724       12.05       0.008
Residual                  6         0.52630        0.08772

Total                    11         5.04069


***** Tables of means *****

Variate: Yield

Grand mean   7.149

Seed_treatments          0.           100.          150.
                       6.590         7.256         7.601


*** Standard errors of differences of means ***
Table              Seed_treatments
rep.                      4
d.f.                      6
s.e.d.                 0.2094
```

Figure 21.2 Analysis of variance

where μ is the overall mean of the experimental units, β_i is the *effect* of block i, t_j is the effect of treatment j, and ε_{ij} is the residual for that plot (representing the unexplained variability after allowing for differences between treatments and between blocks).

In this analysis, the residuals are assumed to have independent normal distributions with zero mean and equal variances. The variance ratio of 12.05 for treatments in the analysis of variance table can then be assumed to have an F distribution on two and six degrees of freedom (the degrees of freedom from the treatment and residual lines respectively), leading to the probability value of 0.008 in the right-hand column, and the differences between the means divided by the standard error of difference can then be assumed to have a t distribution with six degrees of freedom (the degrees of freedom for the residual).

The effect t_j of treatment j represents the difference between the mean for treatment j and the overall mean. So when we are assessing whether the treatments are identical, we are actually seeing whether there is evidence that their effects are different from zero.

This way of representing the analysis becomes more useful in experiments when the treatments given to the units may differ in several different ways. For example, we may have several different fungicides to study and we may also want to try a range of different amounts; or we may want to investigate the effect of varying the amounts of several different types of fertiliser; or we may want to see how well different varieties of wheat are protected by different makes of fungicide. Each of these types of treatment is then represented by a different treatment factor, with levels defined to represent the various possibilities. One of the great advantages of a designed experiment is that it allows you to examine several different treatment factors at once. Suppose

```
***** Analysis of variance *****

Source of variation      d.f.          s.s.         m.s.        v.r.       F pr.

Block stratum             2         0.03793      0.01896       0.33

Block.Plot stratum

N                         2         4.59223      2.29611      40.19      <0.001
S                         3         0.97720      0.32573       5.70       0.005
N.S                       6         0.64851      0.10808       1.89       0.127
Residual                 22         1.25683      0.05713

Total                    35         7.51269


***** Tables of means *****

Grand mean   1.104

N                             0          180          230
                          0.601        1.313        1.398

S                             0           10           20           40
                          0.829        1.155        1.167        1.266

N             S               0           10           20           40
0                         0.560        0.770        0.524        0.552
180                       0.894        1.289        1.525        1.545
230                       1.032        1.404        1.454        1.700

*** Standard errors of differences of means ***

Table                     N            S            N
                                                    S
rep.                     12            9            3
s.e.d.                0.0976       0.1127       0.1952
```

Figure 21.3 Analysis of variance

that we have two treatment factors N (nitrogen at levels 0, 180 and 230) and S (sulphur at levels 0, 10, 20 and 40) and we wish to examine all their combinations, again in a randomised complete block design. The factors N and S are said to have a crossed or factorial structure, and we can represent the yield y by the model

$$y_{ijk} = \mu + \beta_i + n_j + s_k + ns_{jk} + \varepsilon_{ijk}$$

We now have three terms to represent the effects of the treatments: the parameters n_j represent the main effect of nitrogen, s_k represent the main effect of sulphur, and ns_{jk} represent the interaction between nitrogen and sulphur.

The analysis of variance table shown in Fig. 21.3 contains a line for each of these, to allow you to decide how complicated a model is required to describe the results of the experiment.

When analysing a factorial experiment we would like to find a simple model to explain the situation. The full model above will estimate the means for the sulphur and nitrogen treatments as shown opposite.

S × N means	N0	N180	N230
S0	0.560	0.894	1.032
S10	0.770	1.289	1.404
S20	0.524	1.525	1.454
S40	0.552	1.545	1.700

=

μ
1.104

+

n_j: N0	N180	N230
−0.503	0.209	0.294

+

s_k	
S0	−0.276
S10	0.051
S20	0.063
S40	0.162

+

ns_{jk}	N0	N180	N230
S0	0.234	−0.144	−0.090
S10	0.118	−0.075	−0.044
S20	−0.141	0.148	−0.007
S40	−0.211	0.071	0.141

It will be much easier to describe what is happening if there is no interaction. The model will then be

$$y_{ijk} = \mu + \beta_i + n_j + s_k + \varepsilon_{ijk}$$

leading to a table of means:

S × N means	N0	N180	N230
S0	0.326	1.038	1.122
S10	0.652	1.364	1.448
S20	0.665	1.377	1.461
S40	0.763	1.475	1.559

=

μ
1.104

+

n_j: N0	N180	N230
−0.503	0.209	0.294

+

s_k	
S0	−0.276
S10	0.051
S20	0.063
S40	0.162

and you will notice that we can decide on the best level of nitrogen without needing to consider how much sulphur is to be applied, and on the best level of sulphur without needing to think about the level of nitrogen on the plot. This is what we mean by saying that the two factors do not interact: the *interaction* assesses the way in which the changes in yield caused by the various levels of nitrogen differ according to the amount of sulphur or, equivalently, the way in which the response to amount of sulphur differs according to the level of nitrogen.

This idea can be extended similarly to three or more factors. These *factorial* arrangements thus have the advantage that we can examine several different types of treatment at once. If there are no interactions we can present one-way tables of means and these will each have the same replication (number of units for each level of the treatment) as they would have had if we had performed individual experiments of this size for each treatment factor in turn. The only difference is that the factorial experiment has fewer residual degrees of freedom, but 22 (above) is ample. More important, by examining the interaction, we can assess how valid our conclusions for each factor are over a range of values of other factors.

Treatment factors need not always have a crossed structure. They can also be nested one within another. For example, we may have several strains of two different species of aphid, Mp and Rp, and wish to examine their esterase levels. Suppose that we have strains $Mp_1 \ldots Mp_4$ and $Rp_1 \ldots Rp_3$ with several individuals of each strain. We will certainly be interested in assessing differences between Mp and Rp. We may also be interested in how much variation there is amongst $\{Mp_1, Mp_2,$

Mp_3 and Mp_4} and amongst {Rp_1, Rp_2 and Rp_3}; that is, whether there is variability of the strains beyond the variability of the individual aphids. The model of interest (assuming that there is no blocking) would then be

$$y_{ijk} = \mu + s_i + st_{ij} + \varepsilon_{ijk}$$

where the parameters s_i represent the effects of the species ($i = 1, 2$), and st_{ij} represent the strain within species effects ($j = 1, \ldots, 4$ for $i = 1$; $j = 1, \ldots, 3$ for $i = 2$).

Notice that the model does not contain a strain main effect. The actual number allocated to each stain is only a labelling; it does not imply any special similarity, for example, between the strain numbered 2 for Mp and the strain numbered 2 for Rp.

OTHER TYPES OF BLOCK STRUCTURE

Sometimes more complicated blocking structures may be required. For example, there may be more than one way of forming the units into groups. Perhaps we need to cater for large fertility trends running both along and across the field; or we may have insufficient pens in an animal experiment to complete the experiment all at once and need to subdivide the animals, from several different breeds, into batches to be examined in successive weeks. One possibility, if we have two blocking factors each with the same number of levels as the number of treatments that we wish to examine, is to use a *Latin square*. An example, for five dietary treatments, is shown in Table 21.1.

Notice that each diet occurs once in each row and once in each column. So we have simultaneously blocked the units by rows (Week), and by columns (Breed). In the analysis we will be able to estimate and eliminate both the row differences and the column differences, leading to a smaller residual mean square, and thus smaller standard errors for differences between the treatment means. The table shows the plan before randomisation. To randomise we need to select a random permutation for the rows and then another one for the columns.

We have now seen two types of block structure. The randomised complete block design has a nested structure with the individual units nested within the blocks, while the Latin square has a *crossed* structure of rows crossed with columns. These operations of nesting and crossing provide the basis for the more complicated arrangements that are sometimes needed for sophisticated trials. For example, the *split-plot* design extends the ideas of the randomised block design to have a further nesting of *sub-plots* within plots. Alternatively, we may have replicated Latin squares (rows crossed with columns, all nested within replicates).

All of these designs can be generated using menus in GenStat for Windows. Further examples can be found in Cochran and Cox (1957), and Payne (2000b, Chapter 4).

Table 21.1 Latin square example

5 × 5 Latin square (before randomisation)	Breed 1	Breed 2	Breed 3	Breed 4	Breed 5
Week 1	Diet A	Diet B	Diet C	Diet D	Diet E
Week 2	Diet B	Diet C	Diet D	Diet E	Diet A
Week 3	Diet C	Diet D	Diet E	Diet A	Diet B
Week 4	Diet D	Diet E	Diet A	Diet B	Diet C
Week 5	Diet E	Diet A	Diet B	Diet C	Diet D

ASSUMPTIONS OF THE ANALYSIS

Analysis of variance assumes, first, that the model is additive; that is, differences between treatment effects must remain the same however large or small the underlying size of the variable measured. So, for example, in a randomised-block design, we are assuming that the theoretical value of the difference between two treatments remains the same within a block where the recorded values are generally low, as in one where the values are generally high. If your design has more than one replicate of each treatment within each block you can check this by fitting block × treatment interactions, but usually this is not possible. An alternative method, which checks for the common form of non-additivity where treatment effects are proportional, is to fit Tukey's single degree of freedom for non-additivity. Non-additivity can cause interactions between treatment factors but, of course, these may also occur for genuine reasons, for example caused by one treatment modifying the mode of action of another.

Secondly, the variance must be homogeneous: the variability of the residuals should be the same at high values of the response variable as at low values. If this assumption does not hold, the standard errors presented will be too large for differences between treatments with low means and too small for differences between larger means, causing incorrect conclusions to be drawn. Homogeneity of variance can easily be assessed by plotting the residuals against the fitted values: if the variance is homogeneous, the residuals should lie within a uniform band.

Thirdly, the residuals are assumed to have independent normal distributions. Non-normality can be assessed by plotting the residuals as a histogram or by plotting the residuals, sorted into ascending order, against values that would be expected from a normal distribution (a *normal plot*). Non-normality is usually also associated with non-homogeneity of variances.

TRANSFORMATIONS

Failures of the assumptions can often be corrected by transforming the data. The transformations described in most textbooks are designed to stabilise the variance (assumption 2); for example, the square root transformation for counts or the angular transformation for percentages. A frequent mistake is to use the angular transformation blindly, without regard to the way in which the percentages have been obtained; it is important to realise that it is appropriate only when they are based on binomial data (for example a number r diseased out of n examined).

However, it is equally if not more important to consider the additivity of the model. Otherwise, as mentioned above, the resulting interactions can make the results difficult if not impossible to interpret.

In some situations, a transformation can be chosen both to provide additivity and to stabilise the variance. With data where the treatments take the effect of a proportionate increase (or decrease), the standard errors will often be proportional to the means; a logarithmic transformation will then correct both aspects. With percentages representing proportions of diseased material, treatment effects are often found to be approximately proportional to the amount infected for low percentages, while for percentages near to 100 per cent they tend to be proportional to the amount uninfected. If the percentages are obtained by visual assessment of areas such as infected parts of leaves, the standard errors tend to show the same pattern: for low percentages the eye tends to examine the amount infected, while nearer to 100 per cent it is the amount uninfected that is assessed. In this situation, a logit transformation, $\log(p/(100 - p))$, would be appropriate.

Further information about model assumptions and transformations can be found in Mead (1988, Chapter 11), Mead and Curnow (1983, Chapter 7) or John and Quenouille (1977, Chapter 14).

GENERALISED LINEAR MODELS

If additivity and homogeneity of variance cannot both be corrected simultaneously by transformation, a generalised linear model should be used (McCullagh and Nelder 1989). However, although these are readily available in statistical systems such as GenStat and GLIM, they do require rather more statistical expertise to specify the models and to interpret the results than in ordinary analysis of variance.

SPATIAL COVARIANCE MODELS

If you have many treatments to compare, as for example in a variety trial, it may by impossible to put one of each into a uniform block. Specialist designs, such as *Alpha* designs, are available for these situations and can be constructed by systems such as GenStat. The analysis uses a rather more complicated method known as REML (Residual Maximum Likelihood). One advantage of this method, however, is that you can model the fertility trends in a more flexible way, by specifying models to describe the covariances between the plots (Gilmour *et al* 1995). This can result in substantial increases in precision. Further details are given in Chapter 5 of Payne (2000*b*), or Chapter 7 of Harding *et al* (2000).

REPEATED MEASUREMENTS

Special care is needed with experiments where the same units are observed at successive times. *Repeated measurements* like these can show complicated correlation patterns, and you may not be able to assume that the necessary *distributional* assumptions hold for analysis of variance (see the section on *assumptions of the analysis*). A statistician should be able to advise on alternative methods such as the analysis of summary statistics, multivariate analysis of variance, the use of antedependence structure, or the modelling of the inter-time correlation structure (see Chapters 5 and 8 of Payne 2000*b*).

CONCLUSIONS

We have illustrated above the three main principles of experimentation (known as the three Rs):

*   *replication*: the need to have more than one unit for each treatment so that you can ascertain the intrinsic level of variability of the units and so decide whether the differences between the treatments go beyond what we might expect to occur by chance;
*   *randomisation*: the need to allocate units to treatments at random, to avoid any biases;
*   *blocking*: ways of grouping the units in order to improve the precision of the experiment.

These concepts, together with the ideas of factorial treatment structure, are fundamental to a successful experiment, whether in agriculture or in any other research area.

REFERENCES

Cochran WG and Cox, GM (1957) *Experimental Designs* (2nd edn) (New York: Wiley).

Dyke, GV (1988) *Comparative Experiments with Field Crops* (2nd edn) (London: Griffin).

Gilmour, AR, Thompson, R and Cullis, BR (1995) Average Information REML, an efficient algorithm for variance parameter estimation in linear mixed models. *Biometrics* **51**, pp 1440–1450.

Harding, SA, Lane, PW, Murray, DM and Payne, RW (2000) *GenStat for Windows* (5th edn) Introduction (Oxford: VSN International).

John, JA and Quenouille, MH (1977) *Experiments: Design and Analysis* (London: Griffin).

McCullagh, P and Nelder, JA (1989) *Generalized Linear Models* (2nd edn) (London: Chapman and Hall).

Mead, R (1988) *The Design of Experiments: Statistical Principles for Practical Applications* (Cambridge: Cambridge University Press).

Mead, R and Curnow, RN (1983) *Statistical Methods in Agriculture and Experimental Biology* (London: Chapman and Hall).

Payne, RW (ed.) (2000a) *The Guide to GenStat, Part 1 Syntax and Data Management* (Oxford: VSN International).

Payne, RW (ed.) (2000b) *The Guide to GenStat, Part 2 Statistics* (Oxford: VSN International).

Pearce, SC (1983) *The Agricultural Field Experiment* (Chichester: Wiley).

22 Survey research

David de Vaus

WHAT IS A SURVEY?

Survey research and questionnaire research are not the same thing. Although questionnaires are frequently used in surveys, there is no necessary link between surveys and questionnaires. There are two distinguishing characteristics of surveys: the form of data and the method of data analysis. Neither of these features requires questionnaire-based data collection: in-depth interviews, observation, content analysis and so forth can also be used in survey research.

Form of data

Surveys are characterised by a structured or systematic set of data that I will call a *variable-by-case data grid*. This involves collecting information about the same variables from a sample of cases. This information is placed in a grid (see Table 22.1) in which each row represents a case (person) and each column represents the variables or information collected about each case.

Method of analysis

While experimental studies rely on control groups, random allocation to groups, and experimental interventions (see Chapter 19), surveys rely on existing variation in the sample rather than creating it with interventions. Surveys also control for the influence of external factors by using statistical controls in data analysis while experiments control external factors by random allocation to control groups (de Vaus, 2001*a*).

DIMENSIONS OF SURVEYS

Units of analysis

Not only are surveys not restricted to questionnaires, but they are also not restricted to studies of individual people. The units about which information is collected (the unit of analysis) may be

Table 22.1 A variable by case data grid

| Cases | Variables | | | |
	Sex	Age (years)	Political orientation	Social Class
Person 1	male	36	progressive	working
Person 2	male	19	moderate	lower middle
Person 3	female	30	progressive	upper working
Person 4	male	55	traditionalist	upper middle
Person 5	female	42	traditionalist	middle

countries, years, organisations, events or some other unit. If a unit of analysis other than a person is used (such as countries) the names of countries would be placed on the side of the data grid and we would collect information pertaining to countries (such as population size, area, density, unemployment rate, literacy rate, life expectancy).

TYPES OF SURVEYS

Descriptive

Social researchers can try to answer two fundamental questions about society. *What* is going on (descriptive research) and *why* is it going on (explanatory research). Surveys can be an effective way of describing a phenomenon and have been used widely for this. Most governments conduct surveys to obtain an accurate description of population size and characteristics (censuses), unemployment levels, expenditure patterns, experience of crime, housing needs, health levels and health behaviours. Repeated descriptive surveys taken over time can describe changes such as changing patterns of family formation and changes in employment levels.

Explanatory

Explanatory surveys try to account for the phenomena they describe. Why are some people poorer than others? Why are people having fewer children? Why is the level of home ownership declining? Our initial, non-empirical attempts to answer these questions are our theories. These speculative theories require testing and these theories guide the design of the survey, the data we collect and the way we analyse the data.

CONTENT

When constructing a survey, we need to identify what sort of information we need to collect. In descriptive surveys we must collect information about the phenomenon we are seeking to describe. This requires being clear about precisely what this phenomenon is. This requires clarification of the concepts implied in the research question. For example, if we want to describe unemployment levels what do we mean by *unemployment*. Are women who are not in the paid workforce because they are looking after young children unemployed? Are students without paid work unemployed? Is a retired person unemployed? What about someone who works only one hour a week? As well as defining our terms, the following questions help focus the description further.

- What is the *time frame* for the description: the present time, some time in the past or are we looking at change over time?
- What is the *location* of the interest: a particular region, a country, a comparison of countries?
- How *specific* is the interest? Do we want to look at a population overall or do we want to break down our analysis into subgroups (such as men *cf* women; young versus old; urban *cf* rural)?

An explanatory survey will need to be clear about:

- what is to be explained (dependent variable)?
- what are the possible causes (independent variables)?
- on which possible causes will the survey focus?
- what are the possible mechanisms (intervening variables) by which the causal factors might produce their effect?

When specifying the content of a survey try to be very clear about the type of information you need. For example, in a survey of individuals the information you require will normally fall into one of the following categories.

Attributes: such as gender, age, class occupation.
Behaviour: what people *do* (such as: hours worked, participation in voluntary groups, alcohol consumption).
Knowledge: what does the respondent know about the topic.
Beliefs: what a person thinks is *true* or *false* (such as: do they believe that capital punishment reduces crime?).
Attitudes: what a person thinks is *desirable* (such as: *should* capital punishment be introduced?).

QUESTIONNAIRE DESIGN

Although survey data can be obtained with other methods, the structured questionnaire remains the most common method of obtaining a structured set of survey data. It is therefore the method of data collection on which I will focus for the remainder of this chapter.

Concepts to questions

In designing a questionnaire the first step is to develop specific questionnaire items for the concepts that are employed in the research question. This involves translating what are often vague and abstract concepts into specific and concrete indicators of the concepts. This process involves 'descending the ladder of abstraction'. This involves:

- defining the concept;
- identifying different dimensions of the concept;
- identifying sub-dimensions;
- developing indicators for these dimensions/sub-dimensions (see de Vaus 2001*b*).

Principles in designing questions

There are at least eight principles to guide the design of questionnaire items (for more detail see de Vaus 2001*b*).

1. *Reliability.* Assuming that the person does not actually change, a reliable question is one to which respondents give the same response on different occasions. Ambiguous or vague wording must be avoided to ensure that respondents would 'read' the question consistently on different occasions.
2. *Validity.* We must be sure that a question actually measures what we say it does. For example, if we ask about church attendance to measure religiousness we must be sure that it actually does measure this concept.
3. *Discrimination.* Explanatory survey analysis relies on variation in the sample of key variables. Good measures should be sensitive to measuring real and meaningful differences in a sample. For example, if you want to look at the effect of heavy work demands on family well-being then the measures of these concepts must be able to tap meaningful differences in work demands and family well-being.

4. *Response rate.* Non-response to questions needs to be minimised both because of the loss of information and the data analysis difficulties it introduces. Intrusive, insensitive, irrelevant or repetitive questions as well as those that are difficult to understand and answer, or have insufficient response categories, can produce frustration and non-response.

5. *Same meaning for all respondents.* If different respondents interpret a question in different ways they effectively answer different questions, thus making the survey analysis largely meaningless. For example, if I use the term 'old people' in a question then respondents will define 'old' in quite different ways and, in effect, be answering different questions.

6. *Relevance.* Each question must earn its place in your survey. For each question ask yourself whether it really is necessary.

7. *Exhaustiveness (inclusiveness).* There must be sufficient response alternatives so that all respondents can answer the question.

8. *Inclusiveness.* The alternative responses should be mutually exclusive so that only one response for each variable is applicable to any respondent.

QUESTION WORDING

Table 22.2 provides a checklist for evaluating questions. An answer of 'yes' to any of the questions in the table indicates that a question requires further revision. These ideas are expanded in the Bibliography (de Vaus 2001*b*, Foddy 1994, Sudman and Bradburn 1982, Bradburn and Sudman 1979, Alreck and Settle 1995).

Response formats

There is a wide variety of response formats in questionnaires. When framing a question you must first decide whether it will be a closed question in which respondents select from a number of preset responses or whether it will be an open question to which respondents frame their own responses. There are advantages and disadvantages to both sorts of questions but, in general, you are best advised to minimise the number of open questions you use (Foddy 1994, Sudman, and Bradburn 1982, Bradburn and Sudman 1979).

With each closed question you will need to decide on a response format. There is insufficient

Table 22.2 Question wording checklist

1. Is the language complex?	9. Can the question be shortened?
2. Is the question double-barrelled?	10. Is the question leading?
3. Is the question negative?	11. Is the respondent unlikely to have the necessary knowledge?
4. Will the words have different meanings for different people?	12. Is there a prestige bias?
5. Is the question ambiguous?	13. Is the question too precise?
6. Is the frame of reference for the question unclear?	14. Does the question artificially create opinions?
7. Does the question have dangling alternatives?	15. Is the question wording unnecessarily detailed or objectionable?
8. Is the question a 'dead giveaway'?	16. Does the question contain gratuitous qualifiers?

See http://www.infopoll.com/tips.htm for a useful set of tips in question design space here to go into each type but see de Vaus (2001b) and Alreck and Settle (1995) for a fuller discussion.

1. *Rating scales.* These require respondents to select one alternative from a set of ordered categories. This format comes in different styles including:
   - Likert scales
   - Numerical rating scales
   - Feeling thermometers
   - Score out of 10
   - Semantic differential.
2. *Rankings.* These require respondents to rank a set of alternatives.
3. *Checklists.* These involve providing a list of items and asking respondents to select all that apply to them.
4. *Selecting between alternative attitudes statements.* This format involves describing alternative attitudes towards some matter and asking which of the attitudes is closest to their own

WHICH RESPONSE CATEGORIES

Number of categories. There is no agreement about how many response alternatives should be provided (Schwarz *et al* 1985).

No opinion and don't know responses. Although some people do not offer these alternatives it is generally desirable to do so since there are many issues to which people genuinely have no opinion. Forcing them to express an opinion where they really do not have one is to create false and unreliable answers (Bishop *et al* 1980).

Including a middle alternative. There is disagreement about whether a middle alternative such as 'neither agree nor disagree' should be provided. While excluding this option stops people 'sitting on the fence' this faces the danger of artificially creating opinions (Presser and Schuman 1980).

Response alternatives

For questions where the response categories can be ranked from high to low in some respect, the websites in Table 22.3 provide some excellent example of well evaluated sets of response alternatives.

LAYOUT AND STRUCTURE OF THE QUESTIONNAIRE

There are five areas to which attention needs to be given when assembling questions into a questionnaire (see Table 22.4 for various sources of questions). The particular ways of dealing with these matters will vary somewhat depending on the way in which the questionnaire is administered (see later discussion).

Table 22.3 Sample sets of response alternatives

Response alternatives
http://www.au.af.mil/au/hq/selc/smpl-h.htm

The intensity of words
http://www.au.af.mil/au/hq/selc/smpl-g.htm

Table 22.4 Sources of questions

Rather than unnecessarily developing new questions it makes sense to use well developed and tested questions that have been used in reputable surveys. The sites below are excellent sources of questions and provide ideas about question format and structure

1. *The Question Bank*
   http://qb.soc.surrey.ac.uk/nav/fr_home.htm
2. *Zeus data base*
   http://zeus.mzes.uni-mannheim.de/ab_data.html
3. *General social survey*
   http://www.icpsr.umich.edu/GSS99/subject/s-index.htm

In addition, many of the online survey design packages and questionnaire design packages include libraries of questions (see Table 22.5). There are also a number of excellent handbooks of collections of questions on a range of topics. References to these collections are available from my website: http://www.social-research.org.

Answering procedures. Ensure that the way in which questions are to be answered is clear (such as circle responses, tick boxes).

Instructions. The questionnaire should include:

- general instructions, such as when to complete, how to return the questionnaire, do not consult;
- section introductions;
- question answering instructions;
- navigational instructions that instruct respondents which question to answer next when they are required to skip questions.

Filter questions. Since some questions may only apply to subsets of respondents it is best to use questions to filter the sample so that respondents are directed to questions that apply to them but skip those that do not apply.

Use of space. In self-administered paper questionnaires, avoid cluttering the questionnaire. Make use of margins, list question responses down the page and leave sufficient room for open-ended questions.

Question order. Question order can affect response rates and the way in which people answer particular questions. There are several general principles in ordering questions.

- Ensure that the flow of the questionnaire makes sense.
- Commence with questions respondents will enjoy answering (easy, factual and concrete and relevant).
- Group related questions together.
- Leave open-ended questions to near the end if possible.
- Introduce a variety of question formats to make the questionnaire interesting.

SOFTWARE FOR PRODUCING QUESTIONNAIRES

The task of questionnaire layout has been made easier by the power of word processors. Specialised software developed for electronic surveys has made the process even simpler. Some of these packages are listed in Table 22.5. This software, for which evaluation versions are available for downloading, can produce both electronic and professional-looking paper questionnaires.

Table 22.5 Internet survey software

Sphinx survey	http://www.scolari.co.uk/frame.html?http://www.scolari.co.uk/best/
InfoPoll Designer	http://www.infopoll.com/designer.htm
SurveyWriter	http://www.surveywriter.com/HomePage.html
Survey Tracker	http://www.surveytracker.com/
SurveyWin	http://www.raosoft.com/products/interform/index.html
Survey Said	http://www.surveysaid.com/

MODES OF QUESTIONNAIRE ADMINISTRATION

Questionnaires can be self-administered or administered by trained interviewers. With the development of computer technologies we now have both 'low-tech' questionnaires that rely on traditional pencil and paper approaches, and sophisticated computer-based 'high-tech' questionnaires. Table 22.6 summarises the main ways in which questionnaires are administered.

The use of particular low-tech and high-tech questionnaires will depend on the methodology for administering questionnaires. There are four main ways in which questionnaires are administered:

1. *Face to face*: administered by a trained interviewer; these may be PAPI or CAPI interviews.
2. *Telephone*: a trained interviewer using CATI techniques and equipment usually conducts these interviews.
3. *Postal*: these self-administered questionnaires are usually PAPI style but some are DBM or CASI-style interviews.
4. *Internet based*: there are two broad ways in which Internet surveys are administered:

   (a) *E-mail* is used to distribute and collect questionnaires. These e-mail questionnaires come in different formats including:

   - plain text questions inserted as part of an e-mail;
   - an e-mail message formatted in HTML;
   - a formatted questionnaire sent as an e-mail attachment;
   - an interactive questionnaire in the form of an executable file can be sent as an e-mail attachment.

Table 22.6 The technology of administering questionnaires

PAPI	Paper and Pencil Interview
CAPI	Computer Assisted Personal Interview
CATI	Computer Assisted Telephone Interview
CASI	Computer Assisted Self Interview
DBM	Disk By Mail interview
E-mail	Plain text in body of e-mail
HTML e-mail	Questionnaire in body of e-mail or as attachment formatted in HTML (Hypertext Mark-up Language – the formatting language of the web)
E-mail with executable questionnaire	CASI/DBM-style questionnaire distributed by e-mail
Web-based HTML survey	Questionnaire written wholly in HTML and distributed via a web based site
Dynamic Web survey	Questionnaire written with a Survey writing software package that has similar interactive features to a CAPI, CATI or CASI questionnaire.

Table 22.7 Online questionnaire design and administration sites

SurveyWriter	http://www.surveywriter.com/HomePage.html
Response-o-matic	http://www.response-o-matic.com/home.htm
Internet – rogator	http://www.internet-rogator.com/htm/make.htm
Instant Survey	http://www.instantsurvey.com/settings/fstPage.asp

(b) *Web pages.* Questionnaires can also be administered through web pages on the Internet. Interactive questionnaires with features similar to those of CAPI and CASI methods are available with Internet questionnaires.

Web-based questionnaires can be designed easily with the aid of special software. Further information about the range of software with which to conduct computer-assisted surveys can be found at http://www.macer.co.uk./rscentral/rscentral.html.

Demonstration and evaluation versions of software are available at many of these sites. Further information about web surveys can be obtained from http://surveys.over.net/method/topics.html.

Web surveys can also be designed and administered online. There are a number of sites where this can be done at no charge. Examples are given in Table 22.7.

ETHICS

Survey researchers should adhere to ethical principles when conducting surveys. The researcher has responsibilities to at least four categories of people.

The public. The responsibility here is to ensure that the survey results are presented fairly in public and to correct any distortions in the way others use your survey results in public.

Clients/sponsors. Researchers should respect the confidentiality and rights of sponsors and not make unwarranted claims about one's expertise or about the value of the techniques that will be employed.

The profession. It is important not to act in ways that will discredit the profession or make it difficult for other researchers in the future to conduct research because of your actions.

Respondents. The responsibilities to respondents involve conducting the survey in such a way as to ensure that:

- informed consent is given by the respondent;
- participation is voluntary;
- confidentiality is protected;
- no harm comes to participants.

The full codes of ethics of a number of different professional organisations provide a much fuller outline of the types of ethical issues that must be taken into account in social science research, and survey research in particular (see Table 22.8).

Table 22.8 Codes of ethics for survey and social science research

American Association of Public Opinion Research	http://www.aapor.org/ethics/
Council of American Survey Research Organizations	http://www.casro.org/casro.htm
American Sociological Association	http://www.asanet.org/members/ecoderev.html
British Sociological Association	http://www.britsoc.org.uk/about/ethic.htm

PRACTICALITIES

When conducting a survey there are many practical issues that need to be built into any proposal or plan. These matters will affect the type of survey you end up conducting. The practical considerations will often mean that the survey you do is not necessarily the survey you want. The real survey may be different from your ideal survey. To assist with covering the practical side of the survey design, ensure that you have answered the following types of questions.

1. Will you realistically have access to the type of sample that your research problem assumes? Will the sample produce the variability on the key variables that you require?
2. What is your sample size? Will the sample size be large enough to test your propositions, to divide it up in order to analyse sub groups and to generalise?
3. What are the difficulties in contacting the sample?
4. How important is it to be able to generalise beyond the sample?
5. What are your time lines? How realistic are these? Be serious!
6. Have you planned for something to go wrong and for most things to take considerably longer than you anticipate?
7. What is your 'Plan B' if your response rate is too low?
8. Have you obtained ethics clearance?
9. Have you established ways in which respondents can contact you?
10. What is your budget?
11. Is the survey a solo or a team effort?
12. Do you have the expertise to conduct the survey?
13. Do you have experts who can give advice and provide feedback?
14. Have you arranged to conduct a pilot test? (You should!).
15. How will coding be conducted?
16. How will data be checked and cleaned?
17. Who will enter data? By what means will data be entered (automatic, manual, optical scan)?
18. Have you thought through how you will analyse the data? Do you have all the questions you require to do the analysis you plan to conduct? Are variables at the right level of measurement for the analysis you plan? Is the sample type appropriate for your data analysis plans (such as probability sample)?

It is not possible to recommend one method of questionnaire administration over others. Each has its strengths and weaknesses and these strengths and weaknesses will be context-dependent. They will depend on your topic, your own skills, resources and time, the characteristics of your sample and so forth.

Rather than urge a particular method of data collection, it is more useful to provide a checklist to guide your choice in the context of your own survey. When comparing the methods for your survey consider how well each is likely to perform in relation to these matters?

Response rates

*   General samples
*   Special purpose samples

Representative samples

- Availability of unbiased sampling frame
- Nature of likely sample bias and relevance of this to study
- Avoidance of refusal bias
- Control over who completes the questionnaire
- Gaining access to the selected person
- Locating the selected person

Effects on questionnaire design

- Ability to handle:
  Long questionnaires
  Complex questions
  Boring questions
  Item non-response
  Filter questions
- Control over order in which questions are read/answered
- Appropriateness in obtaining full text responses to open ended questions
- Special question modules possible
- Enjoyment of completing questionnaire
- Ability to have follow-up questions
- Range of 'stimulus' materials that can be used (e.g. graphics, audio, lists, video)
- Appropriateness for sensitive questions

Quality of answers

- Minimise socially desirable responses

Ability to avoid distortion due to:

- Interviewer characteristics
- Interviewer opinions
- Influence of other people
- Allows opportunities to consult
- Avoids subversion
- Automatic coding (ease and reduction of error)
- Error checking
- Item non-response controls
- Enables anonymity

Implementing the survey

- Ease of finding suitable staff
- Speed of data collection/returns
- Speed of deployment

- Cost
- User friendliness
- Ease of feedback to respondents
- Ability to follow up non-responders
- Ease of use
- Confidentiality and privacy protection
- Accuracy (opportunity for human error)
    respondent
    coder
- Level of automation
- Respondent access to help to clarify questions or answering procedures
- Longitudinal studies
    Respondent tracking
    Piping (also within survey)

BIBLIOGRAPHY

Alreck, P and Settle, R (1995) *The Survey Research Handbook* (New York: McGraw-Hill).

Bishop, G, Oldendick, R, Tuchfarber, A and Bennett, S (1980) Pseudo-opinions on public affairs. *Public Opinion Quarterly* **44** (2), pp 198–209.

Bradburn NM and Sudman, S (1979) *Improving Interview Method and Questionnaire Design* (San Francisco, CA: Jossey-Bass).

de Vaus, DA (2001*a*) *Research Design in Social Research* (London: Sage).

de Vaus, DA (2001*b*) *Surveys in Social Research*, 5th edn (London: Routledge).

Dillman, D (1978) *Mail and Telephone Surveys: The Total Design Method* (New York: Wiley).

Dillman, D (1999) *Mail and Internet Surveys: The Tailored Design Method, 2nd edn* (New York: Wiley).

Fink, A (1995) *How to Sample in Surveys* (Thousand Oaks, Sager: CA).

Foddy, WH (1994) *Constructing Questions for Interviews and Questionnaires: Theory and Practice in Social Research* (New York, NY: Cambridge University Press).

Kalton, G (1983) *Introduction to Survey Sampling* (Beverly Hills: Sage).

Marsh, C (1982) *The Survey Method: The Contribution of Surveys to Sociological Explanation* (London: George Allen & Unwin).

Miller, DC (1991) *Handbook of Research Design and Social Measurement* (Newbury Park: Sage).

Presser, S and Schuman, H (1980) The measurement of the middle position in attitude surveys. *Public Opinion Quarterly* **44**(1), pp 70–85.

Rosenberg, M (1968) *The Logic of Survey Analysis* (New York: Basic Books).

Rossi, PH, Wright, JD *et al* (eds) (1983) *Handbook of Survey Research. Academic Press* (New York: Academic Press).

Schwarz, N, Hippler, H, Deutsch B and Strack F (1985) Response scales: effects of category range on reported behaviour and comparative judgements. *Public Opinion Quarterly* **49**(3), pp 388–395.

Sudman, S and Bradburn, N (1982) *Asking Questions: A Practical Guide to Questionnaire Design* (San Francisco: Jossey Bass).

Measurement

23 Principles of sampling

Peter Lynn

INTRODUCTION

In much research it is necessary to *sample* units for study. Examples include the following.

- A geographer who wishes to estimate the prevalence of a certain plant in a field will not study the entire field but will divide the field into small areas and sample some of those areas.
- A sociologist who wants to ascertain the proportion of the population who have experienced a certain event will not interview the whole population but will select a sample.
- In everyday life you may
    taste your cooking to see if a dish is ready;
    sample cheese before you buy it.

In all of these situations it is important *how* the sample is selected. If the sample is not typical of the total set of units in which you are interested it will fail to serve its purpose.

WHY SAMPLE?

It is usually possible, at least in principle, to study all of the units that form the population of interest to the study. Reasons why this is rarely done are cost, feasibility and quality.

Cost

There is often a real marginal cost associated with the inclusion of each unit of study: the cost of the time of the researcher, experimenter, interviewer, field worker and the cost of equipment and materials. So the budget may constrain the sample size. Even without that constraint, a smaller sample may leave more money for other stages of the project or for other projects.

Feasibility

If a study of the quality of an industrial output involves destruction of the samples, there is no point in studying the entire output. If results are needed by a particular deadline, there may be insufficient time to study all units.

Quality

Concentration of effort on a sample can increase the quality of the research, which may then lead to more accurate results (see the section on bias, variance and accuracy). For example, in an interview survey with a modest sample size it should be possible to recruit a team of highly capable d provide them with personal training and briefing. With a much larger sample it e difficult to find enough high quality interviewers, and it may be infeasible to brief onally. This could adversely affect the quality of data.

e main reasons for sampling are:

Cost
* Feasibility
* Time
* Quality

SAMPLE DESIGN

The procedures and mechanisms that collectively constitute the method of sample selection are known as the *sample design*. At its simplest, a sample design is a *sampling frame* (the list of units from which the sample will be selected), with a specification of the procedures to sample from the frame. In scientific study, the procedures are usually *objective*, with units chosen by a chance mechanism rather than by subjective selection. Thus, if the same sample design is applied repeatedly, it is likely that different units will be sampled each time due to chance.

INFERENCE

Scientific sampling is to provide a means of making *inferences* about the population of interest using observations made on the sample. The observations are collectively called *sample statistics*, whereas the unknown descriptors of the population are called *population parameters*. So, sample statistics are used to make inferences about population parameters. For example, if we observe a sample mean, $\bar{x}$, we might then make an inference about the probability of the corresponding population mean, μ, being within a certain distance of $\bar{x}$. We might decide on the appropriate probability and distance, using information about how the sample was selected and information about the composition of the sample. A particular sample statistic may be called an *estimator* of a particular population parameter. For example, the sample mean might be an estimator of the population mean. The particular value of that sample statistic observed by the study will be called the study *estimate*. Therefore, if the sample mean is 12.6, then 12.6 is the estimate of the population mean.

There are two basic approaches to inference. One is the *design-based* approach and the other is the *model-based* approach. Chapter 10 of Thompson (1992) provides an introduction to similarities and differences between the two approaches, which are described and discussed in Cassel *et al* (1977) and Särndal (1978).

The design-based approach relies on the randomisation present in the design to provide the theoretical basis for estimation. This approach produces estimation methods that are unbiased, and the precision of which can be estimated, without requiring knowledge of the population structure.

With the model-based approach, the researcher must develop a statistical model that adequately describes the distribution of variables. With this method, the sampling mechanism is irrelevant, and the accuracy of estimators depends on the adequacy of the specification of the model. Great care must be taken with this approach. An adequately specified model can prove an impossible goal.

In the remainder of this chapter, we assume application of the design-based approach to inference.

BIAS, VARIANCE AND ACCURACY

Any method of selecting a sample for scientific study should be objective and should result in a *representative* sample (Kiaer 1895). Objectivity is usually interpreted as meaning that the selection method should not permit any subjective influence, and should be *unbiased*. If a sample design is unbiased, then the average value of a sample statistic, across a large number of repetitions of the study, will equal the corresponding population parameter. (Sections 4.3 and 5.1 of Moser and Kalton 1971). This does not mean that the statistic based on the one sample actually selected will necessarily equal the population value. There could be a lot of variation across the different samples that could be selected. This variation is measured by the *sampling variance* (Section 4.3 of Moser and Kalton 1971, and Section 3 of Mohr 1990). The smaller the sampling variance, the greater the chance that the sample statistic based on the one sample actually selected will be close to the corresponding population parameter.

Bias and variance are properties of the sample design, not of the particular sample selected. The complete set of all estimates that could be obtained, corresponding to all the samples that could be selected using the chosen sample design, is known as the *sampling distribution*. A sampling distribution may be summarised in tabular form, or as a histogram or graph. For example, Fig. 23.1 shows three sampling distributions produced by three different sampling designs, all proposed to measure the same thing. Design A produces a symmetrical distribution, centred on the value of the population parameter. Therefore design A is unbiased. Design B has an identically shaped sampling distribution to design A but is not centred on the population parameter. Design B is therefore biased and is inferior to design A if other factors, such as cost and ease of implementation, are equal. Design C also has a symmetrical sampling distribution, centred on the same value as design B, so it is equally biased. However, the distribution is more compact. Design C has a smaller sampling variance than B. So C is superior to B, other things being equal.

One question is left unanswered by Fig.23.1: is design A superior to C? If we consider bias, A is preferable, but if we consider variance, C performs better. The concept of *error* provides a means of answering the question. Error is a property of a particular selected sample not of the sample design. It is simply the difference between the sample estimate and the population parameter. A sensible objective is to minimise the expected magnitude of error. A design can never guarantee an

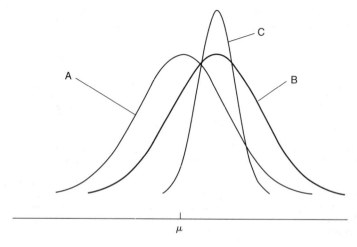

Figure 23.1 Three different sampling distributions produced by three different sample designs, A, B and C, where μ is the population parameter

error-free estimate unless it is unbiased and has zero variance. This can be achieved, using the concept of *statistical accuracy*, a performance criterion that encompasses bias and variance simultaneously.

Accuracy can be measured by a quantity known as *root mean square error (RMSE)*. The RMSE of an estimator can be thought of as a measure of the average magnitude, across the sampling distribution, of the difference between the estimate and the population value: the average error (see Kish 1965, pp 13 and 60 for a precise definition). RMSE might not always be the most appropriate criterion for comparing the desirability of different research designs. In general, however, it is a very useful concept, and has the advantage of ease of interpretation. A biased design with low variance can produce a more accurate estimator than an unbiased design with higher variance.

Another term sometimes used when discussing estimators is *precision*. Precision is simply the converse of variance. A precise estimator is one with low sampling variance, and vice versa. If unbiased designs are being considered, then precision is synonymous with accuracy. In general, precision is only one component of accuracy; bias is the other.

Precision is usually measured by a quantity known as the *standard error* (see Sections 4.3 and 4.4 of Moser and Kalton 1971, for a definition and discussion). For many sorts of unbiased estimators, the standard error has a known and fixed relationship to the area under the curve of the sampling distribution. For example, in most situations the population parameter plus or minus two standard errors will encompass approximately 95 per cent of the area under the curve (see Fig. 23.2). In other words, 95 per cent of the possible samples under the specified design will produce an estimate within plus or minus two standard errors of the true population value. It is this relationship that allows the computation of confidence intervals and the testing of hypotheses (Mohr 1990).

Precision (sampling variance) is determined by three factors: the inherent variation among the population, the sample size, and other aspects of the sample design such as clustering and stratification. The sample size, n, is an important determinant of precision (larger samples yield greater precision) but it is not the only one. In most situations, variance is approximately inversely proportional to n, so doubling the sample size will halve the sampling variance. The number of units in the population, N, is virtually irrelevant. However, it is possible to obtain precise estimators with small n. It is equally possible to obtain imprecise estimators with large n, if the sample is not appropriately designed. It is the *design* of a sample that should give us faith in a study's results. Sample size alone is a fairly meaningless indicator.

Cost is important in the design of a study. It has a valid influence on study design. A main aim

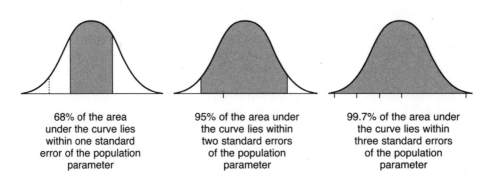

| 68% of the area under the curve lies within one standard error of the population parameter | 95% of the area under the curve lies within two standard errors of the population parameter | 99.7% of the area under the curve lies within three standard errors of the population parameter |

Figure 23.2 Relationship between area under the curve (probability) and distance from the population parameter (width of confidence interval)

of the researcher, although not often stated explicitly, should be to maximise accuracy per unit cost. It is nearly always possible to improve the accuracy of a procedure, but this usually incurs a cost. The task of the research designer is to effect an appropriate balance between cost and accuracy.

NON-PROBABILITY SAMPLING

There are sometimes compelling reasons for a researcher to consider sample designs that involve selecting the more easily accessible units in the population. *Accessibility sampling* is the term for designs where this is the main consideration. Such designs can have cost and administrative benefits and are common in some fields of research. But there is a drawback. There is a risk of bias and the design provides no means of assessing this bias. For example, if the health of fish in a lake was assessed by measuring the first ten fish caught from the most convenient place on the shoreline, the design would be biased if the propensity to be in that part of the lake and to be caught was in any way related to health.

To reduce the risk of such bias, the research may turn to *purposive sampling*. With purposive sampling, the researcher recognises that there may be inherent variation in the population of interest. They attempt to control this by using subjective judgement to select a sample that they believe to be 'representative' of the population. Purposive sampling *can* lead to very good samples, but there is no guarantee that it will. Its success depends on two assumptions:

1. The research can identify in advance the characteristics that collectively capture all variation.
2. The chosen sample will correctly reflect the distributions of these characteristics.

Two factors likely to cause contravention of these assumptions are imperfect knowledge of the population structure, and prejudiced selection. Yates (1935) showed that even experts are generally unable to purposively select an error-free sample.

Accessibility and purposive sampling are often combined, as with quota sampling methods used in some interview surveys (see Chapter 24). However, any design that involves an element of purposive selection is open to criticism. Such designs do not necessarily lead to 'unrepresentative' samples but there is no way to measure the likely quality of the samples. Probability sampling provides the means to do this.

PROBABILITY SAMPLING

Probability sampling or *random sampling* (they mean the same thing) is often thought the only defensible selection method for serious scientific study, unless such sampling is simply not feasible. This is a natural corollary of the design-based approach to inference (see the earlier section on inference).

Probability sampling refers to sample designs where units are selected by some probability mechanism, allowing no scope for the influence of subjectivity. Every unit in the population must have a known and non-zero selection probability. Note that the probabilities need not be equal. The advantages of probability sampling are that it enables the avoidance of selection biases and that it permits the precision of estimators to be assessed, using only information that is collected from the selected sample. Furthermore, because precision can be estimated, this provides a tool for making informed estimates of the likely effect of changes to aspects of the design. Thus, you can choose between competing potential designs, according to precision and cost.

The theory of probability sampling is well developed. Thompson (1992) provides a good introduction with references to more specialised texts. There are practical strategies for implementing probability sampling designs in various fields. For example, see Cochran (1977) or Kish (1965) on surveys; Cormack *et al* (1979) on biological studies; Hohn (1988) on geological studies; Keith (1988) on environmental sampling; Ralph and Scott (1981) on sampling birds; Seber (1982, 1986) on sampling animals; Deming (1960) on business research; Metcalfe (1994) on industrial and engineering research. See also Chapters 19 to 22 of this book.

The simplest form of *probability sampling*, and the one with which other forms can be compared, is *simple random sampling*. This is the design under which every possible combination of *n* units from the population of *N* units is equally likely to be selected. Note that this implies that each individual unit has an equal selection probability. Simple random sampling is therefore *design-unbiased*.

Systematic sampling

Systematic sampling is another design that gives each unit an equal selection probability. The population units are listed and a sample is taken by selecting units at fixed intervals down the list. For example, to sample 100 from a list of 2000 you would generate a random start between 1 and 20 and select that unit and then every 20th unit thereafter until the end of the list was reached. Each unit has an equal chance of selection because each of the 20 possible samples, corresponding to the 20 possible random start points, has an equal probability of being selected and each unit belongs to one, and only one, of those 20 samples. However, it is not simple random sampling because there are only 20 samples that could be drawn. Any other combination of units cannot be selected.

There are two main reasons for sampling systematically. One is administrative convenience. It may be easier for the sampler to count through a list or a set of files than to sample randomly. The other is that systematic sampling incorporates an element of stratification if the list is ordered in a way that is related to the subject of the study.

Stratified sampling

The aim of *stratification* is to guarantee that the sample reflects the structure of the population, at least in terms of one or more important variables. For example, if the sample design for a medical study is to select patients systematically from a list ordered, or stratified, by age, the sample will be certain to reflect the age distribution of the population. If age is related to the variable(s) of interest, this is beneficial. Simple random sampling would not guarantee reflection of the age structure. You might, just by chance, select all the older patients. Stratification can be incorporated within a probability sample design. It does not violate the principle of random sampling.

Stratification can be either implicit or explicit. *Explicit stratification* requires the creation of distinct strata, the determination of a sample size and the selection of a sample from each stratum. For example, the geographical region of interest to a study may be divided into grid squares, each of which would be assigned to one of three strata: densely inhabited, sparsely inhabited and uninhabited. Within each stratum, a simple random sample of grid squares could be selected for study. One advantage of explicit stratification is that it enables the use of unequal sampling fractions, described below.

With *implicit stratification* the sample frame is sorted before it is sampled systematically. The sample size in each stratum is not fixed in advance although it will not vary much. One advantage of implicit stratification is that you can stratify using continuous variables without losing information by having to create broad bands as strata.

Stratification usually brings modest gains in precision (see the earlier section on Bias, variance and accuracy) and is worth doing unless it is prohibitively time consuming and expensive.

Unequal sampling fractions

Sometimes different proportions of units are required in different strata: *unequal sampling fractions*. Explicit stratification is necessary. One reason for unequal sampling fractions is to provide sufficiently large samples for separate analysis in each stratum. For example, in a study of the population of England and Wales, a sample of 2000 people might provide sufficient precision for many purposes. But if separate estimates were required for each of the two countries, the sample in Wales may be too small for estimates to be useful – simple random sampling may select 1900 in England and only 100 in Wales. An unequal sampling fraction could be imposed to ensure a sample of 1725 for England and 275 for Wales, say.

Unequal sampling fractions may be used if it is impractical to give all units an equal selection probability. For example, in line-intercept sampling of vegetation cover, the size of a patch of vegetation is measured whenever a randomly selected line intersects it. This results in large patches having higher probabilities of inclusion in the sample.

Unequal fractions may be used to increase the precision of estimates based on the total sample. This can be achieved by using larger sampling fractions in strata that are inherently more variable (Moser and Kalton 1971, pp 93–99, Thompson 1992, pp 107–108). That this is sensible can be seen by considering an extreme situation where the population falls into two strata, within one of which there is no variation at all. There would be no point in selecting more than one unit from that stratum because knowledge of any one unit confers knowledge of the complete stratum. The sampling fraction should consequently be much higher in the other stratum.

In the examples above, unequal sampling fractions were obtained by specifying an exact sample size for each stratum. Another method is *weighted sampling* in which units in one stratum would have a different probability of selection than units in another. In the study of England and Wales, each person in Wales may have a selection probability three times that of each person in England. To produce unbiased estimates for England and Wales as a whole it is necessary to *weight* the data to restore the correct distribution across the strata, and this can cause a loss in precision.

Multi-stage sampling

It is sometimes desirable to select the sample in two or more stages, to reduce cost or effort. For example, in a survey where people are interviewed in their own homes, a sample of small geographical areas such as postcode sectors or electoral wards may be selected first followed by a sample of addresses drawn from each sampled area. This provides efficient workloads for interviewers, and is much more cost-effective than a sample spread thinly over the whole country. Similarly, a survey collecting data from patients' medical records might first select a sample of GP practices, and then a sample of patients registered at each practice. This reduces the number of practices that need to be contacted, thus easing study administration.

Multi-stage sample designs are efficient solutions in many contexts but they may result in less precise estimators than single-stage samples of the same size. This is because study units within each first stage entity are often less variable than units in the whole population. This increases sampling variance. For example, two people living in the same postal sector, or registered at the same GP practice, may be more similar than two people sampled at random from the whole population, in terms of many variables. The homogeneity of first stage entities can be measured by the *intra-class correlation coefficient*, ρ, (Kish 1965, Section 5.4). The higher the intra-class correlation, the more detrimental it will be, in precision, to cluster the sample.

In multi-stage sampling, the selection probability of each unit will be the product of the probability of selecting the first-stage entity to which the unit belongs and the conditional probability of selecting the unit given that the first-stage entity has been selected. Thus, the relationship between these probabilities needs to be considered carefully when the sample is designed and the probabilities must be recorded carefully to allow appropriate weighting (see the section on weighting below).

CAPTURE–RECAPTURE SAMPLING

The classic use of *capture–recapture sampling* is to estimate the total number of units in a population. There are variants of the technique, but the basic idea is to select a sample, attach an identifying mark to each sample unit, return these units to the population, select another independent sample, and observe what proportion of the second sample has already been included in the first sample. If both samples are truly independent, this proportion should be an unbiased estimator of the population proportion included in the fist sample. Thus, population size can be estimated as the size of the first sample divided by this proportion.

Capture–recapture sampling has been used on many animal populations and on elusive human populations such as the homeless. See Cormack (1979) and Chapter 18 of Thompson (1992) for further discussion.

ADAPTIVE SAMPLING

Adaptive sampling is frequently used to sample rare or elusive populations. It requires an initial selection and the study of a probability sample. Then, whenever a unit exhibits a high or interesting value of the variable of interest, a further sample of units is taken close, usually geographically, to the interesting unit. For example, in a survey of a rare mineral resource, a probability sample of small areas might be studied. Most areas would reveal a zero occurrence of the mineral but where the mineral is found there might be an increased probability that adjacent areas will also host the mineral. This intuitive idea of increasing the study coverage often brings increases in precision.

Adaptive sampling is used in the study of rare animal and vegetation populations, as well as in geology, and in epidemiological studies of human populations. Thompson (1988, 1990 and 1992 chapter 24) provide further discussion.

SAMPLE SIZE

An important element of sample design is the determination of the sample size. As described in the section on bias, variance and accuracy, sample size affects the precision of estimators, although it is not the only element of sample design to do so. This means that if the research can specify in advance the required level of precision, it is possible to determine, at least approximately, the sample size that would be required to deliver that precision. See Barnett (1991, Sections 2.5 and 2.9).

WEIGHTING

Weighting is when a numerical coefficient is attached to an observed value, usually by multiplication, so as to give that value a desired degree of importance. There are several reasons why it may be desirable to *weight* data before analysis. The most common are as follows.

To correct for unequal selection probabilities

If different units in the population had different selection probabilities, sample estimates would be biased unless each sampled unit is given a weight proportional to the reciprocal of its selection probability. For example, in the unequal sampling fractions discussed in the section on probability sampling, units sampled in Wales should be given a weight one-third that of units in England.

To adjust for non-response

If there are some selected units for which no data could be collected (this is common in interview surveys and in medical studies) then sample estimates will be biased if the propensity to respond is related to any of the variables of interest. Non-response bias may be compensated by weighting. This requires some knowledge about the relationship between responding and non-responding units, or between responding units and the total population in terms of some characteristics that may be related to propensity to respond and to variables of interest. There are various ways to develop such weighting. See, for example, Elliott (1991, 1999).

To correct for the effects of sampling variance

The proportion of units (in a random sample) that have a certain characteristic may happen, by chance, to differ greatly from the corresponding population proportion. If the characteristic is believed to be related to variables of interest to the study, the data could be weighted to match the population profile. This will tend to reduce the variance of estimates (whereas the other two motivations for weighting, described above, will tend to reduce or eliminate bias).

Calibration weighting is a term used to describe a class of methods that involve ensuring that the weights used to determine the sample distribution meet certain constraints. A subclass of calibration methods is known as *post-stratification*. This involves weighting a sample to match the known population profile in terms of certain strata and thus has similarities with stratified sampling. Post-stratification and its likely effects are discussed in Holt and Smith (1979). The development of general calibration methods is outlined in Deville and Sändal (1992). In practice, calibration methods will tend to counteract multiple sources of error simultaneously, not just sampling variance. Lundström and Särndal (1999) propose that calibration is appropriate for non-response adjustment, for example.

SUMMARY

Sampling is a complex discipline, yet it is of primary importance in many studies. It is the foundation on which much study is built. For many purposes it is not necessary to be closely familiar with even the few sampling techniques mentioned in this chapter but it is always important to consider how a sample is to be drawn and what effect that sampling method might have on the data. Sampling methods for scientific study should be objective and should maximise the accuracy of estimation, per unit cost, as far as possible. This will require the strict application of appropriate probability selection methods, which will then allow estimation of the accuracy obtained.

The particular sample design issues that are of primary importance vary between disciplines and are discussed in other chapters of this book.

REFERENCES

Barnett, V (1991) *Sample Survey Principles and Methods*, 2nd edn (London: Edward Arnold).

Cassel, CM, Särndal, CE and Wretman, JH (1977) *Foundations of Inference in Survey Sampling* (New York: Wiley).

Cochran, WG (1977) *Sampling Techniques*, 3rd edn. (New York: Wiley).

Cormack, RM (1979) Models for capture-recapture. In Cormack, RM, Patil, GP, Robson, DS (eds) *Sampling Biological Populations* (Fairland, Maryland: International Co-operative Publishing House).

Deming, WE (1960) *Sample Design in Business Research* (New York: Wiley).

Deville, JC and Särndal, CE (1992) Calibration estimators in survey sampling. *Journal of the American Statistical Association*. 87 pp 376–382.

Elliot, D (1991) *Weighting for Non-response* (London: OPCS).

Elliot, D (1999) *Report of the Task Force on Weighting and Estimation*, National Statistics Methodology Series Report No 16, Office for National Statistics (London).

Fisher, RA (1966) *The Design of Experiments*, 8th edn (New York: Hafner).

Hohn, ME (1988) *Geostatistics and Petroleum Geology* (New York: Van Nostrand Reinhold).

Holt, D and Smith, TMF (1979) Post stratification. *Journal of the Royal Statistical Society, series A* 142, pp 33–46.

Keith, L (ed.) (1988) *Principles of Environmental Sampling* (American Chemical Society).

Kiaer (1895) Observations et experiences concernment des denombrements représentifs. *Bulletin of the International Statistical Institute*, 8, book 2, pp 176–183.

Kish, L (1965) *Survey Sampling* (New York: Wiley).

Lundström, S and Särndal, CE (1999) Calibration as a standard method for treatment of nonresponse. *Journal of Official Statistics*, 15, pp 305–327.

Metcalfe, AV (1994), *Statistics in Engineering* (London: Chapman and Hall).

Mohr, LB (1990) *Understanding Significance Testing*. Paper 73 in the series Quantitative Applications in the Social Sciences (Newbury Park: Sage).

Moser, CA and Kalton, G (1971) *Survey Methods in Social Investigation* 2nd edn (Aldershot: Gower).

Ralph, CJ and Scott, JM (eds) (1981) *Estimating Numbers of Terrestrial Birds: Studies in Avian Biology No 6* (Oxford: Pergamon).

Särndal, CE (1978) Design-based and model-based inference in survey sampling. *Scandinavian Journal of Statistics* 5, pp 27–52.

Seber, GAF (1982) *The Estimation of Animal Abundance*, 2nd edn (London: Griffin).

Seber, GAF (1986) A review of estimating animal abundance. *Biometrics* 42 pp 267–292.

Thompson, SK (1988) Adaptive sampling. *Proceedings of the Section on Survey Research Methods of the American Statistical Association*, pp 784–786.

Thompson, SK (1990) Adaptive cluster sampling. *Journal of the American Statistical Association* 85 pp 1050–1059.

Thompson, SK (1992) *Sampling* (New York: Wiley).

Yates, F (1935) Some examples of biased sampling. *Annals of Eugenics* 6 pp 102–213.

24 Sampling in human studies

Peter Lynn

INTRODUCTION

This chapter describes the main issues to be considered when designing a sample for a study of a human population. Sample units may be individual persons or may be groups of people, such as households or families. A common research method used with human subjects is the interview survey and much of the discussion is about sampling for interview surveys. The central issues are similar for any research that collects data directly from the selected sample. Important sampling issues for other research methods will be mentioned. These have much in common with interview surveys.

Much of this chapter refers specifically to studies in the United Kingdom, particularly the section on sampling general populations. Some of the issues may be similar for research in other countries but you should seek the advice of a local expert.

IMPORTANT CONSIDERATIONS

Target population

Before you embark on the design of a sample, think carefully about the definition of the population about which you intend to make inferences. This is the *target population* (Chapter 23 describes the concept of inference). For example, consider a study about the attitudes of parents towards schools. Is the study concerned only with parents who currently have a child in school? Or are the views of those whose children will soon be starting school also relevant? And what about those whose children have recently left school? How should the study treat foster parents and other carers? Are you interested only in schools that cater for a particular age range? Is the study about all schools? Or only state schools? What about grant-maintained schools? Are you attempting to represent the whole of the United Kingdom? Or Great Britain? Or England and Wales?

Only when you have defined the population of interest *precisely* will you be able to work out the best way to sample it. Then, if you realise that it is not possible to give all members of the population a chance of selection, you must restrict the *survey population* more than the target population. You should make this distinction explicit and acknowledge it in your thesis. Consideration of the nature of the excluded part of the target population may lead you to conclude that you cannot reasonably make inferences about the target population but that, instead, you should make statements only about the survey population. See Section 3.1 of Moser and Kalton (1971) for further discussion of the problem of defining the population.

Efficient fieldwork

Much research involves visits to members of the sample to collect information from them. For example, you might interview people, or measure them, or observe certain behaviour. You therefore need to consider, and perhaps control, the geographical location of the sample.

For example, for large scale interview surveys it is common to select a sample of small areas, such as postcode sectors, and then a sample of addresses within each. It is possible to sample the areas so that, by taking an equal number of addresses in each area, you will have an equal-probability sample (see the following section on clustering). Then the number to sample within each area can be set to provide an efficient workload for one interviewer, bearing in mind the amount of work that one interviewer may want to do.

Even if you are doing all the fieldwork yourself, you will want as large a geographical spread of the population of interest as possible. This may be achieved by sampling some small areas and then concentrating your sample of people within those areas. It is better to use a probability sample, rather than purposive selection, for the reasons given in Chapter 23.

Fieldwork efficiency for some research methods is not related to the geographical distribution of the sample. An example is where the data are to be collected at a central point using a self-administered postal questionnaire or the telephone.

Clustering

The samples from sample designs where the study subjects are concentrated in several small areas are called *clustered* samples. Samples may be clustered in ways other than geographical, although geographical clustering is the most common form. Some degree of geographical clustering can be achieved indirectly, by sampling first-stage entities that provide some implicit clustering of study subjects, even though the geographical boundaries of the entities may overlap.

For example, in a study of hospital outpatients, it is likely that most outpatients will live close to the hospital where they were treated. If several hospitals are sampled at the first stage, the resultant sample will be clustered even though it might contain a few people who live a long distance from the hospital they attended.

In the rest of this chapter, for simplicity, first-stage entities within a sample design will be called *areas*, although the arguments apply equally to other sorts of first-stage entities.

Multi-stage sampling (see Chapter 23) is a necessary, but not sufficient, pre-requisite for clustered sampling. There is usually a trade-off between the reduced costs achieved with a clustered design and reduced precision.

Multi-stage designs should result in equal probability samples. The two simplest ways to achieve this are:

1. Select an area with equal probabilities and then select individuals with equal probabilities.
2. Select areas with probability proportional to size (*PPS sampling*: see Lynn and Lievesley 1991, pp 16–17) and then select individuals with probability proportional to the reciprocal of the selection probability of the area to which they belong.

The first method uses the same sampling fraction in each area so the sample size will vary across areas in proportion to the population sizes. In the second method, the same number of individuals is selected in each area so the fraction is inversely proportional to the area population size. The second method is preferable, for fieldwork planning and for statistical efficiency, but it is not always possible as a suitable measure of size for each area must be known in advance.

Samples of the general population in the United Kingdom are typically clustered within administrative areas, such as electoral wards or polling districts, or areas defined by postcodes such as postal sectors (Lynn and Lievesley 1991, Bond and Lievesley 1993). The choice of clustering unit is often influenced by the choice of sampling frame (see the section on sampling frames).

Stratification

If you need to over-sample some sub-groups of the population so that you can analyse them with reasonable precision, then the sub-groups must be identified before sample selection. There may be other reasons to stratify (see Chapter 23) so you must consider carefully what stratification factors are available and how they should be used.

SAMPLING FRAMES

The list of population members from which a sample is drawn is known as the *sampling frame*. The frame may have a physical existence, such as a printed list or a computer file. Alternatively, it may result from the application of a sampling method. In this section, we discuss the important properties of a sampling frame or sampling method. These are:

- no omissions (up-to-date);
- no ineligibles listed;
- no duplicates;
- frame units correspond to study units;
- units are uniquely and fully identified;
- frame permits stratification and clustering;
- easy and inexpensive access;
- familiarity.

These properties are discussed in more detail by Lynn and Lievesley (1991, Section 2.3). These characteristics of a frame will not always be attainable, as lists and records used in frames may have been compiled for purposes different from the purpose of the study.

The frame should completely cover the target population. However, there may be omissions because the frame was not designed to include all of your study or because some people have been excluded for other reasons. Reasons for omissions should be investigated and careful consideration given to the extent that they might bias the results of your study.

The frame should not include individuals who are not part of your target population, otherwise your results may be distorted or, at best, you may have to expend some time identifying and excluding ineligible sampled cases. Similarly, duplicate entries may introduce bias unless the number of entries for each individual is known.

Ideally, the units listed on the frame should correspond exactly with the study units. If this is not the case, there should be a known linkage to enable calculation of selection probabilities. For example, to sample households, addresses are usually selected from a frame such as the Post Office's file of addresses (see the following section on sampling general populations). There is not always a unique one-to-one link between an address and a household, but field workers can establish the number of households at each sampled address and whether each sampled household could have been selected via any other address.

The information on the frame should be sufficient to identify unambiguously each sampled individual and allow easy location on the ground. If this is not the case, it may be worth looking for supplementary information from other sources, such as better quality address details, before starting field work.

For multi-stage sampling, the frame must identify suitable areas. Preferably, these should be areas for which there is also information available for stratification. The frame should be inexpensive and easy to use and there are advantages in using a frame that has already been used as a sampling frame on previous occasions. You can learn from previous experiences and minimise the possibility of nasty surprises.

SAMPLING GENERAL POPULATIONS

Populations that might be of interest to particular studies can broadly be classified as either *general* or *special*. There is no precise definition of the difference between the two but a general population can be thought of as one that includes a large proportion of the total population in the geographical area of interest to the study, perhaps a quarter or more. This would include 'all adults', 'all households with a telephone', 'all married women'. A special population would be a smaller proportion of the total. It may be called a *minority* population.

Methods commonly used to sample general populations are quite distinct from those used to sample special populations. In this section we discuss the former; in the following section, the latter.

Address-based sampling

General population sample designs in the UK usually involve the selection of addresses followed by the identification of relevant individuals associated with each selected address, using some clear definition of association. This is because there are no comprehensive lists of individuals available from which to sample directly in this country. The one exception is the electoral register, which is used to sample electors but it has a rather biased coverage of adults as a whole.

The two lists most commonly used as sampling frames of addresses in the UK are the Postcode Address File (PAF) and the Electoral Register (ER). An outline follows of these two frames and how they might be used. See Lynn and Lievesley (1991, chapter 3) for further details. Council tax lists are also used sometimes but generally for local studies, as they can be accessed only through local authorities. Area sampling (Kish 1965, pp 301–358) is another way to sample residential addresses and is commonly used in North America. It has no advantages in Great Britain where good lists of addresses exist. A general population sample can also be selected by non-probability methods, such as quota sampling. These methods are generally easier and cheaper to implement than probability methods but have the serious defects described in Chapter 23.

The ER is a list of all people eligible to vote and includes the name and address of each person. It is compiled annually by each local authority district (see Hickman 1993). Because it includes addresses, it can be used as a frame of addresses rather than individuals. This is its most common use as its coverage of addresses is better than its coverage of individuals (Smith 1993, Foster 1993). However, about 5 per cent of inhabited residential addresses are not listed on the ER and this can introduce bias. Coverage is particularly poor for some ethnic minorities, people who have moved recently, people aged 20 to 24, and inner London. The main advantage of the ER is that addresses can be selected with probability proportional to the number of registered electors. This can be efficient if you want a sample of individuals, rather than households, and do not want to select more than one individual at an address.

The PAF is a computerised list of every address to which the Post Office delivers mail in the UK. It is split into two files: *large users* and *small users*. The latter is the one used to sample residential address, although it includes some non-residential property too. The PAF contains no information about the occupants at each address so the only way to sample addresses is with equal probability. The main advantage of the PAF over the ER is greater coverage of residential addresses: only 1 per cent or 2 per cent are missing. It is also generally more up-to-date than the ER and, because it is computerised, complicated and large samples can be drawn with relative ease. The PAF is available free of charge from the UK Data Archive at the University of Essex for academic research purposes. Alternatively, samples can be commissioned from computer agencies, although their charges may be high. ER samples can be drawn by hand from public documents at either the National Statistics Library, in Titchfield, Hampshire, or the British Library in London. Alternatively, one computer agency, CACI Ltd, markets a computerised version of the ER, although this omits a small percentage of ER entries.

Telephone number sampling

If you intend to survey by telephone, it is not advisable to start by sampling addresses as described above. Neither PAF nor the ER includes telephone numbers, so these would have to be obtained via directory enquiries or some equivalent commercial look-up service. It is unlikely that you would succeed in finding telephone numbers for more than half of the sampled addresses, leading to severe coverage problems.

Instead, telephone numbers should be sampled directly. Published phone books should not be used as a sampling frame, as the high incidence of unlisted (ex-directory) numbers in the UK can introduce considerable bias. Instead, a sampling method that gives a known chance of selection to all working numbers should be preferred. This can effectively be done by generating random numbers within ranges that are in service: a procedure known as *random digit dialling*. This approach has been feasible in the UK only in recent years (Nicolaas and Lynn, forthcoming). Alternative ways to sample telephone numbers include *plus-digit sampling* and *list-assisted sampling* methods (Collins 1999).

SAMPLING SPECIAL POPULATIONS

Broadly there are three methods to sample a special, or minority, population:

1. Screening a general population sample
2. Sampling from an existing administrative list
3. Constructing a sampling frame.

A brief description of each follows. There is fuller treatment in Hedges (1978) and Kalton and Anderson (1986).

Screening a general population sample

Screening involves the selection of a sample of addresses, as you would for a general population sample, and then checking each sampled address (called a *screen interview*) to identify members of the population of interest. Those identified can then be interviewed. This process can involve a large amount of work. Its viability depends largely on the incidence of the special population in the general population. For example, if each of only 1 per cent of addresses contains a member of the special population, then to find 300, say, you would need to screen 30 000 addresses. If the incidence were 10 per cent you would need to screen only 3000.

The amount of detail that needs to be collected in the screen interview is important. In some situations it may be possible to screen by methods other than personal interviewing, such as with a postal questionnaire or by telephone. *Screening errors* could also be important, particularly if the definition of membership of the special population is complicated. If the screening questions are designed to be conservative, in the sense that some people identified as eligible turn out to be ineligible when the detailed data are collected by the main study instrument, then some effort will have been wasted in interviewing these *false positives*. On the other hand, if the questions are tightened to minimise the risk of false positives, some eligibles might be missed. These are *false negatives*. This could introduce bias. A balance has to be struck.

Sampling from an existing administrative list

It is sometimes possible to identify an existing list that is adequate as a frame. However, there may be problems of access that have to be negotiated carefully. The main problems to confront when you use an existing list are those of coverage (omissions and ineligibles) and selection probabilities (duplicates). A clustered sample for fieldwork efficiency may be difficult to design, as administrative files are often inflexible. Sometimes a choice must be made between the use of an imperfect existing list and the screening of a general population sample. For example, it might be possible to use the DVLA (Driver and Vehicle Licensing Authority) files of registered keepers of motorcycles to sample motorcycle riders. But a keeper is not the same as a rider. Some people will keep more than one motorcycle each and will be listed more than once. On the other hand, there are around one million motorcycles in Britain so it might be feasible to screen a general population sample, although it would be expensive.

Constructing a sampling frame

It may be possible to construct a frame where none exists. Perhaps several existing lists, each of which covers part of the population of interest, could be combined. *Snowballing* techniques (Goodman 1952) may be used to expand the frame. The main problem could be to assess the completeness of the constructed frame. When you combine lists, you should pay special attention to overlap, with duplicate entries on the combined list.

It may not be necessary to construct a frame of the individuals of interest if a frame can be constructed of first-stage units that can be sampled before enumeration of individuals within each sampled unit. For example, it would be an enormous task to identify all families who live in bed-and-breakfast accommodation in a particular area and to list them. It might, however, be possible to identify and list all bed-and-breakfast *establishments*, a sample of which could be drawn, and to identify eligible families in each.

WEIGHTING

As described in Chapter 23, study data should usually be weighted, for several reasons. With general population samples, different units will usually have different selection probabilities. This will certainly be true if the design is to select addresses and then to sample one person at each address. In this situation, people who live alone will have a greater chance of selection than those in multi-person households. The data should be weighted to correct the imbalance (see Lynn and Lievesley 1991, Chapter 4).

In studies of human subjects, there will almost always be some non-response. If the sampling frame provides some information about each individual, this information could be used to develop weighting to adjust for non-response. Even if the frame does not contain any useful information, as with the general population frames of addresses, it may be possible to obtain some basic details about non-respondents as well as respondents, by observation in the field. For example, variables related to housing type and area characteristics could be observed. If variables observed for all sample members are related to the propensity to respond, and also to survey measures, then the information can be used to reduce non-response bias (Elliott 1991, Lynn 1996).

General population samples can also be compared with external population data, such as the decennial census of population. If discrepancies are apparent, weighting can be used to adjust the sample profile. If discrepancies can be assumed to be caused by non-response bias or by sampling variance then weighting is an appropriate remedy. However, you should be careful when you compare your data with external data. Differences, even quite subtle ones, in the definitions used, question wording and data collection mode, can produce an artificial outcome to your analysis. In this situation, weighting might do more harm than good by introducing biases.

REFERENCES

Bond, D and Lievesley, D (1993) Address-based sampling in Northern Ireland. *Journal of the Royal Statistical Society (series D: The Statistician)* **42**, pp 297–304.

Collins, M (1999) Editorial: sampling for UK telephone surveys. *Journal of the Royal Statistical Society Series A*, **162**, Part 1, pp 1–4.

Elliot, D (1991) *Weighting for Non-response* (London: OPCS).

Foster, K (1993) The electoral register as a sampling frame. *Survey Methodology Bulletin number 33* (London: OPCS).

Goodman, LA (1952) On the analysis of samples from k lists. *Annuals of Mathematical Statistics* **23**, p 632.

Hedges, B (1978) Sampling minority populations. In Wilson, M (ed.) *Social and Educational Research in Action* (London: Longman).

Hickman, M (1993) *Compiling the Electoral Register 1992* (London: HMSO).

Kalton, G and Anderson, D (1986) Sampling rare populations. *Journal of the Royal Statistical Society Series A* vol 149 65–82.

Kish, L (1965) *Survey Sampling* (New York: Wiley).

Lynn, P (1996) Weighting for Survey Non-Response. In *Survey and Statistical Computing 1996* Banks, R *et al* (eds) (Chesham: Association for Survey Computing).

Lynn, P and Lievesley, D (1991) *Drawing General Population Samples in Great Britain* (London: National Centre for Social Research).

Moser, CA and Kalton, G (1971) *Survey Methods in Social Investigation* 2nd edn (Aldershot: Gower).

Nicolaas, G and Lynn, P (forthcoming) Random digit dialling in the UK: viability revisited. *Journal of the Royal Statistical Society Series A*.

Smith, S (1993) *Electoral Registration in 1991* (London: HMSO).

25 Sources of population statistics

Jonathan Smith

INTRODUCTION

The population statistics considered in this chapter relate to the numbers of people in given areas and their basic demographic characteristics (such as age, sex and marital status). The main focus is on UK population data: the Census, intercensal population estimates and estimates of population in future years (projections). We shall also look at international sources for use in comparative studies.

Population statistics that are combined during research and analysis need to be on a comparable basis. It is important to be aware of potential sources of incompatibility. Population data can refer to different geographical areas or different points in time, they can be on different population bases or they may have been produced using different methodologies. Users of population statistics need to consider all of these aspects before collecting and processing data to avoid misleading results.

One of the most significant enhancements in recent years in the publication of demographic data has been the increasing importance of electronic data formats, in particular with regard to the Internet. Websites can provide a huge amount of information about data and methodologies as well as links to related sites of interest. They are fast becoming the first point of reference for many researchers.

CENSUS OF POPULATION AND HOUSING

By far the most comprehensive exercise in the collection of population data is the Census. In the UK, the Census is taken in ten-year intervals: the last three were taken in 1981, 1991 and 2001. It involves a comprehensive enumeration of the population compiled directly from information given by each individual at a snapshot in time. As well as providing high quality direct information about the population, the data provide a baseline that can then be used to produce population estimates and projections during the intercensal period.

A range of information is available from the Census at individual and household level. International requirements and longitudinal comparability mean that the main demographic questions are always included (such as age, sex, housing). While a primary function of the Census is to give population information in small areas, cross-classified by other key variables, it also enables the collection of information on a broader range of socio-economic topics. These included, in 2001, the following:

- Usual resident population
- Age and gender structure
- Living arrangements (single, married, cohabiting, divorced)

- Migration (usual address a year ago)
- Country of birth, ethnic group and religion
- Limiting long term illnesses, general health and provision of care
- Economic activity, occupation and industry
- Hours worked
- Information on students
- Academic and vocational qualifications
- Professional qualifications
- Distance and method of travel to work
- Travel to work patterns
- Socio-economic classifications
- Housing type, tenure and landlord
- Composition of household (size, relationships within household)
- Rooms, amenities, central heating and floor level
- Possession of car/van.

One of the main features of the 2001 UK Census is improved access to output material, resulting from the *Census Access Project* and increased reliance on electronic forms of publication. Standard local area statistics are available free over the Internet.

Standard local area statistics consist of key statistics, standard tables and Census area statistics. These are aimed at different users and are explained below. Further products, including samples of anonymised records (SARs), and migration and workplace statistics are also available.

Key statistics

The 2001 key statistics provide data on around 300 of the most significant variables from across the Census. They are designed to facilitate comparison between areas, and to complement the more detailed standard tables. A printed version of the key statistics is available at local authority level and above. Electronic versions are also available.

Standard tables

Standard tables are designed to meet customers' requirements at ward level and above. They are centred on six major topics:

- demographics;
- culture;
- health;
- labour market;
- accommodation;
- communal establishments.

Theme tables provide cross-classified variables. Unlike data produced for the 1991 Census, the standard tables for the 2001 Census are published in electronic form as standard, although there will be a print-on-demand service.

Census area statistics (CAS)

Census area statistics are based on the standard tables and are for output areas (the lowest geographical area used in the Census) as well as higher level standard geographies. These tables are broadly similar to the small area statistics (SAS) supplied from the 1991 and earlier Censuses. Where possible, the 2001 CAS are comparable with the 1991 SAS. Because output areas are smaller than the geographical units used in standard tables (the target size for output areas in England and Wales and Northern Ireland is 100 to 125 households, in Scotland it is 50 households), the level of detail is reduced to maintain confidentiality.

Ad hoc data requests

Non-standard outputs can be obtained from Census customer service at the ONS (Office of National Statistics) and from the relevant authorities in Scotland and Northern Ireland (see contacts list below). Such requests may be necessary for researchers with less standard data needs or methodological queries.

Legislation dating back to the 1920s is aimed at maintaining the confidentiality of individuals with regard to the information they supply in the Census. Disclosure control measures are therefore in place so that data supplied will not enable users to identify disclosure information about individuals.

CENSUS RESEARCH

The diversity and accuracy of Census information stimulates a large amount of research. The ONS publishes its own research on topics of particular interest. For example, the 1991 Census included an ethnicity question on which a series of analytical volumes were produced.

SARs

Samples of anonymised records (SARs) are also available following the Census. This resource is useful for micro-level analysis within the constraints of the Census principle of confidentiality.

There are two files within the SARs. The individual file is a 2 per cent sample of individuals living in private and communal accommodation. This may be enhanced to a 3 per cent sample in the 2001 SAR. Within these files, data are available on a wide range of variables including age, sex and accommodation. Again, the 2001 SARs may be enhanced by bringing down the minimum population size on which records are available from 120 000 (as in 1991) to between 60 000 and 90 000.

A second household file is based on a smaller 1 per cent sample. These data provide a full range of Census variables, although at a much higher level than the individual SARs. In 2001, Government Office Regions (GORs) replaced the Standard Statistical Region (SSR) as the principal geographic unit for the household sample.

The most up to date information about SARs is available from the Census and Microdata Unit at the University of Manchester, which is responsible for providing this information. Its website includes useful contacts, news and information on current research using this source (see list of contacts).

Academic users can access these data sets as long as they (and their institution) agree to not pass on the data to unauthorised users and to respect the condition of confidentiality.

POPULATION ESTIMATES

Because the Census is held at only ten-year intervals, researchers have to use estimates of population during the intercensal period. The ONS produces mid-year population estimates, referring to 30 June each year. These intercensal estimates are published approximately one year in arrears.

The estimates are produced routinely for each of the countries within the UK (England, Wales, Scotland and Northern Ireland) and are based on the most recent Census with an allowance for under-enumeration in the Census. The *cohort component* method is used. This updates the previous mid-year estimate, adding births, subtracting deaths over the past year and allowing for net migration. A technical guide to the methodology used is available on the ONS website.

The ONS can provide the size of the resident population by age (quinary groups, age last birthday), gender and location. Marital status is also available for England and Wales and for Scotland, although not Northern Ireland.

Intercensal estimates are available at the following locations:

* government office regions (GORs);
* counties;
* metropolitan districts;
* London boroughs;
* county district and unitary authorities;
* health authorities.

Estimates for England and Wales are available on CD-ROM/disk, via the Internet at http://www.ons.gov.uk (on the StatBase database) and from the ONS. For Scotland and Northern Ireland, enquires should be made to the General Register Office and the Northern Ireland Statistics and Research Agency respectively.

POPULATION PROJECTIONS

The official population projections in the UK, be they at national or sub-national level, are trend based. They represent scenarios without sudden or substantial shifts in the assumptions of mortality, fertility and net migration.

National population projections

The national level projections are produced by the Government Actuary's Department (GAD) for the UK, England, Scotland and Northern Ireland, in consultation with ONS and the Registrar Generals for Scotland and Northern Ireland, and the National Assembly for Wales. Projections are broken down by single year of age up to 90 years, and gender. They are primarily for a 25-year period from the base year, although longer term projections are also included. The national projections are available as a reference volume, CD-ROM, via the Internet on the GAD website www.gad.gov.uk and by request.

Sub-national projections

Projections at below national level for England are produced by ONS. Long term projections are produced roughly every three to five years and project 25 years from the base year. They are produced in consultation with local authorities and other users. Long term projections are not produced immediately before the Census since the base population is subject to change shortly after Census estimates become available. Short term projections are generally produced every second year in which long term projections are not produced, and project ten years from the base. They are updates on the long term projections, and are primarily produced for the Department of Health (DH); there is no consultation with local authorities. Sub-national projections are produced by the same geographical areas as mid-year estimates.

Long term sub-national projections for England are published as a reference volume, on CD-ROM, on the Internet via StatBase (the ONS database for national statistics, http://www.ons.gov.uk) and by requests. Short-term projections appear in the ONS publication *Population Trends*, on the Internet and by request.

Sub-national population projections are published for Scotland by the General Register Office for Scotland (GROS), for Wales by the National Assembly for Wales (NAW), and for Northern Ireland by the Northern Ireland Statistics and Research Agency (NISRA).

INTERNATIONAL COMPARISONS

National trends can be compared between countries. The following sources may help.

Source	Format	Area	Available statistics
United Nations Population Projections	Paper	Global	Total population (by age group and gender), TFR, CDR, Net migration, Time series (50 years backwards and forwards)
Eurostat *NewCronos Database* – www.eurostat.com[1]	Internet	Europe	Time series data on population (by gender and age), fertility (by parity and age of women), mortality, migration
Council of Europe – Recent Demographic Developments in Europe	Paper	Europe	Total population (by age and gender), population pyramids, total births, abortions, TFR, net reproduction rate, mean age at childbirth, mean age at first marriage, live births by order, international migration, natural increase, life expectancy, longitudinal data
World Factbook – www.odci.gov/cia/publications/factbook	Internet	Global	Total population, age structure, growth rates, net migration, life expectancy, IMR, ethnicity, TFR
World Population Datasheets – www.worldpop.org	Internet	Global	Total population, density, birth rates, population policy, CBR, CDR, TFR, IMR, %Married, %over 65, %Urban, Projections 2025 and 2050

TFR = Total Fertility Rate, IMR = Infant Mortality Rate, CDR = Crude Death Rate, CBR = Crude Birth Rate.
[1] Password may be required for more specific requests.

When making comparisons across countries, be aware that differences in methodologies may affect results.

CONCLUSIONS

Sources of population statistics in the UK have become increasingly accessible in recent years. With the increasing move towards Internet access, this will continue. CD-ROMs and paper copies (where still available) should be found in university and local libraries. Data in this format can also be found at The Stationary Office and at the national statistics offices listed below.

CONTACT DETAILS FOR POPULATION STATISTICS

Office for National Statistics
Census Customer Services
Census.customerservice@ons.gov.uk
Tel: +44 (0)1329 813 800
Fax: +44 (0)1329 813 587

Population Estimates
Pop.info@ons.gov.uk
Tel: +44 (0)1329 813 281
Fax: +44 (0)1329 813 295

Migration and Sub-national Population Projections Unit
Subnatproj@ons.gov.uk
Tel: +44 (0)1329 813 865
Fax: +44 (0)1329 813 295

Office for National Statistics
Segensworth Road
Titchfield
Hampshire PO15 5RR
www.ons.gov.uk

Government Actuary's Department (National Population Projections)
projections@gad.gov.uk
Tel: +44 (020) 7211 2640

New King's Beam House
22 Upper Ground
London SE1 9RJ
www.gad.gov.uk

Samples of anonymised records

The Census Microdata Unit
ccsr@man.ac.uk
Tel: +44 (0)161 275 4721
Fax: +44 (0)161 275 4722

Manchester University
Manchester M13 9PL
www.les1.man.ac.uk/ccsr

The Stationary Office Publications Centre
Tel: +44 (0) 20 7873 0011
PO Box 276
London SW8 5DT

Northern Ireland

Northern Ireland Statistics and Research Agency
Dmb.nisra@dfpni.gov.uk
Tel: +44 (0) 28 9034 8132
McAuley House
2–14 Castle Street
Belfast BT1 1SA

Scotland

Customer Services
customer@gro-scotland.gov.uk
Tel: +44 (0) 28 9034 8132
Population Statistics Branch
General Register Office for Scotland
Ladywell House
Edinburgh EH12 7TF

Wales

Demographics Section
Glyn.jones@wales.gov.uk
Tel: +44 (0) 2920 825 058
National Assembly for Wales
Cathays Park
Cardiff CF10 3NQ

26 Interviewing

Mark Hughes

INTRODUCTION

Interviews play an important part in the lives of most people. While there are similarities between research interviews and other interviews (for example job interviews) there are also differences. As a researcher, you need to be rigorous and methodical whilst doing research interviews (subsequently referred to as interviews). The aim of this chapter is to introduce you to interviewing and the choices that you will need to make if you use interviewing for your research.

The chapter starts with a discussion of the appropriateness of interviewing as a research method. The different types of interview and interview questions are introduced and this is followed by a discussion of interviewing as a process. Analysis of interview data is discussed in terms of a five-stage model. The chapter ends with a summary in the form of a series of key questions and answers.

It is not easy to define an interview because of the variety of types of interview. The following is a useful starting point.

> *The purpose of interviewing is to find out what is in and on someone else's mind. We interview people to find out from them those things we cannot directly observe.*

(Patton 1990)

The central theme throughout the chapter will be that there is no one best way to conduct an interview. You should choose those methods that are most appropriate to your particular project. In considering the appropriateness of this method of data gathering, it is worth considering the strengths and weaknesses of the method.

RATIONALE FOR INTERVIEWING

The appropriateness of interviewing on a particular project may be considered in terms of the strengths and weaknesses of this form of data collection (Marshall and Rossman 1999).

Strengths of interviewing

The strengths of interviewing are:

- face to face encounter with informants;
- large amounts of expansive and contextual data quickly obtained;
- facilitates cooperation from research subject;
- facilitates access for immediate follow-up data collection for clarification and omissions;
- useful for discovering complex interconnections in social relationships;

- data are collected in natural setting;
- good for obtaining data on non-verbal behaviour and communication;
- facilitates analysis, validity checks, and triangulation;
- facilitates discovery of nuances in culture;
- provides for flexibility in the formulation of hypotheses;
- provides background context for more focus on activities, behaviours and events;
- great utility for uncovering the subjective side, the *native perspective* of organisational processes.

Weaknesses of interviewing

The weaknesses of interviewing are:

- data are open to misinterpretation due to cultural differences;
- depends on the cooperation of a small group of key informants;
- difficult to replicate;
- procedures are not always explicit or depend on researcher's characteristics;
- data often subject to observer effects;
- obtrusive and reactive;
- can cause danger or discomfort for researcher;
- depends especially on the honesty of those providing the data;
- depends greatly on the ability of the researchers to be resourceful, systematic and honest, to control bias.

The strengths demonstrate why the interview is a favoured method of data gathering for social scientists. In particular, the emphasis upon cooperation with research subjects and an emphasis upon the *native's perspective* are important elements for the social scientist.

This position can appear contradictory to the natural scientist's concerns with objectivity and hard facts. However, within the weaknesses of interviewing, some of the problems of working with accounts of people's subjective experiences become apparent. This polarised depiction does not fully acknowledge the diversity of disciplines that have employed the method: accountancy, sociology, anthropology and medicine.

TYPES OF INTERVIEW

In deciding upon the type of interview, the phrase 'continuum of formality' (Grebenik and Moser 1962) captures the options open to interviewers. The informal conversational interview is at one end of the continuum and the closed quantitative interview is at the other end. Patton (1990) defines four types of interview and their strengths (+) and weaknesses (−).

Informal conversational interview

Questions emerge from the immediate context and are asked in the natural course of things: there is no predetermination of question topics and wording.

  (+) Increases the salience and relevance of questions.
  (−) Different information collected from different people with different questions.

Interview guide approach

Topics and issues to be covered are specified in advance, in outline form. Interviewer decides sequence and wording of questions in the course of the interview.

(+) The outline increases the comprehensiveness of the data and makes data collection systematic for each respondent.

(–) Important and salient topics may be inadvertently omitted.

Standardised open-ended interview

The exact wording and sequence of questions are determined in advance. All interviewees are asked the same basic questions in the same order.

(+) Respondents answer the same questions, thus increasing comparability of responses. Data are complete for each person on the topics addressed in the interview.

(–) Little flexibility in relating the interview to particular individuals and circumstances.

Closed quantitative interviews

Questions and response categories are determined in advance. Responses are fixed: respondent chooses from among these fixed responses.

(+) Data analysis is simple. Responses can be compared directly and aggregated easily.

(–) Respondents must fit their experiences and feelings into the researcher's categories. May be perceived as impersonal, irrelevant and mechanistic.

These different interview types offer a range of options for the researcher. At the outset of research, informal conversational interviews can be effective for refining and tightening the focus of your research. As the research progresses, more standardised forms of interview can be used.

It is possible, within an interview, to use more than one type of interviewing style. For instance, a personal preference is not to use too structured an approach at the beginning of an interview. The type of interview must be appropriate for your project. The structured nature of the closed quantitative interview may be inappropriate for interviewing a senior person within an organisation, but could be appropriate if you want to compare the views of 50 employees.

Three permutations of the above are worth considering when selecting the most appropriate method for your particular research.

Telephone interviewing

Telephone interviewing keeps costs down if respondents are geographically spread out. However, it may prove difficult to develop a rapport over the telephone.

Group interviewing

Group interviewing might be used when the respondents are part of a group or when the collaboration of the respondents in the research is an objective (for a discussion of group interviewing see Mullings 1985).

Elite interviewing

An elite interview is a specialised treatment of interviewing that focuses on a particular type of respondent. Elites are considered to be the influential, the prominent and the well-informed people in an organisation or community (Marshall and Rossman 1999).

INTERVIEW QUESTIONS

While the content of the interviews will depend upon the particular research and the interview type, the following ideas may aid the creative process. Patton (1990) suggests that there are six kinds of questions that can be asked of people:

- Experience/behaviour questions: what a person does or has done.
- Opinion/value questions: to understand the cognitive and interpretive processes of people.
- Feeling questions: to understand the emotional responses of people to their experiences and thoughts.
- Knowledge questions: to discover factual information the respondent has.
- Sensory questions: questions about what is seen, heard, touched, tasted and smelled.
- Background/demographic questions: to identify characteristics of the person being interviewed.

Each of these questions can be asked in the present, past or future tense. Do not place too much emphasis upon questions about the future as this requires an element of crystal-ball gazing.

INTERVIEW PROCESS

Ackroyd and Hughes (1981) place interviewing within context and provide a fascinating account of the interview process. They challenge the position that methods are more or less tools. The tools play an important role in the conduct of research, but have little meaning if divorced from the context of the research. This leads to the following suggestion for good interviewing.

> *That is the prescription for good interviewing should be read as a set of propositions on how the interviewer and the respondent should interact to achieve the aims of scientifically collecting verbal data.*

(Ackroyd and Hughes 1981)

We can think of the interview as a process. While the process may vary with the interview type and the setting, the successful interview involves a series of linked activities rather than a single event.

Stage 1: preparations

Access to interviewees is likely to influence interviews (Bell 1999, Buchanan *et al* 1988). Respondents may start to form impressions about you when first introduced to the research. In this sense, the interview process begins before any questions have been asked. There are frequent warnings in the methods literature about the demands interviewing makes upon time (Wragg 1980 and Bell 1999). These pragmatic considerations should not be overlooked, particularly in terms of preparation time required.

For an effective interview you should

- gather background information on host organisations;
- check interview guides;
- check tape recorders;
- have maps of locations;
- plan to arrive on time.

Stage 2: introductions

Variables such as, age, race, gender and social class have been identified as bearing upon interviews. This is expressed by Kane (1990) as:

> ... *the closer the interviewer is to the respondent in class, sex, age and interests, the greater chance the interviewer has of being successful.*

This is an ideal position, rather than a prerequisite for interviewing.

Body language plays a significant role in interviews. The respondent will be observing your body language and you will be observing the body language of the respondent. At this stage, friendly smiles are important to allay any fears of a forthcoming inquisition.

At the outset of the interview, there is a need to establish the purpose of the interview. While the research will have been introduced at the time of setting up the interview, this non-threatening material can make for a neutral starting point.

The research interview may be a new experience for the respondent. Whenever possible it is worth agreeing the format of the interview with the respondent. Respondents usually agree to your format, but you should ask.

Stage 3: the uneven conversation

The conventional social rule of 'you speak, then I speak' is suspended. The interviewer's role should be to listen.

> *The most important thing a researcher should remember to do in an interview is to listen. Interviews are primarily a way to gather information, not a conversational exchange of views.*
>
> (Howard and Peters 1990)

Sometimes a respondent gives a misleading impression, which is not necessarily intentional. Whyte (1982) has identified three explanations for this: ulterior motives, a desire to please the interviewer and idiosyncrasy.

Respondents occasionally give answers to questions which you might challenge in the course of a conventional conversation. However, part of the uneven conversation is about listening to the respondent's view. There is a need for neutrality that is effectively captured by Patton.

> *Rapport is a stance* vis-à-vis *the person being interviewed. Neutrality is a stance* vis-à-vis *the content of what that person says.*
>
> (Patton 1990)

Such a view of the interview process allows the necessary rapport to develop without the interviewer introducing personal bias.

Stage 4: the ending

To end an interview would initially appear straightforward. However, if sufficient rapport has developed during the interview, an abrupt exit becomes impossible and undesirable.

Questions can send out subtle signals. A useful question at the end of the interview is to enquire: *are there any questions you would like to ask?* As well as signalling the conclusion of the interview, such a question sometimes leads to further information being provided.

Stage 5: after the interview

Great emphasis is placed upon field notes (Patton 1990), particularly those notes made immediately after the interview. Contact summary sheets and data accounting sheets (Miles and Huberman 1994) provide a vehicle for the summary of the main points of the interviews and to check that research questions have been addressed.

Interviews can be intense experiences, requiring complete attention and frequent thinking on your feet. The disclosure of personal details presents a considerable responsibility, but can leave you feeling exhausted. There can be a feeling of uneasiness after interviews, which it is difficult to rationalise. This stems from the respondents opening up and apparently sharing their inner thoughts. After opening up these areas to gain the information, the researcher disappears. A letter of thanks can demonstrate appreciation for the time the respondent provided for the questions. Also, it is in the research tradition of helping to keep the door open for future research (Bell 1999).

RECORDING INTERVIEW DATA

Before you conduct an interview, you should decide how your interviews will be recorded. Three possible options are: note taking, tape recording or a combination of the two. Do keep in mind that the respondent may not allow you to tape record the interview.

The following personal example highlights the significance of this choice. I had obtained access to seven senior managers at the head office of a large organisation. At the outset of one of the interviews, I asked if I could tape record the interview. The manager agreed and we conducted the interview with the tape recorder running. We concluded the interview and went for lunch. Over lunch, the manager confided that he would have answered questions very differently if the tape recorder had not been present. Instead of portraying a successful organisation, he would have described the low morale and problems within the organisation.

The following questions should help to determine which form of recording is appropriate for your research.

- How sensitive are the issues you wish to address? If the roles were reversed, would you feel comfortable being tape recorded?
- Do you have the ability to record the interview in note form?
- Does the type of interview that you are adopting require you to make notes to act as probes about certain topics as they arise?
- Do you have the resources to have the tape recordings transcribed? This can prove very costly in terms of your own time or paying somebody to transcribe the interviews.

If you decide to use tape recorders, the following supplementary notes may be useful.

Buchanan *et al* (1988, p. 61) found refusals to allow tape recording to be rare, describing tape recorders as now 'accepted technology'. While respondents agreed to be tape recorded there were times when the tape recorder was switched off and they spoke off-the-record (Howard and Sharp 1989).

While there can be a strong desire to use tape recorders from the start of the interview, the recorders can make respondents suspicious. Consequently, it is often necessary to avoid using the tape recorder for at least the first five minutes. During this time the tape recorder remains out of sight.

In terms of transcription, Patton (1990) offers a series of helpful tips on how to keep transcribers sane. Alternatively, Buchanan *et al* (1988) provide a strong rationale for typing your own transcripts.

ANALYSING INTERVIEW DATA

While there may be a desire to partition analysis from the conduct of interviews, Miles and Huberman (1994), among others, encourage interweaving analysis and data collection. They suggest that there are five main stages to qualitative data analysis, and that the researcher has a range of options to conduct each stage.

1. Collect the data
2. Data reduction
3. Data display
4. Draw conclusions
5. Verify findings

By interweaving data collection and data analysis, it is possible to test the effectiveness of your interviewing and make amendments where necessary.

Silverman (1993) in his book, subtitled *Methods for Analysing Talk, Text and Interaction*, is critical of much work done in this area, but offers a range of methods that can be used.

SUMMARY

Here are some key questions to consider when you use interviews as a method of data collection.

What is the rationale for interviewing?

The strengths of interviewing as a method of data collection include the following:

*   face-to-face encounter with informants;
*   obtains large amounts of contextual data quickly;
*   useful for discovering complex interconnections in social relationships;
*   data are collected in natural setting;
*   good for obtaining data on non-verbal behaviour and communication;
*   great utility for uncovering the subjective side, the native's perspective of organisational processes.

What types of interview exist?

Patton (1990) identifies four main types:

1. Informal conversational interview
2. Interview guide approach
3. Standardised open-ended interview
4. Closed quantitative interviews

Variations include telephone interviewing, group interviewing and elite interviewing.

What type of questions can be asked?

- experience/behaviour questions;
- opinion/value questions;
- feeling questions;
- knowledge questions;
- sensory questions;
- background/demographic questions.

What are the implications of considering interviewing as a process?

The interview process has the following broad stages:

1. Preparations
2. Introductions
3. The uneven conversation
4. The ending
5. After the interview

If you consider each of these stages, your interview should enable you to gather the data you require.

How should I record the interview data?

- tape recorder;
- notes;
- tape recorder and notes.

What options exist for analysing interviews?

There are many options, but it is important to consider analysis as the five linked stages mentioned previously.

1. Collect the data
2. Data reduction
3. Data display
4. Draw conclusions
5. Verify findings

POSTSCRIPT

People's accounts of aspects of their lives can be fascinating, as each respondent has his or her own unique story to tell. You must be interested in people if you are to conduct effective interviews.

> *I'm personally convinced that to be a good interviewer you must like doing it. This means taking an interest in what people have to say. You must yourself believe that the thoughts and experiences of the people being interviewed are worth knowing.*

(Patton 1990)

In this chapter, I have introduced the main tools in the interviewer's toolkit and introduced the interview process. However, for this particular research method you, as the interviewer, are an integral element.

REFERENCES

Ackroyd, S and Hughes, JA (1981) *Data Collection in Context* (London, Longman).

Bell, J (1999) *Doing Your Research Project: A Guide for First Time Researchers in Education* (Milton Keynes: Open University Press).

Buchanan, D, Boddy, D and McCalman, J (1988) Getting in, Getting on, getting out and getting back, In Bryman, A (ed.), *Doing Research in Organisations* (London: Routledge).

Grebenik, E and Moser, CA (1962) Society: problems and methods of study. In Welford, AT, Argyle, M, Glass, O and Morris, JN (eds), *Statistical Surveys* (London: Routledge and Kegan Paul).

Howard, K and Peters, J (1990) Managing management research. *Management Decision* **28**(5).

Howard, K and Sharp, J (1989) *The Management of a Student Research Project* (Aldershot: Gower).

Kane, E (1990) *Doing Your Own Research* (London: Marion Boyars).

Marshall, C and Rossman, GB (1999) *Designing Qualitative Research* (Newbury Park: Sage).

Miles, MB and Huberman, AM (1994) *Qualitative Data Analysis: An Expanded Sourcebook* (Beverley Hills: Sage).

Mullings, C (1985) *Group Interviewing* (University of Sheffield: Centre for Research on User Studies).

Patton, MQ (1990) *Qualitative Evaluation and Research Methods* (Beverley Hills: Sage).

Silverman, D (1993) *Interpreting Qualitative Data: Methods for Analysing Talk, Text and Interaction* (London: Sage).

Whyte, WF (1982) Interviewing in field research. In Burgess, RG (ed.), *Field Research: A Sourcebook and Field Manual* (London: George Allen and Unwin).

Wragg, EC (1980) *Conducting and Analysing Interviews*, Rediguide 11 (Nottingham University).

27 Problems of measurement

Jim Rowlands

LOOKING FOR TROUBLE

In any programme of research involving measurement, it is essential to consider critically, at the outset, the likely quality of the data that the system of measurement will provide. No amount of data analysis will save the situation if the data are unsound or insufficiently informative.

Always try to identify and counteract sources of *bias* that may distort the picture. For example, in a study of a certain disease in which measurements on a group of diseased individuals are to be compared with measurements on a control group of individuals who are free of that disease, if it is possible that the control group has its own peculiarity and so is not representative of the general disease-free population then an observed difference between the groups may not mean what it appears to mean. If nothing is done about this beforehand, such as selecting the control group from the disease-free population at random, then the conclusions of the study may be unsound and will be open to challenge.

If the output of a system is measured over a period of time and two measured variables move together during that period, such that one is high when the other is high and low when the other is low, then it will be impossible to determine which variable has the greater effect on the output. The two variables are said to be *confounded*. It is possible for the effect of a measured variable to be confounded with the effect of some unconsidered variable. For example, if the level of a stimulus is increased gradually over time, then the changes in the response may not be due to the changes in the stimulus. They could be due solely to the action of some other variable that happens to be changing with time. One countermeasure is to randomise the time order in which the different levels of the stimulus are applied. The question of whether an unconsidered variable is in play can then be investigated by comparing the graph of the response plotted against time with the graph of the response plotted against the levels of the stimulus.

Try to ensure that the *information content* of the data set will be sufficiently high for its intended purpose. It is important to appreciate that merely increasing the number of measurements will not necessarily achieve this. For example, in a study of the effects of a number of variables on the thickness of an extruded material, eight strips of material were produced. Each strip was produced under a different combination of settings of the variables. Subsequently, thickness was measured with negligible error at frequent intervals along each strip, so creating a sizeable data set. The investigator was disappointed to find that the results shed little light on the question of which variables influence thickness. Doubling or tripling the number of thickness measurements made on each strip could not help; quite enough was known about the thickness profiles of the eight strips already. What were needed were more strips. The root of the problem was that setting up the extruder to produce material under a given set of conditions was an error-prone exercise, so that each set-up would produce a strip with a somewhat different average thickness even under the same nominal conditions. A pilot study in which a small number of strips were produced under the same set of conditions, with the extruder being set up afresh each time, would have revealed this and prevented puzzlement later.

It is easier to guard against problems that complicate the interpretation of results, such as bias and confounding, for some types of investigation than for others. At one end of the spectrum are experimental studies in which the system under study is set up and controlled by the investigator. At the other end of the spectrum are pure observational studies (Cochran 1983) where the investigator has no control over the collection of the data. This type of study can arise in an industrial context. Experimenting on an industrial plant in full-scale production is usually out of the question. On the other hand, massive amounts of data may be provided on many variables by automatic measuring devices. Unfortunately, the information content of such data can be very low even when every measuring device is operating satisfactorily. Continual compensatory adjustments made by operators or by automatic controllers can cause confounding between key variables. By contrast, the data may have nothing to say about the effects of some other key variables because the operating policy is to hold these constant throughout.

Another consideration is the *sampling rate*. This can be set too high. Values of measurements on the same variable taken closely together in time can be highly correlated. If this is so, then the amount of data to be analysed can be reduced without serious loss of information by working with a sub-sequence of the stream of measurements. A simple graphical method can be used to examine the correlation between successive measurements. This is the construction of a scatter plot of the time-ordered sequence of measurements against the same sequence offset by one time unit. For example, seven successive time-ordered measurements such as 6.2, 6.5, 8.4, 5.0, 9.0, 9.9, 9.7 yield the six points (6.2,6.5), (6.5,8.4), (8.4,5.0), (5.0,9.0), (9.0,9.9), (9.9,9.7) on the scatter plot. Figure 27.1(a) shows such a scatter plot in a case where there is little or no correlation between successive measurements, while Fig. 27.1(b) shows a case where successive measurements are highly positively correlated.

It is best not to take measurements provided by other people entirely on trust. Always investigate how they were really obtained. In one investigation it was discovered that values of pressure recorded on a data sheet were in fact eyeballed averages obtained by viewing six separate pressure gauges simultaneously. In another investigation, measurements that should have been made at

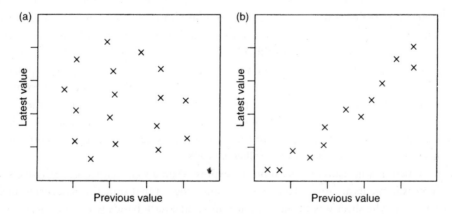

Figure 27.1 Scatter plots showing (a) no correlation, and (b) high positive correlation, between successive time-ordered measurements

three different times of the day were found to have been made all at the same time. Also, important information may not be made available because no one thought to give it and the researcher did not think to ask for it. In one case, flow rate, which turned out to be a key variable, was not included on the data sheet. The rate had to be estimated using measurements of pressure and viscosity and Poiseuille's formula. Only later was it discovered that flow rate was being measured directly and routinely with comparatively little error. In another case, an investigation of the strength of a material made little progress until it was discovered that the recorded strength was actually the average of longitudinal strength and transverse strength. The material had no obvious grain but it was found that these two strengths behaved quite differently. Consequently, their average had little meaning.

WHAT SHOULD I MEASURE, EXACTLY?

The choice of what to measure is not always straightforward. Ideally, the measurement should

- characterise the property or phenomenon of interest;
- be easy to obtain;
- be largely error-free.

The final choice usually represents what is felt to be the best compromise between these three requirements.

Special subject matter knowledge is often needed in order to satisfy the requirement that the measurement should characterise the phenomenon of interest. Always try to speak to an expert about what it is best to measure before making an irrevocable decision. The aim of an experimental programme described by Grove and Davis (1992) was to study *submarining* in car crashes, where the lap portion of the seat-belt rides up and crushes the abdomen of the wearer. As Grove and Davis remark, it would have been highly inefficient merely to record at each trial whether submarining occurred or not. Instead, the investigators measured a number of characteristics known to be associated with the tendency to submarine. One such characteristic was the angle (in radians) that the wearer's back makes with the vertical at the moment of maximum restraint. It is unlikely that someone unfamiliar with the subject would have thought to measure this variable.

The crashes in the seat-belt study were in fact simulated on a computer. Therefore, to ensure the correctness of the results it was necessary to calibrate the simulation model using data obtained from a limited number of real crash tests carried out on dummies under various conditions. The use of calibration curves (or surfaces) is a feature of many measurement processes. For example, the concentration of a chemical that is difficult to measure directly might be obtained indirectly by using a calibration curve that relates the value of an easily measured surrogate response, such as electrical resistance, to the concentration of the chemical. The calibration curve is constructed in the first place by measuring the surrogate response at standard concentrations of the chemical. The scientific challenge is to find a surrogate response that is specific to the quantity of interest. For a discussion of the statistical aspects of calibration curves, such as the construction of confidence intervals, see Mandel (1984) or Carroll *et al* (1988).

It can happen that measurements cannot be expressed on a well-defined quantitative scale or that such measurements are unavailable. For example, a defect that sometimes occurred in a type of transparent acrylic sheet was the appearance of parallel dark bands when the sheet was lit at an angle. The number of dark bands per unit length was easily measured but it would not matter how many bands there were if they were not dark, that is if they were invisible. Consequently, the characteristic of most interest was the darkness of the bands. In principle, the degree of darkness could have been measured on a continuous scale by referring it, directly or indirectly, to some physically meaningful standard but such a measure was not available at the time of the study. Instead, darkness was assessed on an ordered classificatory scale. The scale values chosen were zero (no bands visible), one (bands just visible), two (bands quite dark) and three (bands very dark). Sheets were produced under a number of different conditions. Each one was then inspected visually and assigned to one of the categories zero, one, two or three. Once all the sheets had been classified in this way, the complete data set consisted of the counts for the four categories for each set of conditions.

Classificatory data should not be analysed as if they consisted of measurements made on a well-defined scale even if, as was the case in the above example, the categories can be arranged in a meaningful order. Special methods of analysis are required. For further reading see Siegel (1956), Maxwell (1961), Dobson (1983), McCullagh and Nelder (1989).

In subject areas such as education or the behavioural sciences, researchers are on the safest ground when attention is confined to classificatory data. Much progress has been made since the nineteen sixties but early attempts at meaningful quantification in these areas were often unsatisfactory. A familiar example is IQ testing. The testing procedure produces a partial ordering of the subject population but it is not clear what it actually measures. For further reading, see Roberts (1979) and Michell (1990).

It may be necessary to measure more than one property or response so as to characterise the feature of interest, that is, the complete measurement may be a vector. This was the case in the seat-belt study discussed above. Another example is provided by the measurement of colour. Any particular colour is characterised by the values of three quantities, conventionally denoted by L, A and B. These are related to the electromagnetic spectrum. A polar transformation of L, A, B gives a characterisation of the colour in terms of its hue, chroma and intensity.

For some kinds of measuring device, the output is not a vector but a curve on a graph. The graph can be difficult to interpret but the method of principal components can be used to analyse the curve and describe the results. See Church (1966).

FALLING INTO ERROR

A series of measurements of a fixed quantity T made under constant conditions will usually vary to some extent. In fact, if the measurements do not vary this may well be an indication that the system of measurement lacks sensitivity. If the series is extended indefinitely then the average or *mean* $\bar{x}$ of the measurements x can be expected to settle down to some constant value μ. The measuring device or method of measurement is said to be *unbiased* if $\mu = T$, so that the measurements cluster around the correct value. Otherwise, the device is said to have a *bias* equal to $\mu - T$.

Comparisons of different quantities involving the *differences* of measurements will not be affected by the existence of a constant measurement bias but, in general, it is important to detect and estimate bias when it exists. If the variation in a run of measurements of a fixed quantity T is not too great then the value of $\bar{x}$ will quickly stabilise. Then, if the value of T is known, the value of $\bar{x} - T$ will give a good indication of the bias of the system of measurement in the region of T.

Youden (1962) discusses how measurement bias can arise as the aggregate of small non-random errors associated with the individual components of a measuring device and describes efficient strategies, known as *weighing designs*, for identifying the most important sources of these errors.

It is good practice to monitor the stability of the measurement system by carrying out short

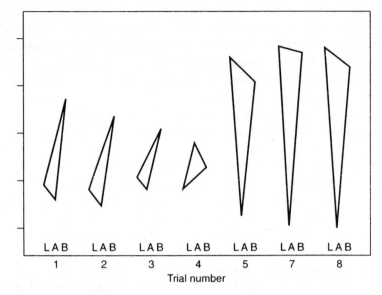

Figure 27.2 Time plot of successive L, A, B colour measurements of the same item

runs of repeat measurements of a reference quantity at regular intervals. Instability may appear over the long term, such as a trend in the results indicating an increasingly serious bias and the need for re-calibration, or it may appear within a single run of repeats. At one manufacturing company, the same item was passed repeatedly through an online colour-monitoring device. The device measured the item's colour in terms of L, A and B at each pass. The values of L, A and B are displayed simultaneously on the time plot shown in Fig. 27.2. The result of each pass is presented as a triangle in which the A-vertex is offset horizontally to the right of the L-vertex by a fixed amount and likewise for the B-vertex. This graphical presentation of the results shows clearly that the device was unreliable.

A measure of the variation in a set of *n measurements* is the *variance* s^2 whose formula is

$$s^2 = \frac{1}{n} \sum (x - \bar{x})^2$$

Unlike the *range*, which is the difference of the largest and smallest measurements in the set, the variance does not tend to increase in size if more measurements are added to the set. The *standard deviation* is the square root of the variance. It is preferable to the variance as a measure of variability in that it has the same units as x.

If the standard deviation is too large then the *precision*, that is the resolution or limit of detection, of the system of measurement will be adversely affected. For example, if there is a need to measure the diameters of fine fibres to the nearest micrometre but the standard deviation is $0.5\,\mu m$ then the desired precision will not be truly attainable. With this standard deviation and assuming no bias, a single measurement whose value is $10\,\mu m$, for instance, could easily have arisen either from a fibre whose diameter is $9\,\mu m$ or from one whose diameter is $11\,\mu m$.

This begs the question of what data should be used in the calculation of the standard deviation. The guiding principle is that the standard deviation should be calculated from measurements of the same nominal quantity made in circumstances where the usual sources of error are allowed to operate. For example, the measurement system should be set up afresh between successive measurements, so that set-up error can make its contribution to the calculated standard deviation. If this is not done then the calculated value is likely to be far too small and will give a false impression of experimental error.

GETTING THE PICTURE

Usually, much of the information contained in a data set is obscured by the detail of the individual values. Data summaries are produced to extract this information and present it in a digestible and useable form. The calculation of the mean $\bar{x}$ of a homogeneous data set, that is one obtained under constant conditions, may be viewed as a way of arriving at a value that typifies the set. Calculating the standard deviation s then gives some indication of the degree of variation around this typical value.

One method of summarisation that sacrifices less information than merely representing the data set by its values of $\bar{x}$ and s is the construction of a *frequency table*. Table 27.1 shows a frequency table that summarises the results of 2608 experimental trials reported by Rutherford and Geiger (1910). Each trial consisted of counting the number of alpha particles emitted from a bar of polonium during an eight minute interval. The table shows, for example, that exactly two particles were emitted during 383 intervals while 11 or more were emitted during only 6 intervals. With the data summarised in this way, a *chi square* test could be used to check the theory that radioactive emissions occur purely at random. (Cramer 1951)

A frequency table may be constructed for measurements made on a continuous scale by counting the number of results that fall in each of a number of non-overlapping arbitrarily chosen *class-intervals*. Table 27.2 shows a frequency table constructed from 550 roughness measurements of a

Table 27.1 Frequencies of intervals containing k alpha particles

k	0	1	2	3	4	5	6	7	8	9	10	≥ 11
Frequency	57	203	383	525	532	408	273	139	45	27	10	6

Table 27.2 Frequency table of 550 roughness measurements (lowest trough to highest peak in μm) of a ship's hull

Roughness (μm)	Frequency
47.5–57.4	7
57.5–67.4	24
67.5–77.4	63
77.5–82.4	42
82.5–87.4	57
87.5–92.4	85
92.5–97.4	78
97.5–107.4	70
107.5–117.4	46
117.5–127.4	26
127.5–137.4	14
137.5–207.4	25
207.5–277.4	13

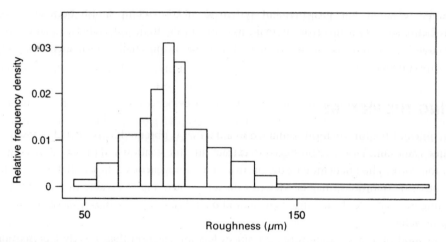

Figure 27.3 Histogram of 550 roughness measurements of a ship's hull. Vertical scale chosen so that total area is unity.

ship's hull as given by Metcalfe (1994). A pictorial representation of this frequency table is the *histogram* shown in Fig. 27.3. It is important to note that the essential feature of a histogram is that the area of each rectangle is proportional to the corresponding class-frequency. It is this that enables the histogram to convey the shape of the distribution of the measurements.

Often, there is not enough data to allow a histogram to be constructed or a less detailed picture of the distribution is all that is required. In either case, a *box and whisker plot* may be used. Here, the central 50 per cent of the ordered data set is represented by a rectangular box and the whiskers are lines drawn from the ends of the box to the largest and smallest results in the set. Finally, the box is divided in two by the *median*, that is, by the middle value of the ordered data set.

Figure 27.4 compares three sets of results obtained under three different conditions A, B and C, by comparing their box and whisker plots. The results are degrees of contamination expressed as percentages and there are 16 results in each set. Despite the wide spread of results, it appears that condition A is preferable to B and C.

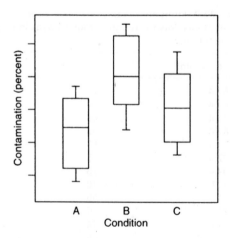

Figure 27.4 Box and whisker plots comparing three sets of 16 results obtained under conditions A, B and C respectively.

It should be noted that means should not be calculated if the data are purely classificatory because addition is not properly defined in that case. In the food industry, for example, taste is usually assessed by using a panel of tasters. Each member of the panel awards each recipe a score on an ordered classificatory scale. The results should be summarised by quoting the median score of each recipe or, better, by constructing a box plot of the scores for each recipe.

The conclusions of a programme of research, and the evidence that supports those conclusions, must be presented clearly. Graphs, such as time plots, scatter plots and histograms, are often the best way to communicate results but this will not be the case if the quality of the graphs is poor. The principles of effective graphical presentation should always be observed. These principles are discussed and illustrated in the book by Cleveland (1985). For example, if the reader is expected to make a visual comparison of two graphs then the scales should be the same for both. Superposed graphs must be easily distinguishable. Zero should not be included in a scale if this will destroy the resolution of the data on the graph. Percentages should not be graphed without indicating the number of results on which they are based. Finally, graphs should be proof-read and their visual clarity should be good enough to survive reduction and reproduction; it is not unknown for key features of a graph to disappear at publication stage when it is too late to do anything about it.

REFERENCES

Carroll, RJ, Spiegelman, J and Sacks, J (1988) A quick and easy multiple-use calibration curve procedure. *Technometrics*, **30**, pp 137–141.

Church, A (1966) Analysis of data when the response is a curve. *Technometrics*, **8**, pp 229–246.

Cleveland,WS (1985) *The Elements of Graphing Data* (Wadsworth).

Cochran, WG (1983) *Planning and Analysis of Observational Studies* (Wiley).

Cramer, H (1951) *Mathematical Methods in Statistics* (Princeton University Press).

Dobson, AJ (1983) *An Introduction to Statistical Modelling* (Chapman and Hall).

Grove, DM and Davis, TP (1992) *Engineering Quality and Experimental Design* (Longman).

Mandel, J (1984) *The Statistical Analysis of Experimental Data* (Wiley).

Maxwell, AE (1961) *Analysing Qualitative Data* (Methuen).

McCullagh, P and Nelder, JA (1989) *Generalised Linear Models*, (2nd edn) (Chapman and Hall).

Metcalfe, AV (1994) *Statistics in Engineering* (Chapman and Hall).

Michell, J (1990) *An Introduction to the Logic of Psychological Measurement* (Lawrence Erlbaum).

Roberts, FS (1979) *Measurement Theory* (Addison-Wesley).

Rutherford, E and Geiger, H (1910) The probability variation in the distribution of α particles. *Philosophical Magazine*, **20**, pp 698–707.

Siegel, S (1956) *Non-parametric Statistics* (McGraw-Hill).

Youden,W (1962) Systematic errors in physical constants. *Technometrics*, **4**, pp 111–123.

28 Instrumentation in experimentation

Anand D Pandyan, Frederike van Wijck and Garth R Johnson

INTRODUCTION

Measurement instruments can be used in all sorts of experiments, ranging from studies during space exploration to mother–infant interactions or the recovery of dexterity after a stroke (Table 28.1 has a few examples).

In this chapter we shall introduce the use of instruments in experimentation. We shall discuss the concept of measurement, consider *what* you might choose to measure and, then, *how* you can measure using instrumentation. We shall describe the basic components of a measurement system and explain their successive functions. We shall illustrate different types of measurement systems with examples of how instrumentation has been used in the measurement of human performance. We shall present criteria on which to evaluate measurement instruments, including aspects of scientific robustness (such as sources of error) as well as practicalities. In the discussion that follows, we encourage you to think about *why* you might want to use measurement technology by considering the balance of potential benefits and drawbacks of using instrumentation in your research. Finally, we shall suggest where you might find help, guidance and resources.

Table 28.1 Some examples of measurement instruments as they may be applied in different areas of research

Topic of interest	Examples of instrumentation used
Cardiac rehabilitation.	Heart rate monitor. Electrocardiogram (ECG).
Alcohol content in the blood stream.	Breathalysers.
Relation between brain and function.	Positron Emission Tomography (PET).
Density profiles across a lipid membrane.	Reflectometers.
Strength (materials, animals including humans and plants).	Strain gauges and signal amplifiers.
Forensic applications (Lie detectors).	Heart rate monitors. Blood pressure monitors. Impedance monitors.
Environmental hazard monitoring. Obstetrics and Gynaecology. Non-destructive testing in engineering. Thickness of polar ice caps.	Geiger and scintillation counters. Ultrasonic transducers and measurement systems.
Breast screening. Insulation protection (Buildings/Transport).	Infrared thermal sensors and cameras.
Archaeology.	Carbon dating with mass spectrometers.

CONCEPT OF MEASUREMENT

What is measurement?

Among many definitions of measurement, we find:

> *Measurement refers to the use of a standard (such as a metric ruler) to quantify an observation*
>
> Kondraske (1989)

He adds:

> *Assessment is the process of determining the meaning of a measurement or collective set of measurements in a specific context.*

Thus interpreted, measurement is instrumental in arriving at objective and accurate inferences from observations. Part seven of this book offers guidance about analysis and interpretation of data.

What can we measure?

Your research data may be categorised as nominal, ordinal, interval or ratio levels of measurement. Table 28.2 provides the characteristics of each level.

Nominal level data pertain to information that can be ordered only into categories that are different, but which lack a hierarchy (such as male/female). Also called **categorical** level data.

Ordinal level data can be classified hierarchically, although the magnitude of the difference between each step in the hierarchy is either unequal or unknown (such as the level of consciousness according to the Glasgow Coma Scale).

Interval level data can be organised into a hierarchy with the magnitude of the difference between each successive step being known and equal, but which lacks an absolute absence of the quantity (such as temperature in °C).

Ratio level data have all the characteristics of interval level data, in addition to an absolute zero (such as velocity, measured in m/s, temperature measured in °K).

You must know the level of data you wish to measure when you decide which statistical methods you will use for data analysis. A general rule is to use parametric tests when your measurements provide ratio or interval levels of data that are normally distributed, and non-parametric tests when your data are either ordinal or nominal (see Chapter 29).

Measurement, as defined by Kondraske, usually involves interval or ratio level data entailing

Table 28.2 Key characteristics of nominal, ordinal, interval and ratio levels of measurement. √ – Condition has to be satisfied. × – Condition need not be satisfied. (Modified from Pandyan *et al* 1999)

Level	Characteristics			
	Hierarchical order	Quantitative measurement	Equal interval lengths	True zero point
Nominal	×	×	×	×
Ordinal	✔	×	×	×
Interval	✔	✔	✔	×
Ratio	✔	✔	✔	✔

standard units. Opinions differ: some authors (see Wade 1992) prefer to use the concepts of 'measurement' and 'assessment' interchangeably. This implies that measurement may also include nominal and ordinal level data, using counts and frequencies.

Before discussing how to measure, you should think carefully about what you wish to measure and why that should be relevant. What is the construct you wish to measure and how does your dependent variable relate to this? (See Parts five and seven of this book.)

MEASUREMENT SYSTEMS: BASIC PRINCIPLES

A measurement system is a configuration of elements that interact with each other to quantify a specific phenomenon for assessment, analysis or control purposes. Figure 28.1 is a simple diagram of a generic measurement system. This consists of the following components: a signal source, a transducer and amplifiers, data display/storage devices and, in some cases, a control device. We will describe the components related to measurement in the following sections.

Signals normally result from an energy conversion process and can be broadly classified into two types: analogue signals and discrete signals. Analogue signals are continuous in time (such as monitoring heart rate), whereas discrete signals occur as discrete events in time (such as maximum and minimum temperature in a 24-hour period). The primary input to the measurement system is the signal: the phenomenon to be measured. Measuring any phenomenon without the assistance of instrumentation generally leads to data of nominal or ordinal levels.

Measurement instrumentation is needed to obtain interval or ratio level data. Elements of this are as follows.

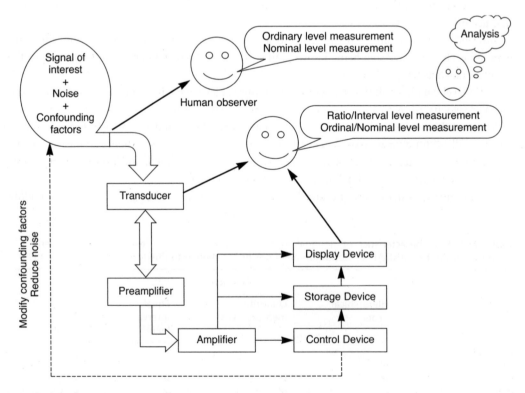

Figure 28.1 Simple diagram of a generic measurement system

Transducers

A transducer converts energy from one form to another. The transducers in these systems convert changes in any form of energy to changes in electrical energy. This process of energy conversion can be passive (such as for example a thermometer) or active (measuring displacement using a potentiometer). An active transducer, such as a strain gauge to measure applied force, must be energised by an external power source.

Preamplifiers and amplifiers

It is often possible to use a passive transducer, such as a thermometer, for direct measurements. However, in many applications this is not the case. The output signals from a transducer have low amplitude and are contaminated by noise and other confounding factors. Also, it may not always be possible to take measurements at the site of recording, such as when monitoring harmful radiation or measuring rapid eye movement (REM) during sleep. Preamplifiers are then used to obtain meaningful measurements. A preamplifier provides the first stage of amplification. For example, in space exploration and radio transmission, the signals collected by the transducers/microphones need to be amplified many times before they can be transmitted without contamination. At this stage, the signals from the transducer are amplified to a sufficient stage to allow for transmission of the signals to the main amplifier. This transmission may be by wires, such as when angular displacement is measured with a flexible electro-goniometer; or it may be by a cordless system such as when measuring muscle activity in tests of normal walking. At the amplifier, the signals are further amplified and processed before being displayed or stored.

Filters

Transmitted signals often become contaminated with unwanted variation. This random signal contamination, known as noise, often arises from interference from the mains power supply but may also originate at the point of observation (Fig. 28.1). For example, any movement of a sleeping person whose REM is being monitored, may appear as noise in the recoded signal. The unwanted noise signals need to be removed for a meaningful interpretation of the recorded signal. This is usually done by filtering. Commonly used filters are:

- *notch* filters: to block selected frequencies in the signal (a 50 Hz notch filter is used to eliminate the mains interference from signals – in the USA, a 60 Hz notch filter is used);
- *band pass* filters: to allow only signals in a selected band to pass through (when measuring muscle activity, signals with frequencies below 20 Hz and above 200 Hz are not normally required so a band pass filter with a band width of 20 Hz to 200 Hz is used). Please be aware that any useful information at the filtered frequencies will also be lost.

Data storage on a PC

Measurement systems are often used in association with personal computers. If you use a personal computer in your research, you can take data in the form of an analogue signal from an amplifier and convert it into a digital signal that is a series of bits. You do this with an *analogue-to-digital converter* (ADC) card. Most commercial ADC cards provide 12-bit or 16-bit conversion. The 12-bit ADC is less sensitive than the 16-bit ADC. Suppose you have a signal that varies from 0 V to 10 V.

A 12-bit ADC card has a resolution of 4096 (2^{12}). Therefore, the 0 V signal will be equivalent to 0 on the ADC and 10 V will be equivalent to 4095. Thus, a change of 1 V from the amplifier will cause an ADC signal to change by approx 409 units and one ADC bit will measure approximately 2 mV.

The interface between an amplifier and your PC can be established either with a serial or with a parallel port. Many commercial programmes are available for data collection on a PC. However, commercial programmes may not have the flexibility you need for your research. Instead, you can develop your own data collection programme using high level programming languages such as HpVee, Labview, Matlab or with a general purpose programming language such as C++. Whatever your approach, you should test that the ADC card matches the data collection programme to be purchased or developed.

PERFORMANCE OF MEASUREMENT SYSTEMS

Although Fig. 28.1 identifies the individual components of a measurement system, you must remember that there is a high degree of interaction between them.

An ideal transducer (or amplifier) will not draw any energy from the signal source (or transducer). In reality, all transducers extract some energy during the measurement process. For example, a thermometer will absorb heat when it measures temperature. If a transducer or amplifier extracts a disproportionate amount of energy from the signal source, it will affect the quantity being measured and thus bias the outcome. When you select a transducer, you should select one that will minimise this bias. This is usually achieved by selecting a transducer with a *high input impedance* (impedance is the technical term for a complex resistance). The higher the input impedance of the transducer, the less energy it will draw from the signal source. At the output from the transducer, the process has to be reversed: the impedance has to be low so that the preamplifier/amplifier will be able to extract the signal from the transducer without any contamination. The general rule for all the components in Fig. 28.1 is that the input impedances should be much higher than the output impedances of the preceding stage.

Confounding effects corrupt the signal but cannot be eliminated by filtering. For example, the ambient temperature may influence the output from a strain gauge. Therefore, ideally you should choose a transducer whose output will not be influenced by any factor other than the signal of interest. However, if a confounding effect cannot be avoided, you may be able to compensate for its influence or you may be able to measure it separately and so allow for it in data analysis. A common example is that of correcting for the influence of ambient temperature on measurements of interest.

EVALUATION OF MEASUREMENT INSTRUMENTATION

In this section, we discuss several criteria that may help in choosing instrumentation for your research.

Health and safety

A risk assessment of both the measurement system and the process of measurement is important before implementation. If your research involves human beings, pay special attention to their safety and comfort. Verify with the manufacturer if there are any health hazards, called *contra-indications*, for a particular type of equipment. For example, the use of an electromagnetic measurement device may be dangerous for anybody who has a pacemaker. In Europe, any piece of equipment should bear the CE mark. This tells you that it meets European safety standards.

Threshold and resolution, accuracy and precision, sample frequency

Threshold and *resolution* indicate the sensitivity of a measurement system. When the input to the measurement system is increased from zero, at one particular value of the input the measurement system will record an output – this is the threshold of the measuring system (Doebelin 1983). Any signal with a magnitude below the threshold cannot be measured. Resolution is the smallest detectable change in input that can be measured by the measurement system (Doebelin 1983).

Accuracy and *precision* express the quality of data that a system will measure. See also Chapter 27. Accuracy is the difference between the measured and true value of a variable (Doebelin 1983). The manufacturer will usually provide information about the accuracy of a system. However, it is important to understand that the accuracy of an instrument refers to the system as a whole, as it functions in a specific environment using specific methodology. Therefore, accuracy may change over time, through use or by damage, and may also be subject to factors such as room temperature (Durward *et al* 1999). Because of this, it is important to *calibrate* your measurement system before data collection. Calibration is the procedure in which the input to the system is systematically varied over the range of values expected in the experiment and is compared with the output.

Precision indicates the ability of a system to yield the same value for repeated measurements (Durward *et al* 1999) and thus indicates how much the value of a discrete sample varies from the mean of a group of measurements. The smaller this variation, the more reliable the system. Since the precision of a system may vary within a measurement range, you should estimate precision throughout the full range required for the experiment.

The *sample frequency* of the measurement system is the number of times per second data are collected. If the sampling frequency is equal to, or less than, the frequency of the input, the reconstructed signal becomes distorted. This phenomenon is known as *aliasing*, defined as an error between the sampled and the original signal (Cohen 2000). The minimum sampling frequency that can be allowed, the so-called *Nyquist frequency*, is based on the *sampling theorem*. This theorem postulates that the sampling frequency should be greater than, or equal to, twice the frequency of the original signal (Cohen 2000). However, exact application of this rule has serious limitations and we advise you to sample at more than five times the signal frequency.

Linear measurement systems – in which any change in input over a defined range produces a proportional change in the output – are generally recommended. However, although some transducers may not be linear, this should cause no problem provided that the relationship between the input and the output can be quantified and is reproducible.

Sources of error

Before you use the measurement system to collect experimental data, you should establish any sources of error and their magnitudes. For example, when you use an optoelectronic movement measurement system, stray infrared light, caused by reflective material, may cause errors. Fluctuating air temperature may disturb measurement systems that involve sound.

Crosstalk, which is said to occur when the output of one signal is contaminated with that from another, may be another source of errors. It can occur when different measurement components are at work at the same time (Durward *et al* 1999). Hence, before you collect data, check if there are any signs of crosstalk. By systematically changing the input to one channel only and monitoring the output of all other channels, you can examine whether only the channel to which you changed the input has registered a change. During this test, you should ensure that channels with no active inputs are grounded.

Hysteresis is the phenomenon where the output of a system depends on its immediate past history of perturbation. For example, in measuring the stiffness in a joint such as the elbow, a therapist will move the joint about its full range of movement. If the therapist were to move the joint twice with an interval of 15 seconds between measurements and record the stiffness, then the stiffness encountered during the first test would be higher than the stiffness in the second. See Durward *et al* (1999) for a detailed discussion of hysteresis. Hence, if you suspect that your measurement instrument is susceptible to hysteresis, you should test it repeatedly through its entire measurement range with values ascending and descending.

User-friendliness

Is your instrument practicable? Questions that you should ask about any proposed equipment are:

- *Set up*: Is it easy to set up? This is important, especially if you intend to use it routinely or if you want to use it in several different places.
- *Calibration*: Is calibration automatic and quick?
- *Automatic data collection*: Is data collection automatic? If it is, it will be fast and help to avoid errors caused by the operator. It will also ensure that all trials are automatically indexed so that there is no confusion between them later.
- *Real-time display*: Will it display data in real time? This will enable you to check data integrity during capture. If you detect errors, you can correct them in the following trial.
- *Automatic analysis*: How much of the data analysis process can be automated? Be aware, however, that analysis by system software might not approach the analysis in the way that you would like; it may obscure interesting features that more careful examination could reveal.
- *Data storage*: Is data storage easy and efficient? Does it automatically identify each trial?
- *Synchronisation*: When you have several instruments to collect data, can they be synchronised automatically? An example of a situation where you may need several instruments is in lie detection, where heart rate, blood pressure and galvanic skin response are measured simultaneously.
- *Wider database*: Will your system easily enable you to input the data into a wider database?

Other practicalities

- *Cost*: Estimate the costs of purchase, maintenance and running of equipment. Also remember you will need to account for training costs, costs involved in data collection and analysis. For example, in some clinical centres expensive devices are purchased for routine measurement, however, due to resources constraints associated with trained personnel and data analysis, many of these device are rarely used.
- *Environment*: Where will you have your equipment? Is there enough space? Is there other equipment nearby or are there other activities that could interfere with your process and introduce errors into data collection?
- *Sturdiness*: Is your equipment robust enough? Where this is required: is it portable enough?

Table 28.3 A summary of the main benefits and drawbacks of implementing measurement instrumentation in research.

	Potential benefit	Potential drawback
Outcome	• Additional information • Greater accuracy • Greater precision • Greater resolution • Data of higher level (interval/ratio)	• Information overload; additional information not necessarily relevant • Differences are not necessarily relevant
Process	• Data acquisition and analysis: standardised to a high level • Using a computer enables data to be stored, accessed and analysed *post hoc*	• Calibration is often required and repeated calibration will need to be done. • Costs • Time • Training • Dedicated space

DISCUSSION

Why measure?

Before you start to implement measurement systems in your own research, you should weigh the potential benefits against the drawbacks. You may wish to consider both the outcome of measurement (the quality of the information obtained) as well as the process of measurement. Table 28.3 summarises the main benefits and drawbacks of implementing measurement instrumentation in research.

Outcome of measurement

A benefit of using instrumentation may be that it provides additional information. For example, in agriculture, measuring soil acidity provides farmers with additional information on which to base decisions regarding the types and amounts of fertilisers. The downside of this may be that – unless you carefully think about what you need to measure – this additional information may not be relevant and only lead to information overload.

Instrumentation allows you to improve accuracy and precision. Without instrumentation, your measurement system would be just the assessor (Fig. 28.1); it would depend only on his or her observational skills and interpretation of the observations.

Most sensing, processing and presentation of experimental data are now done with standard routines that yield quantitative outputs, as depicted in Fig. 28.1. Measurement technology does not eradicate measurement errors. Rather, the sources of error are of a different nature, as discussed earlier. The main issue is: when only quantitative measurement methods are employed, can the magnitude of such errors be determined, corrected for or taken into account (Tourtellotte and Syndulko 1989).

Measurement tools with quantitative scales provide much greater resolution, a much higher level of detail, than qualitative scales (which are widely used in the humanities, medicine and allied professions, and in environmental studies). Thus, smaller changes may be registered that would otherwise remain undetected. For example, measuring the concentration of toxins in river water allows local authorities to monitor the effectiveness of measures to reduce industrial pollution and detect problems at an early stage, i.e. before flora and fauna become affected.

Many qualitative scales provide nominal or ordinal levels of measurement. This restricts the range of statistics that can be applied to the data (Tourtellotte and Syndulko 1989). For example, it may seem convenient to calculate a total score from individual test items in the Bayley Infant Scales or the IQ test. However, such an operation is statistically invalid. Summary statistics, such as sample means and standard deviations, are valid only with interval and ratio variables (Durward *et al* 1999). In other words, information obtained using measurement technology is generally more powerful because the magnitude of change can be reported.

ACKNOWLEDGEMENTS

Anand D Pandyan was supported by a grant from Action Research, UK. Frederike van Wijck was supported by a grant from Action Research, UK and the EC Telematic Applications Programme DE 4203 (Elderly and Disabled).

WEBSITES FOR SOFTWARE AND HARDWARE

www.adeptscience.co.uk/	A commercial site for information on HpVee, data collection software and hardware and analysis software.
www.ni.com/labview/what.htm	A commercial site for information on Labview, data collection software and hardware and analysis software.
www.mathworks.com/products/matlab/	A commercial site for information on Matlab, data collection software and hardware and analysis.
msdn.microsoft.com/visualc/default.asp	A commercial site for information on C++.
www.amplicon.co.uk/	A commercial site for information instrumentation for measurement.
www.analog.com/	A commercial site for information on instrumentation and sensors for measurement.
www.dspguide.com/pdfbook.htm	An online resource for digital signal processing
www.engineers4engineers.co.uk/metrics.htm	A resource site for information on units, measurement and instrumentation

WEBSITES ON SAFETY AND STANDARDS

gallery.uunet.be/esf/	Website for the European Safety Federation
www.mdss.com/	Website for the Medical Device Safety
eur-op.eu.int/	Office of the official publications of the EU
www.medical-devices.gov.uk/	Medical Device Agency, UK.
www.fda.gov/default.htm	Food and Drug Administration, USA
www.iecee.org/default.html	International Electrotechnical Commission (IEC) System for Conformity Testing and Certification of Electrical Equipment.

REFERENCES

Cohen, A (2000) Biomedical signals: origin and dynamic characteristics; frequency-domain analysis. In Bronzino JB (ed.) *The Biomedical Engineering Handbook*, 2nd edn, Vol. 1 pp 52–1 to 52–24. Co-published by CRC Press & Springer.

Doeblin, EO (1983) *Measurement Systems: Application and Design*, 3rd edn, (New York: McGraw-Hill). A more recent edition of this book exists: Doeblin, EO (1990) *Measurement Systems: Application and Design*. 4th Edn (New York: McGraw-Hill).

Durward, BR, Baer, GD and Rowe, PJ (eds) (1999) *Functional Human Movement: Measurement and Analysis* (Butterworth Heinemann).

Kondraske, GV (1989) Measurement science concepts and computerized methodology in the assessment of human performance. In Munsat TL (ed.) *Quantification of Neurologic Deficit* (Stoneham: Butterworths) pp 33–48.

Neumann, MR (2000) Physical measurements. In Bronzino JB (ed.) *The Biomedical Engineering Handbook*, 2nd edn, Vol. 1, pp 47–1 to 48–1. Co-published by CRC Press & Springer.

Pandyan, AD *et al* (1999) A review of the properties and limitations of the Ashworth and modified Ashworth Scales. *Clinical Rehabilitation* 3(5) pp 373–383.

Tourtellotte, WW and Syndulko, K (1989) Quantifying the neurologic examination: principles, constraints and opportunities. In Munsat, TL (ed.) *Quantification of Neurologic Deficit* (Butterworth) pp 7–16.

Wade, DT (1992) *Measurement in Neurological Rehabilitation* (Oxford University Press).

PART 7 | Analysis

29 Elementary statistics

David Hand

INTRODUCTION

Statistics is an unusual word because it has two meanings. It refers both to (typically) numerical data describing some phenomenon, and to the science of collecting and analysing those data. The first of these meanings is, of course, subject specific: what the numbers are, what they mean, and the implications of them, will depend on what they are describing. In contrast, the other meaning, sometimes expanded to *statistical science*, describes methods that can be applied in any domain. It is this second meaning that is the concern of this and the next chapter.

Statistics is a vast subject. It is far too large for any single person to be an expert in all its various sub-domains. It follows that all I can hope to do in these few pages is to try to orientate you, to give you an idea of the motivation behind statistical methods, to show you some very basic tools, and to give you pointers to further reading that will provide the details of what you need to know. Before we get down to it, however, a word or two about the nature of modern statistics is appropriate.

Statistics has long suffered from a bad press in two regards. One is the view that it, like politicians, can bend the facts to suit any purpose. The second is that it is a tedious and boring subject. The first of these criticisms arises because it is easy to mislead people who are statistically naive. By misrepresenting the facts, by presenting only some of the numbers rather than their entirety, by focusing on only particular aspects of the results, and generally by distorting the data to be analysed, of course one can mislead. But here it is the improper use of statistical methods that is the appropriate target of the criticisms rather than the statistical methods themselves. It is unfortunate that the mud flying around from such misuse has sometimes adhered to the tools being used rather than to those using them improperly.

The second criticism may once have had some truth. In the days when even a relatively simple analysis involved endless hours of mechanical numerical manipulations by hand, how could the subject be regarded as exciting? But things are not like that nowadays. Now we have the computer to take over the tedium. The computer enables us to concentrate on the higher level tasks, the seeking for patterns and structures in data, the comparison of our theories with the data, without subjecting ourselves to the tedium of endless arithmetic. This has two consequences. The first is that the reputation of statistics as boring is now completely wide of the mark.

A geologist recently commented to me that he envied me. 'Statisticians,' he said, 'have the best part of scientific research. They don't have to put up with the boredom and repetition of collecting the data. They come in at the most exciting stage – when one is looking at the data one has collected.' He was forgetting the role of statisticians in deciding how to collect data (in experimental design and sampling) and he was also failing to recognise that many statisticians prefer to get some hands-on experience, as it can give a better idea of the aims and difficulties of the study.

Nevertheless, what he said had some truth in it. And when you have reached the stage of analysing your data, of looking to see if the information it contains matches the ideas you have had, you will also find that statistics is entering at the most exciting stage.

The second consequence of the development of the computer is that, at least at this introductory level, we do not have to dwell on the algebra and arithmetic of statistical methods. For all but the most basic of operations on very small data sets, you will use a calculator or computer. Hence, in what follows, we have attempted to focus on statistical concepts and the properties of statistical methods rather than on the mechanics of how to do what electronics will do for you.

This is the first of three chapters on statistics. It introduces the basic ideas. The other two chapters cover, respectively, more advanced statistical methods and computer software.

SCALES

Data come in several forms and it is useful to distinguish between them. First we can distinguish between *numerical* and *non-numerical* measurements. Examples of the former are a person's age or weight and the size of a family. Examples of the latter are the position of a mark on a scale indicating one's extent of agreement with some statement, and scores of mild, moderate or severe on a pain scale. Numbers can, of course, be used to score the latter examples, but they do not have quite as strong empirical force as the numbers used in the former cases and sometimes one must be careful about how one analyses such data.

A second distinction we can make is between *continuous* and *categorical* data. Continuous data are measurements that can (at least in principle) take any value within a certain range. Age, weight and the agreement score above are examples of this. Categorical variables, in contrast, can take only one of (normally) a few values: size of family and the pain scale illustrate this. Sometimes it is not clear which class a variable is in (age, for example, might be recorded just to the nearest year) but this does not usually cause any problems.

It is often useful to divide categorical variables further, into *nominal* and *ordinal* variables. The former have no natural ordering – like the various religions, for example – while the latter do (as in the pain scale example).

BASIC MEASURES

If one looks at a raw table of numbers, it can be difficult to see what is going on. Consider Table 29.1, for example. This (from Frets 1921) shows head lengths (in mm) of 25 men. Even in such a small table, it is not easy to see what head size is typical and what is extremely large or small. It is not easy to see if large extremes are rarer than small extremes. It is not easy to see if there are striking exceptions to the general size of head. This being the case with only 25 values, the difficulty of coping with larger data sets will be obvious.

Table 29.1 Male head lengths (mm)

191	174	189	181	208
195	190	197	175	186
181	188	188	192	183
183	163	192	174	197
176	195	179	176	190

First let us find a way to describe 'typical' head length. A number of statistics are in common use. (And this introduces us to a third use of the word statistics – as the plural of 'statistic'. A statistic is some summary value calculated from or derived from a set of data.). We shall consider three here: the *mean*, the *median*, and the *mode*. These are different kinds of *averages*.

Given a sample of n numbers adding to a total T, the *mean* of the sample is that number (often denoted) $\bar{x}$ such that n copies of it also add up to T. Obviously $\bar{x}$ is smaller than the larger numbers in the sample and it is larger than the smaller ones. It is an average or *representative* value. Numerically it can be found simply by calculating the total in the sample and dividing by the sample size. For Table 29.1, we find that the mean is:

$$(191 + 174 + \ldots + 190)/25 = 185.72$$

The *median* of a sample is the mid-point of the sample: half the sample values are smaller than it and half are larger. In fact, we have to specify things a little more precisely than this. We order the sample in terms of size and if there are an odd number of values in the sample, then the median is the middle one. In the above example the reordered sample is 163, 174, 174, 175, . . . 197, 208 and the middle one has value 188. The median is thus 188. If, however, there are an even number of values in the sample then there isn't a 'middle one'. In this case, we define the median as being half way between the two middle ones. For example, in the ordered sample 10, 14, 15, 17, 18, 18, the median is half way between 15 and 17. That is 16.

Finally, the *mode* is the most commonly occurring value in the sample. In our example above, there is in fact no single value which is the most common. Several values occur twice, but no value occurs more than twice. Such a data set it said to be *multi-modal* – it possesses several modes. In circumstances like this the sample mode is of limited use as a summary of the data. (More sophisticated methods based on identifying the values of the several modes can be useful, but they are beyond the scope of this chapter.) For continuous data, in which the sample values are all different, each value will occur once – hence, again, there will be no unique mode.

Sometimes averages such as those above are termed *measures of location*. This arises from the idea of viewing the sample values as plotted points on a number line. The mean, median, and (if it exists) the mode, are also points on the line, showing, in some sense, the 'average' position of the sample of points. Such a representation cannot be used with nominal data and is of doubtful value with non-numerical data.

The median tells us that sample value which has half the sample below it. Sometimes it is also useful to know what value has a quarter, 25 per cent of the sample below it. This value is called the *lower quartile*. A similar definition, with 75 per cent of the sample below it, gives the *upper quartile*.

So much for measures of location. These tell us the rough size of the sample of values we are dealing with, but they do not tell us how widely distributed are the data about those values. Perhaps the data are very closely clustered about the mean; or perhaps the mean is a very poor summary of the values because the constituents vary greatly. We need to supplement the mean (or median or mode) with another value giving an idea of the *spread* or *dispersion* of the sample.

One simple measure is the *range*. This is simply the difference between the largest and smallest values in the sample. For the data in Table 29.1 the range is $208 - 163 = 45$.

As a measure of spread the range is easy to interpret and understand. But it has the disadvantage that it is not very *stable*. Another sample from the same population is quite likely to have a substantially different range because, in calculating the range, only the two most extreme values are considered. An alternative measure of dispersion which overcomes this variability and is less variable from sample to sample is the *inter-quartile range*, defined as the distance between the upper and lower quartiles.

Another measure of spread that overcomes this variability, and which is the most popular measure of dispersion, is the *standard deviation*, often abbreviated to *sd*. This is most straightforwardly defined as the square root of the *variance*. First, therefore, we have to define variance. The variance of the sample is the average size of the squared differences between the sample values and their mean.

Often the divisor $(n - 1)$ is used in place of n when calculating the mean because the resulting statistic has attractive properties. We need not go into these here – and, in any case, for even moderately large n the difference will be negligible. In our example above, and using the $(n - 1)$ divisor, the sample variance is 95.29.

It follows that the sample standard deviation is the square root of this, namely 9.76. Taking square roots means that the sample sd is measured in the same units as the raw data. (The variance will be in square units: kg^2, inches squared, or whatever, because of the squaring operation in its definition.)

So far, we have discussed measures of location and measures of dispersion. One other simple summary statistic, important because it often indicates when common statistical methods may be reliably used, is skewness. The *skewness* of a distribution of values is a measure of *asymmetry*. For example, does it have many small values and few very large values (*positively* or *right skewed*) or does it have lots of large values and few small values (*negatively* or *left skewed*). Income and wealth distributions, with a very few people earning or owning a lot, tend to be positively skewed. Negatively skewed distributions are less common.

You will notice that we have slipped the word *distribution* in here. This is a technical term in statistics, which fortunately has much the meaning one might expect it to. One can speak of the distribution of a sample, and also of the distribution of a *population*: the set of values that might have been chosen for the sample. We remarked above that the computer and calculator allowed us to sidestep the arithmetic details in a brief exposition such as this. For this reason we shall not give a formula for skewness. If you are keen on that sort of thing then you can find calculation details in the further reading given below.

One of the attractive features of modern statistical technology is the ease with which plots and diagrams can be produced. Again the computer has taken all the drudgery out of the exercise. An example is given in Fig. 29.1. The data summarised here (Cox and Lewis 1966) are time intervals between 800 successive pulses along a nerve fibre, measured in seconds. The diagram shows a *histogram*, produced by grouping the observations according to their size and plotting vertical bars whose heights indicate how many fall into each group.

SIMPLE DISTRIBUTIONS

We have already introduced the term *distribution*. Some distributions are particularly important in statistics, either because they are very common or because they have attractive mathematical properties (quite what this means we will see in a moment!).

Bernoulli distribution

The *Bernoulli* distribution arises when there are two possible outcomes, with probabilities p and $1 - p$ (say). A classic example is the toss of a coin, and if the coin is 'fair' both p and $1 - p$ will equal

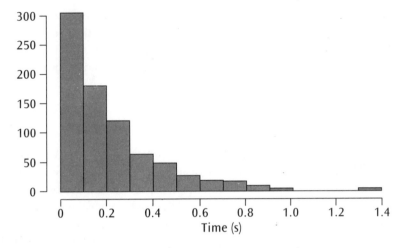

Figure 29.1 Histogram of 799 interpulse waiting times

1/2. Other examples are an application to college, which can be successful or unsuccessful, and whether it will rain or not on your birthday.

Binomial distribution

An extension of this is the *binomial distribution*. This arises as the sum of a number, n say, Bernoulli outcomes. For example, instead of being interested in whether a single toss of a coin will come up heads or tails, we might be interested in the proportion of 100 tosses that come up heads: what is the probability that 50 will produce heads? Or 49? And so on. Or we might be interested in how many of the ten applicants to college from a particular school will be successful. Or we might want to know on how many of your next ten birthdays it is likely to rain.

For situations like this to be modelled by the binomial distribution, certain conditions have to be satisfied. In particular, we require that the individual events have *the same probability of occurring* and are *independent*. If the probability that the coin came up heads differed from throw to throw (because, for example, someone tampered with it by attaching chewing gum to one side), then the binomial distribution would not be an adequate model for the physical situation. *Independence* is a rather more complicated, and very important, concept. Two events are said to be independent if the occurrence of one does not affect the probability that the other will occur. This is likely to be satisfied for tosses of a coin. But suppose we had asked about the number of the next ten days on which it rained. Rain on consecutive days is not independent: if it was dry today it is more likely to be dry tomorrow than if it was wet today. The binomial distribution is unlikely to be a good model for this situation.

Poisson distribution

The binomial distribution is one possible model for *counts*. Another one is the *Poisson* distribution. Suppose, again, that n independent events are considered, with each of them having two possible outcomes (A and B, say), with the same probability that A will occur each time. Then, if n is large and the probability of A is small, the total number of times A occurs can be well approximated by a *Poisson* distribution. Such a distribution might be a good model for the number of misprints in a book: there is a small chance that any particular letter will be misprinted, but there are a lot of them. Of course, we will need to consider whether or not the conditions of independence and equal probability are sufficiently closely satisfied.

Normal distribution

So far we have only considered *discrete* distributions in which the outcome can take only one of a discrete set of values (such as 0, 1, 2, . . .). In other situations, any value can occur (perhaps from a certain range). As above, these are called *continuous* distributions. The most important example of these is the *normal* or *Gaussian* distribution. This is a uni-modal distribution (one peak) which tails off symmetrically to high values and to low values. Consequently, scores that are *r* units above the mean have exactly the same probability of occurring as scores that are *r* units below the mean. The most likely values are those around the mean, and very large or small values are very unlikely.

The normal distribution is often a sufficiently accurate approximation to empirical distributions that occur in real life, and this is one reason for its importance. Another is that, when large samples are involved, the normal distribution is often a good approximation to the distributions of statistics calculated from data. For example, suppose that a sample of 1000 people were asked their ages and an average (the mean) calculated. If this was repeated, 100 times say, we would obtain 100 slightly different mean values, and we could study the distribution of these 100 values. We would find that the majority were clustered together, with few large values and few small values. Moreover, similar numbers of samples would have very small values and very large values – the distribution of the 100 means would be roughly symmetric. To summarise, the distribution of the 100 means, each based on a sample of 1000 people, would be roughly normal.

This sort of thing often occurs, especially when the means (or other statistics) are based on large samples (such as the 1000 in our example). This striking property of the normal distribution makes it of fundamental importance in statistical theory: if exact distributions cannot be worked out, maybe a reasonable approximating normal distribution can be used.

ESTIMATING PARAMETERS

The statistics calculated from samples can often be regarded as *estimates* of *parameters* of the populations from which the samples were drawn. For example, consider the population of the United Kingdom. This entire population will have an age distribution and it will have an average value (a parameter, *a defining characteristic*, of the population). We could discover this average value by asking everyone their age and calculating the average (though we would have to move quickly; people are getting older all the time!). Alternatively, we could take a sample of far fewer people and simply find its average. This sample average is a statistic. It turns out that the variation in such a sample average is inversely related to the square root of the sample size. So, by taking a large enough sample, we can make the variation in our sample average as small as we like. Put another way, we can make the sample average as close as we like to the population average (or, at least, we can specify an interval, a *confidence interval*, such that the probability that the interval contains the true value can be as high as we like).

TESTING HYPOTHESES

These basic ideas can be used to test theories in the following way. Suppose we want to compare two treatments for some disease – treatment A and treatment B, say. We give A to one group of people and B to another group (the two groups being selected by *random allocation*, so as to ensure that there is no bias in terms of the likely recovery rates). And we compare the recovery rates in the two groups. If the two treatments were equally effective (the *null hypothesis*) we could work out the probability of obtaining any particular difference between the proportions recovering under A and under B. In particular, we can work this out for differences as large as, or greater than, the difference we actually obtained. This tells us how likely we are to obtain a difference as large as, or larger than, that actually observed if the groups are really equally effective (if the null hypothesis is true). If this probability is very small it casts doubt on our initial assumption that the two treatments are equally effective. If it is small enough, it may lead us to reject that initial assumption (that is, to reject the null hypothesis). What is 'small enough' here will depend on the experimental situation and the investigators carrying out the work. Common values chosen are 1%, 5% and 10%.

In the above, we used sample statistics to make an inference about a population value: about the difference between the proportion who would recover if everyone received A and the proportion who would recover if everyone received B. Such a technique is called a *hypothesis test* because we are testing a hypothesised value of a population parameter. This basic idea can be extended to a vast number of situations. A fairly straightforward extension of the above situation allows one to compare the means of two groups, using what is called a *t-test*.

An entirely different situation is as follows. Suppose we have two categorical variables – say the three-valued pain scale introduced above and the sex of the patients in the study. Data arising from such a situation can be arranged in a three by two *cross-classification* called a *contingency table*. We might wish to know whether resistance to pain differs between the sexes: whether the distribution of female patients across the three pain categories is the same as the distribution for male patients. This question can be expressed in several alternative but equivalent ways. Is the ratio of the number of males to females the same in each of the three pain categories? Are the two categorical variables, pain and sex, independent? A hypothesis test of this question begins by assuming that the distributions in the populations are the same and, based on this assumption, derives the probability that one would obtain a sample difference between the observed distributions as great as, or greater than, that actually obtained. Again, if this probability is sufficiently small, one will feel that the initial assumption (the null hypothesis of independence) is untenable. This forms the basis of a *chi-squared* test for independence.

Sometimes particular tests make fairly stringent assumptions about the distributions involved in the situation being investigated. For example, the *t*-test mentioned above assumes that the populations from which the samples are drawn follow normal distributions. Such tests are called *parametric* tests. Other tests, *non-parametric* or *distribution-free* tests, relax these assumptions, and so are more generally applicable. Having said that, however, if the assumptions of the parametric test are justifiable, they are generally more *powerful*. This means that they are more sensitive to departures from the null hypothesis.

CONCLUSION

Given the limited length of this chapter, it is obvious that we could not go into great depth here. This means both that we have only been able to scratch the surface of the ideas we have outlined and also that we have only been able to present a very few central ideas. The books listed in the reading list go into more detail and if you are involved in analysing data in your work, you are encouraged to obtain one.

To conclude, however, there is a further general point that should be made. This is that modern statistics, although a tremendously exciting discipline, is also a complex one. Research is very seldom a question of looking at the data, deciding what technique to apply, running the computer to produce a single numerical value, and writing things up. Typically, all sorts of complications arising from the complexities of real life intervene. Because of this, you are advised to seek statistical advice both before collecting your data and before analysing it. Such a precaution could prevent a great waste of time and a good deal of mental anguish.

REFERENCES

Cox, DR and Lewis, PAW (1966) *The Statistical Analysis of Series of Events* (London: Chapman and Hall).

Daly, F, Hand, DJ, Jones, MC, Lunn, AD and McConway, KJ (1995) *Elements of Statistics* (Wokingham: Addison-Wesley).

Frets, GP (1921) Heredity of head form in man. *Genetica*, **3**, pp 193–384.

30 Further statistical methods

David Hand

INTRODUCTION

Chapter 29 outlined some basic statistical ideas and methods. Here we move on to describe some more advanced techniques. Given their advanced nature, the best we can do is scratch the surface. However, we hope that this will be sufficient to indicate the sort of thing that can be accomplished using modern methods. Naturally, if you do have data that needs such methods, you are advised to seek professional advice. Although statistical software is now very readily available, statistical understanding is not so easy to come by. A few minutes discussion with an expert could save endless weeks of frustration.

We begin by distinguishing between techniques for *prediction*, where there is a *criterion* variable that has to be predicted from the other variable or variables, and techniques where the variables are all equivalent. The former is used for prediction as well as for understanding, while the latter is mainly used for understanding what is going on in a set of data: for deciphering the relationships between variables and objects.

REGRESSION ANALYSIS

Regression analysis is a statistical model building technique. It relates a single *response* or *dependent* variable to one or more *predictors* or *independent* variables. The model, a mathematical equation, can be used as a summary of the relationship between the response and the predictors and it can also be used to predict the value of the response given values of the predictors.

We shall illustrate the use of data on the output of wind-powered generators of electricity (Joglekar *et al* 1989). The predictor here is wind velocity (in miles per hour, mph) and the response variable is direct current output. Our regression equation will then permit us to answer questions such as:

- On average, for the generator being studied, what extra current output results from an extra 1 mile per hour in wind velocity?
- Given a wind velocity of 3 mph, what average current output should we expect?

Such a model is constructed as follows. We begin with a set of data. In this case, we need a sample of measurements of wind velocities and the associated current outputs. Let us denote the values of the response variable, current, by y and the values of the predictor variable, wind velocity, by x. Then our sample provides us with a collection of pairs of values, one pair for each measurement occasion. The data are shown in Table 30.1.

Now, let us conjecture that a suitable model relating output to velocity is that output is 0.25 times velocity. A glance at the data shows that this is certainly not a perfect model. The first pair has a velocity of 2.45 so that $0.25 \times 2.45 = 0.613$, which is not equal to the given output of 0.123.

Table 30.1 Wind velocity and direct current output

x	y	x	y
2.45	0.123	6.00	1.822
2.70	0.500	6.20	1.866
2.90	0.653	6.35	1.930
3.05	0.558	7.00	1.800
3.40	1.057	7.40	2.088
3.60	1.137	7.85	2.179
3.95	1.144	8.15	2.166
4.10	1.194	8.80	2.112
4.60	1.562	9.10	2.303
5.00	1.582	9.55	2.294
5.45	1.501	9.70	2.386
5.80	1.737	10.00	2.236
		10.20	2.310

Nevertheless, examination of the other values shows that multiplying velocity by 0.25 gives current outputs in the right ballpark. But how can we find a better value?

What we need is some overall measure of *goodness-of-fit* between our model and the data. Each pair gives us a separate measure of goodness-of-fit: the difference between the output value predicted from the model (0.613 in the above illustration) and the observed output value (0.123 above). So, for this pair alone, its goodness-of-fit measure is 0.613–0.123 = 0.5. But how can we combine the separate results for each pair into a single overall measure?

We could add them up, but this would have the problem that predictions which were too small (and which had negative goodness-of-fit measures) would tend to cancel out predictions which were too large (and which, therefore, had positive goodness-of-fit values). This problem is over-come by squaring the individual goodness-of-fit measures – so making them all positive.

So, the overall goodness-of-fit measure is the sum of squared differences between the output predicted from the model and the observed value.

We can calculate such a measure for a range of conjectured values for the constant relating output to velocity. For example, in addition to 0.25 we could try 0.2, 0.21, ..., 0.3, ..., 0.4. And then we could choose that which best fitted the data.

In fact, there is a better way. The sum of squared differences criterion is a common measure in statistics and the optimum value of the constant can be found mathematically. In practice nowadays, of course, it will normally be found by a computer (see Chapter 31). The value of the constant that defines the relationship between output and velocity is called the *regression coefficient* for the regression of output on velocity. Based on the sample of data we have, our computer will have given us an estimate of that coefficient.

We started the above example by saying that we needed a sample of pairs of measurements. Great care must be taken when this sample is selected. We can distinguish two situations.

In the first situation, the sample is a *random* sample from the population of interest. If this is the case, then hypothesis tests, as outlined in Chapter 29, can be done. So, in our example, we might take a random sample of pairs of measurements. Then we can test whether or not there is any relationship between velocity and current in general: you would ask: 'how likely is it that, if there is no general relationship between velocity and current, we would have obtained the value for the *sample* regression coefficient that was actually obtained?' (The answer is 'unlikely'. Less than 5 per cent would lead you to reject the hypothesis of no relationship between velocity and current.)

If the sample has not been randomly selected then the basis of the hypothesis test to answer this question is invalid. If we had deliberately chosen pairs of values that had low current associated with high velocity and high current associated with low velocity then we might have found an apparent inverse relationship: more wind meaning less output, on average. This would have been nonsensical in terms of statements about the overall relationship between wind velocity and current output.

The second way to choose the sample arises when you can exercise control over the predictor variable. For example, we might want to know whether increasing the concentration x of a chemical X leads to an increase in product Y. To explore this we could do a series of experiments, measuring output Y for various *predetermined X* levels. As it happens, the statistical inferences described above are also valid with this approach.

So far we have described what is called *simple regression*. Simple regression involves a single predictor variable: wind velocity in the above example. *Multiple regression* extends this to model the simultaneous effect of several predictors on the response variable. So, to illustrate, in the above example we might have been concerned about the effect of wind velocity, air temperature, and humidity on the current output. The mathematical model would then involve a separate constant multiple for each of these predictor variables.

Put in mathematical terms, the predicted value of the response is expressed as a weighted sum of the values of the predictors, where the weights are the regression coefficients.

We could have done three separate simple regressions, one for each of the three predictor variables. It is important to understand the distinction between this and the multiple regression involving all three simultaneously. The regression coefficients from the former tell us how the response will change when there is unit change in one of the predictors. The latter tells us how the response will change when there is unit change in one of the predictors *keeping the other predictors constant*. The multiple regression tells us the unique effect of each predictor over and above that of the others.

At first exposure, this idea, like so many others in statistics, is not easy to grasp. But it is an important one. Which of the two types of analysis to do, whether to report several separate univariate analyses or a single multivariate analysis, will depend on the research objectives.

LOGISTIC REGRESSION

In the preceding section, the model formulated to predict the value of a response variable had the form of a simple weighted sum of the predictor variables. This is probably the most ubiquitous statistical model there is: it has a long history and has been used in just about every area of human endeavour. However, despite its power, it is not a universal answer. It has been extended in a number of ways and this section and the next consider two of these extensions. Here we look at what happens when the response can take values only in a certain range, and in the following section we look at what happens when the response is restricted to just two possible values.

Suppose we were exploring the relationship between the dose of a drug and the probability of being cured. One way we could set about this would be to make up several different doses of the drug and administer each of these doses to a group of patients. This is the same sort of way of drawing the sample as the second method described in the previous section on regression analysis.

People vary, so in each group we would expect some would recover and others would not. If the chance of cure increases with increasing dose, then we might expect more people to get better in those groups that were receiving the larger dose. This is beginning to look rather similar to the set-up described in the last section: we could, perhaps, model 'chance of recovery' as the response variable in a regression with 'dose' as the predictor.

This is a perfectly reasonable thing to do and is often done. However, it does have a drawback. This is that probability cannot be greater than 1 or less than 0. (A probability of 1 means certainty, and you can't get more probable than that! Similarly, a probability of 0 means impossible, and you can't get less probable than that.) If we model the probability of recovery as some constant times the dose, then:

- for sufficiently large doses the predicted probability of recovery would be greater than 1; and
- for sufficiently small doses the predicted probability of recovery may be less than 0. (Actually, this will depend on the data. Whereas there is, in principle, no limit to the maximum dose that can be given, there is a limit – zero – to the smallest.)

To cater for this, so that our model will only give reasonable predictions, we modify it slightly. Instead of using the weighted sum (in our case, just the constant times the dose) to predict probability of recovery, we *transform* the model so that its predictions always lie between zero and one. The most common type of transformation used is the *logistic* transformation. If the raw, un-transformed model predicts a value above one, the transformed version predicts a value below one, but the nearer to one the greater the un-transformed prediction. A similar thing applies to low predictions.

Because of the central role of the logistic transformation in such models, this technique is called *logistic regression*.

DISCRIMINANT ANALYSIS

Prognosis means determining the likely future outcome, and is important for people who have suffered a head injury. It will depend on many factors, including age, response to stimulation, and change in neurological function over the first 24 hours after the injury. We would like to predict the future outcome, say recovery or not, on the basis of some of these variables. Again, we shall build a model to do this, and again we will base our model on a sample of people. In particular, we will have a sample of people who have known predictor variable values (such as age) and whom we have followed up so we know their outcome.

Then one way to approach the problem is as follows. First consider the 'recovered' group. Such people will have a range of ages, a range of responses to stimulation, and so on. In a word, they will have a *distribution* across the possible predictor variables. The same applies to the other, non-recovered, group. If these distributions differ it means that for some combinations of age and response to stimulation, one of the two 'recovery' categories is more likely than the other. By modelling the distributions we can identify the combinations that are most likely to correspond to membership of each of the two 'recovery' groups.

There are many ways in which the distributions might be modelled, but the most common assumes a particular class of forms for the distributions. This method leads to what is known as *linear discriminant analysis*. It is called this because it leads to a predictive model that has the form of a weighted sum (a *linear combination*) of the predictor variables. Large values of this weighted sum are associated with combinations of the predictor variables that characterise one of the recovery groups and small values are associated with combinations that characterise the other recovery group. That is, the type of model used in linear discriminant analysis, for permitting one to allocate an object to one of two classes, has the same basic structure as the models discussed in the preceding paragraphs.

ANALYSIS OF VARIANCE

In the above, we described several *predictive* statistical techniques and pointed out that they all had the same underlying form: a weighted sum of the predictor variables. Another very common type of technique, which also has this underlying structure, although this is often concealed in elementary descriptions, is *analysis of variance*. This is aimed at describing the differences between groups of objects, so it is closely related to the discriminant analysis of the previous section. In fact, there are various different kinds of links between all of the techniques described in this chapter. That is one of the exciting things about statistics: its methods are not isolated tools; they form a complex and inter-linked system of ideas and methods.

Suppose that each of the predictor variables is categorical. That is, they can each take one of only a few possible values. For example, age might have been partitioned into young, middle, old; sex will be male or female; and some other measure might be graded as bad, impaired and good. We shall suppose that the response variable is numerical.

The cross-classification of the predictor variables forms a set of *cells*, for example, young males with impairment; old females with impairment. And now we can ask questions such as: do the males differ from the females? Does the response decrease as one moves from young to old? Does the effect of age differ between the two sexes?

To answer such questions, a linear model (a weighted sum) is again constructed and hypothesis tests are done. However, since designs involving categorical variables in this way are so common, special ways of describing the results have been created, and such analyses are summarised by means of an *analysis of variance table* that shows the influence of (in this example) sex, age, and the other predictors on the response, as well as how the effect of each of these predictors differs according to the levels of the other predictors.

OTHER METHODS

So far, all the techniques we have discussed are predictive in the sense that they seek to determine the likely value of one variable given an object with known values of the other variables. Not all questions are like this, however. Another whole class of models is concerned with describing the relationships between variables and objects when no variable can be separated out as a response. *Principal components analysis* is one such. This technique allows us to determine which combinations of variables explain the most differences between the objects in the sample.

In a study of the patterns of consumption of psychoactive drugs, (Huba *et al* 1981) data were collected on 1634 students showing the extent to which they had used cigarettes, beer, wine, spirits, cocaine, tranquillisers, drug store medications used to get high, heroin, marijuana, glue and other inhalants, hallucinogenics and amphetamines. Study of this data set using principal components analysis showed that the greatest range of differences between the students could be explained in terms of the overall extent to which they used the substances. After this, most of the remaining differences between the students could be explained in terms of whether or not they used illegal substances. In effect, what principal components analysis has done is reduce the very complex array of data to a simple and comprehensible description of the main features that distinguish between the students.

TIME SERIES

All of the methods we have outlined above involve multiple measurements on each object. Typically, there will only be a few (or a few tens) of such measurements and there will be several or many objects. In a sense, such situations lie in the middle of a continuum, at one end of which lie *univariate* problems, with single measurements on each object (methods for analysing data of that kind are described in Chapter 29). At the other end of this continuum lie *time series*.

Time series are characterised (at least, in their simplest form) by having just a single object but on which many measurements have been taken: the responses at each of a set of consecutive times.

Time series are ubiquitous forms of data. Examples are: stock closing prices at the end of each trading day; temperature at a particular location measured at midday each day; daily rainfall; and an individual's body weight measured at 8.00 am each day.

Such data sets are important for several reasons. *Forecasting* is an obvious one. It would be immensely useful if we could predict tomorrow's, next week's or next year's FTSE index! Understanding is equally important: is the economy showing an underlying upward trend or are the short-term figures deceptive?

There are several approaches to modelling time series. Some focus on modelling these series in terms of underlying components, such as trend, seasonality and superimposed random terms. Others focus on the probability that a particular value will occur in the next period given that the current (and, perhaps, preceding) periods have the observed values. More complex models include the effects of other variables on the score at each time.

OTHER TECHNIQUES

Statistics is a vast domain, with methodological research going on all the time; new methods for new problems and improved methods for old problems are being developed. Recently, stimulated in part by the possibilities presented by the growth in computer power, new classes of flexible multivariate techniques have attracted a great deal of interest. These include neural networks, projection pursuit regression, radial basis function models and multivariate adaptive regression splines. To some extent, these methods avoid the need to think carefully about what kind of model might be appropriate for the problem in question. But this is a two-edged sword: some insight into what is going on can prevent problems and also lead to better classes of models.

FURTHER READING

Huba, GJ *et al* (1981) *Journal of Personality and Social Psychology*, **40**, pp 180–193.

Joglekar, G, Schuenemeyer, JH and LaRiccia, V (1989) Lack-of-fit testing when replicates are not available. *American Statistician*, **43**, pp 135–143.

Krzanowski, W (1988) *Principles of Multivariate Analysis* (Oxford: Clarendon Press).

Lovie, P and Lovie, AD (1986) *New Developments in Statistics for Psychology and the Social Sciences, Volume 1* (London: British Psychological Society).

Lovie, P and Lovie, AD (1986) *New Developments in Statistics for Psychology and the Social Sciences, Volume 2* (London: British Psychological Society).

31 Computer support for data analysis

Clifford E Lunneborg

INTRODUCTION

In the 21st century, no postgraduate student will complete the analysis of his or her research data without turning to a computer. The computer has moved from being a widely available and convenient tool to being both ubiquitous and essential.

However, data should never be analysed by computer. The computer provides invaluable support to the research student in the analysis of data, but it is the researcher who must design, monitor, refine, report and interpret the analysis, guided at all stages by the questions that motivated the research.

The researcher must remain in control of the analysis. Beware of statistical computing packages; they invite the over-analysis of research data. The recent growth of statistical computing resources makes this warning imperative. Statistical packages are fast and easy to use, at least in the sense that they are user-friendly. They span many statistical techniques and offer many options in the implementation of any one technique. All of this makes it tempting to try out all-too-many analyses.

The increase in amount of computing support for data analysis prompts a second warning: Statistical computing resources should be identified while designing the research, *not* after the data have been collected.

FIVE STAGES OF STATISTICAL METHOD

A recent paper by MacKay and Oldford (2001) provides an accessible account of how data analysis needs to be integrated into an over-reaching statistical method. The method is represented as a series of five stages:

1. Problem
2. Plan
3. Data
4. Analysis
5. Conclusion

In the problem stage, the researcher identifies, at least by name, the variates and attributes that must be assessed in the research as well as the aspect of the problem to be studied. Is the goal of research to describe a set of relations, to establish causal links, or to predict future events? In the plan stage, measurement instruments or techniques are selected for the named variates and attributes and decisions are taken as to where and in what amount data are to be collected. The data stage requires continuing data monitoring as well as data storage.

The evolution of the statistical method through the first three stages impacts on the analysis stage, not least on the computing support that will be required. You do not need any unpleasant surprises when you reach the analysis stage. Ensure that computational support will be available for the descriptive, causal, or predictive analysis of the particular amount and kind of data your measurement techniques and research design call for. Make certain that, as data are collected, they remain appropriate to the planned analyses and are stored in a manner compatible with those analyses.

Planning the analysis, including its computational aspects, as you plan your study, protects against nasty surprises and reduces the chances you will expend your energies on fruitless or needless analyses.

CONFIRMATORY AND EXPLORATORY ANALYSIS

Most research programmes will profit from exploratory as well as confirmatory data analyses. Briefly, confirmatory analyses are those that answer the questions that drove your research. Exploratory analyses provide clues about how better to design your next study. Exploratory analyses have been described as unplanned or dependent upon the data, once collected and examined. They may be of that kind, but even so, their value will be the greater if attention is given, in the problem and planning stages, to what might go wrong. Are there additional attributes that could be worth measuring? In what detail should the data be saved for subsequent analyses?

Throughout, and particularly at the conclusion stage, you should distinguish confirmatory from exploratory analyses.

COMPUTING RESOURCES

There are *statistical procedure packages* and *statistical languages*. The former typically offer a limited number of statistical procedures, either standard or specialised, in an environment easily traversed by the user. The latter provide an extensive set of tools that a knowledgeable user could deploy to implement an extremely rich range of procedures.

To an impressive extent, the distinction between statistical procedure packages and statistical languages has dimmed, although it certainly has not vanished. The language programs have added pull-down menus, permitting researchers to carry out standard analyses with a series of mouse clicks. And the procedural packages have added scripting or macro capabilities, giving researchers greater flexibility in carrying out analyses.

Every major statistical computing resource provides far greater capabilities than it did five years ago. Furthermore, most statistical packages have become far more cooperative; data saved in the format of one package, say SPSS, are readily input to a second package, such as S-Plus. As a result, the researcher can often move from package to package, analysing data on one package, for example, and then turning to other packages to prepare presentation graphics or papers for publication.

New versions of statistical packages are released quite often. The capabilities of any one package will have increased between the time this chapter was written and the time the book reaches you. Fortunately, it is quite easy to learn the capabilities of the latest version of a package. The website provided by the package's publisher can be consulted. Web addresses for several statistical packages are provided later in this chapter. The websites of the Royal Statistical Society (http://www.rss.org.uk) and the American Statistical Association (http://amstat.org) provide links to the websites of package publishers. At the time of writing, an impressive list of statistical packages with links to their web sites is maintained on the website of the publishers of the statistical package Stata (www.stata.com/support/links/stat_software.html).

STANDARD STATISTICAL PACKAGES

Many universities have adopted one of the major statistical packages for use across faculties and this package, naturally, will be the one to which you will turn first. Four of the more popular packages are referenced below. There is a wider discussion in Chapter 11 of how you might go about choosing a statistical package, in terms of the nature of your work, your own nature, and the level of the analysis that you might do.

Genstat (from *general stati*stics) is the product of researchers (including the author of Chapter 21) at the Rothamsted Experimental Station and is distributed by the Numerical Algorithms Group (http://www.nag.com). Due to its origins, Genstat is strong on the analysis of designed experiments and on related regression models. The present version, Genstat 5, also provides facilities for a range of multivariate analyses such as cluster analysis, principal components, correspondence analysis, discrimant analysis, and multivariate scaling, as well as the study of time series, survival analysis, and the analysis of geospatial data.

SPSS (statistical package for the social sciences, http://www.spss.com) boasts a host of standard parametric and non-parametric statistical tests and is widely used for standard analyses of variance, for regression modelling, and for factor, cluster and discriminant analyses. The base-level version 10.0 package can be supplemented with add-on modules for, among other applications, categorical predictive models, conjoint analyses, and exact small-sample statistical tests.

Minitab (http://www.minitab.com) has a loyal following among teachers of statistics and may be familiar to you as a student. In version 13, Minitab shares much of the statistical coverage of SPSS and Genstat. It has a worksheet orientation to data and, thus, may appeal to those students who are comfortable with spreadsheets but find spreadsheet programs limited in their statistical capabilities. See the section on Excel.

S-plus, the augmentation of the statistical language S distributed by Insightful (formerly MathSoft, http://www.insightful.com), is the tool of choice of many academic statisticians. The Windows version, S-plus 2000, now supplements a command-line interface with pull-down windows for common analyses and for the preparation of statistical graphics. S-Plus, although strong on graphics, is best known for its extensibility. It is the platform used by statisticians for developing new procedures. If yours is a novel statistical application, S-Plus may be the best environment for your analyses. Venables and Ripley (1999) give an excellent survey of S-Plus with a good indication of its adaptability. If you become serious about developing new applications, Venables and Ripley (2000) provide valuable assistance.

SPECIALISED STATISTICAL PACKAGES

The Microsoft spreadsheet program, Excel, is increasingly popular as a statistical analysis platform, particularly in business schools. The statistical capabilities of Excel (including those provided by the Analysis ToolPak supplied with the program) cover the range of procedures associated with an introductory course (such as Berk and Carey, 1999). For more advanced analyses, third-party add-ons may be available. For example, XLSTAT (http://www.xlstat.com) provides a set of 25 tools to facilitate data management and to implement a variety of non-parametric tests, analyses of variance, and the more popular multivariate analyses. The XLSTAT website provides links to other

Excel statistical products and to Visual Basic programming resources for those who need to create new statistical applications for Excel.

BUGS (Bayesian inference Using Gibbs Sampling, http://www.mrc-bsu.cam.ac.uk/bugs/) provides the first platform for the study of Bayesian conditional independence models that is relatively easy to use. If you think that models of this kind might be of interest to you, look at the examples at the website; this package may be invaluable.

Resampling Stats (http://www.resample.com) provides a platform for quickly developing applications of permutation (randomisation) tests and bootstrap inference. These non-parametric resampling techniques, which effectively replace difficult if not impossible mathematical analysis with repetitive computations, have grown in importance as the speed of desktop or notebook computers has reached a level where the applications became feasible. Lunneborg (2000) provides an introduction to these techniques.

StatXact (http://www.cytel.com) provides implementations of the more common permutation tests. Some of these features have been imported from StatXact to SPSS.

BLOSSOM (http://www.mesc.usgs.gov/blossom) is another package of specialised permutation tests. The package features permutation applications to multiple-response data and linear models. BLOSSOM is available at no cost from the US Geological Survey.

CONCLUSION

Only a few of the many statistical packages have been mentioned. The Stata web site link mentioned above runs to 12 pages and provides access to the websites of 170 software publishers.

If the computing resources of your university or laboratory are not appropriate to your research, search the list for more appropriate candidates. If the search is not successful, you may need to develop a statistical application for your own needs. This will seem somewhat more difficult than the prospect of running a mainstream statistical application, but do not be daunted. A statistical computing platform such as S-Plus, with 3800 data handling functions to build upon, should enable you to meet your goals.

If your computational requirements are not only novel but also demanding, you may have to develop your application in a lower-level (but faster executing) language. FORTRAN and C++ have been the standards for developing statistical algorithms. S-Plus, among other statistical packages, provides a well-documented pathway for incorporating FORTRAN or C routines. In this way, you need code only those parts of your application that are computationally most sensitive while using standard functions for the balance of the analysis.

As a research student, you are gaining skills and knowledge of lifetime value. Each data analysis is an opportunity to learn more about an ever-expanding range of computational resources.

Good learning and good computing!

REFERENCES

Berk, KN and Carey, P (1999) *Data Analysis with Microsoft Excel* (Pacific Grove, CA: Duxbury).
Lunneborg, CE (2000) *Data Analysis by Resampling: Concepts and Applications* (Pacific Grove, CA: Duxbury).

MacKay, RJ and Oldford, RW (2001) Scientific method, statistical method and the speed of light. *Statistical Science*, 15, pp 254–278.

Venables, WN and Ripley, BD (1999) *Modern Applied Statistics with S-Plus* 3rd edn, (New York: Springer-Verlag).

Venables, WN and Ripley, BD (2000) *S Programming* (New York: Springer-Verlag).

32 Spreadsheets: a few tips

Tony Greenfield

INTRODUCTION

You have been warned in other chapters (10, 11 and 31) about the temptation to try to do all your data analysis in a spreadsheet, notably Excel. The temptation is there because Excel is so widely used throughout universities, industry and commerce for assembling, editing and presenting data for rapid calculations, business plans and domestic accounts. The warning is about analysis. Excel does provide some useful analysis and charting tools and interacts well with Word for the production of reports. However, Excel lacks too many features of statistical analysis packages; some of its analysis features are clumsy to use or are limited; and some of its analyses are suspect.

Nevertheless, Excel has so many advantages for any researcher that it deserves recommendation and some suggestions about how to use it to your advantage. If you plan to use a statistical package, you need not desert Excel. Consider using it at least for data preparation. Do not be afraid that, if you do this, you might have difficulties using your statistical package. All standard packages can read Excel files. In addition, their analysis results can be retrieved by Excel or Word so that you can create well-formatted reports. Unistat (Chapter 11) is even better: it can be used from within Excel, as if its instructions are Excel instructions, and its results appear automatically in well-formatted reports on new worksheets.

In this chapter, therefore, I offer some guidance for starting and a few references for further advice. My purpose is to help you to enter and save your data in a clear structure, in a usable form and without errors. Achieve this and then you can read about advanced features. You will also be more confident about analysis using a statistical package. Many more tips could be offered, but this is my choice.

I shall deal with

- data source;
- planning;
- data entry;
- validation;
- data checking.

DATA SOURCE

What is the source of the data? Have the data come from somebody else on sheets of paper? That's fine; you can plan your spreadsheets as if you had originated the data. However, if the data come already entered into a spreadsheet on a disk, you may be in trouble. Look for that trouble before you start to do any analysis. Faults I have found include:

- String (alphabetic characters) mixed with numeric values in the same column. This will prevent the variables represented by such columns from being available in statistical analysis.
- Zeros used to represent missing values. This will make any analysis worthless. The worst case I have had of this was with some data from an industrial client. A stream of data had been logged automatically into a file; the instrument had recorded missing values as zeros. The company sent the data to me with the message: 'We have tried all standard methods of analysis and found nothing useful. Perhaps you can suggest a different approach'. All they needed was clean data.
- Columns that lack identifying labels.
- Decimal points missing or misplaced.
- Strings used where numeric codes would be better. The simplest are YES/NO and MALE/FEMALE but I have met a study where a string of a dozen characters had been entered. These can be recoded if there are no errors, but there will be some.
- Blanks have been entered as first characters in text.

The section in this chapter on data checking contains advice on how to discover such faults.

If, on the other hand, you are the source of the data in the sense that you are designing your own study and will collect information from a survey, a laboratory or field experiment, or from historical documents such as medical records or a 19th century census, then you should design your data collection form to suit your data entry and storage structure. Do not do one in isolation from the other. Think about your data collection form at the same time as your data storage and analysis. Test the full process of data collection, storage and analysis in a pilot study before you embark on the study proper. Also, be sure that on every data collection form you record:

- source of the data;
- time of data collection;
- what the data represent;
- units of measurement.

PLANNING

Rows and columns

A spreadsheet has rows and columns. Stick to that arrangement when you organise your data. Designate columns to represent variables and rows to represent cases. For example, suppose we are studying a sample of people to discover an association between age, diastolic blood pressure and serum cholesterol, then these characteristics would be called variables and a column would be allocated to each. Provided there was no confidentiality problem, we might add two columns for first and second names. As a check on age, we might add a column to include the date of birth. Every row in the spreadsheet would represent an individual and would contain the values of those variables for that individual. Figure 32.1 shows the first few lines of this spreadsheet.

Unique identity

Have one column, usually the first, that uniquely identifies each individual. In our example (Fig. 32.1), I call each individual a 'case' and start numbering the cases from 1. You could equally use a staff number or a patient number.

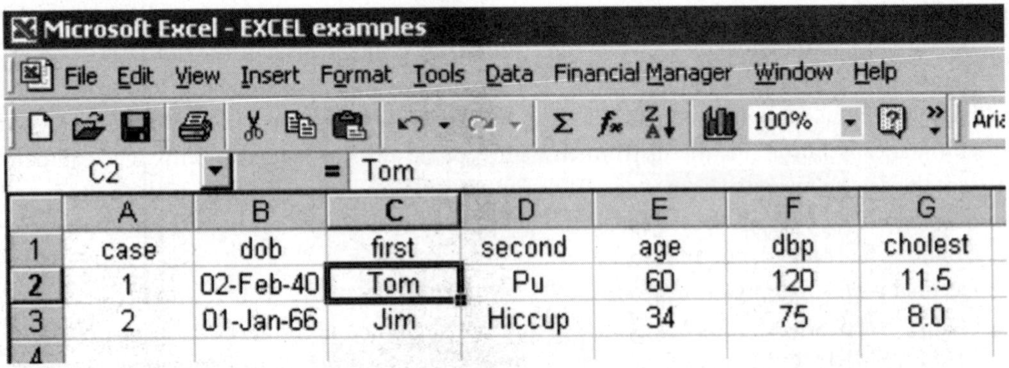

Figure 32.1 The first few rows of a spreadsheet with short labels for columns and unique case numbers for rows

Labels

Every variable should have a name that will be used to identify entries on the *data collection form* (DCF) and for reference in statistical analysis. Create that name when you design the DCF and use it to label the corresponding column on the spreadsheet. The name should start with an alphabetic character (A to Z) and it should have no more than eight characters in it. Few statistical packages will admit variable names of more than eight characters; also, a short name sits neatly at the head of the column. As examples (Fig. 32.1) use: *dob* for *date of birth*; *dbp* for *diastolic blood pressure*; *cholest* for *serum cholesterol*.

Data types

Variables' values can be simply classed as strings of alphabetic characters, as for names of people, and numbers, such as age and blood pressure. The classes are refined to include dates, currencies, integers and decimal values. The classes are known as *data types*. When you first prepare your spreadsheet, before you enter any data, you can specify the data type of a variable or column. If you then try to enter a data value of the wrong type, Excel will warn you of an error. See also the section on validation.

In our example, select column G, which will contain the data values for the variable *cholest*. Do this by placing the mouse pointer over the G and clicking the mouse. On the main menu, click on Format, then on Cells. A simple notation for this instruction is: Format > Cells. The following dialogue box (Fig. 32.2) appears.

In the left-hand pane, headed 'Category:' is a list of the data types from which you can choose one to allocate to your variable *cholest*, which is noted at top right under 'Sample'. Choose to display data values with one place after the decimal point. Without this selection, a value such as 8.0 would appear on the spreadsheet as 8, so you might wonder, when checking your entries if the correct value was present. With it, the zero will appear after the point (see Fig. 32.1). Representation of negative numbers is unimportant since you will have no negative values.

Similarly, you can allocate appropriate cell formats for date of birth, first and second names (text), and case identifiers and age (numbers with no decimal places).

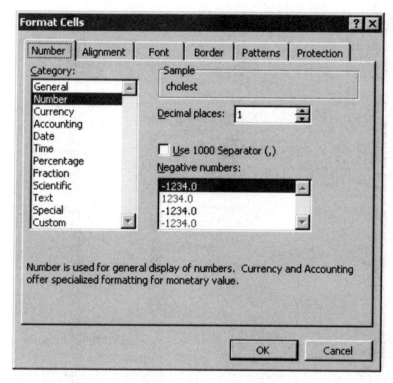

Figure 32.2 The dialogue box for formatting entries of cholesterol values

DATA ENTRY

When you enter your data, copying from your DCF, you can either enter directly onto the spreadsheet, row by row, or use a *data form*.

Direct entry

Keep headings visible

Copy directly from your DCF into a row of data, using the tab (⭾) button to skip from one column to the next. The more rows you enter, the further your current entry is from the first row that contains the column labels. Eventually the first row will disappear from the screen. You can keep the headings in view. Highlight the row below the headings, row two, and select `Windows > Freeze panes`. The headings in row one will always be displayed, no matter how many rows you have entered. You can remove this selection with `Windows > Unfreeze panes`.

Pick from list

Excel offers a useful feature that saves time and avoids boredom and misspellings. As you enter text values for a string variable, Excel automatically generates a list behind the scenes. Figure 32.3 shows an example of a list of receptacle types. Now, if you type just the first letter of a receptacle, such as 'b', the full word, 'box', appears.

The list may grow long; there may be several clashes of first letters. It may be a list of counties,

Figure 32.3 A list is generated

countries, foods, chemical elements. The solution is: select the next blank cell, right click the mouse and a drop-down menu appears (Figure 32.4a). Click on `Pick a list` and the full list appears, in alphabetical order to make it easy (Fig. 32.4b). Click on your choice.

Data form

The data form is an easy way to enter data into a spreadsheet. After you have put the variable names into the first row of the sheet, highlight any row in that sheet then click on `Data > Form`. The form appears automatically. Enter the data into this form and values will be transferred into rows of the sheet.

The data form is an easy means to view, change and delete records in the spreadsheet. You can also use it to find a specific record based on criteria that you enter. You can edit records in the text boxes just as you would edit them on the spreadsheet.

VALIDATION

While you are entering data, either directly or via a data form, you need to know if you have made a mistake. Some mistakes can be flagged automatically by setting criteria. After you have specified the data type for each variable, click on `Data > Validation` and the validation dialogue box will appear (Fig. 32.6).

Repeat this procedure for each variable in turn. The result will be that if you ever enter a value of the wrong data type and outside the limits you have set, a warning message will appear telling you to enter a correct value.

DATA CHECKING

Once you have entered your data, and especially if you have received data files from other people, you must check that the data are clean. Do this even if you have had validation checks in place. *If anything can go wrong, it will.* Several powerful tools are available to help you to check data.

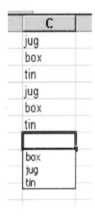

(a)

(b)

Figure 32.4 Pick from list: (a) the drop down menu; (b) alphabetical list

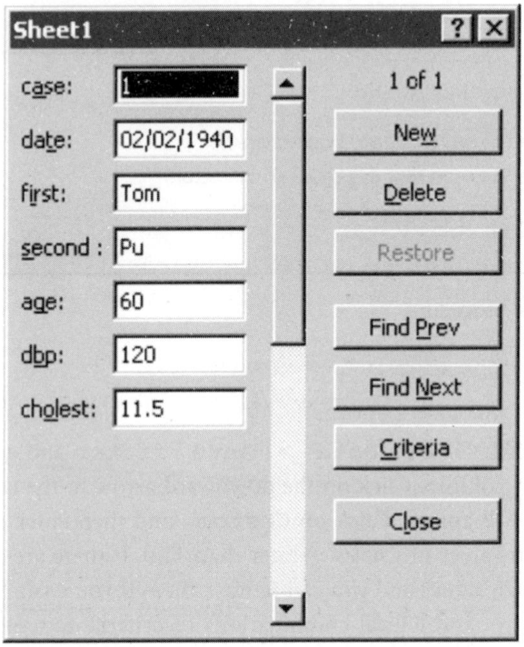

Figure 32.5 The data form

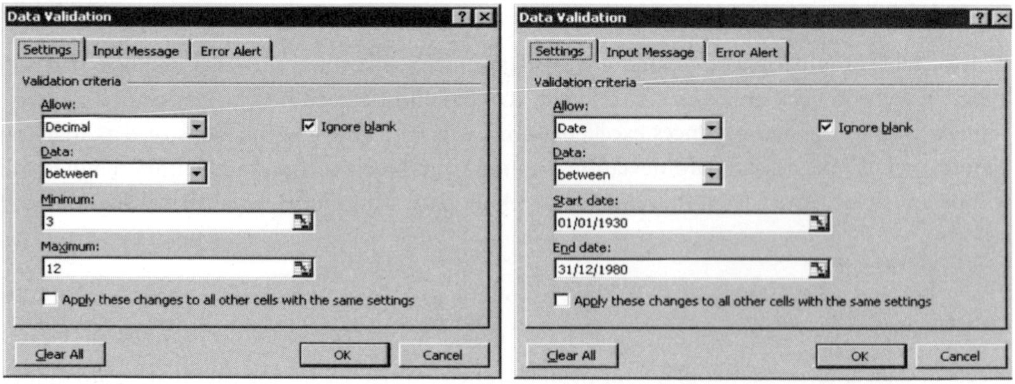

Figure 32.6 The validation dialogue: (a) for a decimal number; (b) for a date

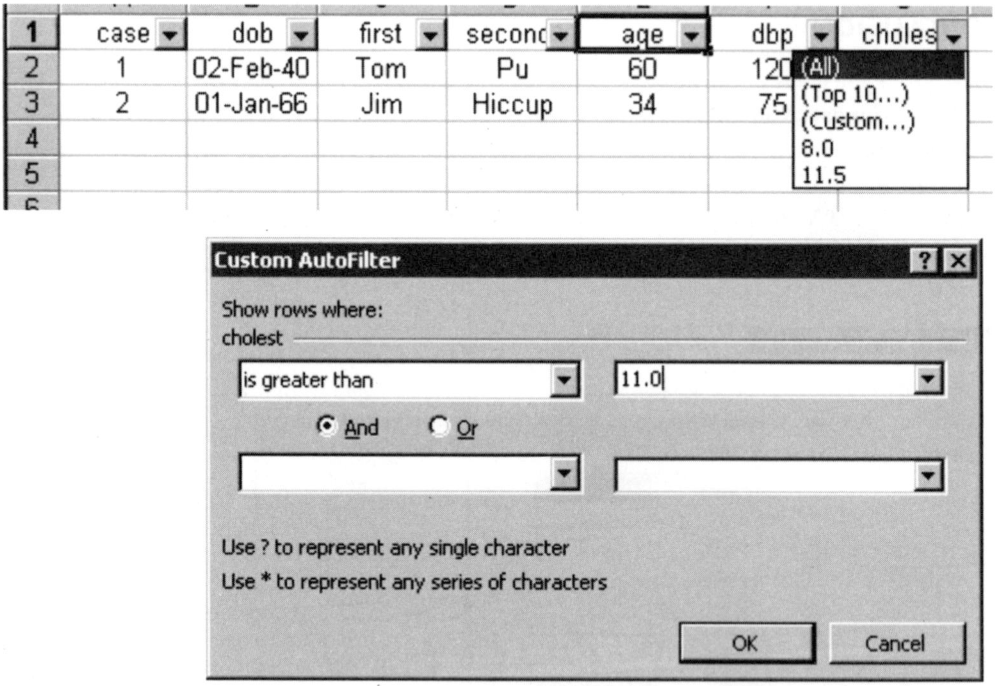

Figure 32.7 The auto filter procedure

Auto filter

Highlight any occupied cell. Click on Data > Auto filter and a downward arrow will appear at the top of every column. Click on the downward arrow in the colum that you want to check. A drop down list will appear. Click on Custom and then enter criteria for search. For example, you can look for values of *Cholest* greater than 11.0. If there are any, the auto filter will find all cases with such high values and you can remove them if you wish. See Fig. 32.7.

You can use comparative and logical combinations of criteria and you can filter on several columns together.

Pivot tables

A pivot table summarises large amounts of data quickly. Excel has a wizard dialogue that will appear when you click on `Data > Pivot Table` and `PivotChart Report`. It is astonishingly easy to use and produces excellent summaries, showing any functions of data that you choose: counts, means, standard deviations, minima and maxima. Try it and within minutes you will be an expert. Apart from its value for checking data, it produces tables that will grace your reports.

Charts

A rule of data analysis is: first plot your data. It will give you a feel for the data that no amount of reading tables will give. Plotting is also a good check: you can easily see if there are any values that are out of range. Use Excel's automatic chart procedures.

CONCLUSION

I have given you a few of the more powerful ways to ensure that your data are free of errors. Once you have clean data, you can proceed to analysis, either with some of the features available in Excel or by moving your spreadsheets to statistical packages. Some references are listed below to help you with this. In addition, there is an organisation called ASSUME (The Association of Statistics Specialists Using Microsoft Excel). Look at its website which has links to many useful sources of information, articles and reviews: www.jiscmail.ac.uk/lists/assume.html

FURTHER READING

Liengme, BV (1997) *A Guide to Microsoft Excel for Scientists and Engineers* (Butterworth-Heinemann).

McCullough, BD and Wilson, B (1999) On the accuracy of statistical procedures in Microsoft Excel 97. *Computational Statistics and Data Analysis* **31** pp 27–37.

Special tools

33 The value of mathematical models

Andrew Metcalfe

INTRODUCTION

We all use simple mathematical models in our everyday lives. The most common example is arithmetic, which we use for calculating monetary transactions, amongst other things. The numbers represent the physical currency, or perhaps electronic credits, but the example is exceptional because no approximation need be involved. A more typical example is provided by the answer to the question: how much wallpaper do you need to redecorate your living room? You could probably model the area to be papered by rectangles, work out their areas, add them up, and make some allowance for matching edges of rolls and so on. Your rectangles will not correspond to the three-dimensional shape of the room, and will not include details such as light switches, but the simple model is quite suitable for calculating the number of rolls of wallpaper you should buy. However, it would not be adequate for working out suitable sizes and positions for central heating radiators.

The mathematical models needed for research programmes are more complicated but the sequence of: stating the problem; formulating a relevant mathematical model; obtaining the solution; and interpreting the solution in the practical context, is common to all applications. We should also monitor the accuracy of our solution, and then refine our model to improve subsequent predictions.

There are many reasons for developing mathematical models. Their use can be traced back to prehistory when people recorded counting by cutting notches in sticks. Practical geometry is now assumed to have been invented by the Egyptians 5000 years ago (see, for example, Roberts 2000). They knew how to calculate the areas of triangles, and so they calculated the areas of fields by dividing them into triangular shapes. The motivation for this was that the waters of the river Nile overflowed every year and swept away the land boundaries. As a consequence of geometry, farmers knew the extent of their land and the authorities could work out the corresponding tax bills. The Egyptians were also aware that a triangle with sides in the ratio 3:4:5 was right angled, and they made use of this fact when constructing pyramids, although there is no evidence that they ever considered proving that this result followed from a set of axioms. The general result, that the square on the hypotenuse equals the sum of the squares on the other two sides, was known to the Babylonians, about 1000 years before Pythagoras set up his school at Kroton (in southern Italy) in 532 BC, but they did not prove it. The proof of the general case, referred to as Pythagoras's Theorem, is perhaps the best known of all mathematical theorems.

The Pythagoreans were secretive, so it is not known for certain that Pythagoras was the first to prove the theorem that bears his name, but his school certainly made amazing contributions to mathematics. The most famous is a proof that the square root of two, which is the length of the hypotenuse in a right-angled triangle that has its other two sides of length 1, cannot be expressed exactly as a fraction (ratio of two integers). It is extraordinary that they posed the question, and the method of proof by contradiction was another insight, yet, in modern notation, it requires only a few lines of school algebra. A further surprise is that the difference between the square root of two and a very close approximating fraction can lead to quite different outcomes in the chaotic dynamic systems that are now proposed as models of weather.

Al-Khuwarizmi (AD 770–840) and his colleagues, the Banu Musa, were scholars at the House of Wisdom in Baghdad. Their tasks included the translation of Greek scientific manuscripts and they also studied, and wrote texts on, algebra, geometry and astronomy (O'Connor and Robertson 1999). The algebra treatise *Hisab Al-Jabr w'al-Muqabilah* is the most famous of Al-Khuwarizmi's works, and is the origin of the word 'algebra'. The purpose of the book was to provide a means of solving practical problems of the time, which included those arising from trade, lawsuits and the construction of canals. His name was adopted in medieval Latin as 'algorismus' and later in English as 'algorithm' to mean 'a sequence of rules for solving a problem, usually, but not always, mathematical'.

Mathematical models have always been crucial for the physical sciences and engineering. The main objectives are explanation and prediction. A renowned example is Isaac Newton's *Philosophiae Naturalis Principia Mathematica*, published in 1687 with the assistance of Edmund Halley, in which he showed how his principle of universal gravitation together with his three laws of motion explained the motions of the planets and the trajectories of, for example, a ball thrown on earth. In brief, he assumed that the force between two bodies is proportional to the product of their masses, and inversely proportional to the square of the distance between them, and that this force produces a change in their velocities. Newton developed the calculus to investigate the consequences of these assumptions. It is remarkable that such a succinct set of premises can explain nearly all observed motion. However, all explanations stop somewhere, and the theory does not attempt to explain what might underlie the apparent inverse square law.

Newton was not the first person to offer a model for the orbits of satellites. By around 190 BC, Hipparchus had developed a theoretical model of the motion of the moon based on epicycles. He showed that his model did not agree totally with observations and it seems to have been Ptolemy who was the first to correct the model to take these discrepancies into account. Hipparchus was also able to give an epicycle model for the motion of the sun, but he did not attempt to give an epicycle model for the motion of the planets (O'Connor and Robertson 1999). Ptolemy's epicycles give a geometric description of orbits but do not provide the depth of explanation offered by Newton's theory and are not so generally applicable. However, even Newton's model is not adequate for dealing with objects that move at speeds approaching that of light. Albert Einstein's Theory of Relativity overcomes this limitation and when British eclipse expeditions in 1919 confirmed his predictions, *The Times* ran the following headline (London, 7 November 1919):

Revolution in science – New theory of the Universe – Newtonian ideas overthrown

It would have been more accurate to say that Einstein's model explains phenomena that Newton's cannot, but the impact of the headline might have been lost. Einstein had written a popular exposition of relativity in 1916, and the 15th edition of the authorised translation was first printed in paperback in 1960 (Einstein 1960).

Although much of the progress in mathematics has been inspired by a desire to solve practical problems, there are important exceptions. Extraordinary innovations, such as introducing i for the square root of minus one in the late 16th century (Sawyer 1943), have turned out to have great practical value. The concept of i is of fundamental importance in mathematics and is extensively used in electrical engineering.

Today, the world of finance, and the lure of stock markets, still provides scope for developments in mathematics, but research work uses probability theory to make explicit allowance for random events. In 1973, Black and Scholes published a formula for pricing share options. Before its use became widespread, any dealers who happened to know of their formula were able to identify underpriced share options and make substantial profits. As a consequence, there was a certain mystique about the result. Fischer Black died in 1995, but Myron Scholes and Robert Merton went on to share the 1997 Nobel Prize in Economics for its derivation.

Mathematical models can make a valuable contribution to work in many disciplines. The Pythagoreans were fascinated by the relationship between mathematics and music. Links with architecture go back to the ancient Egyptians and today justify at least one journal: *Nexus Network Journal – Architecture and Mathematics Online*. Knott (2000) has an interesting web page on the Fibonacci numbers, which includes a discussion of the extent to which the golden section really occurs in architecture, art and music.

Sociological applications are more modern. Shannon and Weaver (1949) wrote a monograph entitled *The Mathematical Theory of Communication*, which has been relevant to electronic communications and linguistics. Poundstone (1992) provides a fascinating mathematical analysis of the 'Prisoner's Dilemma' and associated potential conflict situations. The availability and power of modern computers has led to mathematical models that are used for simulations rather than being manipulated to provide algebraic solutions. For example, a recent computer simulation that was demonstrated on a BBC science programme suggested that a crowd would disperse through an emergency exit more quickly if it had a central divider. People in the crowd were modelled by dots in a plane, and impasses were resolved by various sets of rules, which could include randomisation. Helbing *et al* (2000) present a more sophisticated model of pedestrian behaviour, and suggest practical ways to prevent dangerous crowd pressures.

Logic and mathematics are inextricably linked, and an understanding of the principles of mathematical modelling would be an advantage for research studies in many areas of philosophy. For example, the best non-specialist account of Georg Cantor's work on infinite sets that I have read is given by Reid (1963). The history of mathematics is a well researched subject, as can be seen from the website set up and maintained by O'Connor and Robertson (1999), but it may be more surprising that mathematics can contribute to historical studies. Fairclough (2000) gives a nice example. Sometime around 1640, one Edward Somerset, the Second Marquis of Worcester, demonstrated a machine that gave the impression of perpetual motion, to King Charles I and most of his court. The machine, which was constructed in the Tower of London, was a great wooden wheel, 14 feet in diameter, with 40 cannon balls strung at strategic intervals around the rim. It seems that the Marquis stopped short of claiming perpetual motion and invited his audience to, 'Be pleased to judge the consequences'. Fairclough's analysis is a good example of mathematical modelling.

LEARNING MATHEMATICS

If you are working in any of the physical sciences, life sciences or social sciences, there are at least three reasons why it will be worthwhile revising and broadening your mathematical knowledge:

1. An understanding of mathematics is necessary to understand much of the research literature.
2. Computer software covers a dazzling range of sophisticated techniques for analysing and displaying data. Comprehension of the underlying mathematical principles will enable you to

choose appropriate methods for your research, to understand the computer output, and to be aware of the limitations of the techniques you use.

3. Quite straightforward mathematical models can be used in new contexts, and such applications often lead to publication in reputable journals.

If you are an engineer, mathematician or physicist you will already have had considerable experience of mathematical modelling, and have the necessary concepts to teach yourself new techniques relatively easily. Even so, finding a relevant course, at either postgraduate or undergraduate level, should help you learn new methods more quickly. Kreyszig's book, which is now in its 8th edition (Kreyszig 1998), is a comprehensive general reference work. Zill and Cullen (1999) concentrate on differential equations, vector calculus, and complex analysis. Jeffrey's books, including *Mathematics for Engineers and Scientists* (4th edition) (Jeffrey, 1989), are written in a clear and accessible manner. Academic Press has recently published his *Advanced Engineering Mathematics* (Jeffrey 2001). Croft *et al* (1992) is a book that covers engineering mathematics with examples drawn from electrical engineering. *Engineering Mathematics Exposed* (Attenborough 1994) is a readable text at a slightly lower level. A collection of essays, edited by Bondi (1991), gives an indication of the wide range of topics that can be usefully described in mathematical terms. *Classical Mechanics & Control* (Burghes and Downs 1975) gives a useful insight into mathematical modelling. The books by Clements (1989), Edwards and Hamson (1989), Gershenfeld (1999), Haberman (1977), Murthy *et al* (1990), Shier and Wallenius (2000) are examples of texts on 'mathematical modelling' rather than specialist areas of mathematics. My own introductory statistics book, *Statistics in Engineering* (Metcalfe 1994), emphasises the modelling aspects of the subject.

If your background is in chemistry or the life sciences, such as biology and medicine, or the social sciences, such as business, economics, geography, or sociology, it may be some time since you took any mathematics courses, although advanced mathematical options are often offered in these subjects. In England, the final school examinations are A-levels, and A-level mathematics or its equivalent is a good basis for further reading. However, typical A-level texts tend to be rather detailed and some books that cover the essential material in the context of your subject area should be more relevant. *Mathematics and Statistics for Business, Management and Finance* (Swift 1997) starts from scratch and is very popular. For chemists, rather more advanced mathematics texts are *Mathematics for Chemistry* (Doggett and Sutcliffe 1995), and some of the titles in the *Oxford Chemistry Primers* series (such as Sivia and Rawlings 1999). *An Introduction to the Mathematics of Biology – with Computer Algebra Models* (Yeargers *et al* 1996) is an interesting book that would be a good starting point for postgraduate research. The authors' objectives included making the subject relevant and accessible to students of either biology or mathematics. In the preface they state that two major journals, *Mathematical Biosciences* and *Journal of Mathematical Biology*, had tripled in size since their inceptions 20 to 25 years earlier. Another example is *Mathematics and Computing in Medicine and the Life Sciences* (Hoppensteadt and Peskin 2000). Burghes and Wood (1980) have written a book on mathematical modelling in the life sciences, and *Models in Biology* (Brown and Rothery 1993) contains a wide range of applications. There are many specialist applications of mathematics in geography, such as random spatial fields, aspects of GIS and GPS systems, and so on (see Fujita *et al* 1999). The mathematical treatment of economics is referred to as econometrics and can be considered a specialist branch of probability and statistics (see Hendry 1995).

It may be a good idea to consult several books on a particular topic. If you find one author's exposition hard to follow, another's approach may be clear to you. Also, books written for a general readership such as *Mathematics: the Science of Patterns* (Devlin 1994), *Does God Play Dice?* (Stewart 1997), and *Calculus Made Easy* (Thompson and Gardner 1999) can be very helpful for understanding basic concepts.

Whatever your speciality, it is worthwhile checking other fields. For example, marine technology and aeronautical engineering have much in common. The mathematical techniques associated with engineering control are also used in econometrics. Many research topics, in disciplines as different as civil engineering and medicine, involve the identification and analysis of non-linear systems, and there are many other such examples.

MATHEMATICAL SOFTWARE

Modern computers have greatly reduced the need to learn the detail of mathematical methods and it will often suffice to understand the general principles. For example, the details of efficient algorithms for calculating matrix eigenvalues can be ignored by non-specialists now that software such as Matlab can provide answers at the touch of a button. However, Matlab does not substitute for an understanding of the concept of eigenvalues and eigenvectors. It is usually far easier to understand these ideas for special cases, such as for 2 by 2, or 3 by 3 matrices when they have clear geometric interpretations, than for the general n by n case. Computer algebra, such as Maple, is another valuable aid but a sound knowledge of algebra is needed to make good use of it. Mathematica is another powerful software system for numerical and symbolic computation and scientific graphics. Up-to-date information on all these products, and associated books, can be found on the Internet by typing 'Mathematica', Matlab', or 'Maple' in any search engine, such as Google or Yahoo.

Fortran is still commonly used for research work in engineering, despite the increasing use of C++, and the NAG subroutines are invaluable. Another source of algorithms is Press *et al* (1992). The following website is a useful resource: www.fortran2000.com

The high-level programming language *J* (Iverson Software Inc) also contains powerful mathematical functions (phrases). Spreadsheet software, such as Excel and Lotus, can be used for simple, but effective, mathematical modelling (see Liengme 1997), and has the advantage of being widely available.

READING PAPERS WITH MATHEMATICAL CONTENT

Reading mathematics in papers is usually hard work unless you are very familiar with the techniques used. This is partly because the mathematics is often presented in a very formal manner, with many intermediate steps omitted. In addition, the final logical order may not correspond to the intuitive way in which it was developed. It is best to start by reading the article through fairly quickly to get an overview. If then you decide you need to read it thoroughly, it may help to start by looking at special cases. For example, an exposition in terms of n-dimensions may become far clearer in 1, 2 or 3 dimensions. Try not to be put off by the use of technical terms. These are often a generalisation of concepts that are probably familiar to you, and there are plenty of good dictionaries of mathematics and statistics around. Alternatively, look up the index of a relevant textbook, or try the Internet. Sometimes the use of technical terms is perhaps unnecessary, such as the use of 'sigma-algebra', in a paper from an engineering journal, for the set of values that could be taken by a variable that represented a flow of water in the application being discussed. You can find a definition of sigma-algebra, by typing 'sigma-algebra' in *Yahoo*, at: mathworld.wolfram.com/SigmaAlgebra.html

If you reach an impasse, it may be possible to leave the impenetrable section out and proceed with the remainder of the paper. A difficult piece may seem quite understandable if you return to it on another day. Also, other people will be more inclined to help with a specific section of a paper, than with the paper in its entirety, if they can do so without reading the whole thing. If you have a substantial query that you have not been able to resolve with colleagues' advice, you can always try contacting the author. A final tip is that some people find it worthwhile enlarging mathematical derivations when they photocopy a paper.

You may find that the relevant material from published papers has been incorporated into a recent book, in which case reading the book is likely to be easier, and more convenient, than reading the original papers. Most publishers' catalogues are available on the Internet, and the search facilities provided by the online booksellers are very useful.

PROMOTING APPLICATIONS OF MATHEMATICS

The Society for Industrial and Applied Mathematics (SIAM) was inaugurated in Philadelphia in 1952. The website is at: www.siam.org/nnindex.htm

The goals of SIAM were to

- advance the application of mathematics to science and industry;
- promote mathematical research that could lead to effective new methods and techniques for science and industry;
- provide media for the exchange of information and ideas among mathematicians, engineers, and scientists.

These goals haven't changed; they are more valid today than ever before.

The Institute of Mathematics and its Applications was founded in England in 1964, with similar objectives. Their website is at: www.ima.org.uk

Its bulletin, *Mathematics Today*, contains general interest articles that describe novel applications. They are certainly not restricted to engineering and science. For example, Moiseiwitsch discusses the link between mathematics and art in a recent article (Moiseiwitsch 1999).

ADVANCED COURSES

The London Mathematical Society (LMS), the Isaac Newton Institute for Mathematical Sciences at the University of Cambridge, and the International Centre for Mathematical Sciences (ICMS) in Edinburgh all offer short courses from time to time. For example, the LMS, together with EPSRC, is now advertising a short course in Wave Motion, with an emphasis on non-linear models. The Society's website is at: www.lms.ac.uk/activities/

This is aimed at research students working in the area of mathematical modelling, rather than exclusively research mathematicians. The ICMS is offering an instructional conference on non-linear partial differential equations, which is aimed at postgraduate students at the beginning of their research programmes, and EPSRC is providing financial support for the majority of participants. The ICMS website is at: www.ma.hw.ac.uk/icms/current

If such courses are relevant to your research, attendance would be invaluable. Apply early.

TYPES OF MATHEMATICAL MODELS

I have found it convenient to give more details of applications of mathematics under three chapter headings: deterministic models, stochastic models and simulation, and optimisation methods.

You may find the following summary of some of the main areas of mathematics, under these categories together with some applications, helpful. It is somewhat subjective, and by no means complete. The division between deterministic and stochastic is rather arbitrary, such as: some aspects of signal processing are deterministic rather than stochastic; some control theory is presented in a deterministic context whereas other formulations take account of random disturbances and measurement errors. Also, some, if not all, of the optimisation methods can be thought of as models, such as dynamic programming. Several of the mathematics subject areas in the table are sub-divided into techniques in the relevant chapter, and references can be found there. I have also included a few extra references in the table.

I have omitted explicit mention of statistical methods in this summary because they are discussed elsewhere in this book. However, fitting stochastic models to data is a statistical problem because it involves making inferences about their parameters.

Deterministic models

Area	Physical	Life	Social
Linear dynamics	Vibration of rotors	Population dynamics and epidemiological applications (Diekmann and Heesterbeek 2000)	Economic models: linear differential and difference equations
Non-linear dynamics	Wind induced motion of suspension bridges	Spatio-temporal patterning in biology (Chaplain et al 1999)	Predicting typhoons (Branover et al 1999)
Control theory	Autopilots for aircraft	Biological control (Kirupaharan and Dayawansa 2001)	Robotics (Wiener 1948)
Catastrophe theory	Phase transitions	Non-linear dynamics in nursing care (Lanza 2000)	Economic models: some non-linear (Granger and Terasvirta 1993)
Partial differential equations	Fluid flow	Modelling methane fluxes in wetlands (Segers and Leffelaar 2001)	Production functions such as Cobb–Douglas (Huang 1964)

Stochastic models

Area	Physical	Life	Social
Markov chains	Dam storage	Speech recognition (Juang and Rabiner 1991)	Brand loyalty
Point processes	Rainfall modelling	Birth and death processes	Monitoring effects of road safety measures
Time series	Flood prediction	Epidemiology	Social trends
Spatial processes	Distribution of ore in mining	Diffusion across membranes. (Yeargers et al 1996)	Image processing of satellite pictures

Area	Physical	Life	Social
Signal processing	Instrumentation	Monitoring muscle function in babies	Verbal communication (Shannon and Weaver 1949)
Simulation	Performance of computer systems	Epidemics	Inventory management and production planning

Optimisation

Area	Physical	Life	Social
Calculus	Calculating flight paths of space exploration vehicles	Logistic growth model	Maximization of a consumer's utility.
Descent algorithms	Airfoil geometry (Landman and Britcher 2000)	Chemical reaction rates (Jackels et al 1995)	Debt dynamics (Semmler and Sleveking 2000)
Linear programming	Gas transmission (De Wolf and Smeers 2000)	Emission of greenhouse gases from agriculture (DeCara and Jayet 2000)	Blending problems
Dynamic programming	Control algorithms	DNA sequence analysis (Wheeler and Hughey 2000)	Allocation of water resources
Critical path analysis	Programming techniques for microprocessors (Broberg et al 2001)	Nuclear material safeguards (Booth and Isenhour 2000)	Project planning
Genetic algorithms and simulated annealing	Optical telecommunications networks	Human posture recognition (Hu et al 2000)	Cooperative trade (Sherratt and Roberts 1999)
Artificial neural nets	Engineering applications (Bogdau and Rosentiel 1999)	Processing EEC signals (Peters et al 2001)	Benefits transfer (Delavan 1999)

SUMMARY

- We all use mathematics to some extent.
- Many of the developments in mathematics over the centuries have been motivated by a desire to solve practical problems. However, imaginative innovations, such as introducing i for the square root of minus one, have turned out to be of great practical importance.
- Mathematics is the means for quantifying research findings.
- Research councils in the UK, at least, are actively promoting multidisciplinary research between mathematics and other disciplines and the subject of the first degree is not critical if you have the enthusiasm to study whatever background material is needed for the project.
- Research in mathematics itself continues to be supported and the increased interest in applications should strengthen this.
- There are considerable resources for learning mathematics at postgraduate level: lectures, books and specialist software.

REFERENCES

Attenborough, M (1994) *Engineering Mathematics Exposed* (Maidenhead, UK: McGraw-Hill).

Beckman, D and Killat, U (1999) Routing and wavelength assignment in optical networks using genetic algorithms. *Eur T Telecomm*, **10**(5), pp 537–544.

Bogdau, M and Rosenstiel, W (1999) Application of artificial neural networks for different engineering problems. *Lecture Notes Comput Sci.* **1725**, pp 277–294.

Bondi, C (1991) *New Applications of Mathematics* (London: Penguin).

Booth, D E and Isenhour, T L (2000) Using PERT methodology in nuclear material safequards and chemical process control. *Environ.Model. Assess.* 5(3), pp 139–143.

Branover, H, Moiseyev, S, Golbraikh, E and Eidelman, A (1999) *Turbulence and Structures* (Academic Press).

Broberg, M, Lundberg, L and Grahn, H (2001) Performance optimisation using extended critical path analysis in multi-threaded programs on multiprocessors. *J. Parallel Distr. Comp.* **61**(1), pp 115–136.

Brown, D and Rothery, P (1993) *Models in Biology* (Wiley).

Burghes, D N and Downs, A M (1975) *Classical Mechanics & Control* (Chichester, UK: Ellis Horwood).

Burghes, D N and Wood, A D (1980) *Mathematical Models in the Social, Management and Life Sciences* (Chichester, UK: Ellis Horwood).

Chaplain, M, Singh, G D and McLachlan, J (1999) *On Growth and Form* (Wiley).

Clements, R R (1989) *Mathematical Modelling* (Cambridge, UK: Cambridge University Press).

Croft, A, Davison, R and Hargreaves, M (1992) *Engineering Mathematics* (Longman: Addison Wesley).

DeCara, S and Jayet, P A (2000) Emissions of greenhouse gases from agriculture: The heterogeneity of abatement costs in France. *European Review of Agricultural Economics* 27(3), 281–303.

Delavan, W (1999) Artificial neural nets and benefits transfer. *American J. Agr. Econ.* **81**(5), pp 1296–1297.

Devlin, K (1994) *Mathematics: the Science of Patterns* (New York: Scientific American Library).

De Wolf, D and Smeers, Y (2000) The gas transmission problem solved by an extension of the simplex algorithm. *Management Science* **46**(11), pp 1454–1465.

Diekmann, O and Heesterbeek, H J (2000) *Mathematical Epidemiology of Infectious Diseases* (Wiley).

Doggett, G D and Sutcliffe, B T (1995) *Mathematics for Chemistry* (Longman: Addison-Wesley).

Edwards, D and Hamson, M (1989) *Guide to Mathematical Modelling* (London: Macmillan).

Einstein, A (1960) *Relativity* (Penguin).

Fairclough, T J (2000) The great weighted wheel. *Mathematics Today* 36(4), pp 107–113.

Fujita, M, Krugman, P and Venables, A J (1999) *Spatial Economy: Cities, Regions, and International Trade* (MIT Press).

Gershenfeld, N A (1999) *The Nature of Mathematical Modelling* (Cambridge University Press).

Granger, C W J and Terasvirta, T (1993) *Modelling Nonlinear Economic Relationships* (Oxford University Press).

Haberman, R (1977) *Mathematical Models: Mechanical Vibrations, Population Dynamics and Traffic Flow* (Englewood Cliffs, New Jersey: Prentice Hall). Reprinted (1998) (Classics in Applied Mathematics Series) Society for Industrial and Applied Mathematics.

Helbing, D, Farkas, I and Vicsek, T (2000) Simulating dynamical features of escape panic. *Nature* 407, pp 487–490.

Hendry, D F (1995) *Dynamic Econometrics* (Oxford University Press).

Hoppensteadt, F C and Peskin, C S (2000) *Mathematics and Computing in Medicine and the Life Sciences* (New York: Wiley).

Hu, C B, Li, Y and Ma, S D (2000) Human posture recognition using genetic algorithms and Kalman motion estimation. *Chines. J. Electron.* **9**(4), pp 457–461.

Huang, D S (1964) *Introduction to the Use of Mathematics in Economic Analysis* (Wiley).

Jackels, C F, Gu, Z and Truhlar, D G (1995) Reaction-path potential and vibrational frequencies in terms of curvilinear internal coordinates. *Journal of Chemical Physics* 102(8), pp 3188–3201.

Jeffrey, A (1989) *Mathematics for Engineers and Scientists*, 4th edn, (London: Chapman & Hall).

Jeffrey, A (1990) *Linear Algebra and Ordinary Differential Equations* (Boston, USA: Blackwell Scientific Publications).

Jeffrey, A (2001) *Advanced Engineering Mathematics* (Academic Press).

Juang, B H and Rabiner, L R (1991) Hidden Markov models for speech recognition. *Technometrics* **33**, pp 251–272.

Kirupaharan, N and Dayawansa, W P (2001) Theory of reference frames and biological control. *Math. Comput Model.* **33**(1–3), pp 193–198.

Knott, R (2000) http://www.mcs.surrey.ac.uk/Personal/R.Knott/Fibonacci/fib.html

Kreyszig, E (1998) *Advanced Engineering Mathematics*, 8th edn (New York: Wiley).

Landman, D and Britcher, C P (2000) Experimental geometry optimization techniques for multi-element airfoils. *Journal of Aircraft* **37**(4), pp 707–713.

Lanza, M L (2000) Non-linear dynamics: chaos and catastrophe theory. *Journal of Nursing Care Quality* **15**(1), pp 55–65.

Liengme, B V (1997) *A Guide to Microsoft Excel for Scientists and Engineers* (Arnold).

Metcalfe, A V (1994) *Statistics in Engineering – a Practical Approach* (London: Chapman & Hall).

Moiseiwitsch, B (1999) Mathematics and art, *Mathematics Today* **35**(6), pp 175–178.

Murthy, D N P, Page, N W and Rodin, E Y (1990) *Mathematical Modelling* (Oxford, UK: Permagon Press).

O'Connor, J J and Robertson, E F (1999) ww-groups.dcs.st-and.ac.uk/~history/Mathematicians/Hipparchus.html

Peters, B O, Pfurtscheller, G and Flyvbjerg, H (2001) Automatic differentiation of multichannel EEC signals. *IEEE T. Bio-Med. Eng.* **48**(1), pp 111–116.

Poundstone, W (1992) *The Prisoner's Dilemma* (Doubleday).

Press, W H, Flannery, B P, Reulolsky, S A and Vetterling, W T (1992) *Numerical Recipes in Fortran.*

Reid, C (1963) *A Long Way from Euclid* (New York: Crowell) (1965, Routledge & Kegan Paul Ltd).

Roberts, A (2000) http://www.mdx.ac.uk/www/study/sshtim.htm

Sawyer, W W (1943) *Mathematician's Delight* (Penguin).

Segers, R and Leffelaar, P A (2001) Modeling methane fluxes in wetlands with gas transporting plants 1. Single root scale. *J. of Geophysical Research – Atmospheres* **106**(D4), pp 3511–3528.

Semmler, W and Sieveking, M (2000) Critical debt and debt dynamics. *Journal of Economic Dynamics and Control.* **24**(5–7), pp 1121–1144.

Shannon, C E and Weaver, W (1949) *The Mathematical Theory of Communication* (University of Illinois Press).

Sherratt, T N and Roberts, G (1999) The emergence of quantitatively responsive cooperative trade. *Journal of Theoretical Biology* **200**, pp 419–426.

Shier, D R and Wallenius, K T (2000) *Applied Mathematical Modeling* (CRC Press).

Sivia, D S and Rawlings, S G (1999) *Foundations of Science Mathematics* (Oxford University Press).

Stewart, I (1997) *Does God Play Dice? The New Mathematics of Chaos*, 2nd edn (London: Penguin).

Swift, L (1997) *Mathematics and Statistics for Business, Management and Finance* (MacMillan).

Thompson, S P and Gardner, M (1999) *Calculus Made Easy* (St Martin's Press).

Wheeler, R and Hughey, R (2000) Optimizing reduced space sequence analysis. *Bioinformatics* **16**(12), pp 1082–1090.

Wiener, N (1948) *Cybernetics* (Wiley).

Yeargers, E K, Shonkwiler, R W and Herod, J V (1996) *An Introduction to the Mathematics of Biology* (Boston: Birkhauser).

Zill, D G and Cullen, M R (1999) *Advanced Engineering Mathematics*, 2nd edn (Jones and Bartlett).

34 Deterministic models

INTRODUCTION

A good mathematical model will be as simple as possible, while including the essential features for our application. If we want to calculate an escape velocity for a rocket carrying a spacecraft, such as *Voyager 2*, or a robot, such as *Sojourner Rover*, we can model it as a point mass. That is, its physical extent is ignored in the simplest calculation. As the planet Earth has an atmosphere we should allow for air resistance. As a first attempt we could model the rocket as a cylinder, and we might then improve on this by using a cone to model the housing for *Voyager*. A more accurate answer may lie between the two extremes, but it should be closer to that given by the improved model. If there are astronauts involved in the mission, recovering them requires more detailed modelling. For instance, we need to model the heat distribution in the surface layers of the command module during re-entry.

The success of a model is usually judged in terms of the accuracy of predictions made using it, but we also try to capture something, at least, of the way we imagine the world to be. I have chosen the following examples of mathematical models to illustrate the ranges of techniques and areas of application.

DISCRETE AND CONTINUOUS VARIABLES

Although we perceive time and space to be continuous, and variables that vary over space or time (often referred to as field or state variables) as discrete or continuous, we do not have to model variables in the same way. For example: the size of a population of animals is an integer number, but if it is large it can be treated as a continuous variable; time is continuous but provided we sample sufficiently quickly we can model it as a sequence of discrete steps. The distinction is useful because somewhat different mathematical techniques are used for discrete and continuous modelling. However, distinguishing between models that treat time as discrete, and solution methods that provide a numerical approximation to a continuous time solution of a differential equation in discrete time steps, may be open to interpretation. For instance, I have classified the finite difference method as a discrete space/time model, but you may prefer to think of it as an approximate solution procedure for an underlying continuous space/time model. Many differential equations can only be solved numerically, in discrete time steps, and so on.

LINEAR AND NON-LINEAR

The distinction between linear and non-linear dynamic systems is fundamental.

A system is linear if the response to a sum of input signals is the sum of the responses that would result from the individual input signals. If the input signal is a sine wave, the steady state system response will be a sine wave at the same frequency, but with a change in phase. If the amplitude of the input signal is doubled, the amplitude of the response doubles. In algebraic terms, a differential equation, which models a system, is linear if the sum of any two solutions is also a solution. The theory of linear systems is thoroughly worked out, and has been applied successfully to a wide range of practical problems. Therefore, an attractive approach to modelling non-linear systems is to linearise, locally. However, this may not give satisfactory prediction.

Some algebraically simple sets of differential equations exhibit quite different responses if input conditions are very slightly perturbed. These are known as chaotic systems, and their responses may appear to be random despite being deterministic. Ian Stewart's book (Stewart 1990) is a fascinating and authoritative introduction to chaotic dynamics, which discusses the links with fractals. Stewart's examples include: the tumbling of Hyperion, a moon of Jupiter; the weather; turbulence; and dripping taps. The vagaries of the tidal current under the bridge at Halkida, which connects Evia to the Greek mainland, might be explained by chaotic dynamics. Aristotle was greatly puzzled by the way the tide changed direction so many times during the day, and was not able to provide an explanation. Systems can exhibit many different deviations from linearity, and there is no general theoretical framework corresponding to that for linear systems. There is, therefore, great scope for research projects that involve modelling non-linear systems. Useful texts include Berry (1996), Drazin (1992) and Thompson and Stewart (1986).

VIBRATION CONTROL

Although the simplest way to reduce unwanted vibration is to add dampers to the system, Victorian engineers also designed clever mechanical devices, known as vibration absorbers. These were tuned to counteract forces causing the disturbance (Den Hartog 1956). An interesting application to a wobbly foot-bridge is described by Jones et al (1981). This could be useful for the designers of the Millennium Bridge, a recently constructed footbridge linking the North Bank of the River Thames to the Tate Modern, but the theory assumes the bridge can be modelled as a single mode linear system (analogous to a mass on a spring). This is certainly not realistic for large suspension bridges, because the cables supporting the deck oppose its downward movement but offer little resistance to its lifting. This is an example of non-linearity. In 1940, four months after the Tacoma Narrows Bridge was opened, a mild gale set up resonant vibrations along its half-mile centre span. It collapsed within a few hours. It was a slender bridge and, although some benign longitudinal oscillations had been allowed for in the design, the torsional vibrations that destroyed it were quite unexpected. Billah and Scanlan (1991) and Doole and Hogan (1996) present convincing non-linear models that account for the mechanism of the collapse.

Both dampers and vibration absorbers, which are made up from small auxiliary masses and springs, are passive devices, in so much as they do not require any auxiliary sensors, actuators or power supplies. This is still a significant advantage, despite microprocessors and advances in sensor and actuator designs. However, there are specialist applications where the advantages of active systems outweigh the drawbacks. The possibility of applying control forces with contactless electromagnets is crucial for some of these. Another advantage is their potential to supply energy when required as well as to dissipate it, whereas a passive system can only dissipate and temporarily store energy. They can also produce a force at a point in such a way that the force depends on signals received from sensors that may be far removed from that point. In contrast, passive systems produce a local force that is only related to local variables. A further advantage is that active systems can be adapted to different operating conditions, as these conditions occur, without any outside intervention. Applications include: car suspensions; reduction of vibration of circular saws, which can result in considerable financial savings (Ellis and Mote 1979); high speed centrifuges on magnetic bearings; and the reduction of vibrations of rotating shafts. The modelling of rotating shafts illustrates many of the general issues that arise in mathematical modelling.

VIBRATION CONTROL OF AN OUT-OF-BALANCE ROTOR

A diagram of the rotor, excluding the details of the bearings, is shown in Fig. 34.1. The rotor is a continuous body, but we were content to concentrate on the displacements of nine points on the rotor measured at nine stations (Metcalfe and Burdess 1986, 1990). The first step is to imagine the rotor to be made up of nine pieces, with the mass of each piece concentrated at its centre of gravity, with these masses connected by rods of negligible mass. The theory that describes this situation is well known (see Meirovitch (1986), for example), and the end result is a set of linear differential equations, with constant coefficients, which describe the free vibration of the undamped system. This model of the rotor has 18 degrees of freedom system (nine displacements in the x direction and nine in the y direction). We will return later to the question of whether 18 degrees of freedom will suffice. The general theory of such systems is covered in any text on vibrations or linear differential equations (Jeffrey 1990, Thomson 1993, Weaver *et al* 1990). There will be nine characteristic frequencies (natural frequencies) and nine corresponding mode shapes in the plane containing the x direction and the axis of the shaft, and a similar set of nine frequencies and mode shapes for the y direction. The mode shapes corresponding to the three lowest frequencies are shown in Fig. 34.2. If the rotor is flexed in some way and then released, the resulting motion will be modelled as some linear combination of the mode shapes vibrating at their natural frequencies. According to the model, this vibration will continue for ever, because no damping has

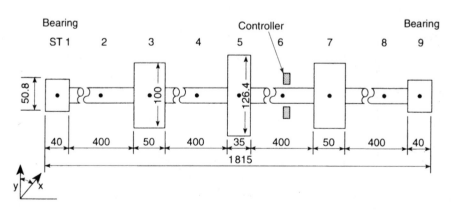

Figure 34.1 Rotor bearing model

Figure 34.2 Typical first three mode shapes

been allowed for. In practice, there will always be damping, caused by factors such as internal friction and air resistance, and the vibration will die down. However, such light damping has little effect on the natural frequencies or mode shapes.

The objective of our work was to reduce the vibration of a rotor caused by its not being perfectly balanced. This mass unbalance produces a disturbing force when it rotates, which will be harmonic at the frequency of rotation. If an undamped linear system is forced at a frequency that equals one of its natural frequencies, the theoretical amplitude of vibration will increase to infinity. This is known as resonance. Despite the light natural damping in structures, resonance is a real phenomenon that causes noise and wear, and is frequently dangerous. Operating speeds of rotors must be well away from their natural (critical) frequencies. We were modelling a rotor in journal bearings, and the oil film provided some damping and increased the stiffness. Holmes (1960) presented an elegant model for a journal bearing, and showed that these effects depend on the speed of rotation. Our model was modified to include: the light damping; a sinusoidal disturbance at the shaft rotation frequency; and the controller with its transducer and actuator, which were positioned at station six.

Although our model includes many differential equations, they are all linear and may be written as an equivalent system of 42 first-order linear differential equations, known as a state-space description. There is a detailed theory of such systems, and of their control, most of which is implemented in Matlab, and its associated toolboxes. Useful texts include Barnett and Cameron (1985), Borrie (1992), Jacobs (1993) and Kwakernaak and Sivan (1972).

In the engineering literature, a numerical solution to a mathematical equation, which purports to model a specific piece of equipment, is often referred to as a (computer) simulation study. This distinguishes it from a scale model, for example. Results of simulations at frequencies from ten radian/s up to 240 radian/s in 10 radian/s intervals, with a low and high controller gain, are shown in Fig. 34.3. The 'sum of squared displacements' is the sum of squares of the x and y displacements at the nine stations sampled over a 2 second interval, which is long enough for the transient response to become negligible. The vertical scale is 20 times logarithm base ten of the ratio of the

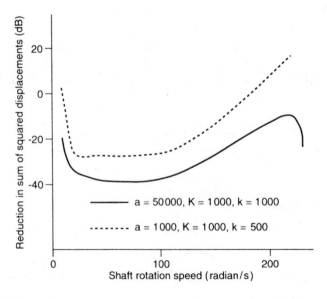

Figure 34.3 Controller performance

controlled to the uncontrolled response (dB). Thus, negative values reflect an attenuation and any values above zero would correspond to a detrimental effect. At a speed of 80 radian/s the vibrations are reduced by a factor of nearly 100. It may appear that further increasing the gain would improve the performance, but this would tend to make the controlled rotor system unstable.

It was not necessary, for this application, to model explicitly the rotation of the shaft. The harmonic forces generated by the shaft's rotation could be represented by the circular functions (sine and cosine). However, one drawback of a relatively simple linear model for the complex dynamics of an out-of-balance rotor is that it does not allow for the possibility of whirling (defined as the rotation of the plane containing the bent shaft and the line of centres of the bearings). Thompson (1993) explains how whirl can be modelled for a single disc. It is a non-linear effect that comes under the classification of self-excited motion (Schmidt and Tondl 1986).

Another simplification was to think of the rotor as made up of nine point masses. This restricted the analysis to nine mode shapes and nine natural frequencies. We are assuming that the ignored modes are of no importance. Although high order modes can often be neglected safely, they can also sometimes have unexpected and potentially disastrous effects. Feedback control systems designed for a finite mode approximation to a physical system can be unstable in practice (Balas 1982). This happens when the controller affects lightly damped modes that were ignored in the model, referred to as control spillover. The movements of these modes are detected by the transducers, observation spillover, and this may cause the controlled system to become unstable.

Unfortunately, it is easier to point out the hazards of ignoring high order modes than it is to give general advice about how many to include. Individual skin panels in an aeroplane fuselage can resonate due to acoustic excitations from the jet engines. This phenomenon is known as drumming and can lead to fatigue failure. The mathematical model for the fuselage does not include high frequency modes of individual panels. In most cases, the interaction between the global bending of the fuselage and the natural frequencies of the panels is small enough for the latter to be analysed separately. But it is unwise to rely on computer simulations, and laboratory experiments with test rigs, and scale models, are often the next step. The possibility of bugs in complex computer software, and hardware, should also be borne in mind.

The rotor example demonstrates the main concept of the finite element model, which is to divide a continuum into a finite number of bits that have simpler geometry than the original. Our bits were hypothetical point masses, joined by rods of negligible mass. In general, each bit (finite element) has a number of nodes that determine the behaviour of the element. Since displacements or stresses at any point in an element depend upon those at the nodes, we can model the structure by a finite number of differential equations describing the motions of the nodes.

FINITE ELEMENT MODELLING

The finite element method is a computational method that is used routinely for the analysis of: stress; vibration; heat conduction; fluid flow; electrostatics; and acoustics problems. Practical applications rely on the power of digital computers, which have provided the impetus for the development of the method over the past 40 years, since early papers by, for example, Turner *et al* (1956).

Original work in elasticity, early in the 19th century, led to differential equations that described the stress–strain relationship for materials assumed to be linear. These equations can be solved for simple bar shapes. The essence of the finite element method is that quite complex

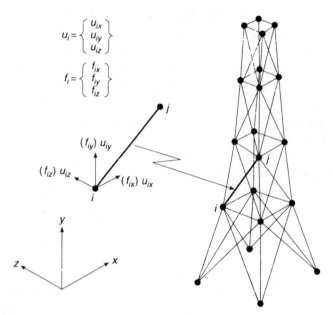

Figure 34.4 A simple bar type structure and its typical 'element'

and realistic structures can be made up from such simple 'elements' (see Fig. 34.4). The use of continuous element was the next step, and applications have included those shown in Figs 34.5 to 34.9. Appleby (1994) gives an ideal introduction to the method, and the associated software FINEL. This is easy to use and is capable of solving fairly large problems of static stress analysis, and field problems such as heat conduction and potential flow for two-dimensional and axisymmetric three-dimension situations. It can also be used to solve two and three-dimensional frame structures.

The following example (Appleby 1994) illustrates the principles involved. A simple triangular bracket, attached to a wall, is loaded at its tip. The bracket is made from thin sheet mild steel, and the load is in-plane, so the equations of plane stress apply. The simplest model of this structure is a single element that deforms in a linear way (the displacements are linear functions of x and y) and the deformed plate remains a straight-sided triangle. With this assumption about the way the

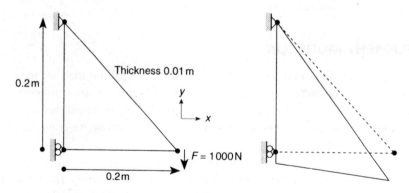

Figure 34.5 One-element model of a bracket (Appleby, 1994)

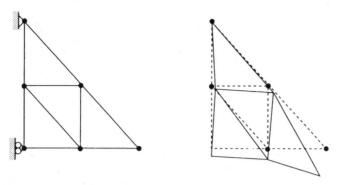

Figure 34.6 Four-element model of a bracket (Appleby, 1994)

structure behaves, we know at the outset that the deformed shape must be something like that shown in Fig. 34.5. Note that we have not so far done any calculation, but simply imposed on the problem a chosen form of solution. Normally, we would choose a form that we expect to be capable of representing the true solution to reasonable accuracy. In this case, the bracket should really bend much more near the tip than we have allowed, and it is not surprising if our model is much stiffer than it should be. We can improve things by using four elements, each of which behaves linearly but which together permit more complex behaviour (Fig. 34.6).

In practice, we often use more than one mesh, of progressively increasing refinement, to help

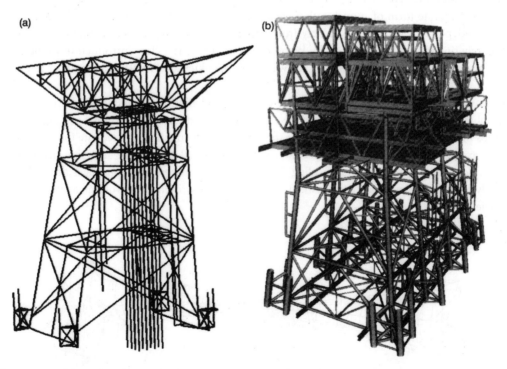

Figure 34.7 (a) Model of gas platform – beam representation (courtesy of M Kirkwood, British Gas Research Station, Loughborough, UK). (b) Model of gas platform – tube and plate representation (courtesy of M Kirkwood, British Gas Research Station, Loughborough, UK)

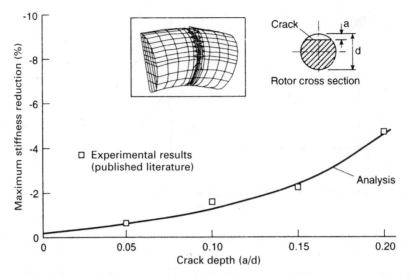

Figure 34.8 Rotor stiffness variation as a function of relative crack depth. Reproduced by kind permission of Imam *et al* (1989)

us assess the likely accuracy of the solution. If the increased resolution makes little difference, it suggests that we may have reached convergence to a practical solution. It is important to realise that convergence may be very slow, so that we are much further from the limiting values than it appears, and convergence to a seriously misleading solution is also possible! We should then use a more accurate form of model, rather than increase the resolution of a simple one. We must have independent verification, if only from experience or an approximate estimate, before we can rely on any results. The book by Woodford *et al* (1992) is a clear introduction to the more sophisticated PAFEC finite element software, and Zienkiewicz (1989) is a standard reference work.

Towards the end of his book on finite element modelling for stress analysis, Cook (1995) emphasises that the linear analysis assumes that response is directly proportional to load, and that loads maintain their original directions as the structure deforms. This is adequate for many practical examples in which displacements and rotations are small, but not for analysing situations in which deflections are large and buckling may occur. As a consequence, non-linear finite element analysis has been developed and Crisfield (1991, 1997) has written a two-volume textbook on the subject.

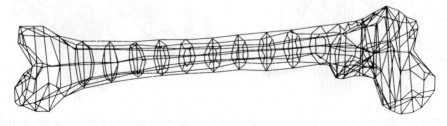

Figure 34.9 A problem of biomechanics. Plot of linear element form only – curvature of elements omitted. Note degenerate element shapes

FINITE DIFFERENCE METHOD

The finite element method applies the exact equations for the idealised elements to a model of the system, made up from these elements. The finite difference method approximates the differential equations describing the original system, by replacing derivatives with ratios of small, rather than infinitesimally small, changes in the variables. The two methods are conceptually different, and although many problems can be solved with either method, the solutions will not, in general, be identical. Gottardi and Venutelli (1993) compare the two methods for solving the Richards equation, which describes flow in unsaturated soil. The pros and cons of different schemes for approximating derivatives are discussed in books on the subject, such as those by Davis (1986) or Smith (1985).

Modelling the impact of pollutants, such as oil spills or seepage from dumps, on groundwater is a topical area of applied research. The models are expressed in terms of partial differential equations, and these are solved for specific scenarios. The whole process can be thought of as simulating the effect of pollution incidents. The basis of the mathematical description of multiphase fluid flow in porous media is the conservation of mass and momentum for each fluid phase. Faust *et al* (1989) present a two-phase flow model based on a three-dimensional, finite difference formulation. They use it to investigate the flow of immiscible, denser than water, non-aqueous fluids, from two chemical waste landfills near Niagara Falls, into the groundwater (Fig. 34.10). One of the

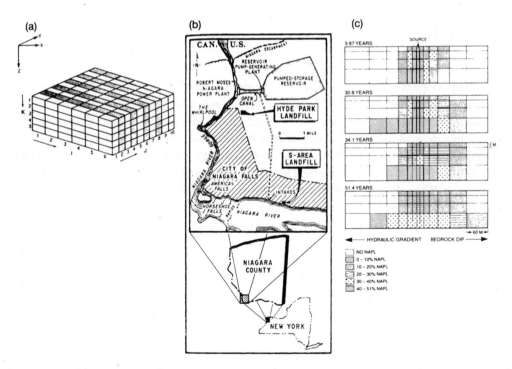

Figure 34.10 (a) Schematic representation showing typical three-dimensional, finite difference grid with alternate slices shaded for SSOR (odd–even) method. Reproduced by kind permission of Faust *et al* (1989). (b) Locations of the Hyde Park and S-Area Landfills, Niagara Falls, New York. Reproduced by kind permission of Faust *et al* (1989). (c) NAPL saturation distribution with time in vertical section through the centre of the source area and aligned with the direction of bedrock dip. Reproduced by kind permission of Faust *et al* (1989). (Faust, C R, Guswa J H and Mercer J W, *Water Resources Research*, Vol. 25, pp. 2449–2464, 1989. Copyright by the American Geophysical Union.)

research issues was the effectiveness of clay as a geological barrier. The mathematical model was a simplification of the three-phase fluid flow equations used for petroleum reservoir simulation (Peaceman 1977).

CONTROL THEORY

There are applications of control theory in almost all disciplines. Novel applications of the H-infinity criterion, minimising the worst case (such as Basar and Bernhard 1995), are still potential research projects. The method is supported by the Matlab Robust-Control toolbox.

A particular feature of chemical processes is that there are often long delays, due to thermal inertia, between applying control action and noticing its effect. This can also occur in other situations, and Ray (1981) gives a detailed treatment.

Many text books include sections on the control of non-linear systems and Slotine and Li (1990) and Khalil (1996) are restricted to them. Robotics provides many challenging applications.

CATASTROPHE THEORY (SINGULARITY THEORY)

René Thom's famous treatise on catastrophe theory, which is now considered part of singularity theory, *Stabilité Structurelle et Morphogénèse*, published in 1972, was the culmination of work, by him and others, over the preceding ten years. He suggested using the topological theory of dynamical systems, originated by Henri Poincaré, to model discontinuous changes in natural phenomena, with a special emphasis on biological systems. Poston and Stewart (1978) give an accessible account of the theory, some fascinating applications, and citations of many more. Wilson (1981) describes applications to urban and regional systems.

The following example is loosely based on one given by Burghes and Wood (1980). Suppose you have started a small business selling T-shirts, with portraits of famous mathematicians and associated formulae printed on them. You wish to model student intention to buy (I). You assume intention to buy depends on personal enthusiasm E and social pressures against purchase S. The personal enthusiasm could be improved by advertisements, which emphasise the high quality of the T-shirts and their educational value. The social pressures against such garments are left to your imagination. When these are high, the postulated 'threshold effect' (Fig. 34.11) is that an increase in enthusiasm will have little effect on intention to buy, until a certain threshold is reached when social pressures are overcome and intention to buy jumps to a new high level. The 'delay effect' is

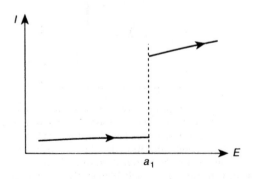

Figure 34.11 The threshold effect – high social normative factors against; increasing enthusiasm

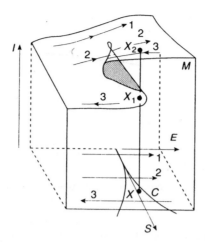

Figure 34.12 Intention to purchase depends on enthusiasm and social factors against

the converse when enthusiasm decreases. The whole scenario is represented in three dimensions in Fig. 34.12.

The projection of the fold onto the $E - S$ plane is a cusp C. If the social factors against purchase are low, the intention to buy increases continuously with enthusiasm (Fig. 34.13 and path 1 in Fig.34.12). If social factors are high, as enthusiasm increases we enter the cusp region and only jump to the top leaf when we reach the right-hand side (Fig. 34.11). However, as enthusiasm decreases from a high value we enter the cusp region from the right, and jump to the lower leaf when we reach the left-hand side (Fig. 34.14). Burghes and Wood (1980) provide a mathematical model for this example.

The concept of structural stability, or insensitivity to small perturbations, plays an important part in catastrophe theory. Chaos is the name given to the pseudo-random behaviour of some deterministic systems, and their extreme sensitivity to small perturbations. Fractal geometry, particularly associated with Benoît Mandlebrot (1982, for example), is closely allied to chaos theory. Fractals exhibit a similar structure over a wide range of scales and provide realistic models for the outlines of coastlines, the shapes of trees and snowflakes, the surfaces of viruses and many other natural phenomena. The idea is that, however much you enlarge portions of a coastline, you will still see 'bays' and 'headlands', even on individual rocks. Fractals have been used to study the

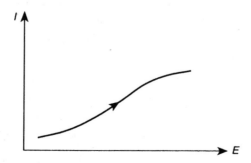

Figure 34.13 Early stages of the lifecycle of new product – low social normative factors against enthusiasm

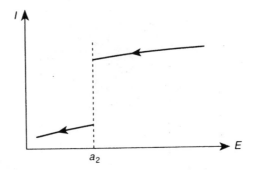

Figure 34.14 The delay phenomenon – high social normative factors against; decreasing enthusiasm

interaction of oil and water, in particular the phenomenon known as viscous fingering in oil wells (Stewart 1990). There are many popular books on the subject. Falconer (1990) gives an introductory mathematical account.

OTHER MATHEMATICAL METHODS

There are many other mathematical methods for modelling systems. Of particular importance are complex variable (see Jeffrey 1990) which can be used for designing aerofoils, vector analysis, which is central to hydrodynamics (see Lamb 1993), and Fourier analysis and integral transforms (see Firth, 1992) which can be used for control system design, fracture mechanics (see Broberg 1999), and the solution of certain partial differential equations amongst many other applications.

REFERENCES

Appleby, J C (1994) *FINEL Software (1 MS DOS Disk) and Tutorial* (University of Newcastle upon Tyne: Department of Engineering Mathematics).

Balas, M (1982) Trends in large space structure control theory: fondest hopes, wildest dreams. *IEEE Transactions on Automatic Control* **AC27** pp 522–535.

Barnett, S and Cameron, R G (1985) *Introduction to Mathematical Control Theory* (Oxford University Press).

Basar, T and Bernhard, P (1995) *H-infinity Optimal Control and Related Minimax Design Problems: A Dynamic Game Approach*, 2nd edn (Birkhäuser).

Berry, J S (1996) *Introduction to Non-linear Systems* (Arnold).

Billah, K Y and Scanlan, R H (1991) Resonance, Tacoma Narrows bridge failure, and undergraduate physics textbooks. *American Journal of Physics* **59**(2), pp 118–124.

Borrie, J A (1992) *Stochastic Systems for Engineers* (New York: Prentice Hall).

Broberg, K B (1999) *Cracks and Fracture* (Academic Press).

Burghes, D N and Wood, A D (1980) *Mathematical Models in the Social, Management and Life Sciences* (Chichester: Ellis Horwood).

Cook, R D (1995) *Finite Element Modeling for Stress Analysis* (New York: Wiley).

Crisfield, M A (1991) *Non-linear Finite Element Analysis of Solids and Structures, Vol 1: Essentials* (Wiley).

Crisfield, M A (1997) *Non-linear Finite Element Analysis of Solids and Structures, Vol 2: Advanced Topics* (Wiley).

Davis, J L (1986) *Finite Difference Methods in Dynamics of Continuous Media* (New York: Macmillan).

Den Hartog, J P (1956) *Mechanical Vibrations*, 4th edn (New York: McGraw-Hill).

Doole, S H and Hogan, S J (1996) A piecewise linear suspension bridge model: non-linear dynamics and orbit continuation. *Dynamics and Stability of Systems* **11**(1), pp 19–47.

Drazin, P G (1992) *Non-linear Systems* (Cambridge University Press).

Ellis, R W and Mote, C D (1979) A feedback vibration controller for circular saws. *Transactions of ASME. Journal of Dynamic Systems, Measurement & Control* **101**(1), pp 44–48.

Falconer, K (1990) *Fractal Geometry* (Chichester, UK: Wiley).

Faust, C R, Guswa, J H and Mercer, J W (1989) Simulation of three-dimensional flow of immiscible fluids within and below the unsaturated zone. *Water Resources Research* **25**(12), pp 2449–2464.

Firth, J M (1992) *Discrete Transforms* (London: Chapman & Hall).

Gottardi, G and Venutelli, M (1993) Richards: computer program for the numerical simulation of one-dimensional infiltration into unsaturated soil. *Computers & Geosciences* **19**(19), pp 1239–1266.

Holmes, R (1960) The vibration of a rigid shaft on short sleeve bearings. *Journal of Mechanical Engineering Science* **2**, pp 337–341.

Imam, I, Azzaro, S H, Bankert, R J and Scheibel, J (1989) Development of an on-line rotor crack detection and monitoring system. *ASME Journal of Vibration, Acoustics, Stress and Reliability in Design* **111**, pp 241–250.

Jacobs, O L R (1993) *Introduction to Control Theory*, 2nd edn (Oxford: Oxford University Press).

Jeffrey, A (1990) *Linear Algebra and Ordinary Differential Equations* (Boston, USA: Blackwell Scientific Publications).

Jones, R T, Pretlove, A J and Eyre, R (1981) Two case studies in the use of tuned vibration absorbers on footbridges. *The Structural Engineer* **59B**, p 27.

Khalil, H K (1996) *Nonlinear System* (Prentice Hall).

Kwakernaak, H and Sivan, R (1972) *Linear Optimal Control Systems* (Wiley).

Lamb, H (1993) *Hydrodynamics*, 6th edn (Cambridge University Press).

Mandlebrot, B B (1982) *The Fractal Geometry of Nature* (San Francisco: Freeman).

Meirovitch, L (1986) *Elements of Vibration Analysis*, 2nd edn (New York: McGraw-Hill).

Metcalfe, A V and Burdess, J S (1986) Active vibration control of multi-mode rotor-bearing system using an adaptive algorithm. *Transactions of ASME Journal of Vibration, Acoustics, Stress & Reliability in Design* **108**(2), pp 230–231.

Metcalfe, A V and Burdess, J S (1990) Experimental evaluation of wide band active vibration controllers. *Transactions of ASME Journal of Vibration & Acoustics* **112**(4), pp 535–541.

Peaceman, D W (1977) *Fundamentals of Numerical Reservoir Simulation* (Amsterdam: Elsevier).

Poston, T and Stewart, I (1978) *Catastrophe Theory and its Applications* (London: Pitman).

Ray, W H (1981) *Advanced Process Control* (McGraw-Hill).

Schmidt, G and Tondl, A (1986) *Non-linear Vibrations* (Cambridge University Press).

Slotine, J-J and Li, W (1991) *Applied Nonlinear Control* (Prentice Hall).

Smith, G D (1985) *Numerical Solution of Partial Differential Equations* (Oxford University Press).

Stewart, I (1990) *Does God Play Dice? The New Mathematics of Chaos* (London: Penguin).

Thompson, J M T and Stewart, H B (1986) *Nonlinear Dynamics and Chaos* (Chichester, UK: Wiley).

Thomson, W T (1993) *Theory of Vibration with Applications*, 4th edn (London: Chapman & Hall).

Turner, M J, Clough, R W, Martin, H C and Topp, L T (1956) *Stiffness and deflection analysis of complex structures, Journal of Aeronautical Science* **23**, pp 805–823.

Weaver, W J R, Timoshenko, S P and Young, D H (1990). *Vibration Problems in Engineering*, 5th edn (New York: Wiley).

Wilson, A G (1981) *Catastrophe Theory and Bifurcation: Applications to Urban and Regional Systems* (University of California Press).

Woodford, C H Passaris, E K S and Bull, J W (1992) *Engineering Analysis using PAFEC Finite Element Software* (Glasgow: Blackie Academic).

Zienkiewicz, O C (1989) *Finite Element Method*, 4th edn (with Taylor R L), Two volumes (McGraw Hill).

35 Stochastic models and simulation

Andrew Metcalfe

INTRODUCTION

The Agora Museum in Athens contains a piece of a Kleroterion, an allotment machine. Names of candidates for senate were placed in an array of slots (typically 50 rows by 11 columns). A funnel at the top contained bronze balls, which were coloured black or white, and a crank-driven device released these, one at a time, down a tube. A white ball corresponded to selection. You can easily find out more from internet sites such as www.alamut.com/subj/artiface/deadMedia/agoraMuseum.html

The concept of random processes can therefore be traced back at least as far as 2 BC. Although 'stochastic' is now synonymous with 'random', Stewart (1990) gives its original meaning in the Greek language as 'skilful in aiming'. This is appropriate because we aim to use probability theory and the theory of stochastic processes to model the occurrences of chance events and to provide the best possible predictions despite the uncertainty. We can also quantify the uncertainty by using, for example, 95% confidence intervals for unknown parameters and 95% prediction intervals for individual outcomes. Apart from short-term predictions, stochastic models are also used to generate many possible long-term scenarios for evaluation of policies that might relate to portfolio management (Ranne 1999) or the construction of flood defences (Wallis 1981).

A stochastic model starts with a deterministic model. It is often, but not always, a simple empirical relationship, and accounts for deviations between the model and data by postulating random 'errors'. These errors encompass: inherent variation in the population being modelled; modelling error; and measurement error. A typical research project will involve: thinking of reasonable models for the situation; fitting these models to existing data and choosing one or two that seem the best, from an empirical point of view; simulating future scenarios; and monitoring the success of predictions. The random errors are modelled by a probability distribution. Generation of random numbers from a given probability distribution is an essential part of any (stochastic) simulation. Ross (1997) gives a thorough account of simulation methods.

I have chosen the following examples of stochastic models to indicate the ranges of both techniques and areas of application. Although we perceive time and space to be continuous, and variables that vary over space or time (field or state variables) as discrete or continuous, we do not have to model variables in the same way. For example, the Markov chain model for dam storage (Moran 1954) treats both volume of water and time as discrete. That is: volume of water is measured in multiples of, typically, 20ths of the total capacity of the dam; and time jumps from the end of one dry season to the end of the next one. The stochastic calculus deals with continuous variables defined over continuous time, and financial applications are a popular research topic. You may find the following summary of some of the main techniques of stochastic modelling, by category, helpful. Although the theory of signal processing techniques, such as spectral analysis, is often nicer

Table 35.1 Example of stochastic models

Field variable	Space/Time	
	Discrete	Continuous
Discrete	• Markov Chain	• point processes
Continuous	• time series models • signal processing of digitised signals • Image processing • Kriging	• field models • spectral and wavelet theory for analogue signals • Ito Calculus, Stratonovich Calculus

when expressed in terms of continuous signals, modern data analysis is almost always performed on the digitised signal. Provided the sampling rate is high enough – and megahertz rates can now be achieved – nothing is lost (see Chapter 28).

There are many books on stochastic modelling. Examples are Ross (2000), Bhattacharya and Waymire (1990), Cox and Miller (1977), Nelson (1995), which concentrates on the modelling of computer performance, and Guttorp (1995) which emphasises scientific applications. Cox and Isham (1980) is a good reference for point processes. There are as many titles on time series. Chatfield (1989) is a nice clear introduction, Pole *et al* (1994) discuss Bayesian methods and include a computer disk with BATS software, and Tong (1990) gives a thorough treatment of non-linear time series. Books on signal processing tend to concentrate on frequency domain techniques. Newland (1993) is written in the context of mechanical engineering and Bendat (1998) is a recent book on non-linear techniques. Although there are many applications for stochastic calculus (such as Oksendal 1995), including quantum theory, the most common are financial (for example, Mikosch 2000). The publisher Springer has an impressive list of books in the field of mathematical finance and insurance.

APPLICATIONS OF MARKOV CHAINS

The Markov property is that the future depends on the present, but not the past, given the present state. In a Markov chain, the process can be in any one of a discrete set of states after each time step. In brand loyalty models, the state is the brand and the time steps are times between purchases. Brown *et al* (1997) ranked pension funds by their financial performance and defined the state as the quarter (within top 25 per cent; . . .; within lowest 25 per cent) in which a pension fund appeared at the end of each year.

More specialist topics include hidden state Markov chains (MacDonald and Zucchini 1997), in which the state is not observed, and which have been used for such diverse applications as the modelling of genome structure, speech recognition and rainfall modelling. Markov chain Monte Carlo (MCMC) methods, such as the Gibbs sampler, are now commonly used for stochastic modelling, such as the joint distribution of floods and their volumes (Adamson *et al* 1999). Casella and George (1992) is a good introduction. The Hastings–Metropolis (see Chib and Greenberg 1995) is more general. Gilks *et al* (1995) includes many practical applications of these techniques.

APPLICATIONS OF POINT PROCESSES AND SIMULATION

In a point process, events, which result in a change of state of the process, occur at instants of time. There are many applications, including machine breakdowns and repairs, and queuing situations.

In a typical queuing model, the state is the number of persons in the system and an event is the arrival of another person or the completion of a service. It is possible to build up more complex models by superimposing point process models and, for example, rectangular pulses, as Rodriguez-Iturbe *et al* (1987) do for rainfall at a point. Simulation of point processes is known as discrete event simulation (Ross 1997).

APPLICATIONS OF TIME SERIES AND SIMULATION

The risk of flooding in the short term has an important bearing on some civil engineering decisions. For example, contractors working on a dam face, from barges or with floating cranes, will benefit from accurate estimates of flood risk. Water engineers responsible for reservoir operation, who need to balance the requirements of flood control, provision of domestic and industrial water supply, public amenity and effluent dilution, will also benefit from up-to-date estimates of the risk of occurrence of high flows. In such cases, the risk of flooding will be influenced by prevailing catchment conditions and weather forecasts, as well as the average seasonal variation. Insurance companies might also have an interest in estimating short-term flood risks.

The most useful indicators of flood risk will be the time of year, a measure of how wet the catchment is (if it is saturated, rain will run off directly into the river rather than soak into the ground), and rain forecasts (although these are not reliable beyond one or two days in the UK, and general tendencies are incorporated in the time of year). Tsang (1991) fitted a stochastic model to data from the River Dearne in South Yorkshire, and then estimated the dependence of flood risk on catchment wetness, during the summer months, by simulation. She used base flow in a river, which she approximated by daily minimum flows, as a measure of catchment wetness. An autoregressive model, so-called because past values of base flow are used to predict today's value, with daily rainfalls over the previous few days as additional explanatory variables, was fitted to the time series of daily baseflow and daily rainfall. The daily rainfall time series was itself modelled as a Markov chain sequence of wet and dry days, with a Weibull distribution of rainfall on wet days. Finally, events were defined as those peak flows for which the rainfall during the preceding two days was at least 14 mm. It was assumed that smaller amounts of rainfall could not lead to flooding. To these peak flows Tsang fitted a Weibull distribution whose parameters were a function of the total rainfall over the two days preceding the day of the event and the baseflow on the day before the event.

The first step in estimating flood risk is to generate a sequence of wet and dry days for the required period using the Markov chain. Next, a random sample of daily rainfalls is generated for the wet days. The autoregressive model can then be used to generate a baseflow sequence. Events with a two-day rainfall total exceeding the rainfall threshold of 14 mm are identified, so at this stage the number of rainfall events is known. Now suppose that the probability of exceeding some critical flow is required. For each rainfall event, the probability of not exceeding this critical flow can be calculated from the Weibull distribution, and hence the risk of flooding during any required period can be calculated.

A computer program was written to calculate the flood risks for seven and 30 days ahead, as a function of current base flow, using the stochastic simulation (Fig. 35.1). The results show a relationship between the flood risk and start-of-period baseflow, which is more pronounced for the predictions seven days ahead. The model can be explained in physical terms and is reasonably straightforward to fit. It would be possible to refine it by, for example, generating correlated random variables for rainfall sequences extending over more than one day, but this will only be

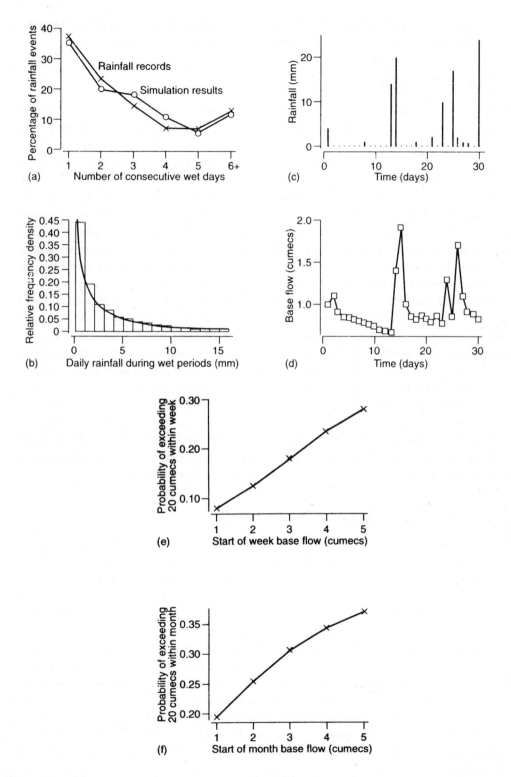

Figure 35.1 (a) Frequency of consecutive wet days. (b) Daily rainfalls during wet periods (mm). (c) Realisation of rainfall over 30 days. (d) Corresponding base flow series. (e) Start of week base flow $(m^3 s^{-1})$. (f) Start of month base flow $(m^3 s^{-1})$

worthwhile if it makes a substantial difference to risk estimates. The need for simulations to compute a flood risk is not a serious disadvantage given modern computing facilities.

SIGNAL PROCESSING

Signal processing covers a vast range of applications. A medical example (McClelland 1997) involves recording the electromyograph (EMG) response to a pseudo-random sequence of taps applied to the biceps muscle. In this context, the biceps muscle is adequately modelled as a single degree of freedom linear system and it follows, from the theory of spectral analysis, that the auto-covariance function of the EMG response is an estimate of the impulse response of the biceps. The importance of the method is that it provides clinicians with a quick painless test to ascertain whether babies are suffering from cerebral palsy. Early detection increases the efficacy of treatment for the condition. A larger scale example (Hearn *et al* 2000) involved the estimation of the frequency response functions for the three translational and three rotational motions of a large motorboat, from data collected during sea trials. Hence, the risks of capsize in extreme sea states, and the accelerations experienced by crew at various stations on board, can be estimated.

The wavelet transform is an important development in signal analysis. Spectral analysis (see for example, Firth 1992, Hearn and Metcalfe 1995) gives an average frequency description of random signals, but is of limited use if statistical features of the signal change over time. Wavelets can be thought of as local Fourier analyses that track the changes. A musical score may be a helpful analogy. An early application was the analysis of earthquake records (Goupillaud *et al* 1984). Newland (1993) gives an introductory account and some Matlab program listings. For a recent review of wavelet analysis and its statistical applications, you can read Abramovich *et al* (2000). Ogden (1997), Walker (1999) and Burrus (1998) are useful reference books. Kaiser (1994) takes the reader from first year undergraduate mathematics to research results in mathematical physics, and his enthusiasm is encouraging. The book edited by Silverman and Vassilicos (2000) includes applications to: astronomy, turbulence, the physiology of vision, acoustics and economics.

A RANDOM FIELD MODEL FOR RAINFALL

The distribution of rainfall, over time and space, is essential information for designers of water resource projects ranging from flood protection to irrigation schemes. Ideally, and provided there were no long-term climate changes, statistics could be calculated from long records over an extensive network of rain gauges. In practice, rain gauge networks are often sparse or non-existent and, even in countries with good coverage, records for periods exceeding 50 years are relatively uncommon. Furthermore, records usually consist of daily rainfall totals, and for some purposes, such as assessment of the hydraulic performance and pollution impact of sewers, finer resolution, down to five-minute rainfall totals, is needed. For some purposes, it may be possible to progress with rainfall at a single site. Other applications need rainfall at several sites, and projects that are more ambitious require a rainfall field model. The development of rainfall field models, and their calibration from radar data, is an active research topic. The rainfall model described below has been coupled with a deterministic rainfall-runoff model of the River Brue catchment in the South West of England and could be used for flood warning and the design of flood protection schemes (Mellor *et al* 2000a).

The structure of the model is shown in Fig. 35.2 (Mellor 1996). An initial random field (i) is produced by randomly generated intersecting prisms, which move along their axes with constant

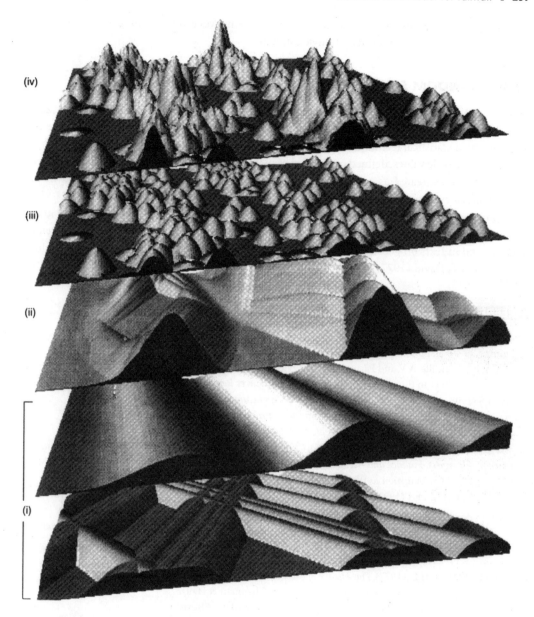

Figure 35.2 Realisation of MTB model (reproduced by kind permission of D Mellor)

velocities. This field is modulated by a function composed of sine waves, which has an independent velocity, and introduces the effect of rain bands. This modulated field (ii) represents a time varying spatial rate of an inhomogeneous Poisson process, which controls the births of rain cells. That is, where the field takes on a high value there is a large probability of rain cells occurring, and where the field is low there is a smaller chance of a rain cell occurring. The rain cells themselves are described as parabolas of revolution (iii), whose heights represent rainfall intensity at the corresponding point on the surface. The peak of a rain cell grows and then decays over time (iv), and all the rain cells are assumed to have the same velocity. In flood warning applications, rain cells and rain bands are identified from radar data and an ensemble of scenarios is stochastically generated up to six hours ahead (Mellor *et al* 2000b). Thus, the system gives limits that have any chosen probability of being exceeded rather than a single estimate.

OTHER RANDOM FIELD MODELS

Another particularly active research area is the analysis of digital images from space probes, electron microscopes, brain scanners, and so on. Noise and blur have to be removed, and there is a wide variety of statistical techniques that can be used. The images are usually considered in terms of discrete grey scale values, defined over a grid of picture elements, typically 1024×1024. The grey scale is sometimes treated as continuous. Some good introductory papers can be found in the Internet directory: http://www.stats.bris.ac.uk/pub/reports/MCMC

Kriging is a method for spatial interpolation between a few point values. It was developed in the mining industry, and this is reflected in some of the terms used, such as the 'nugget effect'. Details can be found in texts on geostatistics, Isaaks and Srivastava (1989) for example. A nice introductory reference is David (1977).

REFERENCES

Abramovich, F, Bailey, TC and Sapatinas, T (2000) Wavelet analysis and its statistical applications. *The Statistician* **49**(1), pp 1–29.

Adamson, P T, Metcalfe, A V and Parmentier, B (1999) Bivarite extreme value distributions: an application of the Gibbs sampler to the analysis of floods. *Water Resources Research* **35**(9), pp 2825–2832.

Bendat, J S (1998) *Nonlinear Systems Techniques and Applications* (Wiley).

Bhattacharya, R N and Waymire, E C (1990) *Stochastic Processes with Applications* (Wiley).

Borrie, J A (1992) *Stochastic Systems for Engineers* (New York: Prentice Hall).

Brown, G, Draper, P and McKenzie, E (1997) Consistency of UK pension fund investment performance. *Journal of Business, Finance and Accounting* **24**(2), pp 155–178.

Burrus, C S (1998) *Introduction to Wavelets and Wavelet Transforms: a Primer* (Prentice Hall).

Casella, G and George, E I (1992) Explaining the Gibbs sampler. *The American Statistician* **6**(3), pp 167–274.

Chatfield, C (1989) *The Analysis of Time Series: an Introduction*, 4th edn (London: Chapman & Hall).

Chib, S and Greenberg, E (1995) Understanding the Metropolis–Hastings algorithm. *The American Statistician* **49**(4), pp 327–335.

Clements, R R (1989) *Mathematical Modelling* (Cambridge, UK: Cambridge University Press).

Cox, D R and Miller, H D (1977) *The Theory of Stochastic Processes* (Chapman & Hall).

Cox, D R and Isham, V (1980) *Point Processes* (London: Chapman & Hall).

David, M (1977) *Geostatistical Ore Reserve Estimation* (Amsterdam: Elsevier).

Firth, J M (1992) *Discrete Transforms* (London.: Chapman & Hall).

Gilks, W R, Richardson, S and Spiegelhalter, D G (1995) *Practical Markov Chain, Monte Carlo* (Chapman & Hall).

Goupillaud, P, Grossmann, A and Morlet, J (1984) Cycle-octave and related transforms in seismic signal analysis. *Geoexploration* **23**, pp 85–102.

Guttorp, P (1995) *Stochastic Modeling of Scientific Data* (Chapman & Hall).

Hearn, G E and Metcalfe, A V (1995) *Spectral Analysis in Engineering: Concepts and Cases* (Arnold).

Hearn, G E, Metcalfe, A V and Lamb, D (2000) All at sea with spectral analysis. *Proc. Conf. Ind. Stats in Action*, Vol II, pp 217–235 (University of Newcastle upon Tyne).

Isaaks, E H and Srivastava, R M (1989) *Applied Geostatistics* (Oxford University Press).

Kaiser, G (1994) *A Friendly Guide to Wavelets* (Birkhauser).

McClelland, V (1997) Excitatory and inhibitory reflexes between muscles of the upper limb in man. PhD thesis University of Newcastle upon Tyne.

MacDonald, I L and Zucchini, W (1997) *Hidden Markov and Other Models for Discrete-valued Time Series* (Chapman & Hall).

Mellor, D (1996) The Modified Turning Bands (MTB) model for space-time rainfall: I model definition and properties, *Journal of Hydrology* **175**.

Mellor, D, Sheffield, J, O'Connell, P E and Metcalfe, A V (2000a). A stochastic space-time rainfall forecasting system for real time flow forecasting I: development of MTB conditional rainfall scenario generator. *Hydrology and Earth System Sciences*, Vol. 4 (in press).

Mellor, D, Sheffield, J, O'Connell, P E and Metcalfe, A V (2000b). A stochastic space-time rainfall forecasting system for real time flow forecasting II: application of SHETRAN and ARNO rainfall runoff models to the Brue catchment. *Hydrology and Earth System Sciences*, Vol. 4 (in press).

Mikosch, T (2000). *Elementary Stochastic Calculus with Finance in View* (Thomas Mikosch).

Moran, P A P (1954) Theory of dams and storage systems. *Australian Journal of Applied Science*, **5**.

Nelson, R (1995) *Probability, Stochastic Processes and Queuing Theory: the Mathematics of Computer Performance Modelling* (Springer-Verlag).

Newland, D E (1993) *Random Vibrations, Spectral & Wavelet Analysis*, 3rd edn (London: Longman).

Ogden, R T (1997) *Essential Wavelets for Statistical Applications and Data Analysis* (Birkhauser).

Oksendal, B (1995) *Stochastic Differential Equations*, 4th edn (Springer).

Pole, A (1994) *Applied Bayesian Forecasting and Time Series Analysis* (Chapman & Hall).

Ranne, A (1999) The investment models of a Finnish pension company. *Vector* **15**(4), pp 63–70.

Rodriguez-Iturbe, I, Cox, D R and Isham, V (1987) Some models for rainfall based on stochastic point processes. *Proc. R. Soc. London A* **410**, pp 269–288.

Ross, S M (1997) *Simulation*, 2nd edn (Academic Press).

Ross, S M (1999) *An Introduction to Mathematical Finance* (Cambridge University Press).

Ross, S M (2000) *Introduction to Probability Models*, 7th edn (Academic Press).

Silverman, B W and Vassilicos, J C (2000) *Wavelets* (Oxford Science).

Stewart, I (1990) *Does God Play Dice? The New Mathematics of Chaos* (London: Penguin).

Tong, H (1990) *Non-linear Time Series: A Dynamical System Approach* (Oxford: Oxford University Press).

Tsang, W W (1991) Estimation of short term flood risk. MSc dissertation, University of Newcastle upon Tyne.

Walker, J S (1999) *Wavelets and their Scientific Applications* (Chapman & Hall).

Wallis, J R (1981) Risk and uncertainties in the evaluation of flood events for the design of hydraulic structures. In *Piene e Siccita*, edited by E Guggino, G Rossi and E Todini, pp 3–36. Fondazione Politecnica del Mediterraneo, Catania, Italy.

36 Optimisation

Andrew Metcalfe

INTRODUCTION

The aim of optimisation is to choose values of variables so that some function of those variables (the objective function) takes its least value. You should be aware that a local minimum value need not be a global minimum, and that the least value does not necessarily correspond to a minimum. This is because it may occur on the boundary of the set of values that the variables are allowed to take. An example is the determination of the most economic cruising speed for a cargo ship given the cost of fuel, the efficiency of the engine as a function of the ship speed, the cost of storing fuel on board the ship, the cost of time at sea, and cost of delays over delivering the cargo. It could turn out that the most economic speed corresponds to the highest speed of which the ship is capable.

Formulating the problem in terms of finding the least value of an objective function is not a restriction because finding the greatest value of a function is equivalent to finding the least value of its negative. Furthermore, setting a function to some preferred value is equivalent to finding the least value of the difference between them. Optimisation problems are widespread and there are many techniques for solving them. These range from the calculus, such as for the linear optimal control problem, to stochastic trial-and-error methods such as genetic algorithms. Although most of these techniques were originally applied to deterministic problems, they have been adapted to deal with optimisation problems that include stochastic terms in their definitions. The subject of operational (or operations) research (OR) is mainly concerned with the application of optimisation methods in industry and commerce. The OR Society in the UK has a website at www.orsoc.org.uk/ and there are many journals devoted to the discipline.

CALCULUS

If the objective function is a continuous and differentiable function of the variables, stationary points can be found, in principle, by setting partial derivatives equal to zero. However, the resulting equations may have to be solved numerically. Constraints can be handled by the technique of LaGrange multipliers (see Stephenson and Radmore 1990, Jeffrey 2001 and, in the context of economics, Chow 1996).

An important application is the general solution of the linear optimal control problem, and its stochastic variant, in which the system is subject to disturbance noise and the observations are subject to measurement noise (such as Kwakernaak and Sivan 1972, Barnett and Cameron 1985). An associated and mathematically equivalent problem is constructing an optimal observer, which is usually referred to as a Kalman filter (Kalman and Bucy 1961).

LINEAR PROGRAMMING

Many optimisation problems are highly structured and there are very efficient methods for their solutions. If you hope to solve optimisation problems with a large number of variables it is essential to use the most efficient algorithm available, and, since the size of the problem usually increases exponentially with the number of variables, this situation will not change with the introduction of more powerful computers. There are particularly efficient algorithms for solving linear programming problems.

The linear programming (LP) problem is to maximise, or minimise, some linear function of variables subject to linear inequalities. Typical examples include blending problems and transportation problems. The inequalities define a feasible region that is bounded by hyper-planes. The optimum corresponds to one of the vertices of this region, and the search can therefore be restricted to vertices. The simplex method for solution of the LP problem moves between vertices so that the value of the objective function improves or, at worst, stays the same.

There are many books written on linear programming, such as Bunday and Garside (1987), and Kolman and Beck (1995), which includes advice about microcomputer software. They recommend LINDO from Lindo Systems, who have a website at www.lindo.com/

Standard LINDO will handle up to 200 variables and the extended version will go up to 100 000 variables. Williams (1993) describes the method of projective transforms for such large problems. The Matlab optimisation toolbox also includes algorithms for the efficient solution of linear programming problems.

Any book on OR will include something on linear programming. Taha (1997) includes a disk with software for solving LP problems.

Stochastic variants of LP are usually discussed under the title of *chance constrained programming* (Taha 1997).

MATHEMATICAL PROGRAMMING

Williams (1990, 1993) includes linear programming (LP), non-linear programming (NLP) and integer programming (IP) under the general heading of *mathematical programming*. The IP methods are important if the variables can take only a few integer values, and the case of all variables being 0 or 1 is quite common. One approach to the NLP problem is to use piecewise-linear approximations to the non-linear functions. Among applications for mathematical programming, there are many in geography and planning (see Killen 1983).

DYNAMIC PROGRAMMING AND SDP

The ideas behind dynamic programming were first formulated by Bellman (1957). The method can be used for a variety of problems, including scheduling of work in factories (Smith 1991) and optimal control (Jacobs 1993). A simple example is that of a traveller who intends to travel from a city A to a city Z in several stages. At each step there are many possible intermediate destinations, and the costs of travel for all possible routes between stages are known. The most efficient way to minimise the total cost is to work backwards from Z. Critical path analysis is a related problem, and programme evaluation and review technique (PERT) is a stochastic version of this.

Fair allocation of water from a network of reservoirs to households, to farms for irrigation, and to industry, is a vital issue in countries with arid climates, such as South Africa. A typical operating policy will specify the amounts of water to be released to the various recipients each month. The decisions that make up the policy depend on the amount of water in the reservoir, the time of the year, and the expected future inflows into the reservoir. These inflows are unknown and are described by a probability distribution. The determination of a policy that will optimise the benefits to the community is an example of a *stochastic dynamic programming* (SDP) problem (see Archibald *et al* 1997). Howard was a pioneer in the methods of SDP and his book (Howard 1960) is an elegant exposition of the principles involved. A more up-to-date textbook is Puterman (1994). Simple SDP problems can be solved by using decision trees.

DESCENT ALGORITHMS

Descent algorithms find a minimum value of a continuous function of several variables by calculating approximations to local derivatives and then proceeding in the direction of steepest descent until a minimum is found along the curve in this direction. The process is then repeated. These algorithms are used as part of a modelling procedure, rather than being a model in themselves. One valuable application is estimating parameters of models, which are non-linear in those parameters, from experimental data (such as the useful non-linear regression routine in SPSS) There are many ingenious modifications of descent algorithms, and good software that implements them is readily available (such as NAG subroutines and the Matlab Optimisation Toolbox). If you do not wish to rely on libraries of subroutines you can use algorithms from *Numerical Recipes* (Press *et al* 1992). The mathematical analysis of optimisation methods can be found in Sundaram (1996), for example.

The simplex method, and modified simplex method of Nelder and Mead, is a somewhat simpler and less efficient, but generally effective, means of finding a minimum. If the objective function depends on two variables only, the simplex method (which is quite different from the simplex method for LP) is easily described. Begin by calculating the values of the objective function at the vertices of a triangle in the plane of the two variables. Then reflect the point corresponding to the largest value of the objective function in the edge joining the other two points. Now calculate the value of the objective function at this new point. Continue in this manner until a point reflects back to itself, and then reduce the size of the simplex until it is sufficiently small to stop. This method has been used for online optimisation of the productivity of chemical processes (Myers and Montgomery 1995, for example). The objective function, to be maximised in this context, is the productivity. The process variables are perturbed, within safe limits, according to the simplex algorithm.

The snag with all these methods is that they may find a local rather than a global optimum. One way to mitigate this is to start from several different sets of values of the variables. An alternative is to try the stochastic methods of the next section.

GAs AND SIMULATED ANNEALING

Simulated annealing is a descent algorithm with small probabilities of moving in the direction of steepest ascent rather than descent. These probabilities become smaller as the value of the objective function decreases. Genetic algorithms (GA) code the values of the variables as binary numbers and link them to form a string of binary digits (referred to as a chromosome). Strings are selected from an initial set with probabilities proportional to their 'fitness', which will increase as the objective function becomes lower in a minimisation problem, and are combined by crossing over sections of the strings. Although these random search methods appear to perform well in some situations, there is no guarantee that they will find the global optimum. The heuristics of the GA make sense when the objective function depends on many dichotomous variables but, somewhat surprisingly, they can be useful with continuous variables as well. Since the GA is a minimisation procedure rather than a model, its use can be justified by the results. A recent book that discusses these methods is Pham and Karaboga (2000).

ARTIFICIAL NEURAL NETS

Artificial neural nets (ANNs) are empirical relationships established between input variables and output variables from a data set referred to as a training set. The objective is to predict the output for cases for which only values of the input variables are known. Formally, ANN include multiple regression models as special cases, but typical ANN applications have little physical interpretation (see Wray and Green 1995 for an interesting exception). They seem to work well if the training set is very large and covers the range of likely values for the input variables. They should not be used for extrapolation outside this range. There is a plethora of applications, including the assessment of credit worthiness of applicants for credit cards (Hand and Jacka 1998). Fitting ANN is a large non-linear least squares problem and many ingenious methods have been proposed. Matlab has an ANN toolbox. Much has been written about ANN, but the recent book edited by Kay and Titterington (2000) would be a good starting point.

REFERENCES

Archibald, T W, McKinnon, K I M and Thomas, L C (1997) An aggregate stochastic dynamic programming model of multireservoir systems. *Water Resources Research* 33(2), pp 333–340.

Barnett, S and Cameron, R G (1985) *Introduction to Mathematical Control Theory*, 2nd edn (Oxford University Press).

Bellman, R E (1957) *Dynamic Programming* (Princeton University Press).

Bunday, B D and Garside, G R (1987) *Linear Programming in Pascal* (London: Arnold).

Chow, G C (1996) *Dynamic Economics: Optimization by the LaGrange Method* (Oxford University Press).

Hand, D J and Jacka, S D (1998) *Statistics in Finance* (Arnold).

Howard, R A (1960) *Dynamic Programming and Markov Processes* (MIT).

Jacobs, O L R (1993) *Introduction to Control Theory*, 2nd edn (Oxford University Press).

Jeffrey, A (2001) *Advanced Engineering Mathematics* (USA: Academic Press).

Kalman, R E and Bucy, R S (1961) New results in linear filtering and prediction theory. *Journal Basic Engineering, Transactions ASME Series D* 83, pp 95–108.

Kay, J W and Titterington, D M (eds) (2000) *Statistics and Neural Networks – Advances at the Interface* (Oxford University Press).

Killen, J (1983) *Mathematical Programming Methods for Geographers and Planners* (London: Croom Helm).

Kolman, B and Beck, R E (1995) *Elementary Linear Programming with Applications*, 2nd edn (San Diego: Academic Press).

Kwakernaak, H and Sivan, R (1972) *Linear Optimal Control Systems* (New York: Wiley).

Myers, R H and Montgomery, D C (1995) *Response Surface Methodology* (Wiley).

Pham, D T and Karaboga, D (2000) *Intelligent Optimisation Techniques: Genetic Algorithms, Tabu Search, Simulated Annealing and Neural Networks* (New York: Springer-Verlag).

Press, W H, Flannery, B P, Reulolsky, S A. and Vetterling, W T (1992) *Numerical Recipes* (Cambridge University Press).

Puterman, M L (1994) *Markov Decision Processes: Discrete Stochastic Dynamic Programming* (New York: Wiley).

Smith, D K (1991) *Dynamic Programming – A Practical Introduction* (New York: Ellis Horwood).

Stephenson, G and Radmore, P M (1990) *Advanced Mathematical Methods for Engineering and Science Students* (Cambridge University Press).

Stewart, I (1990) *Does God Play Dice? The New Mathematics of Chaos* (London: Penguin).

Sundaram, R K (1996) *A First Course in Optimisation Theory* (Cambridge University Press).

Taha, H A (1997) *Operations Research*, 6th edn (Prentice Hall).

Williams, H P (1990) *Model Building in Mathematical Programming*, 3rd edn (Chichester: Wiley).

Williams, H P (1993) *Model Solving in Mathematical Programming* (Chichester: Wiley).

Wray, J and Green, G G R (1995) Calculation of the Volterra kernels of nonlinear dynamic systems using an artificial neural network. *Biological Cybernetics* 71(3), pp 187–195.

PART 9 | Presentation

37 Writing the thesis

Tony Greenfield

INTRODUCTION

A thesis or a dissertation is a work of scholarship that is published and made available for others to read. Even if you do not publish your work, or parts of it, as papers in academic journals, your thesis will be published by being placed in the university library, provided your examiners are satisfied with it. You may believe that the final stage of your work is the presentation of your thesis to your examiners but that is not so. If they grant your higher degree, the thesis will be available for anybody to read for all time. Through your work, any reader may judge the scholarship of your department, of your university, and of the examiners. It is in the university's own interests that your work should withstand criticism. You will fail the university if in any way your work lacks quality and, if it does, the examiners will be right to refuse or defer your degree.

You must therefore ensure that, in every respect, your thesis or dissertation is of the highest achievable quality. There are several good texts that may help you, including other chapters in this book. Paul Levy offers some wise counsel in his entertaining chapter on presentation (Chapter 38). In this chapter, I summarise a few points which I, as an examiner, see as important. These will include a suggestion, but not a rule, for overall *structure*, guidance on *style*, and advice about the *presentation of statistics*. But first I shall distinguish between a thesis and a dissertation.

A *dissertation* is a formal treatment of a subject, usually in writing. When the word is applied to undergraduate or postgraduate research it usually refers to work done, either as a review of a subject or as the application of established methods to the study of a specified problem. A dissertation is usually submitted as part of an examination for a master's degree such as an MSc, MA or MPhil, for a post graduate certificate and sometimes for a first degree.

A *thesis* is a dissertation resulting from original research. It is usually submitted as the only document for examination for a doctorate such as a PhD, a DPhil, or an MD. It may be submitted for a master's degree. Originality is the essential feature of a thesis and if you are submitting a thesis you must make clear which ideas were *yours*, which original work you did, and which was done by others.

In the rest of this chapter I shall refer to the thesis but most of my advice applies equally to the dissertation.

STRUCTURE

The obvious structure is: introduction; background; materials and methods; results; conclusions. This suggests that there need be no more than five chapters and indeed one academic supervisor I know insists that six should be the limit. But there is *no* limit to the number of chapters nor to the number of words in your thesis unless it is imposed by your department. Brevity is better than prolixity provided you do not skimp on information.

You must interest your readers and not bore them. You must catch and keep the readers' interest so that they will read every word of your thesis with understanding, approval and pleasure. You must convince the readers that you know your subject and that you have contributed new ideas and knowledge. You must not deter nor offend them with bad spelling, bad grammar, poor printing, uninformative diagrams, disorderly presentation, false or incomplete information, inadequate explanation, weak argument.

Here, in more detail, with some comments, is my guidance for structure with the headings.

1. Title
2. Summary
3. Keywords
4. Contents
5. Introduction
6. Background and choice of subject
7. Methods, results and analysis
8. Discussion
9. Conclusion and recommendations
10. References and bibliography
11. Appendices
12. Glossary
13. Notations
14. Diary
15. Acknowledgements

Title

It is not easy to devise a title for a thesis. It must be short. It must identify your work so that anybody working in your subject area will immediately recognise it. Beware, however, of the possibility of misclassification. You may be amused to find a book about traction (for treatment of spinal injuries) in the transport section of a library but you wouldn't want that to happen to your work. Do not use abbreviations or words that may be difficult to translate into other languages without misinterpretation.

On the title page you should add

- your full name and existing qualifications;
- the name of the degree for which you are a candidate;
- the names of your department, faculty and university;
- the date of submission.

Summary

You must tell your reader what your work is about, why you did it, how you did it and what conclusions you reached. This is also your first opportunity to declare your originality. Can you do this briefly, in no more than 200 words, and simply with no technical terms? If you can, you will encourage your reader to read on.

Keywords

Keywords are needed for classification and for reference. Somebody sometime will be interested in your subject but will not know of your work. You want to help them to discover it through your library's online inquiry service. What words would this person's mind conjure if they want to find the best literature on the subject? Those must be your keywords.

Contents

In many theses that I have read, the contents list has been no more than an abbreviated synopsis: a list of chapter headings. The contents list must tell me where to find the contents so it must include page numbers. This is easy with a word processor. But do not restrict this to the chapter headings. I want to be able find each of the appendices by name and by page number. It is frustrating to be told that a table of data can be found in the appendices. Even if you direct me to Appendix 9, my time will be wasted and my temper frayed if I have to search.

Please, in your contents list, give the page number of every chapter, of every appendix (which should have a name), of the index, of the references, of the bibliography, of the glossary, of your diary, and of your acknowledgements. If you do that, your readers, including your examiners, will be able to find their way through your work.

Include a contents list of illustrations. For example:

> Figure 1   Flowchart of materials   page 23

and so on.

Introduction

Your introduction should be an expansion of your summary and your contents list combined. Your opening sentence should be a statement of the purpose of your research followed by the briefest possible statement of your conclusions and recommendations. Describe the path you followed to go from one to the other in terms of the contents of your thesis. Then your readers will know what to expect. Say who you are and in what department you are working; describe the resources that were available and what difficulties you met.

Review the contents of your thesis, perhaps devoting a paragraph to a summary of each subsequent chapter.

Background and choice of subject

Why did you choose the specific subject? Did you discover an interest in it because of something you had done earlier, or from your reading? Or was it suggested to you by your supervisor? What is the context of your subject: in what broader realm of knowledge does it fit? Is there a history of discovery? Who were the early workers and what did they publish? Describe the narrowing of the field, related problems that others have studied, the opportunities for further study that they have revealed and the opportunities created by scientific and technical advances. Will any human needs, other than intellectual, be met through your research?

This is where you demonstrate your ability to study the literature. Name the most important of the references you found but beware of boring your reader with a long and unnecessary account of every document that you found in your search just because it seemed slightly related. Recount any different viewpoints you may have found in the literature. State your opinion about the reliability of the evidence supporting the different viewpoints and lead into your own. You should state this in terms of questions to be answered and hypotheses to be tested.

Methods, results and analysis

In a short paper you would write a section on materials and methods followed by a section on results. In a longer study you will probably write several chapters each dealing with different aspect of the whole. It may not be easy to separate the methods from the results. Possibly each of several chapters will have a description of methods and results. In some subjects the most important part of the method will be a theoretical development. This must be rigorous and explained so clearly that any intelligent reader will understand it. There is a danger, in referring to theoretical development by another worker, that your reader will not know it and will be frustrated if you simply give the result and a reference. That reference is unlikely to be easily at hand. The reader will appreciate your skill if you can explain the theory in a nutshell without re-enacting the full theoretical development.

Describe technical equipment and techniques for observation and measurement. Compare the costs, reliability and ease of alternative techniques. Did you design and administer questionnaires? Did you have constructive or investigative discussions with individuals or groups? Did you use brainstorming? Be honest about the practical work that you did and what was done by others. Describe the methods of experimental design and data analysis that you used and what computer programs you used. Examiners will not be impressed by a bland statement such as 'the data were analysed by standard statistical techniques'. In describing your experimental design, you should refer to the questions and hypotheses stated in your introduction, perhaps repeating them in detail.

Results are usually best displayed in tables of data with summary statistics. If there are just a few measurements keep them in this section, but if they run into several pages put them in an appendix with clear references. Sometimes graphs will be suitable to illustrate the data but it is not always true that 'a picture is worth a thousand words'. Especially avoid bar charts and pie charts. These are a waste of space and should be reserved for platform presentations. Simple data tables will do.

A chapter on methods and results is not the place to discuss results unless discussion of results at one stage of your research is part of your argument for developing further theory and methods for a later stage. If this is so, be sure to keep your discussion separate from the results through a separate chapter section.

Discussion

There is no need to repeat any results, but only to refer to them, interpreting and commenting on them with reference to your aims, your hypotheses, the work and opinion of others and the suitability of your theory, methods, experimental design, and analysis.

Conclusions

Conclusions follow naturally from your discussion. Have you met your objectives? Have you found or done something new? Have you added to the store of human knowledge, even if you have only demonstrated a negative result? What did *you* contribute? Do you have any recommendations for further study?

Was the course of your research smooth? Did you follow any blind alleys, any deviations from your intended study design? You should report them so that later workers don't repeat your mistakes. Similarly, if you found any negative results you should report them. It is unethical not to do so. Also be clear about what is meant by a negative result. It is rarely a demonstration that 'there is no effect'. Usually it is a statement that 'there is insufficient evidence to conclude that there is an effect', which is not the same.

References and bibliography

References and bibliography are usually lumped together but you could separate them.

In the bibliography list those books that will be useful for background reading and further study and which describe methods and theory that are widely used and accepted such as statistical methods, survey design and analysis, general mathematics, computing, communications, history.

In the references list those books and papers to which specific reference is needed for the development of your argument within the thesis.

In both lists you should consistently follow a standard form for each reference. The most usual standard is the Harvard system.

The standard for a paper is:
authors, date, title, journal (in italics), volume (in bold), issue, pages.

The standard for a book is:
authors, date, title (in italics), publisher (including city).

Be sure that every reference is necessary for the development of the argument and that you have truly read every one. Your examiners will not be impressed by a long list of references of which some are hardly relevant. They may even ask you about individual ones. Be sure too that every reference in your list is actually referred to in the text of your thesis and, similarly, every reference in the text is in your list. A careful examiner will check this. You will help him, and may convince him, if against every reference in your list you put, in square brackets, the pages of your thesis where the references are made.

Please don't try to impress me, if I'm your external examiner, by including references to my papers unless they are truly relevant.

Appendices

Some people collect masses of material (data forms, memoranda, correspondence, company histories, hand written notes) and fill hundreds of pages, which they describe as appendices.

Appendices are valuable only if they comprise material that is germane to your thesis and for which there is some possibility that your reader will make reference. You might describe special equipment, a detailed specification of a computer program that you used, a table of costs, a theoretical argument from other research (but any theory that you have developed should be in the main text), data collection forms, printed instructions to surveyors, maps, or a large table of raw data.

Be sure to give each appendix a name as well as an appendix number, just as you would if it were a chapter of the main text. Number the pages consecutively with the main text so that the reader can easily find any appendix when it is referenced.

Glossary

In your thesis you should highlight the first occurrence of every word and acronym that may be unfamiliar to your reader: underline it or put it in italics or bold or in a sans serif type. Define the word in your main text but then enter the word in to your glossary where you should repeat the definition. If you introduce a lot of technical language your reader may quickly forget a definition and want to be reminded. Give page numbers to the glossary so that it can be found easily.

Notation

You may define notation as you like anywhere in your thesis but, as with technical words, you must keep to your definitions. The symbol π, for example, is normally used to denote the ratio of a plane circle's circumference to its radius. It is also used occasionally to denote probability. If you use it as such, define it in the text and again in a table of notations. Whenever in the text you use a symbol that may puzzle your readers let them check its meaning in this table of notations.

Diary

How did you spend your time? Were you always at your desk or at the laboratory bench? Or were you in the library, at seminars and conferences, visiting equipment suppliers, interviewing, discussing your research with your supervisor or other researchers, or lying on the beach (and thinking)?

A diary of your work will help your examiner to understand the complexity and difficulties of your research and will help those who follow to plan their own projects.

Acknowledgements

I mention acknowledgements last, not necessarily because they should go last but because they are not part of the substantial research report. However, they are important and you could put them immediately after the title.

You did not work on your own. You were guided and helped by your lecturers and demonstrators, by your supervisor, by technicians, by suppliers of equipment, by surveyors and assistants, by other research students with whom you discussed your work, by the secretaries and administrators, and you were sustained by grant awarders and by your family. You should thank them all.

STYLE

At the end of this chapter is a list of some good books about scientific and technical writing. Here are a few points to ponder.

Personal pronoun (I)

There is continuing debate on whether to use the first person, singular, active I. One professional institute banned its use in all reports some years ago. My daughter, as an undergraduate, assured me that she would fail if she used it in her dissertation.

Use of the personal pronoun 'I' is not simply a matter of taste. It is a question of honesty and of the credit that you deserve and need to justify the award of a higher degree. *You* are responsible for ensuring that others recognise what *you* have done, what ideas *you* have had, what theories *you* have created, what experiments *you* have run, what analyses and interpretations *you* have made, and what conclusions *you* have reached. You will not succeed in any of this if you coyly state

- 'it was considered' (write: 'I proposed' or 'I thought')
- 'it was believed' (write: 'I believed')
- 'it was concluded' (write: 'I concluded')
- 'there is no doubt that' (write: 'I am convinced')
- 'it is evident that' (write: 'I think')
- 'it seems to the present writer' (write: 'I think')
- 'the author decided' (write: 'I decided')

But be careful: too much use may seem conceited and arrogant.

Spelling

Every word processor now has a spell checker, yet many published papers and theses are littered with misspellings and misprints. One reason is that the writers are too lazy or ignorant to use the spell checker.

But another reason is that many words, when misspelled, are other correctly spelled words. The spell checker will not identify these. If there are any in your submission you are telling the examiners that you have not read carefully what you have written. Here is a recent example:

> Improved understanding of these matters should acid cogent presentation . . .

The typist had misread 'aid' in poor hand writing as 'acid'. The most common (anecdotally) of scientific misprints is the change from 'causal relationships' to 'casual relationships'. Other common ones, which the spell checker will not find, are:

- 'fro' for 'from' or 'for'
- 'lead' for 'led' (past tense of 'to lead')
- 'gibe' for 'give'
- 'correspondents' for 'correspondence' or 'corresponding' ('changes in watershed conditions can result in correspondents changes in stream flow')

(My favourite malapropism is: 'Sir Francis Drake circumcised the world with a one hundred foot clipper'.)

If you are writing for a British audience, use English rather than American English spelling. Words like 'color' and 'modeling' look wrong to a British eye as do words ending in -ize instead of -ise. On the other hand, if you write for an American audience, use American spelling. Fortunately, word processors offer a choice of appropriate spell checkers.

Abbreviations and points

Do *not* use points except as full stops at the ends of sentences or as decimal points:

- write BSc, PhD *not* B.Sc., Ph.D.
- write UK, UNO, WHO, ICI *not* U.K., U.N.O., W.H.O., I.C.I.

Do *not* contract:

- department into dept. or dept
- institute into inst. or inst
- government into gov't. or gov't
- professor into prof. or prof

Do *not* use:

- e.g. (write 'such as' or 'for example')
- i.e. (write 'that is')
- *et al* (except in references)
- etc. (put a full stop instead, otherwise the reader will wonder 'what are the etceteras?' and if you can't be bothered to tell him he may not want to read further)

The plurals of acronyms may be written with the initials followed by a lower case 's' without an apostrophe (ROMs).

Avoid possessives with acronyms (do not write NORWEB's) by recasting the sentence to eliminate the possessive.

Prefer single quotes to double quotes, but single and double are used in nesting quotes.

Units

Use SI units with standard abbreviations without points. The base units are: m, kg, s, A, K, cd, mol. Note that, by international agreement, including France and the USA, correct spellings are *gram* and *metre*.

Do not use a dash to denote an interval.

Write 'between 20 and 25°C' *not* '20–25°C'.
Write 'from 10 to 15 September' *not* '10–15 September'.

Capitals

Resist a tendency to a Germanic capitalisation of nouns by avoiding capitals wherever possible. Too many of them break the flow of the eye across a sentence. They also make pompous what need not be so. The general rule is that proper names, titles and institutions require capitals, but descriptive appellations do not. Thus, government needs no capital letter, nor does committee or department. The same goes for jobs that are obviously descriptive, such as prime minister, foreign secretary, or even president unless it is used as a personal title ('President Washington' but 'the president'). There are a few exceptions such as Black Rod, The Queen, God.

Laws are lower case (second law of thermodynamics) unless they are named after somebody (Murphy's law).

Integers: In text, write out 0 to 10 (as zero, one, …, ten) but for greater integers use figures (21). If an integer starts a sentence, write it in words.

Things to avoid

- *Ornate words and phrases* such as convey (take), pay tribute to (praise), seating accommodation (seats), utilize (use), Fred underwent an operation (Fred had an operation), we carried out an experiment (we did an experiment).

- *Needless prepositions* tacked on verbs: check up, try out, face up to.
- *Vague words* like considerable, substantial, quite, very, somewhat, relatively, situation (crisis situation), condition (weather conditions), system.
- *Clichés* (last but not least, as a matter of fact)
- *Passive voice*
  - As is shown in figure 1 (Figure 1 shows)
  - It was decided to.
- *Obfuscation*
  I found the following on the World Wide Web. It is attributed to Mark P Friedlander.

  > *Learn to obfuscate*
  > Children, children, if you please
  > Learn to write in legalese,
  > Learn to write in muddled diction,
  > Use choice words of contradiction.
  > Sentences must breed confusion,
  > Redundancy and base obtusion,
  > With a special concentration
  > On those words of obfuscation.
  > When you write, as well you should,
  > You must not be understood.
  > Sentences concise and clear
  > Will destroy a law career.
  > And so, my children, if you please,
  > Learn to write in legalese.
  > So that, my dears, you each can be
  > A fine attorney, just like me.

STATISTICS

Several textbooks offer guidance about the presentation of data and of data analysis. In *A Primer in Data Reduction*, Andrew Ehrenberg (1982) wrote four chapters on communicating data: Rounding; Tables; Graphs; Words. These are worth reading before you write any papers or your report.

Rarely are measurements made to more than two or three digits of precision. Yet results of analysis are often shown to many more digits. Finney (1995) gives an example: $2.39758632 \pm 0.03245019$ 'computed with great numerical accuracy from data at best correct to the nearest 0.1%'. Such numbers are crass and meaningless but computers automatically produce them. Would you then report them, pretending scientific precision, or would you round them to an understandable level that means something?

In his discussion of tables, Ehrenberg says that

- rows and columns should be ordered by size;
- numbers are easier to read downwards than across;
- table lay-out should make it easier to compare relevant figures;
- a brief verbal summary should be given for every table.

The briefest and best (my view) of guides about the presentation of results is reprinted as an article from the *British Medical Journal*: Statistical guidelines for contributors to medical journals.

(Altman *et al* 1983). This has good advice for all research workers, not just those in the medical world, and I suggest that you obtain a copy. Here are a few of its points.

- Mean values should not be quoted without some measure of variability or precision. The standard deviation (SD) should be used to show the variability among individuals and the standard error of the mean (SE or SEM) to show the precision of the sample mean. You must make clear which is presented.
- The use of the symbol ± to attach the standard error or standard deviation to the mean (as in 14.2 ± 1.9) causes confusion and should be avoided. The presentation of means as, for example, 14.2 (SE 1.9) or 14.2 (SD 7.4) is preferable.
- Confidence intervals are a good way to present means together with reasonable limits of uncertainly and are more clearly presented when the limits are given: 95% confidence interval (10.4, 18.0) than with the ± symbol.
- Spurious precision adds no value to a paper and even detracts from its readability and credibility. It is sufficient to quote values of t, x^2 and r to two decimal places.
- A statistically significant association does not itself provide direct evidence of a causal relationship between the variables concerned.

FURTHER READING

Altman, DG, Gore, SM, Gardner, MJ and Pocock, SJ (1983) Statistical guidelines for contributors to medical journals. *BMJ* **286**, pp 1489–1493.

Barrass, R (1978) *Scientists Must Write* (London: Chapman and Hall).

Cooper, BM (1975) *Writing Technical Reports* (London: Penguin).

Ehrenberg, ASC (1982) *A Primer in Data Reduction* (London: Wiley).

Finney, DJ (1995), Statistical science and effective scientific communication. *Journal of Applied Statistics* 22(2), pp 193–308.

O'Connor, M and Woodford, FP (1978) *Writing Scientific Papers in English* (London: Pitman Medical).

Kirkman, J (1992) *Good Style: Writing for Science* (London: E & FN Spon).

Partridge, E, (1962) *A Dictionary of Clichés* (London: Routledge and Keegan Paul).

38 Presenting your research: reports and talks

Paul Levy

INTRODUCTION

One of the more neglected areas of the research process is perhaps the most important: the report and the presentation. Clear and effective presentation of the findings of the research is vital if the researcher wishes the research to be properly understood. It is also important if the conclusions of the research are to have impact and be remembered by the reader.

What was the best piece of writing you have ever read and why? What was the worst piece of writing? What was the best piece of writing you have ever written yourself, and why do you regard it as the best? Whether it is a novel, a newspaper article, a research report, or a poem, good writing contains a number of distinguishing features.

FEATURES OF GOOD WRITING

Good writing

- is well structured;
- has a particular and appropriate style;
- is satisfying for the reader;
- contains an internal logic;
- makes use of the richness of language.

Good writing is well structured

> *I like a film to have a beginning, a middle and an end, but not necessarily in that order.*
>
> Jean-Luc Godard

Some of the best exponents of structure in literature are crime novels, particularly classic whodunnits! A structure is just as important in a research write up as it is in an Agatha Christie! A well structured report will have a clear structure which allows the reader to follow the entire research process from the early stages of formulating the research question, through the research design and choice of research methods, right through to the presentation of findings, analysis and conclusions. Here's a typical structure for a research report:

1. Title
2. Acknowledgements
3. Contents, list of figures, glossary of terms

4. Aims and objectives
5. Background to the research (possibly, including analysis of literature)
6. Research methodology
7. Presentation of research findings
8. Analysis of research findings
9. Conclusions (and possibly recommendations)

This structure is an amalgam of the most common ones to be found in research reports. There are many other structures that can be used (for a more detailed discussion on structure see Chapter 37).

Let us return to the crime novel for a few moments. What is good about a classic crime novel? From the first few lines, the reader is hooked in through a scene-setting which is both interesting and inviting. The plot begins to unfold, and more information is revealed about both events and characters. Through the use of language and suspense, the reader is kept on the edge of his/her seat right to the end. The sign of a good novel is when the reader doesn't want the story to finish, cannot put the book down and is anxious to read another book by the same author. In many cases the structure is described as neat or clever, there might be a twist at the end of the story, a sting in the tail. I am not suggesting that your research write-up should be structured like a crime novel! However, you can learn from the structures of good literature. A checklist for your writing might look something like this:

- Is the structure coherent?
- Does the structure support the reader in understanding the research process and logic?
- Does the structure make reading easier?

Good writing has a particular and appropriate style

People usually have a favourite author. You can pick up a book that a friend has recommended as 'absolutely brilliant' and not be able to get beyond the first page. You wonder what excuses you can give your friend who lent you the book with such enthusiasm. It's all a matter of style. And different styles appeal to different people.

The particular style of writing depends on the personality of both the writer and the reader. As a result, the more particular your style of writing, the more danger there is of enthusing some readers but switching off others (who might be assessing the work!). If there's one maxim worth remembering here it is this: *Remember who you are writing for.*

How should you style your research write-up ? It very much depends on who you are writing for. A write up in a magazine may need a very different style to a formal research report or a chapter in an academic book. The same piece of research may need to be written up differently for different audiences. The magazine article may need a more informal, conversational style. A research report will need to be more formal. A book chapter might combine formal and informal.

In general, research reports should tend towards the formal. Why is this? One of the key reasons relates to the nature of research itself. The research process carries with it the ethical responsibilities of scientific investigation. The researcher is concerned with discovery and the sharing of that discovery with a chosen audience. Clarity of thought on behalf of the researcher, and clarity of interpretation and understanding on behalf of the reader is critical. It is a serious and dangerous business trying to understand the world and its underlying processes! Because of this, the danger of mis-interpretation needs to be minimised. A clear, logical style is therefore appropriate. The formal style can therefore aid understanding, not because it is necessarily the best style to use for that purpose, but simply because you are writing in a scientific tradition and the formal style has been in place in that tradition for over two centuries. As a result, it is embedded in the assumptions of the scientific community. It also has the advantage of ensuring

- logic;
- structure;
- clarity;
- precision.

In general then, a formal, impersonal style tends to be used in most research reports. For example:

> *The research involved the use of questionnaires and interviews . . .*

or

> *The researcher used questionnaires and interviews . . .*

is generally favoured over:

> *I used questionnaires and interviews in the research . . .* (see Chapter 37 for a contrary view)

An autobiographical tone can be appropriate in some research, particularly in inductive approaches where the researcher is very much involved with reflecting on the research as he/she goes along and where this reflection is very much part of the research process. For example:

> At this point I began to discover a number of biases in my own interview style. This was a result of being in the research situation, not only as an observer, but also as a participant . . .

This autobiographical style can help to locate the reader right inside the research situation, and to re-live the thought processes that helped the researcher to make key discoveries from the data. However, you should also be aware that this can be dangerous. With both the reader *and* the researcher *in* the research, the objectivity gained from taking a more distanced view can be lost.

In more traditional research approaches, such as in a typical research project based on a questionnaire survey, a more formal approach, using the thirdperson, is more appropriate.

Good writing is satisfying for the reader

Should reading a research report be a satisfying experience for the reader? Of course it should! There is no reason why research shouldn't be interesting and stimulating and, equally, no reason why readers of that research shouldn't be interested in, and stimulated by, what they read. A satisfying read will come from a number of sources:

- an interesting research topic;
- a well structured piece of writing;
- relevant use of well-presented graphics;
- a well-told research story;
- a perceptive set of conclusions.

An interesting research topic isn't always as easy to find as we may like. Indeed you might be given a piece of research to do that doesn't seem interesting. However, it will be very hard to write up research in an interesting way if you aren't interested in the topic yourself. If this is the case, it is important to make a real effort to get interested. This may involve reading around the subject and perhaps finding a few related videos in the local library. It is possible to reach a threshold where working hard ceases to be hard work! You, the researcher, need to get involved if you want to involve the reader of the research later on.

A well-structured piece of writing is often conducive to a satisfying read.

> *Science is nothing but trained and organised common sense.*
>
> TH Huxley

In a long research report, it is helpful to end chapters with a clear and simple summary of that chapter and to point the reader towards what is coming up in the next chapter. Similarly chapter beginnings may contain a paragraph that takes stock of what has been read so far. Other structural techniques include:

* posing questions at the beginning or end of chapters which are picked up later;
* posing big questions at the beginning of the report which are addressed one or several times throughout the report;
* building a schematic diagram as the report progresses (such as a flow chart of the research process which is added to as the report proceeds);
* returning in the final chapter to the aims set at the beginning of the report.

You may be able to think of others. A useful exercise here is to take a look at past research reports by different authors and look at them purely in terms of structure. Ask yourself:

* What was satisfying about the structure?
* What structural techniques were employed?

Relevant use of well-presented graphics can also support a satisfying read. This will be dealt with in the next chapter. Some readers respond better to the written word. Others are better engaged through the use of graphics and pictures. A further group prefer to hear arguments through the spoken word. It makes sense, therefore, to ensure that you vary your presentation approach to meet the varying needs of your audience!

A lot of people love to hear a good story. Storytelling is a traditional activity that can be found in most cultures in the world. For most people, listening to a good story can be a satisfying experience, particularly if the story has been well told! Storytelling can be a useful mechanism for presenting the chapter on research methodology. The story of the research can be an important support to understanding the research findings and core arguments. It is also a way of reminding the reader that the research process has been carried out by human beings with all the human problems that involves! The story of your research can be told informally in the traditional storytelling style of 'once upon a time . . .' with autobiographical style, possibly conversational in tone. This might be appropriate for a magazine or for stand-up verbal presentation. On the other hand, a more formal style might be used for research reports where a story structure is used but presented using formal language. For example, the methodology chapter might be structured as follows:

1. The background and context to the research
2. Why the topic was chosen
3. What research methods were chosen and why
4. The research process

5. Problems encountered and overcome
6. The outcome of the research.

For a bit of fun, here's that list again related to a typical story:

1. The background and context to the research (describing the lie of the land, the castle and the dark wood where the wicked witch lives)
2. Why the topic was chosen (the quest for the magic key)
3. What research methods were chosen and why (the choice of route and magic charms for the quest)
4. The research process (the adventure)
5. Problems encountered and overcome (battles on the way)
6. The outcome of the research (and they all lived happily ever after!).

Finally, a perceptive set of conclusions will round off the write-up. A sense of roundedness, of circularity, of coming back to the start, is a feature of a lot of good writing and can support the sense of a good read. Many research reports fail to draw sensible conclusions from the research data. For such research to be useful to the world, to avoid being placed in one of the many storage jars of the mind to be found on the dusty shelves of libraries, research should

- draw practical conclusions from the research findings
- suggest areas for further research which lies beyond the scope of the current research project.

Good writing contains an internal logic

Poor research reports make it difficult for the reader to follow the logical thread of the research process. The write-up should enable the reader to follow the stages of the research from beginning to end. It is important to know from the start if you

- are testing a hypothesis (or more than one);
- addressing one or more questions;
- exploring a broad or specific issue;
- measuring variables

or some combination of these.

The reader needs to be clear about

- why you chose your research topic (the background);
- the environment in which the topic is important and/or interesting (the context);
- what type of research you are carrying out (the approach);
- what the key stages are (the methods and processes);
- how the results are presented and analysed (findings and analysis);
- how your conclusions are drawn (conclusions drawing the threads together);
- how you have reached your recommendations (if you have any).

The internal logic of the writing is concerned with creating a logical and coherent path for the reader through all of these stages.

It is always worth showing drafts of the write-up to a colleague or friend to get feedback on the internal logic of the report. What may seem obvious to you may not be to your reader! Here's a list for checking the internal logic:

1. Do the conclusions at the end follow on from the aims set out at the beginning?
2. Does the research process follow a logical path?
3. Are any conclusions at the end not supported by the research data?
4. Do the recommendations arise logically from the conclusions and, if not, what is the justification?
5. Are there any contradictory arguments expressed anywhere in the writing?

Good writing makes use of the richness of language

A good novel, an inspiring poem, an exciting short story, all make use of the richness of language. A reader will not be impressed by

- use of woolly, often-repeated words such as 'nice' or 'interesting' ('It was a nice/an interesting piece of writing');
- use of clichés ('at the end of the day' . . . , 'pros and cons . . .');
- over-formal use of language ('the process was undertaken on a formalistic basis which nevertheless facilitated an iterative process . . .').

Good writing in research makes use of plain English which makes full (and proper) use of language. The key is to maintain accuracy without losing the reader's interest. A number of resources are available to writers to support this process:

- a thesaurus and grammar checker (either on computer or manual);
- wide reading: the best training for a writer is the writing of others; read other research papers, books, novels, poetry;
- a computer spell-checker to find repeated words; combine this with a thesaurus to ensure variety.

Be aware of the two extremes of writing in research work – the *artist* and the *scientist*: (I am, of course, being simplistic and unfair to the great variety of artists and scientists in the world!):

The *artist* is concerned with

- *use of expression;*
- *colour;*
- *image;*
- *representation;*
- *interpretation;*
- *subjectivity;*
- *experience of natural processes.*

The *scientist* is concerned with:

- *use of logic;*
- *objectivity;*
- *rationality;*
- *accuracy;*
- *measurement and control of natural processes.*

Both extremes have something to offer the writer of research. The scientist dominates most research writing. However, you need only read the writings of Darwin, Einstein, Goethe, Gleick and Hawking to see the importance of the artist in such writing as well.

PRESENT YOUR RESULTS

One of the most crucial parts of the research writing process is the presentation of results and analysis.

You should present research results

- in clear language;
- with helpful commentary;
- with supporting use of graphics;
- with proper references between the text and any graphics;
- with appropriate reference to and use of appendices;
- with guidelines to the reader on how the results were obtained and why they have been presented in the way they have;
- with any relevant criticism of the results.

Present research results in clear language

It is all too often the case that the results section of a research report contains a long list of statistics hot out of the mouth of a computer! The key term is *reader friendly*. You should present results in as helpful a way as possible.

- Pitch the presentation at the right level. It is always better to be on the safe side and assume the reader isn't as conversant with the subject as you are.
- Use simple, easy to understand terminology.
- Use helpful and simple graphics of summary data supported by more detailed data in appendices.
- Use formats such as 'bullet points' to list key findings, particularly in summary form at the end of a section or chapter.

Present research results with helpful commentary

Commentary sentences and paragraphs can guide the reader through the chapter, if the results are particularly complex. For example:

> *The chapter is divided into three sections. The first section will . . .*

or

> *Table 5 differs from Table 4 in that it includes the figure for 1995 . . .*

A bullet-point summary of the main findings at the end of the chapter or section may help the reader.

Present research results with supporting use of graphics

A picture really can paint a thousand words! In research writing the use of graphics will help the reader and will also keep the word count down. Some ways to use fewer words are explained in the next chapter. Graphs, tables, diagrams or other types of graphics should support the argument that appears in the text. Remember:

- Never use a graphic that does not support something written in words.
- Never write long sentences when a short sentence supported by a simple graphic will do the trick.

Present research results with proper references between the text and any graphics

Always refer clearly to any graphics that have been employed. This need not be done with verbosity. It needs only a . . .

> *(see Table 1) . . .*

or

> *Diagram 1 shows an example of . . .*

If you do not refer clearly to graphics (and it is very easy to forget), readers will easily become lost, may lose the thread of the argument and, eventually, will become frustrated in their attempts to understand what the research is about.

Present research results with appropriate reference to, and use of, appendices

Many research projects have appendices that are larger than the report itself. Appendices should be used sparingly and should not be a repository for the entire contents of the researcher's filing cabinet. Appendices are the support of a research report. They enable the reader to obtain further detail about

- the research context (there may, for example, be a relevant extract from a report, some laboratory or interview notes, a map of a factory floor, a company report, data about a specific product or process);
- the research methods (a full version of a questionnaire or interview schedule);
- the research findings (a full set of graphs showing research findings);
- other supporting information (such as a glossary of terms, list of references).

To be useful, such appendices need to be page numbered, included in the contents page, and properly referenced in the main text. For example:

> *Appendix 1 contains a full list of the questions contained in the research questionnaire.*

or

> *A fuller, more detailed account of the stages in the experiment can be found in Appendix 2.*

Present research results with guidelines to the reader on how the results were obtained and why they are presented in a given way

Even in a short research write up, there ought to be at least a paragraph or two informing the reader of *how* the results were obtained. If the readers understand the research methods they may understand the results. If the research was interview based, for example, the use of this research method helps to explain why the researcher is presenting the findings in the form of case examples. If the research method was questionnaire based, the presentation of findings in the form of graphs and tables is explained.

Present research results with any relevant criticism of the results

We should be suspicious of any research writing that appears to be presented as perfect. Research is a human process and is therefore open to error. Difficulties usually arise in one form or another and, even in the controlled conditions of a laboratory, the researchers may have taken a philosophical approach to research that may be open to question.

All true research writing will therefore be self-critical, will present to the reader the problems as well as the successes. Good research writing will pre-empt the questions and criticisms that could be expected to arise in the mind of a typical reader. For example, in interview-based research, there is the danger of bias (in interviewer and interviewee); in questionnaire research, there is a danger that respondents misunderstand questions; in a controlled laboratory experiment there is the danger that environmental factors distort results.

In summary, always include a section on what went wrong, as well as what went right, what is problematic about the findings, as well as what is persuasive about them.

THE PROCESS OF WRITING

Different people write in different ways. Some people find writing easy and can throw a report together in an evening. For others it is a slow, painful process taking many days (and even nights!). Are there any general principles and tips to help a writer of research? Below is a set of guidelines and tips for writing research. At least some of the tips should be of use to a writer of any brand.

Tip 1:   a process for writing

Here is a process for writing a piece of research. It can be adapted for different types of research.

1.   Write the final paragraph first! This can be a strong motivator and can help a writer see where he or she is going in the writing.
2.   Get an overview of the whole piece of writing. One way is to draw a map of the report. This could take the form of a flow chart (see Fig. 38.1).
3.   Or, for a bit of fun, you might try something more imaginative. Picture the report as a road journey. This can help get an idea of the 'flavour' of the report. (see Fig 38.2).

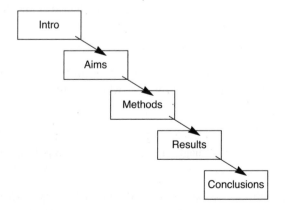

Figure 38.1 A flow chart

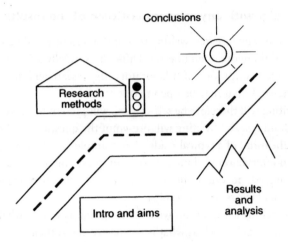

Figure 38.2 Thinking of your report as a journey

4. Write the chapter or section headings first and then make notes under each heading. In that way, you can build up a file that will eventually turn into the final draft.
5. Keep a notebook with you at all times for writing down ideas and references. This could be invaluable to you later.
6. Make several drafts. Always write the first draft by hand. When we type on a computer our fingers tend to run ahead of our thoughts. Three drafts should be enough: the first to get the ideas down on paper, the second to revise and rethink, the final draft for a final check, to polish up, format and ensure good presentation.
7. Find a supportive colleague or friend to check over your drafts.

Tip 2:   ideas on format

Check to see if you are required to provide a particular format or style.

You can centre your text like this
which is good for the title pages

You can format, justifying to the left, which means that all text is aligned along the left hand side of the page. This is standard in a lot of reports.
   Or you can format your text

justified to the right which means that all text is aligned along the
right-hand side of the page which might be of use on headed note
paper, or for formatted questionnaires.

Or you can locate a block of text in a smaller space, which can be useful
for quotations or for placing text next to a diagram or a table. Desk-top publishing
software is very good for doing this.

Finally, you may wish to format the text so that the text is double justified or blocked equally across the page (as the text in this book). This makes the report look neater than left justification.

Tip 3: ideas on the report style

Few people agree on what is the most appropriate style for a research report. It really depends on the audience. Or it may be that the style is specified for you by someone else.

Book style takes the form of text divided into chapters, with chapters divided into paragraphs.

Report style also makes use of chapters which tend to be quite short, are often called 'sections' and make extensive use of bullets points or numbering:

1. Like this
2. And this
3. And this
    * or like this
    * and this
    * or even this
    * and this

A further style of business report which is also used in technical reports involves the use of numbering. For example:

1.0   Each major section is numbered 1.0, 2.0, 3.0 and so on
1.1   While each subsection is numbered 1.1, 1.2, 1.3 and so on
1.1.1   And each sub sub section is numbered 1.1.1, 1.1.2, 1.1.3 and so on.

The book style is used more for more academic research, and the report style is used more in business and technical research. However, there are no firm rules. The main guidelines are:

* be sensitive to the readership;
* check to see if a particular style is required;
* ensure maximum readability;

Tip 4: use the resources available to you to best advantage

* Check spelling and grammar with spell checkers. Beware of computer spell checkers, which can encourage laziness. They cannot distinguish, for example, between 'an' and 'and'.
* Make full use of graphics and, if using computers, use a clear font:

    This is Times, and this is Univers: both clear and acceptable.
    This is Script – a lot of fun, but unreadable and unacceptable!

    A type face with serifs, like Times, should be used for long texts. Sans serif types, like Univers and Helvetica, tire the eyes and should be used sparingly, perhaps for emphasis or for headings.
* If you use a computer printer, ensure that the printout is of reasonable quality, and beware of bad photocopiers.
* Use **bold** or *italic* to emphasise and *italics for quotations* and for paraphrasing.
* Use colleagues for proof-reading and criticism.

Tip 5: plan your writing in detail

Set *aims*. Three should be enough. An aim is a general statement of direction of the research. For example: 'The aim of this research is to explore the link between . . .'.

Set *objectives*. These should arise logically from the aims. They are more specific than aims in that they are explicit about what actions are required to meet the aims. For example: 'The objective of this report is to measure the differences and similarities between . . .'.

PRESENT YOUR RESEARCH STANDING UP

For some, even to stand up in front of a small audience is a terrifying experience. Others seem to love it. Love it or hate it, researchers are often asked not only to give a written version of their research work, but also to stand up and present it verbally. PhD students defend their theses at a viva voce. Professional researchers may be asked to present their findings to a client. Students are often asked to give individual or group presentations to their peers and to the lecturers.

Whether a verbal form of presentation is requested or not, it may be of benefit to the research process to consider it. A verbal presentation can complement the written word through

- direct, live contact with the researcher;
- the researcher's demonstrated enthusiasm for the research;
- the opportunity for questions and discussion.

In general, the verbal presentation of research is not too different from other kinds of verbal presentation, such as business presentations. As in these other types of presentation, the presenter needs:

- to plan properly and rehearse;
- confidence and enthusiasm in voice and posture;
- a structured approach to the material;
- appropriate and supporting use of visual aids.

Few people can stand up and present effectively without any planning or rehearsal. An audience will usually be able to identify lack of preparation through

- an unconfident speaker;
- visual aids that look rushed or simply lifted from the research report;
- contradictions in the main argument;
- a lack of cohesion between the written and verbal material;
- poor time management during the presentation;
- lack of preparation for questions and discussion at the end.

One of the tips for writing mentioned earlier was the importance of drafting. A similar principle applies to stand up presentations.

When you prepare the material you might

- mark the research report with a highlighter pen to identify key areas for inclusion in the talk;
- make notes on cards that can be sequenced to provide a guide for the final version of the talk;
- use report contents as a guide to structure.

When you rehearse the talk you might

- practice in front of a mirror, and again in front of a friend or colleagues;
- audio- or videotape the talk to get an idea of what you look and sound like;

- time the presentation and practice until you are in control of the time available to you;
- sit in on a colleague's presentation and try to identify what was good about it, and what was not so good, so as to draw lessons that you can apply to your own talk.

When you prepare the visual aids you might

- hand-write the materials, such as slides, before committing them to print or foil;
- use large pieces of flip chart paper with pens or crayons to design your slides;
- ensure you know how to use the technology: Do you always put slides the right way up on an overhead projector? Do you know which way up to put slides in the carousel of a 35 mm projector?

The presenter needs confidence and enthusiasm in voice and posture

> *He who whispers down a well*
> *About the wares he has to sell*
> *Will never make as many dollars*
> *As he who climbs a tree and hollers*

(Anon)

No matter how impressive the visual aids are, no matter how important the research findings are, lack of enthusiasm on the part of a speaker will send an audience to sleep. Enthusiasm does not simply mean jumping around a lot, being loud, or arriving inside a huge wedding cake. Particularly in research presentations, the voice and eye contact can be used to

- create enthusiasm at the beginning of the presentation to communicate the importance and interesting nature of the research;
- emphasise key points throughout the presentation;
- highlight conclusions and recommendations.

Here are some tried and tested keys to maintain confidence.

- 'Laughter is inner jogging'. Enjoy it!
- Confidence comes with practice.
- It is never as bad as you think it will be.
- The audience is not the enemy.
- Always prepare properly.
- Relax, and don't forget to breathe!
- Proceed at a pace with which you are comfortable.
- Prepare for questions; don't be afraid to respond 'I don't know'.

Last of all, take a look at yourself in the mirror. Practise your talk. What can you do to improve the basic skills of verbal presentation?

- Voice projection
- Voice clarity
- Voice tonal range
- body posture

- Time management
- Listening and observation
- Control of body language
- Enthusiasm

Pick one area for improvement. Use the presentation as an opportunity to develop yourself.

The presenter needs a structured approach to the material

Unstructured presentations are anathema to research presentations. Research is a structured process and a good presentation should mirror this. Because of this, one of the simplest ways of structuring a research presentation is to follow (at least in part) the written report structure. Here is a suggested simple structure for a slide presentation:

Slide 1   Research project title, your name, department, university, sponsor
Slide 2   Aims and objectives of the presentation
Slide 3   Context/background to the research
Slide 4   Research methodology
Slide 5   Findings (graphical or text)
Slide 6   Analysis
Slide 7   Conclusions
Slide 8   Recommendations

You might also include slides containing

- summary of findings;
- an abstract or executive summary at the beginning;
- a pertinent and/or amusing quotation;
- a cartoon that captures the theme of the research;
- photographs;
- a set of questions for further research at the end.

The presenter needs appropriate and supporting use of visual aids

There is nothing worse than a one hour talk where the only available source of information is the speaker's monotone voice! Just as bad is a speaker who says very little but puts slide after slide on the overhead projector, crammed with too much information, too small to read anyway!

Visual aids should act as a support to a presentation not a substitute for it! There is a range of visual aids available that can be used to present the research effectively and which have different advantages and disadvantages:

Overhead projector

Advantages: simple to use; effective; easy to prepare; slides are relatively cheap; can be used in conjunction with a computer; good for presenting research data graphically.

Disadvantages: projectors can overheat; can be noisy; light can get in the speaker's eyes.

Tips: check that the slides can be seen from all parts of the room, and have a spare bulb ready.

Slide projector

Advantages: can show colour photographs; allows remote control; if slides are professionally made can look very impressive; good for most kinds of data if prepared on computer.

Disadvantages: the world is littered with stories of slide projectors breaking down; slides must be pre-loaded; light can get in speaker's eyes

Tips: check the equipment beforehand; have a spare to hand; check that your slides are all the right way up and in the right order.

White/blackboard

Advantages: allows speaker to write things up; build up research ideas; diagrams.

Disadvantages: messy; requires legible handwriting; unprofessional; in a fixed position unless portable one is available

Tips: use a clean board; erase any previous words written up by someone else; practise writing beforehand; be clear about what you are writing up; write legibly.

Flip chart

Advantages: dynamic; movable; good for small group presentation; very little can go wrong with it; good for building up diagrams and recording questions and ideas.

Disadvantages: too small; relies on speaker's writing; requires pages to be torn off.

Tips: use in conjunction with an overhead projector for writing up questions; before the presentation, draw any items you want to include in light pencil to act as a guide for neat writing and drawing during the presentation.

Video

Advantages: allows pictures to be shown of the live research situation; can create interest for audience.

Disadvantages: danger of technical difficulties; some people do not enjoy TV.

Tips: check the equipment beforehand; try to get a player with remote control; check the room to see that the screen is big enough.

Other visual aids

Other visual aids for research presentations include

- live demonstrations;
- use of supporting notes handed out to the audience;
- use of audio cassette based material;
- posters and exhibition boards;
- drama-based presentations (use actors if you can).

The important point for all of these aids is to ensure

- they are appropriate to the research;
- they are suited to the audience type, size and expectations;
- you can confidently use them.

PRESENT THE RESULTS OF DIFFERENT RESEARCH METHODS

Different research methods indicate different types of presentation. This will vary with type of research project and audience. Here are some guidelines for the main research methods.

Presentation of questionnaires and statistics

Tips:

- Use graphics wherever possible.
- Remove jargon and technical words that will alienate audience members (perhaps support with a glossary of terms handout).
- Do not overload the audience with too many figures.
- Use supporting handouts.
- Select only the major findings for presentation.
- Allow time for questions of clarification, either as you go along, or at the end.
- Use only one graph or table per slide, and make it big enough to read.

Presentation of interviews

Tips:

- Do not put too much information on a slide.
- Use italic style for direct quotations.
- Create summary tables to help audience gain an overview of the research findings.
- Supply a supporting handout with a list of interview questions, a summary of interviewee characteristics, or a research process summary showing how the interviews were done.

Presentation of case studies

Tips:

- Use storytelling where possible.
- Use pictures to give a visual flavour.
- Use summary tables to compare and contrast different cases.

Presentation of experiments (such as laboratory work)

Tips:

- Use storytelling where possible.
- Use graphics and photographs for visual flavour.
- Allow time for questions of clarification.
- Use practical demonstrations if possible and appropriate.

A final word

The presentation of research, like all presentation, is a skill that can be developed. The presentation or research must be designed and delivered to ensure

- understanding;
- clarity and accuracy;
- interest and enthusiasm for both speaker and listener.

Much more could be written about the skills, techniques, equipment, materials and support that can be used to achieve a high standard of presentation. The reading list provided at the end of this chapter is for the speaker who would like to develop these skills a little further. Good luck!

FURTHER READING

Reading on presentation skills

Bell, G (1990) *The Secrets of Successful Speaking and Business Presentation* (Heineman).
Leigh, A and Maynard, M (1994) *Perfect Presentation* (Arrow Business Books).
Peel, M (1995) *Successful Presentation in a Week* (Headway: Hodder and Stoughton).

Reading on writing skills

Bartram, P (1994) *Perfect Business Writing* (Arrow Business Books).
Bell, J (1994) *Doing Your Research Project*, 2nd edn, Chapters 11 and 12 (Open University Press).
Bowden, J (1994) *How to Write a Report*, 2nd edn (How To Books Ltd).
Cooper, B M (1990) *Writing Technical Reports* (Penguin Books).
Daniels, D and Daniels, B (1993) *Persuasive Writing* (Harper Collins).
Goodworth, C (1990) *The Secrets of Successful Business Report Writing* (Heineman).

39 Graphical presentation

Paul Levy

INTRODUCTION

In this chapter, we look at the graphical presentation of information. This is a huge topic and there is not enough space to explore it in depth. Here are some basic guidelines for those who are new to research and wish to put some graphical life into their research reports.

Information expressed visually can be a guide for the writer as well as for the reader. Graphics act as points of light in the writing, beacons, signalling the development of the research from aims, through methods, to findings, analysis and conclusions. Even if you omit them from the final draft, they can help you while you are writing.

Some of the graphics used in research reports are

- graphs;
- pie charts;
- tables;
- diagrams;
- photographs;
- cartoons.

GRAPHS

If you have collected a lot of numbers, and if these numbers are, at least in part, necessary for a reader to understand the research, then a graph of one kind or another will be appropriate. Any book on graph making will talk about the different kinds of graph: bar charts, histograms, line graphs. What is common to them all is that the data, through graphic presentation, is easier to read and understand than in text form.

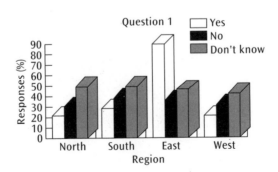

Figure 39.1 A graph with three results side by side

As Fig. 39.1 illustrates (from the first question of a questionnaire), the clear and simple presentation is the key. The responses to a question that requires either a 'yes', 'no' or 'don't know' response are shown for four respondent groups from different parts of a country. The reader is able to get a rough idea of the responses by looking at the graph, without having to read the numbers in detail. These numbers can be contained in an appendix, or in the report itself. But the visual impact is the important thing, particularly when the graph is being presented in a stand-up presentation. The researcher may have a particular point to make about the responses to the questionnaire, and the point can be made on the back of the visual impression the graph creates. In the case of Fig. 39.1 there may be a point to be made about the 'yes' response from the group of respondents from the 'east'.

In Fig. 39.2, there is a second version of the same graph. In this case, by putting the three types of response into one bar for each group, we can get a visual sense of the proportion of responses from each group.

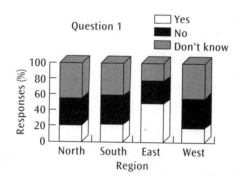

Figure 39.2 The same graph as in Fig. 39.1 showing relative proportions

In Fig. 39.3, we have an example of the wonders of technology: a simple graphic version of Fig. 39.1 generated three-dimensionally. Impressive though it may look, the ability to compare the responses is lessened by the distortion caused by the poor perspective of the three dimensions.

Finally, in Fig. 39.4, the *proportion* graph shown in Fig.39.2 is presented in a different way, allowing the reader a little more accuracy in assessing the proportions. The reader can pick out the different responses and relate them more quickly to the percentages on the scale provided.

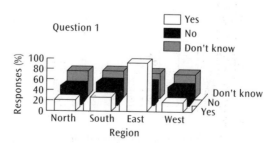

Figure 39.3 A three-dimensional version of Fig. 39.1, lacking clarity for the reader

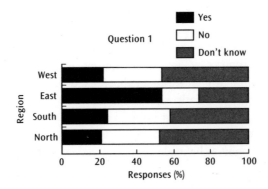

Figure 39.4 Another version of Fig.39.1 presented differently

The choice of the type of graph depends on what you believe should have visual impact. What is the aim of the graph? What response should it elicit in the reader?

The following guidelines may help.

- Check the purpose of the graph from the readers' point of view.
- Do not use too many graphs.
- Label the axes properly.
- Include exact figures on the graph if this is required.
- Keep the amount of data on one graph manageable.

Fig. 39.5 shows a graph presenting two kinds of data on one chart. This enables the reader to see a relationship between several variables. Once again, it is important to be clear about the purpose of such a graph.

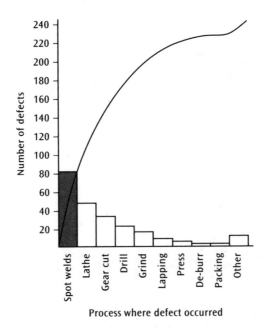

Figure 39.5 An example of a graph showing two kinds of data

Graphs have a range of uses for different kinds of research. They can

- show changes in a research variable over time;
- show relative proportions;
- establish relationships between research variables.

PIE CHARTS

Pie charts can have impact in a stand-up presentation but should not be used in written reports since the few numbers they represent are more easily read in a simple table.

Pie charts can be used

- to show the relative 'share' of different elements;
- as an alternative to the graph shown in Fig. 39.1.

As with graphs, they can be generated easily by computer programs. They are harder to construct by hand. Figure 39.6 shows the simple visual power of a pie chart in showing the results of a question from an attitude survey.

Figure 39.7 is a poor example of a pie chart. It has the same data as those used in Fig. 39.6. In this case, the percentages are missing and the pie pieces have been separated. Clarity is lost and it is very hard to see what the chart is trying to say. However, if, in a stand-up presentation, we only wish to make the simple point that salad is the preferred lunch time food, then this chart does the trick.

Finally, in Fig. 39.8, we have a three-dimensional pie chart. Once again, salad stands out clearly as the preferred food, and the graphic overall looks impressive. There is, however, a small danger

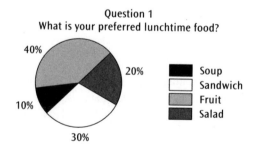

Figure 39.6 A pie chart showing the responses to a question from a questionnaire

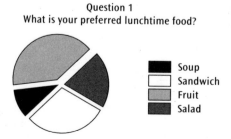

Figure 39.7 A pie chart without numbers attached, giving a rough idea of proportion but lacking precision for the reader

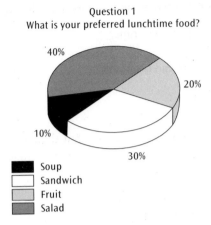

Question 1
What is your preferred lunchtime food?

40%

20%

10%

30%

■ Soup
□ Sandwich
▨ Fruit
▨ Salad

Figure 39.8 Impressive use of three-dimensions, but deceptive on the proportion of each 'slice' of the pie

that the distortion of perspective distorts the reader's view of the data. Compare each of the pie slices in Figs 39.7 and 39.8. What do you think?

In general, pie charts can make for good, impressive visuals. As with graphs, some guidelines should be noted:

- Label the pie chart properly.
- Be clear about the purpose of using the chart.
- Too many pie pieces can make the chart look overloaded with information and hard to read.
- Be careful of the impact of using three-dimensional effects.
- Pie charts can be most effective in stand-up presentation.
- Pie charts should not be used in written reports.

TABLES

Tables can be used in conjunction with other, more visual, charts or they can be used alone. With other charts, the table can be used to hold the detailed data while the chart gives a general visual impression. On its own, a table holds research data that can be read easily and understood by a reader.

Tables are *successful* in research writing when they are

- simple;
- clear;
- not too overloaded with data;
- clearly linked to the text and other graphics.

Tables are *unsuccessful* in research writing when they

- are used as 'dumping grounds' for piles of numbers;
- try to say too much at once;
- 'stand out' alone and are not integrated with the text.

Table 39.1 is a simple table, without any data. It has four columns for data and allows the reader a quick view of the results of a piece of survey work. It is poorly labelled and would rely on proper referencing within the text.

Table 39.1 An empty table which is clear and simple, but poorly labelled

C I Travel Ltd
Survey of favourite holiday destinations

Destination	Tally	Total	Cumulative total	%
Costa del Sol.				
Tenerife				
Florida				
Paris				
Kos				
Blackpool				
Bognor Regis				

In summary, tables depicting research data need

- supporting commentary;
- proper labelling;
- simple and clear presentation;
- links to other types of graphic.

FIGURES

Diagrams can take many forms. Some of their uses in research are:

- to show an experiment;
- depict a process;
- map an organisation;
- link a set of ideas.

A figure will support written research if it

- helps to clarify an argument or a context;
- demystifies a process;
- helps to link critical ideas together;
- improves the visual appeal of a piece of writing.

Figures 39.9 and 39.10 show one researcher's attempts to describe an organisation's philosophy known as 'continuous improvement'. In Fig. 39.9 we have a sense of a number of ingredients (shown on the left) all being important in the creation of the *Continuous Improvement* (CI, on the right). This is clear. What is not so clear is the relationship between each of the elements on the left.

In Fig. 39.10 we have a second version of the model. In this case the elements are depicted as 'cogs in a machine', suggesting a quality of motion in the diagram. They are now viewed by the reader in terms of their relationship to each other: they are interdependent; one cannot move without another. If the researcher's intention was to make this point, then you might think that Fig. 39.9 is less successful than Fig. 39.10. However, the arrangement of the cogs is such that none of them can move!

Finally, in Fig. 39.11, we have an example of a flowchart. A flowchart is useful if you wish to

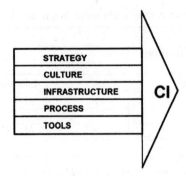

Figure 39.9 The first version of a model taken from an sample research project on 'continuous improvement'

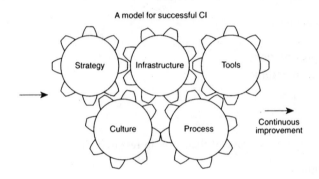

Figure 39.10 A second version of Fig. 39.9 containing an attempt to show 'movement'

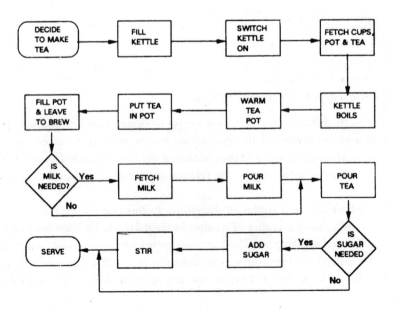

Figure 39.11 A flowchart making a complex process visual for the reader

describe a process. In Fig. 39.11 there is the process of making a cup of tea. The diagram lacks a key to describe the different boxes, but it does give a visual impression of all of the stages required. Perhaps tea making isn't so simple after all!

PHOTOGRAPHS

Photographs are powerful visual aids. They work well in stand-up presentations (used mainly with slide projectors) but can also be used in written reports. Once again, we have to deal with the basic question: what is the purpose of the visual aid? If the research report is to be academically credible then the use of photographs should not be used to create the impression that the write-up is like a piece of journalism, no matter how appealing the pictures!

A photograph can, and should, be used where a real picture is critical to the reader's understanding of the research. For example, in a biological research write up, photographs taken from microscope slides may be appropriate. Or in a piece of engineering research, a picture of a laser machine being studied may be appropriate. What are less appropriate, for example, are snapshots of the researcher in action, or a picture of the interviewer and interviewee shaking hands.

Guidance for using photographs

· Be clear about who owns the copyright on photographs.
· Do not use poor photocopies of photographs.
· Be clear on why a photograph is being used.

CARTOONS

Cartoons can be used cautiously in stand-up presentations. But be wary about using them in a written research report, unless they illustrate a point effectively and are not likely to annoy a reader. The two rules shown in Fig. 39.12 may help.

Computer versus hand drawing

It is now largely standard for research reports and graphics to be word-processed or computer generated. However, programs for drawing on many computers are user-unfriendly and

Figure 39.12 Rules about using cartoons

researchers do not always have the time to spend on learning such programmes. Some strategies are available.

• Get support from a computer literate colleague.
• Use neat handwriting (stencils can be used for slides).
• Write the graphic by hand and use a computer scanner.

Remember: The quality of the graphic may be seen by audiences and readers to represent the quality of the research.

Colour

If colour pens or printers are available, use them! At the simplest level, colour is appealing to look at. At a deeper level colour is a powerful tool for presentation. Colour can be used to

• create identity for different sections of the research, such as blue for methods, green for findings;
• depict emotional data, such as red for problems, green for actions, orange for warnings.

When you draft your report, experiment with different colours. Too much black and white can create the impression of greyness to the reader; however, too many colours can make a presentation cluttered and confusing to the eye.

AND FINALLY . . .

And finally, there are the logos; the icons; sections inside boxes; proper page numbers; a clear contents page; a list of figures and tables; an impressive title page; reader-friendly report covers, the final spell check, and then . . . presenting it to the reader! Phew!

REFERENCE

Tufte, E (1983) *The Visual Display of Quantitative Information* (Cheshire, Connecticut: Graphics Press).

40 Personal home pages on the web

Karen L Ayres

INTRODUCTION

Many universities now allow members of staff and postgraduates to have their own personal home page (PHP) on the university website. Such pages have several uses in postgraduate research. Just as you will be interested in web pages maintained by others working in your area (Chapter 12), they may be equally interested in your current research. Specifically, PHPs may be useful to

- outline the project you are currently working on;
- invite feedback on your research;
- list publications, with downloadable preprints of articles;
- make your software available for download.

In my own experience, a PHP is particularly useful when presenting work at a conference. Fellow researchers can subsequently obtain preprints from the web page, as well as find out more about you and your research.

GET YOUR PAGE ONTO THE WEB

Before you spend time developing a web page, you should check that your university does allow PHPs. You can find out the necessary information from the computer services' personnel at your college, or from the university website. You will also need to find details of how to get your page mounted on the website. The methods are likely to differ between universities but your computer services helpdesk should be able to provide you with simple instructions.

If PHPs are permitted, there are usually some common-sense guidelines that must be followed. For example:

- The university/college coat of arms must not be used on the page.
- The page must not contain, nor link to, any defamatory, pornographic, or other inappropriate material.
- The page should not contain any material that breaches copyright.
- The page should not be used for commercial purposes.
- The page should include a statement to the effect that the university or college is not responsible for, or endorses, the content of the page.

Remember that by being mounted on the university's website, your page is to some degree, representing your college: do not put anything on your page that may bring it into disrepute.

There may also be limits on the amount of webspace you are allowed. You should check this with your computer services' personnel. However, common sense dictates that you should not put large files in your personal webspace.

If you are not permitted to mount your own page on your university's website, you may want to consider purchasing webspace from an Internet Service Provider (ISP). Again, your university computer services centre may be able to give you guidance as to the best options.

HTML – THE LANGUAGE OF THE WEB

Once you have established that PHPs are allowed, you can proceed with designing and writing your homepage. This is a lot simpler than you might initially think!

Webpages are written in HTML (Hypertext Markup Language). This is a text-based computer language: a HTML document consists of a series of opening and closing *tags* surrounding pieces of text. These tags tell the browser how to format the text. Although webpages can be generated by specialist software packages, such as Macromedia DreamWeaver and Microsoft FrontPage, or created by selecting `Save As HTML Document` in programs such as Microsoft Word, these packages are not essential for writing a webpage. Files containing HTML code are ASCII text files (with a .htm or .html extension), and so can be created in any basic text editor. All you need to do is type the commands into the file, save it, and then open it in a web browser: your webpage will be displayed (assuming you haven't made any typing errors). You can easily make changes to the file and reload the page into the browser to see what effect these changes have.

GUIDE TO BASIC HTML

Almost all pages have the standard tags

```
<HTML>
<HEAD>
   <TITLE>My page title</TITLE>
</HEAD>
<BODY>
   Text for actual page
</BODY>
</HTML>
```

The <HTML> tag tells the browser to interpret the file as a HTML document, and <HEAD> contains general commands that are not part of the main page (note that HTML tags can be in lowercase as well as uppercase, though uppercase helps to distinguish the code from the normal text). Any text between the <TITLE> . . . </TITLE> tags will appear in the browser's title bar. For details on other main tags see, for example, Oliver (1998).

The commands for the actual page are placed within the <BODY> environment. Again, the commands are tags that tell the browser how to format the text between them. The basic tags, with descriptions, are:

Headings, paragraphs, and horizontal rules

Pre-formatted headings are available. A major heading (large bold font) is generated via <H1> My heading </H1>, and a minor heading by <H4> My heading </H4>. Intermediate values produce intermediate-sized headings.

Paragraphs should be enclosed within the <P> . . . </P> environment (note that several spaces or carriage returns in the .html file will be interpreted as a single space by the browser, and so paragraphs and line breaks must be specified with HTML code). The HTML command for a line break is a single <BR>, and   should be used to insert an extra space on the page.

To divide the page into sections, you can use a horizontal rule. This is produced by <HR WIDTH="100%">, which will draw a thin line the entire width (100%) of the page.

Text placement and fonts

To centre text, enclose it within <CENTER> . . . </CENTER>. To right-align a paragraph, use <P ALIGN="RIGHT">My paragraph</P>.

Bold font is produced by <B> . . . </B>, and italics by <I> . . . </I>. To underline use <U> . . . </U>, and to display text in a typewriter font use <TT> . . . </TT>.

By default your page will probably appear in Times New Roman (though this depends on individual browser settings). If you want text to appear in a different font, for example Arial, as well as slightly larger, use <FONT FACE="Arial" SIZE=+1> text </FONT>. Correct display will depend on the availability of the font, and also on the particular browser being used (some may not be able to interpret the FACE command).

Lists

A bullet-pointed list is produced with

```
<UL>
    <LI>First item
    <LI>Second item
</UL>
```

For a numbered list, replace UL with OL.

Pictures and links

To place a picture on a page, use the IMG command

```
<IMG SRC="pic.gif" ALT="figure 1">.
```

If the picture cannot be displayed for any reason, then the text 'figure 1' will appear on the page instead.

To include a link to a webpage, the <A> environment is used:

```
<A HREF="http://www.rdg.ac.uk/">click here</A>.
```

Where pictures are to be used as links instead of text, use the <IMG SRC="pic.gif"> command in place of 'click here' – to remove the default border around the picture specify BORDER=0 within the IMG command.

For files that are to be downloaded, simply replace the xxx.html file with the name of the relevant file (such as file.doc). This file must be in your webspace.

To link to an e-mail address (so that the user's e-mail program will be activated when clicking on the link), use the mailto command:

```
<A HREF="mailto:snr96kla@reading.ac.uk">email!</A>.
```

Tables

Tables are important in HTML documents – as well as presenting information concisely, tables give more control over how different parts of the page can be displayed in relation to each other. The basic layout of a (2 by 2) table is

```
<TABLE>
    <TR>
    <TD>row1 col1 text</TD>
    <TD>row1 col2 text</TD>
    </TR>
    <TR>
    <TD>row2 col1 text</TD>
    <TD>row2 col2 text</TD>
    </TR>
</TABLE>
```

where the <TR> . . . </TR> tags enclose information relating to a particular row, and the <TD> . . . </TD> environment contains information for a particular cell within that row. Additional information on tables is in Chapter 15 of Oliver (1998).

FURTHER INFORMATION ON HTML

I have covered only the most basic elements of HTML, and so have not considered topics such as colour or use of frames. The easiest way to learn more about HTML is to look at the code underlying other people's web pages (browsers usually have a *View Source* facility). By doing this, you can see how different parts of the page were produced. Alternatively, there are many books on the subject (for example Burns 1998, Oliver 1998). Your computer services library will probably have some HTML reference books that you can consult.

ENHANCING AND CORRECTING YOUR PAGE

Web pages can be enhanced easily with colour and graphics, as well as JavaScript functions (for example, two images can be transposed as the mouse pointer moves over a specific part of the page). Some websites provide free graphics for people to use on their own sites (see below). However, you should never assume that any graphic on a website is free for you to download and use unless the owner clearly states that such permission is granted. Copyright rules apply to websites, and the creator of an image retains the copyright on their product whether or not they assert it in writing (see Chapter 41). If you are unsure about using pictures from other people's sites (for example graphics for bullet points), create your own. Pictures for web pages can be generated easily by scanning in photographs, or by drawing images in a suitable computer package. Jasc Paint Shop Pro is one program that can create GIF, JPEG and PNG file formats suitable for web pages (see Clark 1998, for a guide to using the package). You should resist the temptation, though, to create very detailed pictures or animations that may take a long time to load over a slow Internet connection.

You might make errors while typing code into your HTML file. Some of these will be easily identifiable, as the page will not display as you intended. Other errors with the code that are fixed by the browser before generating the page can be routinely identified with programs designed to find such bugs (for example, Dave Raggett's *HTML Tidy*, available at www.w3.org/People/ Raggett/tidy/). Note that a browser does not actually change your HTML file when it identifies errors before it displays your page; it is up to you to correct your mistakes.

ONLINE WEB RESOURCES

For further information on writing web pages, and for tips on how to improve your page and make it more professional, you can search the Internet for HTML guides, graphics, and free examples of scripts (code that performs a specific function). Some sites that I have found useful are:

- NCSA HTML Primer
  http://archive.ncsa.uiuc.edu/General/Internet/WWW/HTMLPrimerAll.html
  (*a simple introductory guide to the HTML language*)
- Earthweb's HTML Goodies Tutorials
  http://www.htmlgoodies.earthweb.com/tutors
  (*tutorials for learning basic and advanced HTML*)
- JavaScript Goodies Scripts
  http://www.htmlgoodies.earthweb.com/JSBook
  (*scripts outlined in the JavaScript Goodies book by Joe Burns, 1999*)
- Downloadable GIF icons and images
  http://socsci.colorado.edu/GIF
  (*list of downloadable GIF images for webpages, maintained by the Social Science Data Laboratory at the University of Colorado at Boulder*)

There are many more such pages on the Internet. You can use one of the web search engines to locate additional free resources for web designers.

TYPICAL CONTENTS OF A RESEARCHER'S WEB PAGE

There is much scope for the contents of a PHP, and what you put on your page depends to some extent on your subject area. However, some core items that are likely to be common to all scientific researchers are the following.

Name and current position   (for example: Final year research postgraduate)

Contact details   You should include your university postal as well as e-mail address, and telephone and fax number.

Research interests   Provide a brief outline of your current projects. List those people with whom you are working, including your supervisor. If your thesis title is finalised, you can state that. Give details of your current source of funding, with a link to their website.

Publications   If you have had articles relevant to your research published, particularly in peer-reviewed journals, list them on your page. Include full details just as you would if you cited the paper in another article. You should not include copies of the papers for downloading unless you have received permission to do so from the publishers. You can also give details of papers that have been accepted for publication, but have not yet appeared in print. If you want to give further information about any of the articles listed, include a brief abstract on the page.

Karen L. Ayres
Final Year Research Postgraduate, Applied Statistics

POSTAL ADDRESS: Dept. of Applied Statistics, University of Reading, PO Box 240, Earley Gate, Reading, RG6 6FN, UK.

Email: snr96kla@reading.ac.uk

Fax: +44(0) 118 975 3169

Welcome to my homepage!

RESEARCH INTERESTS

I am currently a final year PhD student, working on MCMC methods for estimating genetic correlations within and between loci (and their implications for forensic identification). My PhD is supervised by Professor David Balding, and is funded by a studentship from the UK EPSRC.

I am a student member of the Royal Statistical Society and the International Biometric Society.

PUBLICATIONS

- **Ayres, KL** and Balding, DJ (1998). Measuring departures from Hardy-Weinberg: A Markov chain Monte Carlo method for estimating the inbreeding coefficient. *Heredity* **80** pp 769–777.

BACKGROUND

1995–

> Studying for a PhD in the *Department of Applied Statistics* at the *University of Reading* with Professor David Balding (first year completed at Queen Mary & Westfield College, London, prior to supervisor moving to Reading).

1994–1995

> M.Sc. in Statistics at the *London School of Economics.*

1991–1994

> B.Sc. in Pure Mathematics (1st class honours) at *Queen Mary & Westfield College,* University of London.

Last updated Aug. 1998

Figure 40.1(a) A simple postgraduate homepage, outlining research interests, publications, and background

Preprints If you have submitted papers to journals and these have not yet been accepted but you want others to benefit immediately from your research, you can include preprints of your manuscript on your page for downloading. However, you should *always* check with your supervisor as well as any other co-authors before you make your manuscripts available for download.

Software If your project involves developing software, you may want to make your programs available for download. Again, you should check first with your supervisor, and any others who are involved with the project. See Chapter 41 for further information on intellectual property rights.

```
<HTML>
<HEAD>
    <TITLE>Karen L. Ayres, University of Reading</TITLE>
    <META NAME="Keywords" CONTENT="Ayres, postgraduate, statistical genetics, forensic identifica-
tion, estimating genetic correlations">
</HEAD>
<BODY>
    <HI><I>Karen L. Ayres</I></H1>
    <H2>Final Year Research Postgraduate, Applied Statistics</H2>
    <HR WIDTH="100%">

    <P><B>POSTAL ADDRESS: Dept. of Applied Statistics, University of Reading, PO
Box 240,
    <BR>Earley Gate, Reading, RG6 6FN, UK.
    <BR>Email:<A HREF="mailto:snr96kla@reading.ac.uk">snr96kla@reading.ac.uk</A>
    <BR>Fax: +44(0) 118 975 3169</B></P>
    <HR WIDTH="100%">

    <P><B>Welcome to my homepage!</B></P>

    <H3>RESEARCH INTERESTS</H3>
    <P>I am currently a final year PhD student, working on MCMC methods for estimating
genetic correlations within and between loci (and their implications for forensic
identification). My PhD is supervised by
    <A HREF="http://www.rdg.ac.uk/~snsbalng/">Professor David Balding</A>, and is
funded by a studentship from the UK <A HREF="http://www.epsrc.ac.uk/">ESPRC</A>.</P>
    <P>I am a student member of the <A HREF="http://www.rss.org.uk/">Royal Statistical
Society</A> and the <A HREF="http://www.tibs.org/">International Biometric
Society.</A>
    </P>

    <H3>PUBLICATIONS</H3>
    <UL>
        <LI><B>Ayres, KL</B> and Balding, DJ (1998). Measuring departures from
        Hardy-Weinberg: A Markov chain Monte Carlo method for estimating the
        inbreeding coefficient. <I>Heredity</I> <B>80</B> pp 769-777.
    </UL>

    <H3>BACKGROUND</H3>
    <DL>
    <DT><B>1995 - </B>
        <DD>Studying for a PhD in the <A
        HREF="http://www.rdg.ac.uk/Statistics/">Department of Applied Statistics</A> at the
        <A HREF="http://www.rdg.ac.uk/Statistics/">University of Reading</A> with
        Professor David Balding (first year completed at Queen Mary &amp; Westfield College,
        London, prior to supervisor moving to Reading).
        <BR><BR>
    <DT><B>1994-1995</B>
        <DD>M.Sc. in Statistics at the <A HREF="http://www.lse.ac.uk/">London School of
        Economics.</A>
        <BR><BR>
    <DT><B>1991-1994</B>
        <DD>B.Sc. in Pure Mathematics (1st class honours) at
        <A HREF="http://www.qmw.ac.uk/">Queen Mary &amp; Westfield College</A>,
        University of London.
    </DL>
    <HR WIDTH="100%">
    <P><FONT SIZE=-1><I>Last updated Aug. 1998</I><FONT></P>
</BODY>
</HTML>
```

Figure 40.1(b) HTML code for the homepage given in Fig. 40.1(a) – this code was typed into a basic text editor and saved under the filename home.html.

Background   Potential employers, such as senior researchers working in your area, may visit your homepage. For this reason, as well as to give a more complete picture of your education to date, it is a good idea to list all your relevant qualifications (post A-level will usually suffice).

Other items that you might want to put on your page include:

* a list of conferences you plan attending;
* a list of links to useful web pages;
* research organisations to which you belong.

An example of a postgraduate PHP is given in Fig. 40.1(a). This page is essentially the same as my first homepage, developed while I was studying for a PhD at the University of Reading. It is simple, but contains those areas listed above that were relevant to me at that time. The home.html file that contains the HTML code for the page is given in Fig. 40.1(b).

Your page does not need to consist only of research-related material. It is still a personal page, so you can include a list of your leisure interests, for example. I usually do. However, these should be the last items to appear on the page. Remember, as a researcher, your main reason for creating a PHP is to communicate your research to others in the field.

AND FINALLY . . .

Now that you have written your page, you need to make it available on the web. Ask your computer services staff how to do this. The procedure is generally simple. Further guidance can be obtained from others in your department who already have their own web pages.

Once your page is online, you will need to advertise it so that other researchers can find it easily. One option is to submit your site to one or more of the internet search engines. Some search engines, such as Excite (www.excite.co.uk), periodically catalogue sites automatically and so you need do nothing. If your department maintains a web page that lists current research postgraduates, you should ask that your page be linked to that list. Similarly, if the university maintains a list of PHPs, ask for a link to that.

The best way to advertise your site is routinely to include the web address along with your other contact details in all research-related correspondence. Furthermore, as well as your e-mail address you should include your web address on the title page of all conference presentations and other seminars and posters. If appropriate, tell conference delegates that they can obtain preprints from the site.

A website should not be a one-off creation. It should be updated periodically. It is very disappointing to read someone's web page and then to discover that it has not been updated in over a year. In addition, if you move on to another university and subsequently set-up a new homepage, you should ensure that your old page directs people to the new one. Guidance on web page redirection can be found on pages 358–361 in Oliver (1998).

REFERENCES

Burns, J (1998) *HTML Goodies* (Indianapolis, USA: Que).
Burns, J (1999) *JavaScript Goodies* (Indianapolis, USA: Que).
Clark, TM (1998) *SAMS Teach Yourself Paint Shop Pro in 24 Hours.* (Indianapolis, USA: SAMS).
Oliver, D (1998) *SAMS Teach Yourself HTML 4 in 24 Hours* 3rd edn (Indianapolis, USA: SAMS).

PART
10

Future

41 Protecting and exploiting technology

Laura Anderson

We hear much, nowadays, of the importance and value of technology and intellectual assets. In many cases, the value of new technology is determined by the ability of the proprietor to prevent others from obtaining access to that technology, or at least from obtaining access for free.

While the law does not protect technology as such, it does provide protection through various intellectual property rights that seek to protect the results of the creative intellect.

In this chapter, we discuss the following issues:

- What intellectual property rights exist and in what do they subsist?
- How can intellectual property rights be protected?
- Who owns the intellectual property rights in any particular technology?
- How can intellectual property rights be exploited?

The comments that follow are intended to provide a generous overview of considerations relevant to those involved in the development of technology and its exploitation. These comments are based on the law at March 2001. The law is, however, complex and is constantly developing. Accordingly, before applying any information in this chapter to particular circumstances, professional advice should be taken from a lawyer or patent agent, as appropriate. Additionally, the comments in this chapter relate to English law. For other jurisdictions, advice should be sought from lawyers or patent agents qualified to practise in the relevant country.

INTELLECTUAL PROPERTY RIGHTS

Under English law, the most important forms of intellectual property that are relevant to academic research institutions are

- patents;
- copyright and database rights;
- industrial designs (registered designs and unregistered design rights).

Know-how (unpatented confidential technical information) is commonly described and treated as a form of intellectual property. However, as know-how is information, it is not, strictly speaking, a property right.

In addition, there are other forms of intellectual property protection that may be relevant to certain technology, including semiconductor topography rights and petty patents or utility models that may be available in some countries in the event that the inventive step requirements of patentability are not satisfied (see below).

PATENTS

A patent is a monopoly right granted by the state in return for adequate disclosure to the state and, in turn, the public, of a new invention which the inventor could otherwise have kept secret. The invention may, for example, be a product such as a novel designer drug or a process such as the method for manufacturing that drug. The disclosure is made by the inventor submitting a written specification of the invention to the relevant state body, the patent office.

Patents are available only for novel inventions. To be new, the invention must not have been used or in any way disclosed in public, in the UK or elsewhere, by the inventor or anyone else before its priority date, normally the date the patent application is filed. There must also be an inventive step. In other words, when looked at through the eyes of a person skilled in the particular area of technology concerned, the invention must not be obvious when compared with everything that is known at the priority date claimed. Patentable inventions must also be capable of industrial application.

However, there are limitations on patentability. For example, discoveries, scientific theories and mathematical or business methods are not patentable *per se*, although their application to a product or process may be patentable if there is a technical effect. The patentability of computer programs is the ongoing subject of debate. In the absence of a new technical effect, patent protection for computer programs has not been granted in Europe, copyright being the chosen medium of software protection (see below). The effect of this requirement of technical effect is that patents for software and Internet-related business methods are much more readily available in the US than in Europe, leading to calls for the revision of European patent law in this respect.

Ownership of a patent gives its registered proprietor the exclusive right to exploit the product or process claimed for up to 20 years from the filing date and the right to prevent others from doing so unless authorised by the registered proprietor. As such, patents can be extremely valuable rights, especially at the time of entering a new market. Time is often needed to establish a new product and recover research and development costs before competitors arrive on the market.

Where a patentable invention may have been developed, it is crucial not to disclose details of the invention to any other person before a patent agent has drafted and filed the patent application. If the invention is disclosed, the patent application may be prejudiced on the grounds of lack of novelty and, even if the application is granted, the validity of the patent may later be brought into issue. Care should, therefore, be exercised when publishing or presenting papers at conferences or to colleagues at seminars to ensure that the invention is not accidentally disclosed. The same issue applies when demonstrating the invention on departmental open days.

If a potential industrial partner wishes to evaluate technology belonging to an institution that is potentially patentable, it is important to ensure that before representatives of that prospective industrial partner see or have disclosed to them any such technical information, they are told and have acknowledged that such demonstrations and/or disclosures are being made to them in confidence. They should be required to sign a *confidentiality agreement* confirming this. Professional advice should be taken on the form of such an agreement. Many academic institutions, however, already have their own standard form agreement.

A possible disadvantage of patenting an invention, rather than merely keeping it secret, is the often substantial cost involved in obtaining and, once granted, maintaining the patent. In addition to paying renewal fees, this could include defending claims that the patent is invalid. As a result, patents are not always the most appropriate form of protection for an invention.

KNOW-HOW

Know-how is a general term used to describe technical information, which is often unpatentable, and which is confidential to its originator. Formulae, recipes and process descriptions are common examples. The commercial value of know-how resides in its confidential nature. Clearly, this gives rise to a conflict between, on the one hand, academic freedoms and the requirement to publish the results of research work and, on the other, the necessity to keep know-how confidential to preserve its value.

Keeping technical information confidential has some advantages over patent protection. No formalities are required and hence there are no application and renewal fees to pay. Furthermore, unlike patents, which are territorial in nature, no such restrictions apply to confidential information. However, the commercial value of such information is destroyed if it loses its confidentiality, either because it leaks out or because someone else independently develops the same know-how and publishes it. Once a product is on the market, it may also be possible to discover its formula or its manufacturing method by reverse engineering. Accordingly, whilst in theory the life of know-how is perpetual, in practice it is uncertain. This is a major disadvantage compared with patent protection.

The following ground rules can help to prolong the life of know-how. Marking documents containing such information 'confidential' and permitting access to the information only on a need-to-know basis are obvious steps. Storing confidential documents in a secure place, minimising the number of copies made, and protecting access to information stored on a computer with a security code are further practical steps that should be taken.

Disclosure of know-how often accompanies the granting of a licence to exploit an associated patent on a commercial scale. The recipient of that information should be required to keep it confidential, not to disclose it to anyone else, and not to use it for any purpose other than that specified. In certain circumstances, such duties can be implied by law. The prudent course of action, however, is to ensure such obligations are recorded in legally binding documents, signed before the information is imparted, and in which the relevant information is clearly identified. There still remains, however, the risk of those obligations being ignored and the information leaking into the public domain. It is therefore important that practical steps such as those outlined above are also imposed upon the recipient.

Confidentiality is frequently an issue when an academic research body collaborates with a commercial partner. For the former, it is often important to publish results wherever possible, but for the latter this may prejudice the patentability or confidentiality, and ultimately the commercial value, of the technology whose development the partner has financed. Usually, a compromise will be reached under which the research body is permitted to publish important scientific discoveries, perhaps after scrutiny by, and the approval of, the commercial partner. The publication of theses by research students must also be taken into account, bearing in mind any relevant university regulations.

COPYRIGHT

Copyright protects the particular expression of an idea rather than the idea underlying the expression. It subsists in original written materials provided certain qualification requirements are met, such as by the author being a UK resident. Common examples of works protected by copyright are laboratory notebooks, instruction manuals, graphs and preparatory design materials. It is also the principal legal medium for protecting computer software.

One advantage of copyright is that there are no registration or other formalities for it to subsist. It arises automatically on creation of the work. The owner of the copyright in a work will be the person who created it, unless an employee made it during the course of his employment, in which case the owner will usually be the employer. Establishing ownership of copyright, however, can sometimes be difficult. This may be facilitated by the use of a copyright notice as follows:

© [insert name of copyright owner] [insert year of creation of work]

It is also important to keep all original works and records of the dates on which all copyright works were produced.

Copyright in a work generally subsists for the life of its author plus 70 years. Copyright in the UK gives its owner the exclusive right to do certain acts, such as copy the work or issue copies of the work to the public. It is an infringement of copyright to do any of the acts the copyright owner has the exclusive right to do, unless that owner gives permission. Special provisions apply for making back-up copies of, and decompiling, computer programs.

Like a patent, copyright is also a national right but, by virtue of various international conventions, protection may extend beyond the country in which copyright protection originally arises.

Copyright also protects certain types of databases where, as a result of the selection or arrangement of the contents of the database, the database constitutes the author's own intellectual creation. Where the compilation of a database has not entailed the requisite degree of selection or arrangement for copyright protection, the database may still be protected by a separate but related database right. The database right prevents against the unauthorised extraction or re-utilisation of all or a substantial part of any database if there has been a substantial effort entailed in putting the database together. The database right subsists for the shorter period of 15 years from the end of the year in which the database is created.

DESIGNS

Design right in the UK protects an original design that relates to any aspect of the shape or configuration of a three-dimensional article, such as a design for a part of a machine. There are exceptions, however, for those features of shape or configuration which 'must fit' or 'must match' with another article. The design right is an unregistered right that arises automatically provided the design qualifies for protection by reference, for example, to the citizenship of the designer and it has been recorded in a design document or an article has been made to the design. The design right may give rise to protection for up to 15 years.

If a design has 'eye approval' then more extensive registered design protection may be available. Registration gives the proprietor of the design certain exclusive rights for up to 25 years. To be registrable, the design must be novel and must be applied to an article by an industrial process. Protection is not, however, available if the design depends on the appearance of another article of which it forms an integral part (such as a car body panel).

HANDLING INTELLECTUAL PROPERTY RIGHTS IN PRACTICE

It is helpful for all research staff to have a basic knowledge of the intellectual property rights described above and the technologies in which they are likely to arise.

Maintaining detailed and accurate laboratory notebooks and records (including dates) of any inventions made is extremely important to facilitate intellectual property protection. Procedures should be implemented to prevent any accidental disclosure of intellectual property rights; in particular, technical information that needs to be kept confidential. All publications, theses, abstracts and seminar materials should ideally be screened by the academic institution concerned before sending for publication or being presented and amended accordingly.

Identifying what intellectual property rights are available for exploitation is a key step in any technology transfer programme. This can be done by means of a technology audit. In the same way as accountants audit books, there are specialist technical auditors who can identify what intellectual property rights may subsist in the technology concerned, evaluate them and advise on their protection and exploitation.

PRELIMINARY POINTS BEFORE EXPLOITING TECHNOLOGY

Having identified some intellectual property rights that may be suitable for exploitation, the preliminary matters set out below should be considered.

Who owns the intellectual property rights?

It is important to establish the ownership of the intellectual property rights concerned as, generally speaking, it is only the owner of those rights who has the right to exploit them or to grant or transfer that right to others.

In the case of an academic institution, this is often a complex issue. There are several possible candidates ranging from the academic institution itself to the research supervisor, the graduate student, any collaborative partner or any other funding body. Legal rules set out for each type of intellectual property who owns that particular right in law. In certain cases, these rules may be set aside by agreement.

In addition, many academic institutions have policies on the ownership and exploitation of intellectual property rights by their academic staff and research students, but employment contracts, terms upon which research grants are awarded, or collaborative agreements, would need to be checked in conjunction with these.

How are the intellectual property rights owned?

Intellectual property rights may be owned by the academic institution alone, or perhaps jointly with a collaborative partner or even an academic. Patents, for example, may be exploited by each joint owner without recourse to the other, but a licence under a jointly owned patent can be granted only by all joint owners, unless the owners have previously agreed otherwise.

By whom are the intellectual property rights to be exploited?

Often academic institutions will set up a limited liability technology transfer company that will be responsible for exploiting the technology and associated intellectual property rights developed at the institution. Commercial contracts are then entered into by that company (to whom the intellectual property rights will have been transferred) rather than the institution. This is an important way to reduce the risk of prejudicing the institution's tax and charitable status.

COMMON WAYS OF EXPLOITING TECHNOLOGY

Two common routes of technology exploitation used by academic institutions are assignment and licensing.

Assignment

An assignment is the legal term for an outright transfer of the property right concerned (or the interest held in that right), including the right to sue infringers. Parts of that property right may even be carved out for assignment in certain cases.

To be valid, assignments of patents, protected designs or copyright must all be in writing, but there are different rules on execution. It is advisable to seek professional help on the form and scope of the assignment, especially where the technology concerned may be required as a basis for further research.

An assignment is likely to be appropriate where the proprietor of the relevant rights is not able to exploit the rights and the purchaser is prepared to pay full market value for the technology and needs the title to those rights for its purposes.

Licensing

The alternative route to an assignment is usually to grant a licence. A licence does not transfer any property right as such to the licensee. Rather, it allows the licensee to use the intellectual property rights concerned in accordance with the terms agreed, the use of which would otherwise be an infringement.

Licences can be granted expressly or by implication and on an exclusive, non-exclusive or sole basis. A written agreement is preferable so as to define the scope of the licence and to ensure adequate control over the licensing arrangement. Biotech, pharmaceutical and IT contracts, in particular, require specialised provisions to take account of the nature of the relevant technology.

An *exclusive licence* is the closest to an assignment as it permits only the licensee to use the licensed rights. The licensor is also precluded. The licence may be restricted to certain fields of use. For example, an exclusive licence under a pharmaceutical patent could be limited to the production of the substance claimed for use in only one therapeutic area. This might be appropriate where an institution wishes to grant additional rights under the same patent to other licensees for different fields of use.

To enable the institution to protect its income stream, the licence agreement could contain provisions enabling the institution to terminate the licence if the licensee fails to exploit the technology to its full potential, and so to look for another licensee, or perhaps to alter the licence to a non-exclusive basis.

If the licensing institution also wishes to be able to exploit the technology then a *sole or non-exclusive licence* should be considered. A non-exclusive licence is usually more appropriate for a technology that has many applications. The institution will be free to use the technology itself as well as to grant non-exclusive licences to others. Under a sole licence, only the licensor and licensee are entitled to use the relevant technology.

More elaborate ways of dealing with intellectual property rights are possible. For example, intellectual property rights can be used as consideration for the issue of shares in an exploitation company or mortgaged in the same way as a house as security for borrowing.

The consideration for the transfer of the intellectual property rights concerned is usually a matter for negotiation. It could, for example, be a lump sum payable on the granting of rights or, more commonly, a percentage royalty on sales of the product resulting from their exploitation. Combinations of these routes and more sophisticated arrangements are always possible.

Finally, national and European competition rules and taxation consequences should always be considered when deciding how to exploit intellectual property rights.

CONCLUSION

Provided appropriate steps are taken, academic institutions can endeavour to exploit the technology arising from their research efforts to produce income for further research, thus reducing the need to rely on external sources of funding. However, technology transfer programmes require specialist assistance at all stages, whether it is in identifying and protecting intellectual property rights or in their subsequent exploitation.

42 Career opportunities

Ralph Coates

INTRODUCTION

In this chapter, I present some views and information about sectors of employment together with some useful tips to help you locate and apply for appropriate posts.

A postgraduate degree (at doctorate or master's level) does not in itself guarantee you employment. However, your skills, abilities and some of the specialised knowledge derived from your postgraduate study will most certainly assist when matching yourself to both the requirements of an employer and the demands of a job. Recognition of what you have to offer is crucially important so that you can effectively explore the appropriate job market and project yourself competitively within it.

SECTORS OF EMPLOYMENT

Teaching and education

In the area of higher education, a postgraduate degree coupled with evidence of a good record of research interests and experience is normally a pre-requisite for lecturing posts in most institutions of higher education.

Post-doctoral fellowships of between three and five years duration are available in universities throughout the world. Many are funded by an appropriate research council and will provide opportunities for researchers to continue working in their specialist areas.

There are occasionally some short-term appointments of one to three years as demonstrators or research assistants.

If, however, you are contemplating a teaching career in schools then, despite your higher degree, you are strongly recommended to take a *Post Graduate Certificate in Education* (PGCE) course. All state schools, and increasingly public schools and sixth form colleges, require teachers to have this teaching qualification. Without it, your future promotion opportunities could be adversely affected.

International Agencies

The *Commonwealth Development Corporation* (CDC) recruits a small number of staff each year on agriculture-, engineering- and science-based projects related to the developing world.

Postgraduate qualifications together with experience are frequently required.

The *Consultative Group on International Agricultural Research* (CGIAR) is an association of countries, international and regional organisations and private foundations dedicated to supporting a network of 13 agricultural research centres and programmes around the world. These centres offer the opportunity for research in developing countries with excellent facilities provided by the World Bank and other agencies.

The *European Commission*, the largest of the institutions of the European Union, occasionally has vacancies. In particular, the *Joint Research Centre* employs postgraduate and postdoctoral researchers in physical and computer sciences, engineering and related disciplines to work on joint projects.

The *Overseas Development Administration* (ODA) recruits experienced staff for tours of duty in many countries in Africa, Latin America, the Middle East and South-East Asia. The disciplines required include agriculture, engineering and the sciences. The ODA also handles recruitment for several other international organisations.

Civil Service (including government laboratories) and industrial research centres. Each year the civil service (and its many research establishments) and major industrial companies (with established and active research centres) will recruit, as necessary, people with a sound background of higher education in research techniques coupled with some proven experience.

A report in 1993 by the Institute of Employment Studies suggests that

> there is no evidence of any significant broadening of the PhD science labour market beyond its traditional scientific research employment areas, except possibly in mathematics. However the market is made up of a number of different types of employers, only a small minority of whom are those which can demonstrate a discrete demand for newly qualified PhD science graduates.

I suspect that the same is true for newly qualified PhD engineering graduates.

Business and industrial companies

In the 1993 report by the Institute of Employment Studies, referred to above, the view was expressed that 'based on present economic trends, overall demand by industrial, commercial and public sector employers for PhD graduates is likely to remain fairly steady to the end of the decade with possibly a slight increase overall.'

Many employers in this sector do not make any significant distinction between those with a master's degree and an applicant with a bachelor's level of qualification, although the particular study topic undertaken at the postgraduate level may, in some cases, be regarded as 'useful to have' as an area of knowledge. The doctorate level of degree may appeal to some employers because they will recognise the nature of the individual study as evidence of many of the skills required for the jobs they have available.

The European and overseas connection

The notion of working outside of the UK has considerable appeal to many postgraduates and, with the widening of the European Union together with a policy of internationalism on the part of many companies, it is likely that more opportunities will arise. However, such posts will require proven and relevant experience, perhaps with some previous overseas contact, as well as a postgraduate qualification. A facility with languages will undoubtedly be advantageous if you intend to live and work abroad.

Skills employers seek

Employers expect postgraduates to have trained minds, with the abilities to apply their intellects to business or technical situations and to continue learning throughout their careers. Some vacancies require postgraduates with specific expertise. Whatever qualifications are sought for the vacancy, employers also expect the postgraduate applicant to have acquired a wide range of personal skills.

There are many different ways of expressing skills and abilities that can sometimes cause confusion when trying to pinpoint exactly what employers really want. The following list of core skills and definitions have been distilled from

- work by members of the Careers Advisory Board and my former colleagues in the Careers Service of the University of Newcastle upon Tyne;
- regular surveys of employers' graduate recruitment brochures and application forms;
- the skills module of PROSPECT (HE), the computer assisted guidance system for students in higher education.

Communication

The ability to operate three distinct modes of communication.

- Written communication:
  - write well-expressed, grammatical documents (especially reports and letters) appropriate to the needs of the readers.
- Interpersonal communication:
  - listen attentively and seek to understand what other people say;
  - ask probing questions, consider differing views;
  - negotiate with people to reach agreement on a point of view or course of action;
  - speak in clear and succinct language.
- Oral presentation:
  - make lucid and confident oral presentations, appropriate to the audience.

Teamwork

The ability to

- recognise and understand the attitudes, actions and beliefs of the other members of a group;
- establish a good rapport with others and work effectively to meet an objective or complete a task;
- contribute to the planning and coordination of a group's work;
- assist the working process of a group by helping to resolve conflicts, recognising the strengths of others and encouraging them to contribute;
- when appropriate, take a leadership role, setting the direction and winning the commitment of others.

Planning and organising

The ability to

- take a long term view and set challenging but achievable objectives;
- decide priorities for achieving targets;

- make a plan and organise resources to follow it through;
- draw up a work schedule and meet deadlines;
- effectively manage personal time and handle a range of activities simultaneously.

Problem-solving

The ability to:

- assimilate, analyse and evaluate complex information, identify key issues and principles, and draw well-reasoned conclusions;
- think critically, learn from mistakes, challenge established assumptions and make well-supported judgements;
- take a broad view, seeing less obvious connections and interdependencies;
- think conceptually and creatively; generate ideas that pay off in practice;
- implement action based on the assessment of all available data.

Initiative

The ability to:

- take appropriate action un-prompted; be a self starter
- set demanding personal goals and overcome difficulties to achieve them;
- pursue an activity to a high standard and rise to challenges;
- take well-researched decisions quickly.

Adaptability

The ability to:

- respond readily to changing situations and priorities;
- recognise potential for improvement;
- re-apply known solutions to new situations;
- initiate change and make it happen: be pro-active not reactive
- tolerate stress and remain effective under pressure.

Employers may look for other skills, most commonly:

- *numeracy* – the ability to understand and use numbers accurately;
- *computer literacy* – the ability to use word-processing and spreadsheet software, and databases, competently;
- *languages* – the ability to speak, write or learn foreign languages.

Finally, each person has a *unique profile of skills and knowledge*. Employers may well expect postgraduates to have reached informed career choices by assessing how well their own knowledge and skills match those required by the job or career sought. Awareness of personal strengths and weaknesses will be looked for in the candidates. You will be asked to explain your career choices and to give reasons for the specific job application.

WHERE TO FIND THOSE ADVERTISED POSTS

You will find science-, engineering- and technology-related vacancies regularly advertised in the major national newspapers, and scientific and technical journals, some of which are listed below with their websites.

The Independent (Monday)	www.independent.co.uk
The Daily Telegraph (Tuesday & Thursday)	www.jobs.telegraph.co.uk
The Evening Standard (Wednesday)	www.thisislondon.co.uk
The Guardian (Thursday)	www.jobsunlimited.co.uk
The Times (Friday)	www.thetimes.co.uk
The Observer (Sunday)	www.observer.co.uk
The Sunday Times	www.sunday-times.co.uk
The Sunday Telegraph	www.jobs.telegraph.co.uk
New Scientist	www.newscientist.co.uk
Nature	www.nature.com
Biologist	
Chemistry in Britain	
Chemistry and Industry	www.enviro.mond.org
The Chemical Engineer	
New Civil Engineer	
Professional Engineering	
IEE Recruitment	
Materials World	www.instmat.co.uk

For teaching and lecturer posts, you will need to refer to:

The Times Educational Supplement (TES)	www.tes.co.uk
The Times Higher Educational Supplement (THES)	www.thesis.co.uk

The appointments department of the Association of Commonwealth Universities also circulates vacancy details to the universities careers services.

Prospects Today (available from most university careers services), www.prospects.csu.ac.uk, is a fortnightly publication that advertises vacancies for graduates. Some of the posts will specify opportunities for those with postgraduate qualifications.

If you are seeking particularly to work abroad, then *Overseas Jobs Express* (www.overseasjobs.com) is a fortnightly publication with advertisements for jobs based overseas, some of which will require postgraduate qualifications.

Recruitment agencies, many of which advertise in the national newspapers, technical journals and on the Internet, are worth contacting, particularly if they work for employers in a specialised work sector.

TAKING ACTION

Advertised posts

Responding to an advertised post is fairly straightforward. You get some indication of what the job involves and what the employer is expecting of the applicant. Moreover, you get a clear instruction of how they want you to make application: by letter and CV, or with an application form.

Whatever the style of approach, always remember it is your first and maybe your only opportunity to impress the selector enough to be invited to an interview. So, write about yourself in a positive way. Your application must have impact, be of quality and match the job specification. Remember, you are a quality product in a highly competitive market. Your potential will be judged largely on your track record of performance and achievement in the major periods of your life so far (such as university, school, working experiences and even some of your extra-curricular activities). So, this is not the time to be over modest!

Once you are over this first hurdle and have been invited to an interview, it is important that you are able to keep your story line going and live up to the impression you have so far created.

Speculative applications

In some cases, you may consider it appropriate to make speculative applications to employers, organisations or institutions to tell them of your existence and hope to influence them into considering you as a possible candidate either immediately or at some future date. To make the necessary impact, you must have a good perception of the employer's business and work activities and recognise where you believe you can make an appropriate and effective contribution by applying your skills, abilities and expertise.

If you are contemplating this more open job search, you may find it helpful to talk to members of academic staff in your university department about your plan of action. They may have information about the type of work you are seeking and may also have some useful contacts to enable you to make that first approach.

Your application, usually by letter and CV, must have impact and illustrate your self-confidence. Try to find the name and designation of the person to whom it would be most appropriate to send your letter and CV.

Speculative applications are certainly worth trying in a carefully controlled way.

CONCLUSION

Finally, for further information about any of the employment sectors or help in dealing with applications, get in touch with your university careers service.

Index